SUPERMAN

SAVAGE DAWN

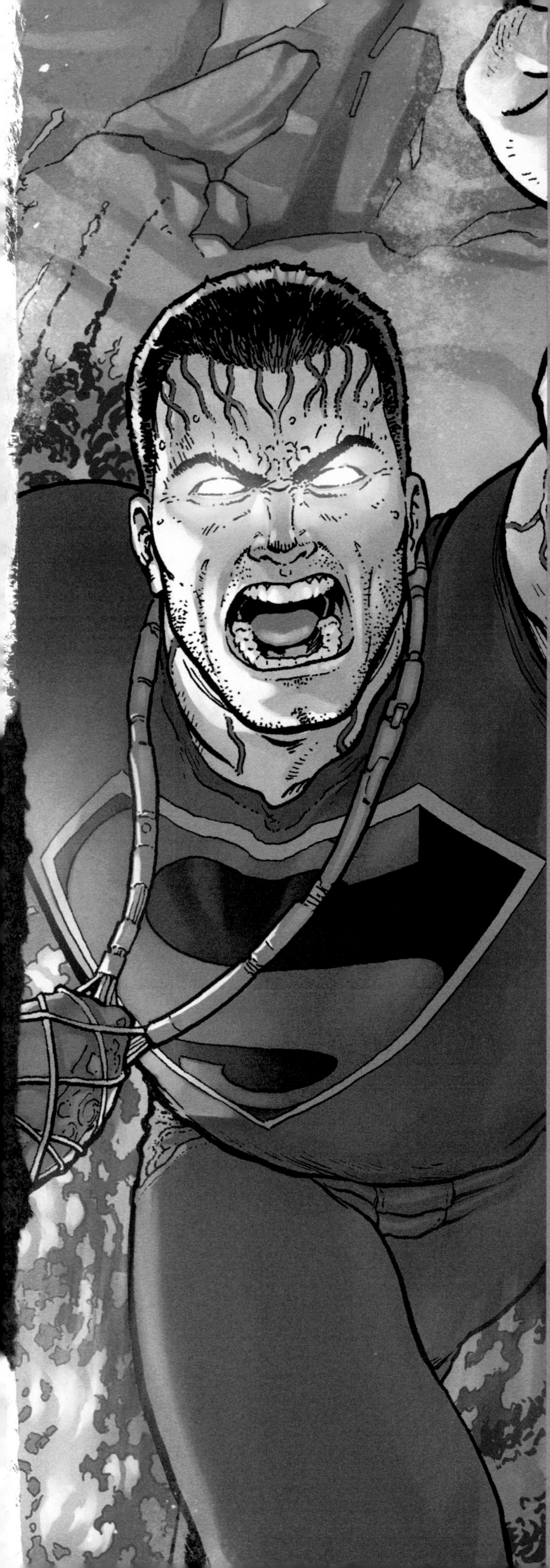

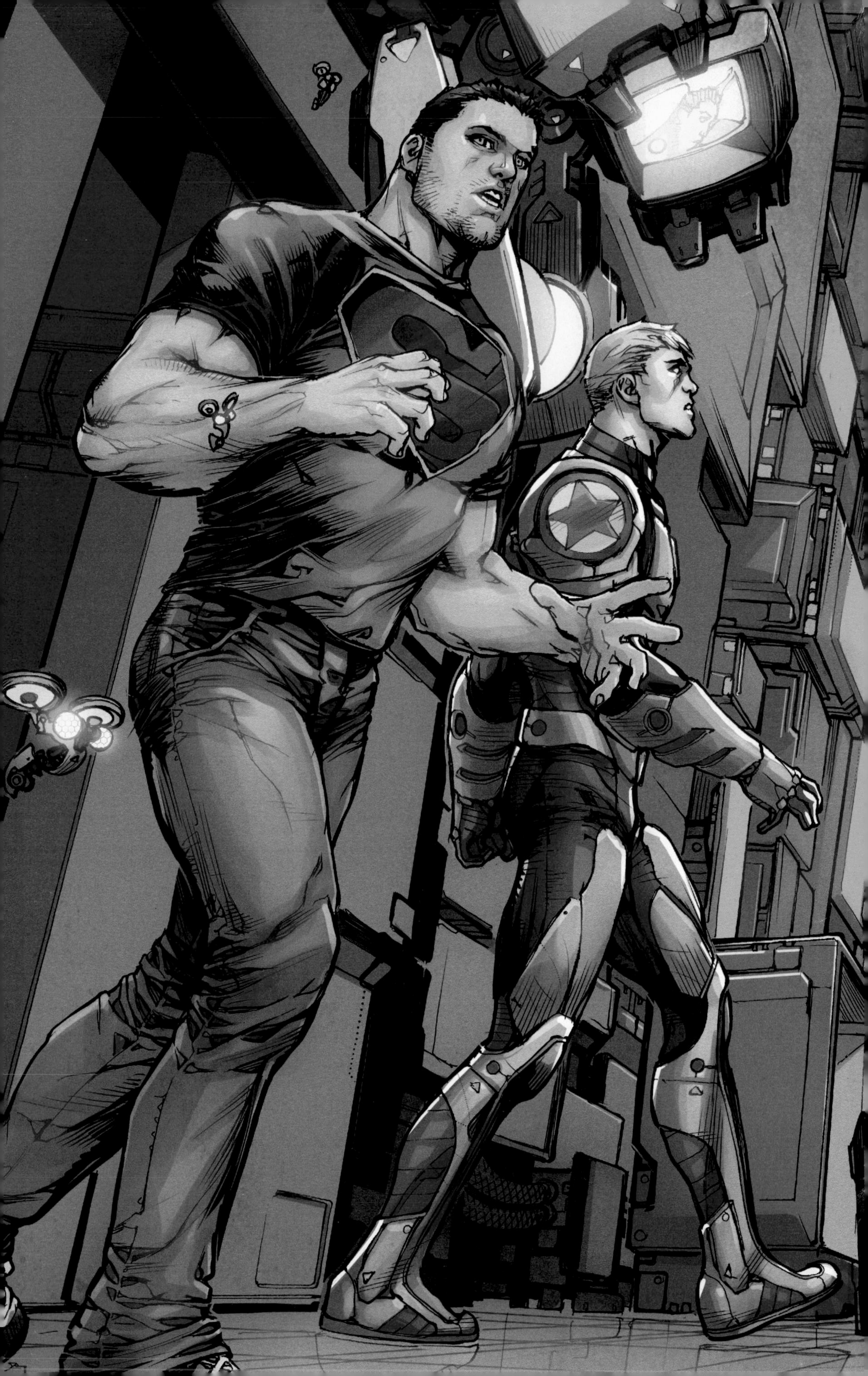

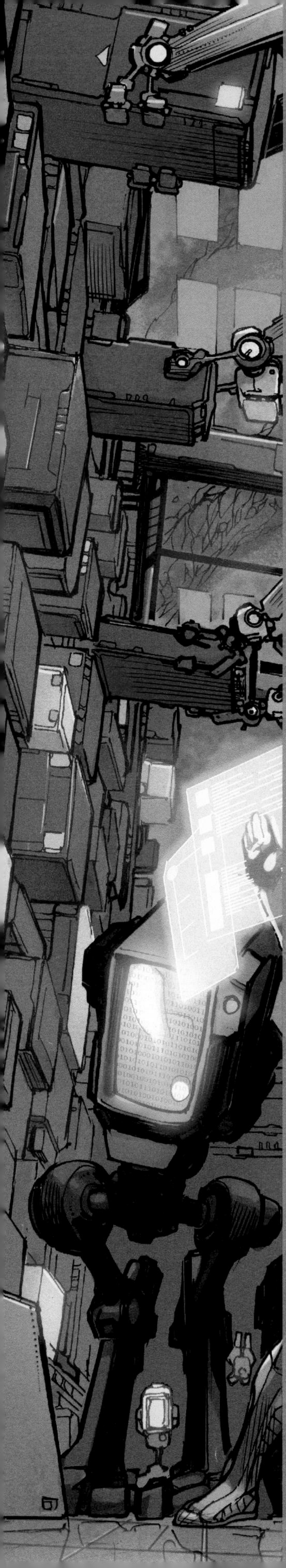

SUPERMAN

SAVAGE DAWN

WRITTEN BY
AARON KUDER GREG PAK
PETER J. TOMASI GENE LUEN YANG

LAYOUT ART BY
AARON KUDER

PENCILS BY
JON BOGDANOVE VICENTE CIFUENTES
JAVI FERNANDEZ AARON KUDER
JACK HERBERT DAN JURGENS DOUG MAHNKE
DAVID MESSINA BEN OLIVER HOWARD PORTER
BRUNO REDONDO CLIFF RICHARDS
RAFA SANDOVAL ARDIAN SYAF
PATRICK ZIRCHER

INKS BY
JUAN ALBARRAN JON BOGDANOVE
GAETANO CARLUCCI VICENTE CIFUENTES
JAVI FERNANDEZ JONATHAN GLAPION
SCOTT HANNA JACK HERBERT DON HO
SANDRA HOPE AARON KUDER
HOWARD PORTER DOUG MAHNKE
JAIME MENDOZA JEROME K. MOORE
BEN OLIVER CLIFF RICHARDS
BILL SIENKIEWICZ ARDIAN SYAF
JORDI TARRAGONA PATRICK ZIRCHER

COLORS BY
BLOND HI-FI LEE LOUGHRIDGE
TOMEU MOREY TRISH MULVIHILL
BEN OLIVER ARIF PRIANTO
WIL QUINTANA

LETTERS BY
A LARGER WORLD STUDIOS
ROB LEIGH STEVE WANDS

COLLECTION COVER ART BY
AARON KUDER TOMEU MOREY

SUPERMAN CREATED BY
JERRY SIEGEL
AND JOE SHUSTER
BY SPECIAL ARRANGEMENT WITH THE JERRY SIEGEL FAMILY

WONDER WOMAN CREATED BY
WILLIAM MOULTON MARSTON

ANDREW MARINO Assistant Editor – Original Series
DAVID WOHL Editor – Original Content
EDDIE BERGANZA Group Editor – Original Series
JEB WOODARD Group Editor – Collected Editions
SUZANNAH ROWNTREE Editor – Collected Edition
STEVE COOK Design Director – Books
DAMIAN RYLAND Publication Design

BOB HARRAS Senior VP – Editor-in-Chief, DC Comics

DIANE NELSON President
DAN DIDIO and JIM LEE Co-Publishers
GEOFF JOHNS Chief Creative Officer
AMIT DESAI Senior VP – Marketing & Global Franchise Management
NAIRI GARDINER Senior VP – Finance
SAM ADES VP – Digital Marketing
BOBBIE CHASE VP – Talent Development
MARK CHIARELLO Senior VP – Art, Design & Collected Editions
JOHN CUNNINGHAM VP – Content Strategy
ANNE DEPIES VP – Strategy Planning & Reporting
DON FALLETTI VP – Manufacturing Operations
LAWRENCE GANEM VP – Editorial Administration & Talent Relations
ALISON GILL Senior VP – Manufacturing & Operations
HANK KANALZ Senior VP – Editorial Strategy & Administration
JAY KOGAN VP – Legal Affairs
DEREK MADDALENA Senior VP – Sales & Business Development
JACK MAHAN VP – Business Affairs
DAN MIRON VP – Sales Planning & Trade Development
NICK NAPOLITANO VP – Manufacturing Administration
CAROL ROEDER VP – Marketing
EDDIE SCANNELL VP – Mass Account & Digital Sales
COURTNEY SIMMONS Senior VP – Publicity & Communications
JIM (SKI) SOKOLOWSKI VP – Comic Book Specialty & Newsstand Sales
SANDY YI Senior VP – Global Franchise Management

SUPERMAN: SAVAGE DAWN

DC Comics, 2900 West Alameda Ave., Burbank, CA 91505
Printed by RR Donnelley, Salem, VA, USA. 9/2/16. First Printing.
ISBN: 978-1-4012-7004-9

Library of Congress Cataloging-in-Publication Data is available.

PEFC Certified

Printed on paper from
sustainably managed
forests and controlled
sources

PEFC/29-31-75   www.pefc.org

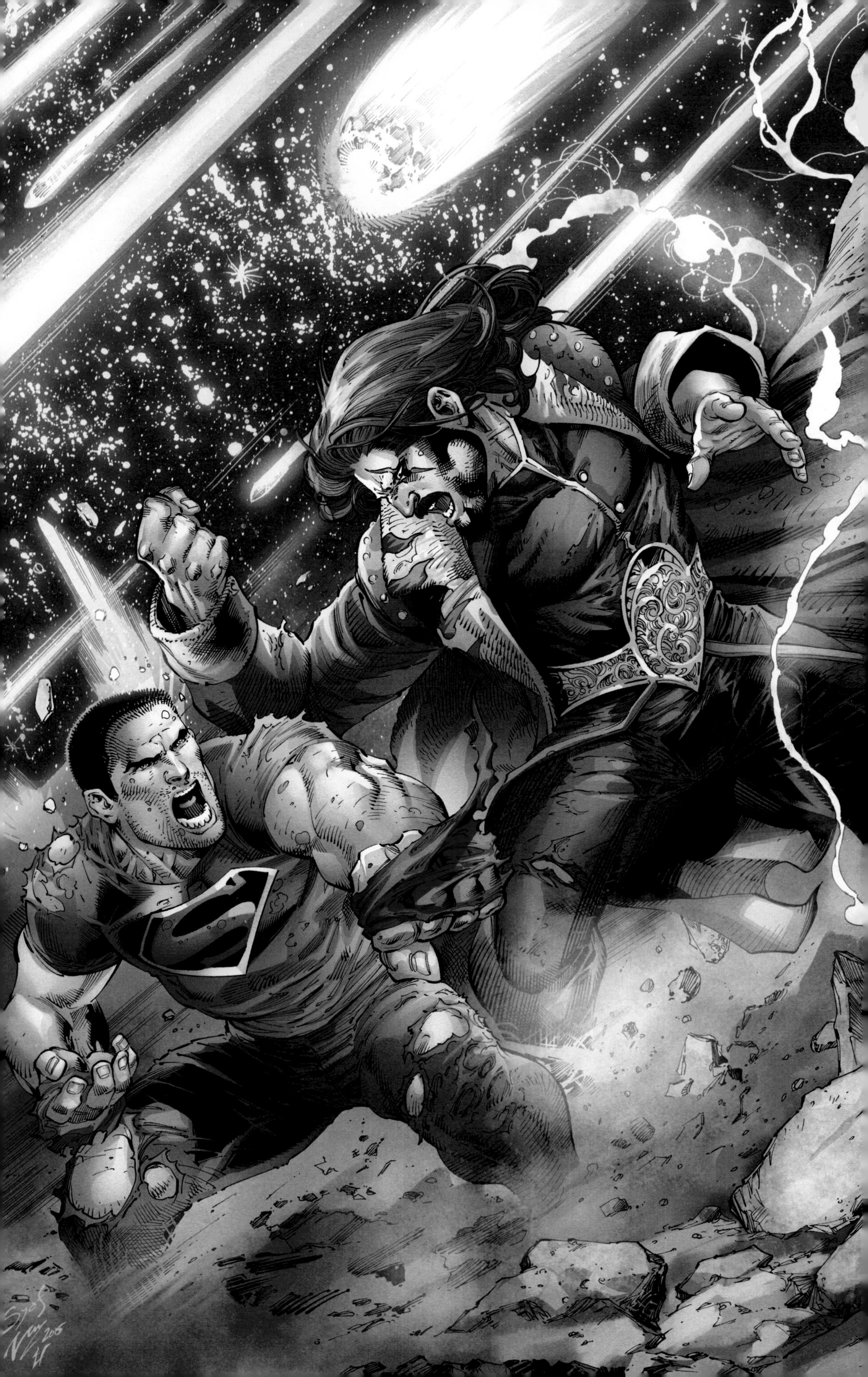

SAVAGE DAWN

GREG PAK GENE LUEN YANG PETER J. TOMASI AARON KUDER writers DAN JURGENS RAFA SANDOVAL BEN OLIVER pencillers BILL SIENKIEWICZ BEN OLIVER inkers TRISH MULVIHILL LEE LOUGHRIDGE TOMEU MOREY BEN OLIVER colorists A LARGER WORLD STUDIOS letterer ARDIAN SYAF VICENTE CIFUENTES ULISES ARREOLA cover

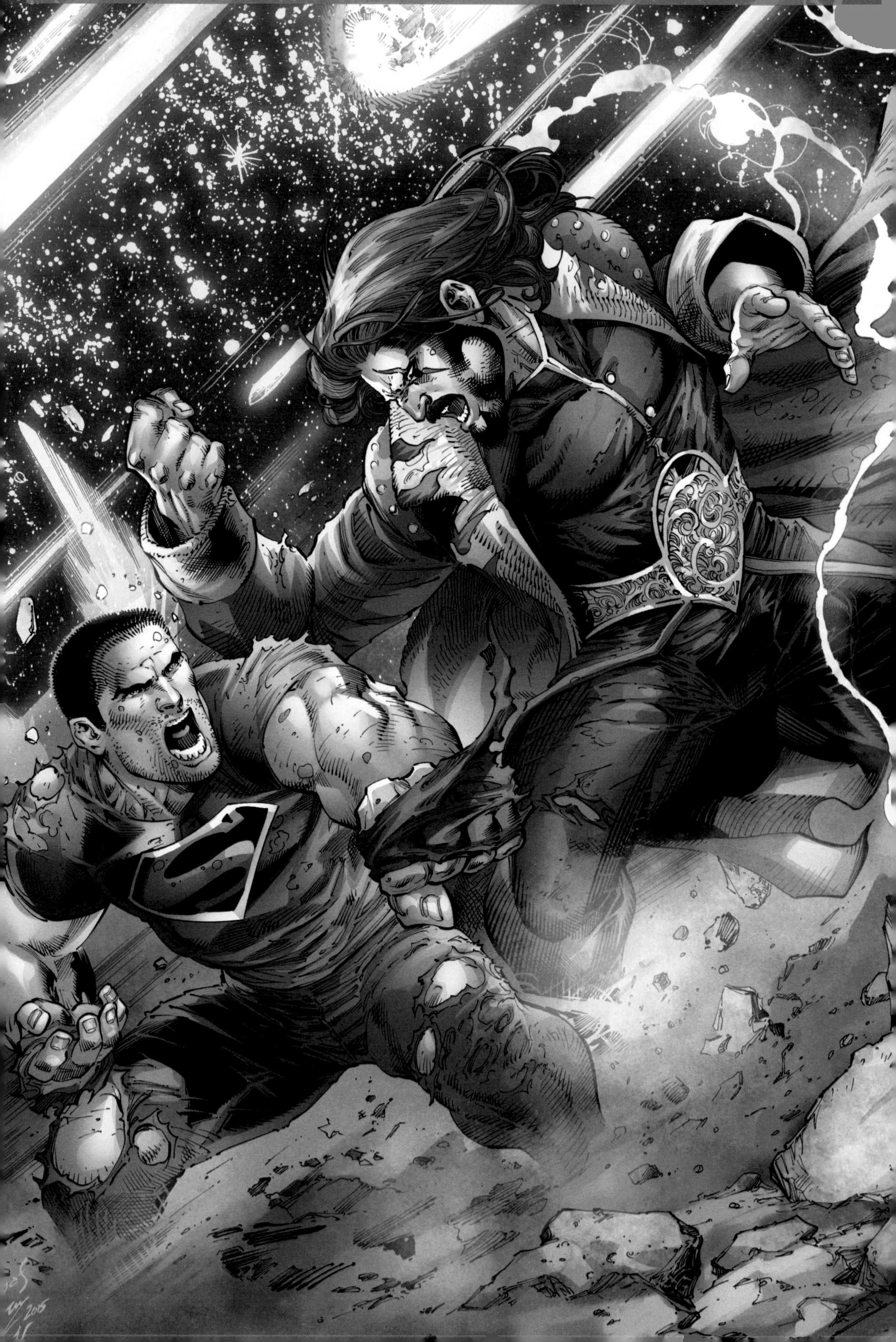

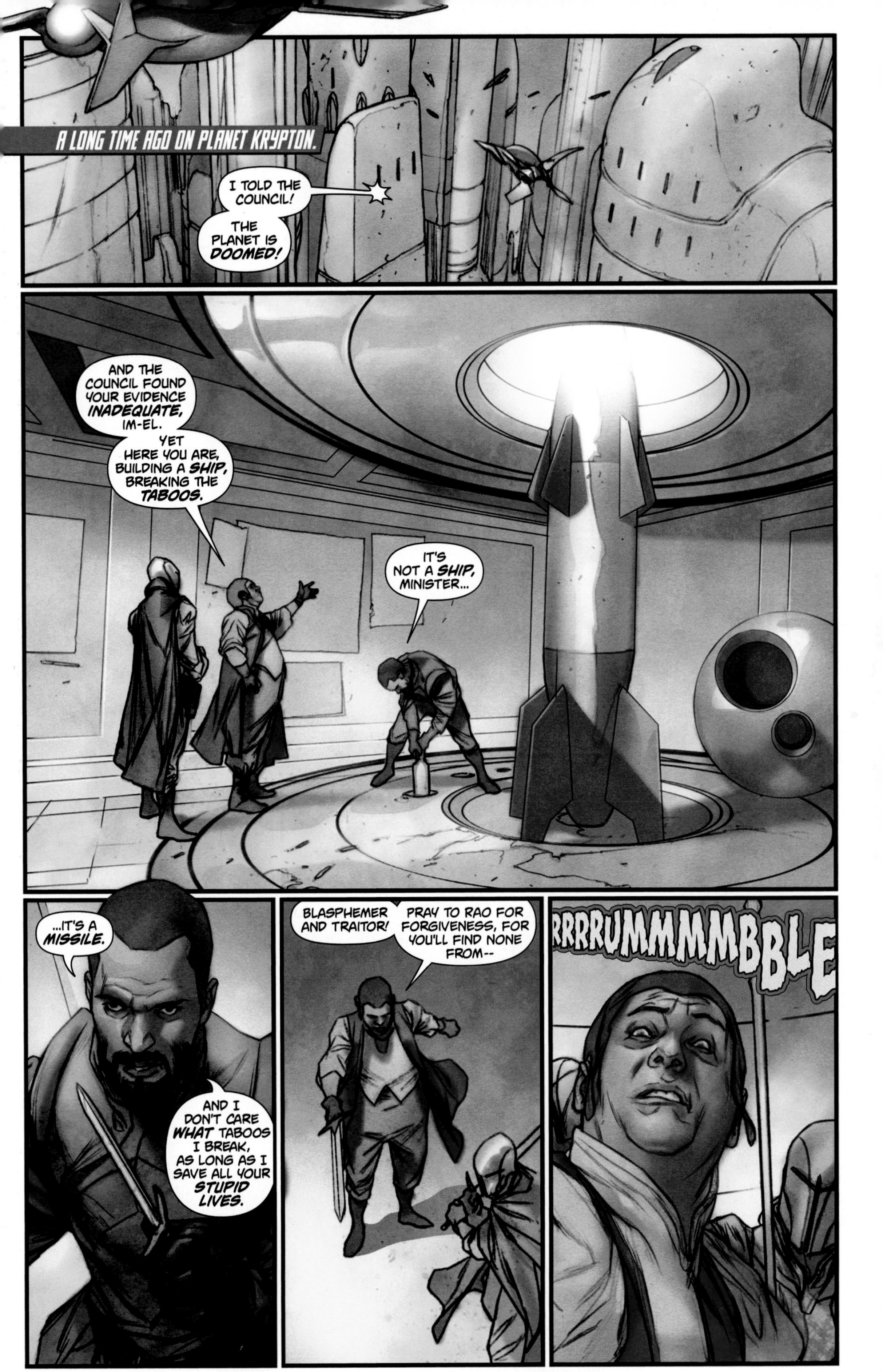
A LONG TIME AGO ON PLANET KRYPTON.
I TOLD THE COUNCIL!
THE PLANET IS DOOMED!
AND THE COUNCIL FOUND YOUR EVIDENCE INADEQUATE, IM-EL.
YET HERE YOU ARE, BUILDING A SHIP, BREAKING THE TABOOS.
IT'S NOT A SHIP, MINISTER...
...IT'S A MISSILE.
AND I DON'T CARE WHAT TABOOS I BREAK, AS LONG AS I SAVE ALL YOUR STUPID LIVES.
BLASPHEMER AND TRAITOR!
PRAY TO RAO FOR FORGIVENESS, FOR YOU'LL FIND NONE FROM--
RRRRUMMMMMBBLE

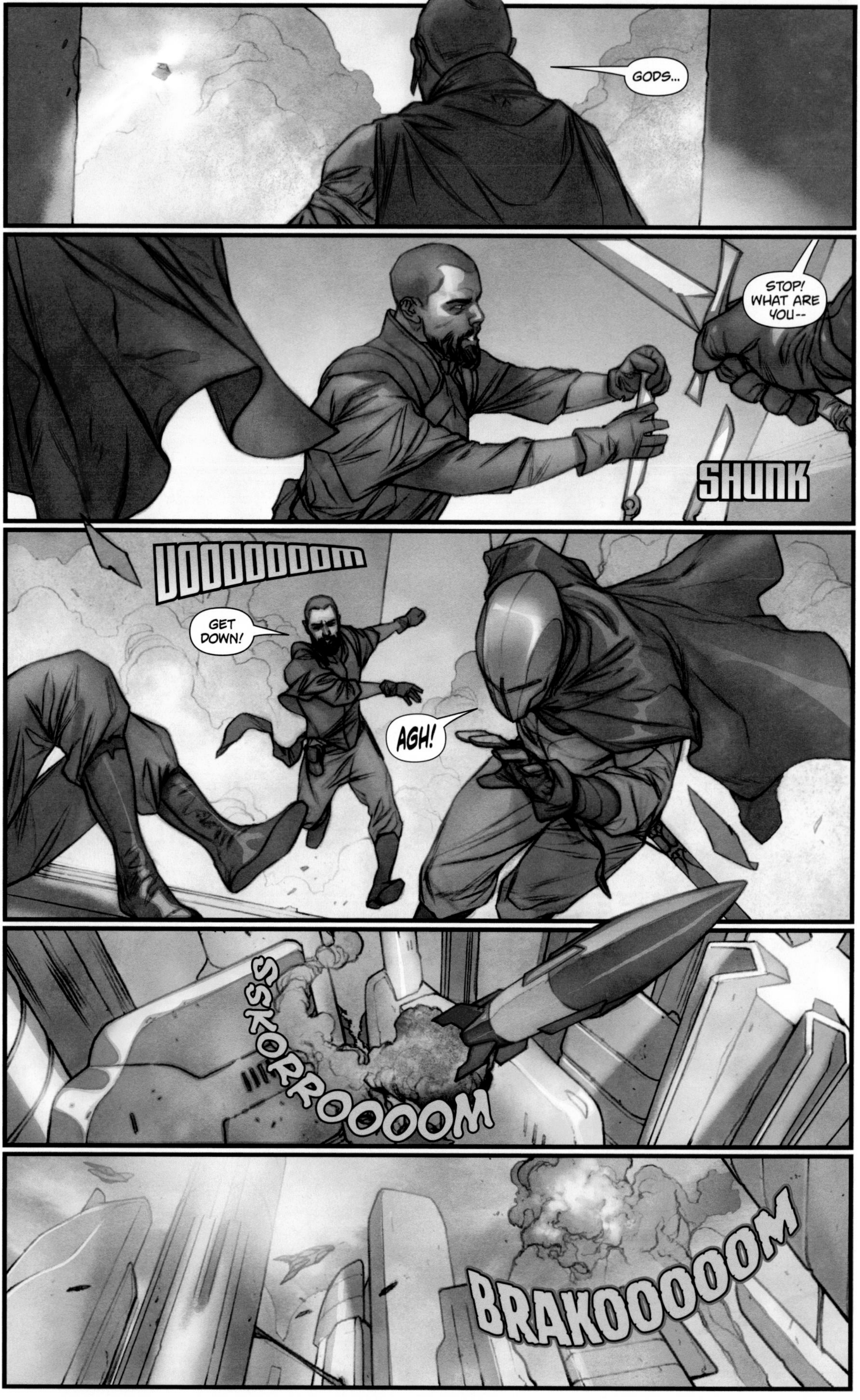
GODS...
STOP! WHAT ARE YOU--
SHUNK
VOOOOOOOOM
GET DOWN!
AGH!
SSKORROOOOOM
BRAKOOOOOOM

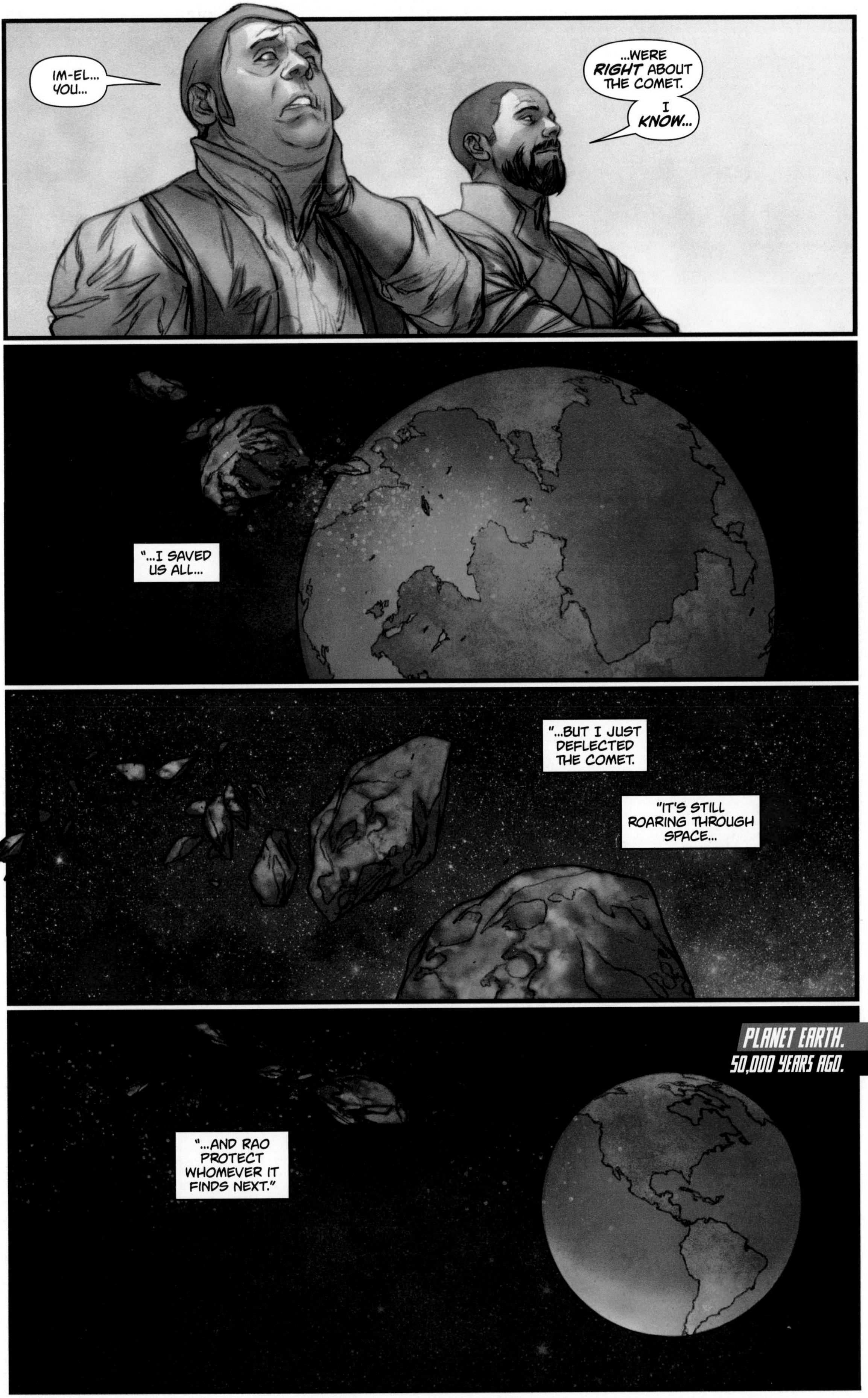
IM-EL... YOU...
...WERE RIGHT ABOUT THE COMET.
I KNOW...
"...I SAVED US ALL...
"...BUT I JUST DEFLECTED THE COMET.
"IT'S STILL ROARING THROUGH SPACE...
PLANET EARTH. 50,000 YEARS AGO.
"...AND RAO PROTECT WHOMEVER IT FINDS NEXT."

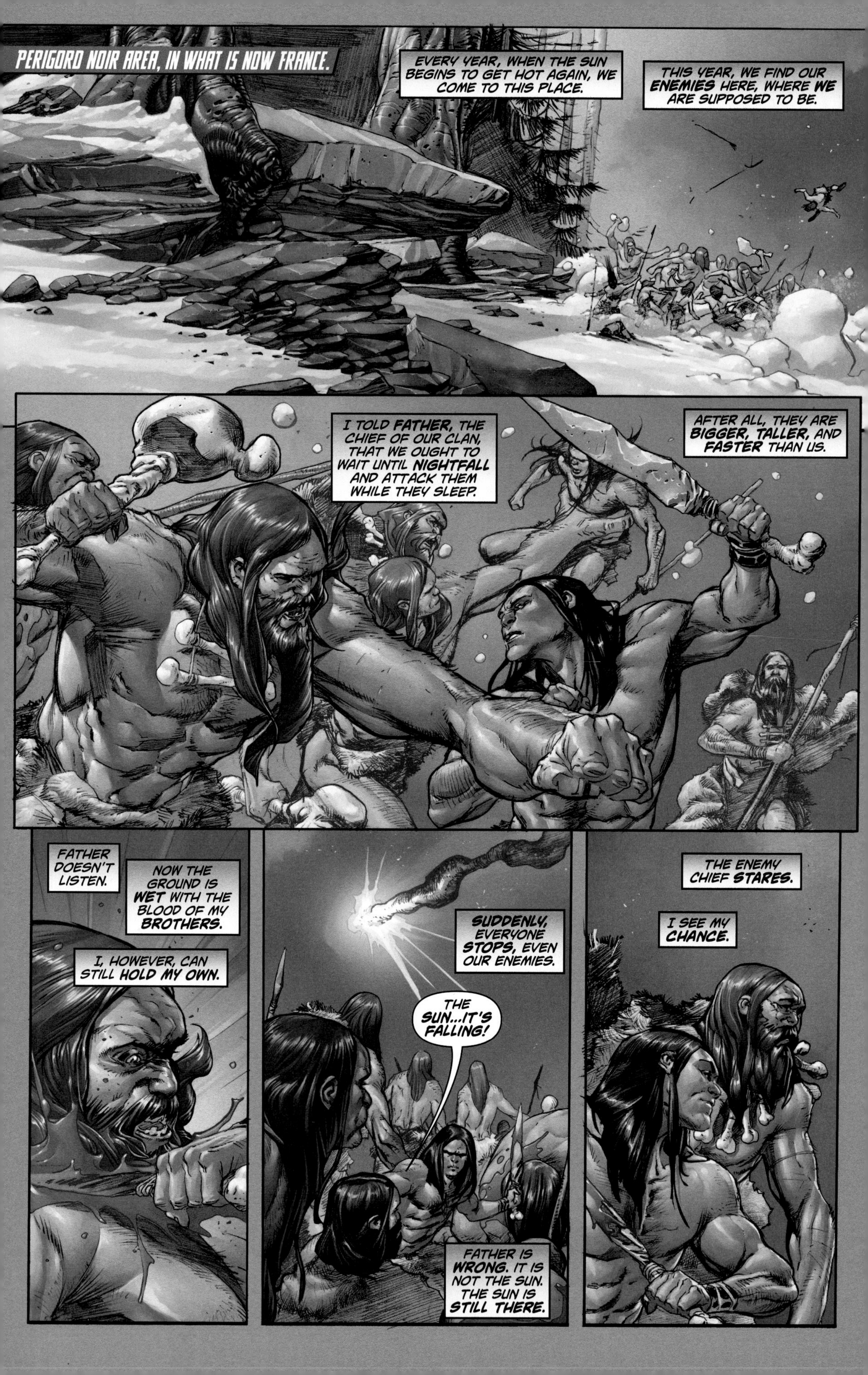
PERIGORD NOIR AREA, IN WHAT IS NOW FRANCE.
EVERY YEAR, WHEN THE SUN BEGINS TO GET HOT AGAIN, WE COME TO THIS PLACE.
THIS YEAR, WE FIND OUR ENEMIES HERE, WHERE WE ARE SUPPOSED TO BE.
I TOLD FATHER, THE CHIEF OF OUR CLAN, THAT WE OUGHT TO WAIT UNTIL NIGHTFALL AND ATTACK THEM WHILE THEY SLEEP.
AFTER ALL, THEY ARE BIGGER, TALLER, AND FASTER THAN US.
FATHER DOESN'T LISTEN.
NOW THE GROUND IS WET WITH THE BLOOD OF MY BROTHERS.
I, HOWEVER, CAN STILL HOLD MY OWN.
SUDDENLY, EVERYONE STOPS, EVEN OUR ENEMIES.
THE SUN...IT'S FALLING!
FATHER IS WRONG. IT IS NOT THE SUN. THE SUN IS STILL THERE.
THE ENEMY CHIEF STARES.
I SEE MY CHANCE.

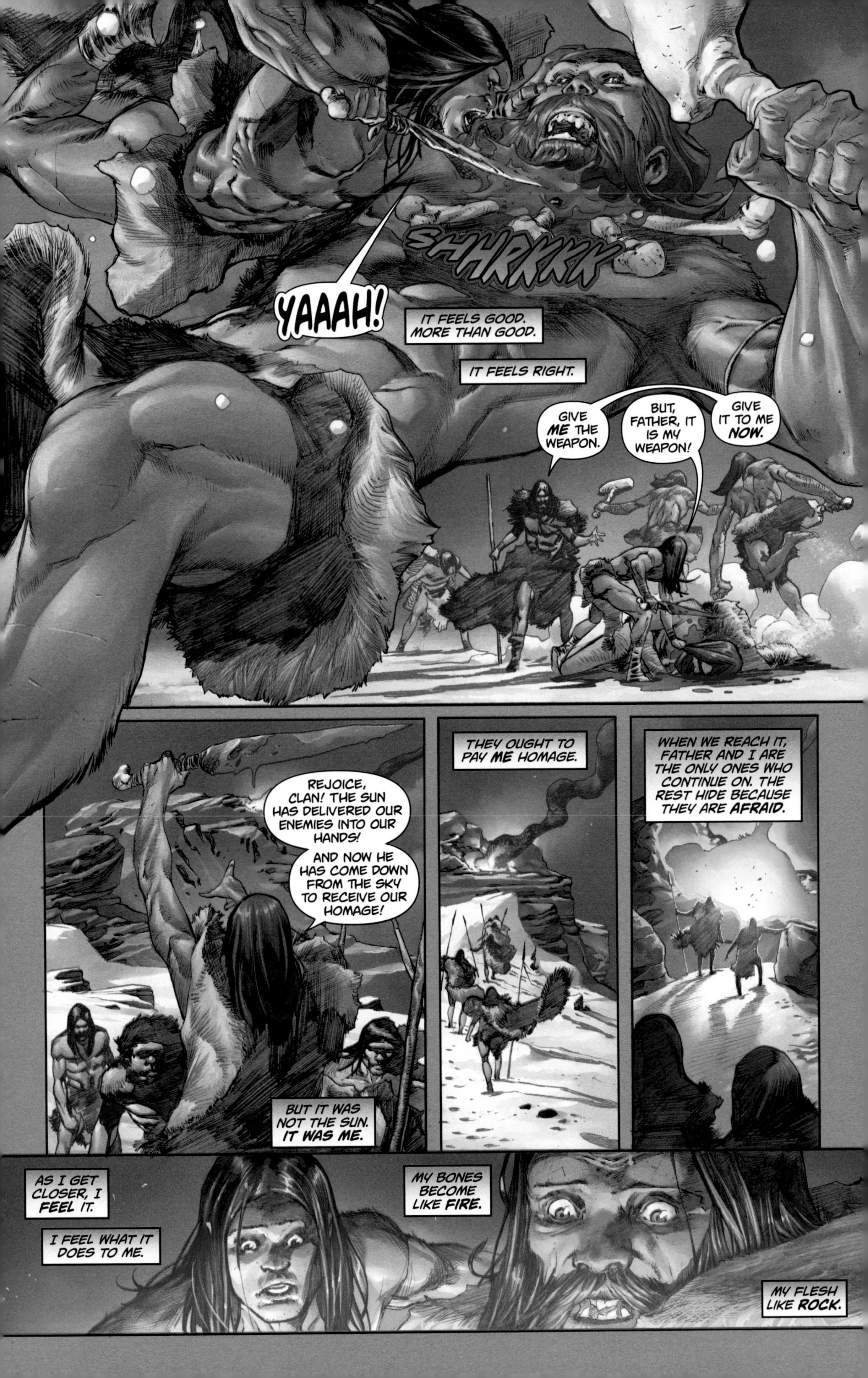
SHHRKKK
YAAAH!
IT FEELS GOOD. MORE THAN GOOD.
IT FEELS RIGHT.
GIVE ME THE WEAPON.
BUT, FATHER, IT IS MY WEAPON!
GIVE IT TO ME NOW.
REJOICE, CLAN! THE SUN HAS DELIVERED OUR ENEMIES INTO OUR HANDS!
AND NOW HE HAS COME DOWN FROM THE SKY TO RECEIVE OUR HOMAGE!
BUT IT WAS NOT THE SUN. IT WAS ME.
THEY OUGHT TO PAY ME HOMAGE.
WHEN WE REACH IT, FATHER AND I ARE THE ONLY ONES WHO CONTINUE ON. THE REST HIDE BECAUSE THEY ARE AFRAID.
AS I GET CLOSER, I FEEL IT.
I FEEL WHAT IT DOES TO ME.
MY BONES BECOME LIKE FIRE.
MY FLESH LIKE ROCK.

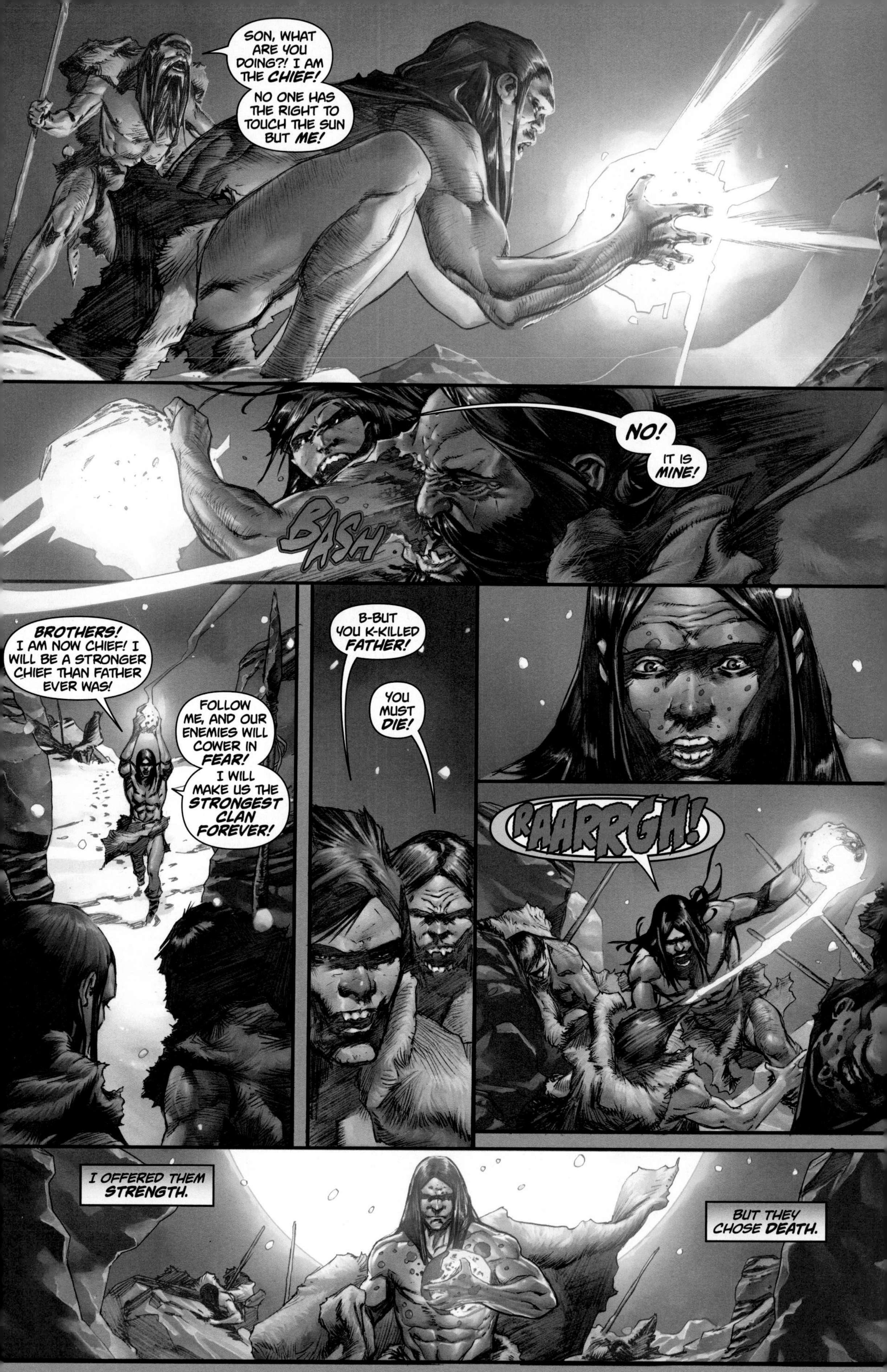
SON, WHAT ARE YOU DOING?! I AM THE CHIEF!
NO ONE HAS THE RIGHT TO TOUCH THE SUN BUT ME!
NO!
IT IS MINE!
BASH
BROTHERS! I AM NOW CHIEF! I WILL BE A STRONGER CHIEF THAN FATHER EVER WAS!
FOLLOW ME, AND OUR ENEMIES WILL COWER IN FEAR!
I WILL MAKE US THE STRONGEST CLAN FOREVER!
B-BUT YOU K-KILLED FATHER!
YOU MUST DIE!
RAARRGH!
I OFFERED THEM STRENGTH.
BUT THEY CHOSE DEATH.

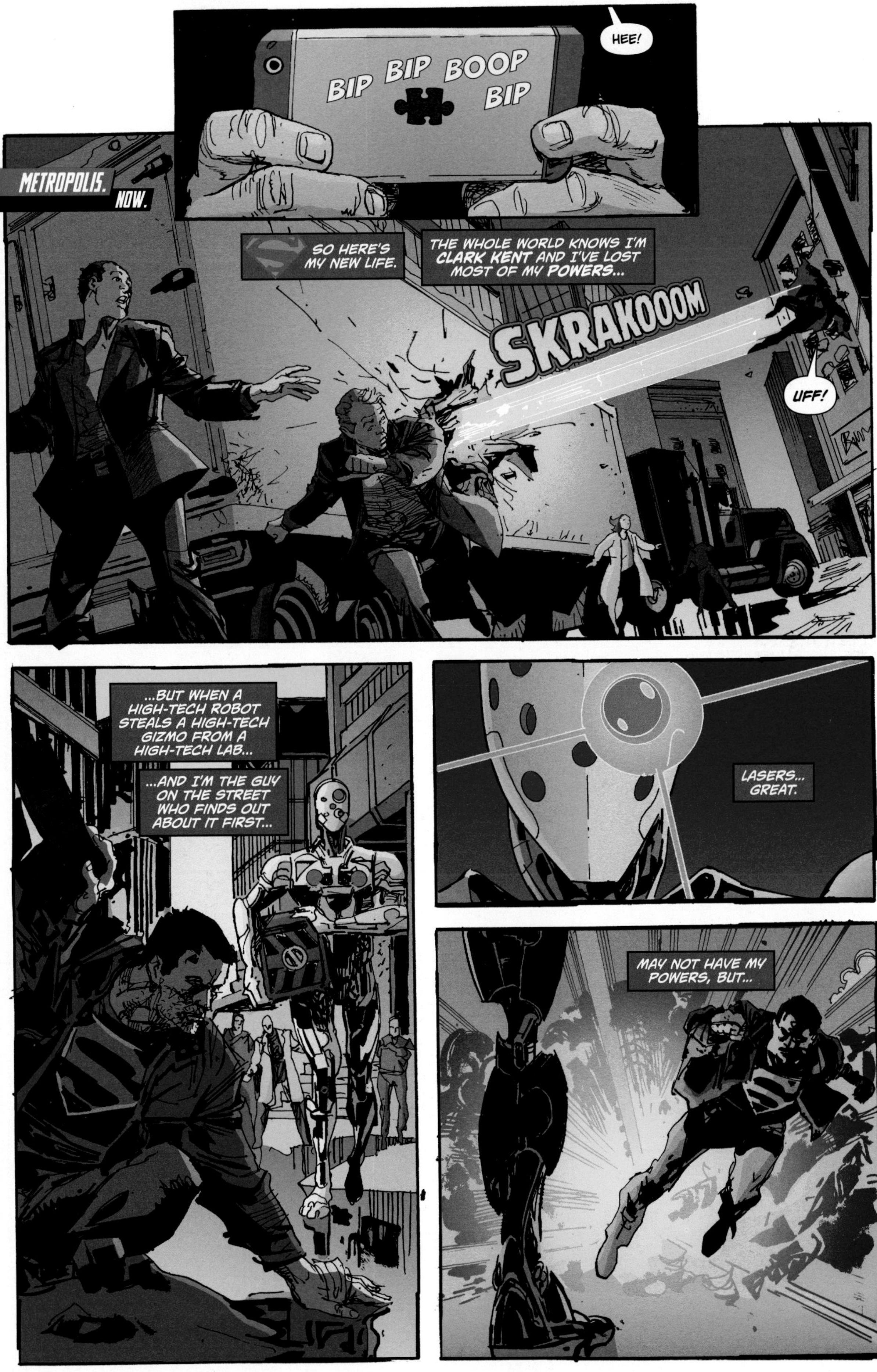

BIP BIP BOOP BIP
HEE!
METROPOLIS. NOW.
SO HERE'S MY NEW LIFE.
THE WHOLE WORLD KNOWS I'M CLARK KENT AND I'VE LOST MOST OF MY POWERS...
SKRAKOOOM
UFF!
...BUT WHEN A HIGH-TECH ROBOT STEALS A HIGH-TECH GIZMO FROM A HIGH-TECH LAB...
...AND I'M THE GUY ON THE STREET WHO FINDS OUT ABOUT IT FIRST...
LASERS... GREAT.
MAY NOT HAVE MY POWERS, BUT...

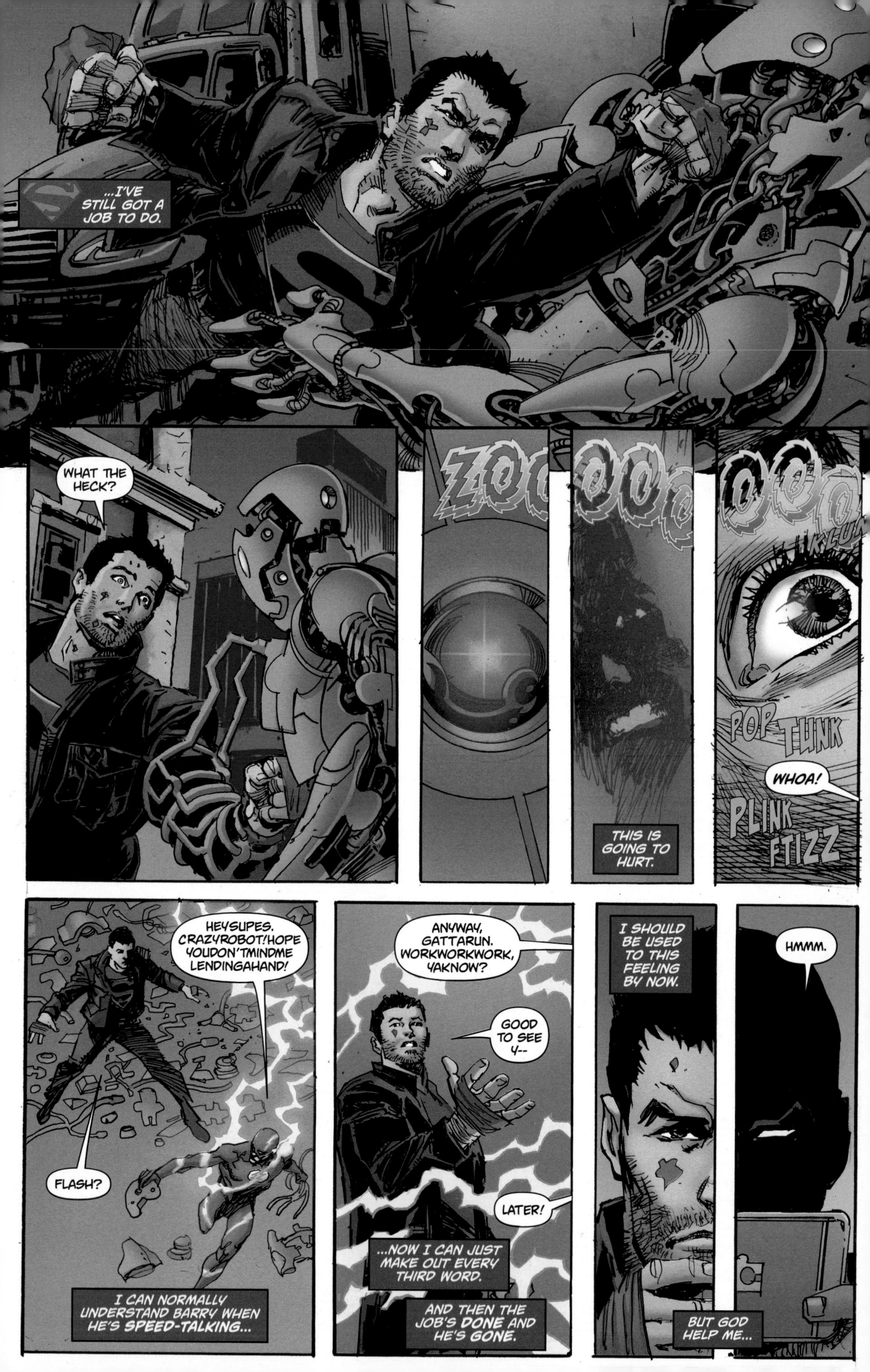
...I'VE STILL GOT A JOB TO DO.
WHAT THE HECK?
ZOOOOOOOOOO
THIS IS GOING TO HURT.
KLUN
POP
TUNK
WHOA!
PLINK
FTIZZ
HEYSUPES. CRAZYROBOT!HOPE YOUDON'TMINDME LENDINGAHAND!
FLASH?
I CAN NORMALLY UNDERSTAND BARRY WHEN HE'S SPEED-TALKING...
ANYWAY, GATTARUN. WORKWORKWORK, YAKNOW?
GOOD TO SEE Y--
LATER!
...NOW I CAN JUST MAKE OUT EVERY THIRD WORD.
AND THEN THE JOB'S DONE AND HE'S GONE.
I SHOULD BE USED TO THIS FEELING BY NOW.
HMMM.
BUT GOD HELP ME...

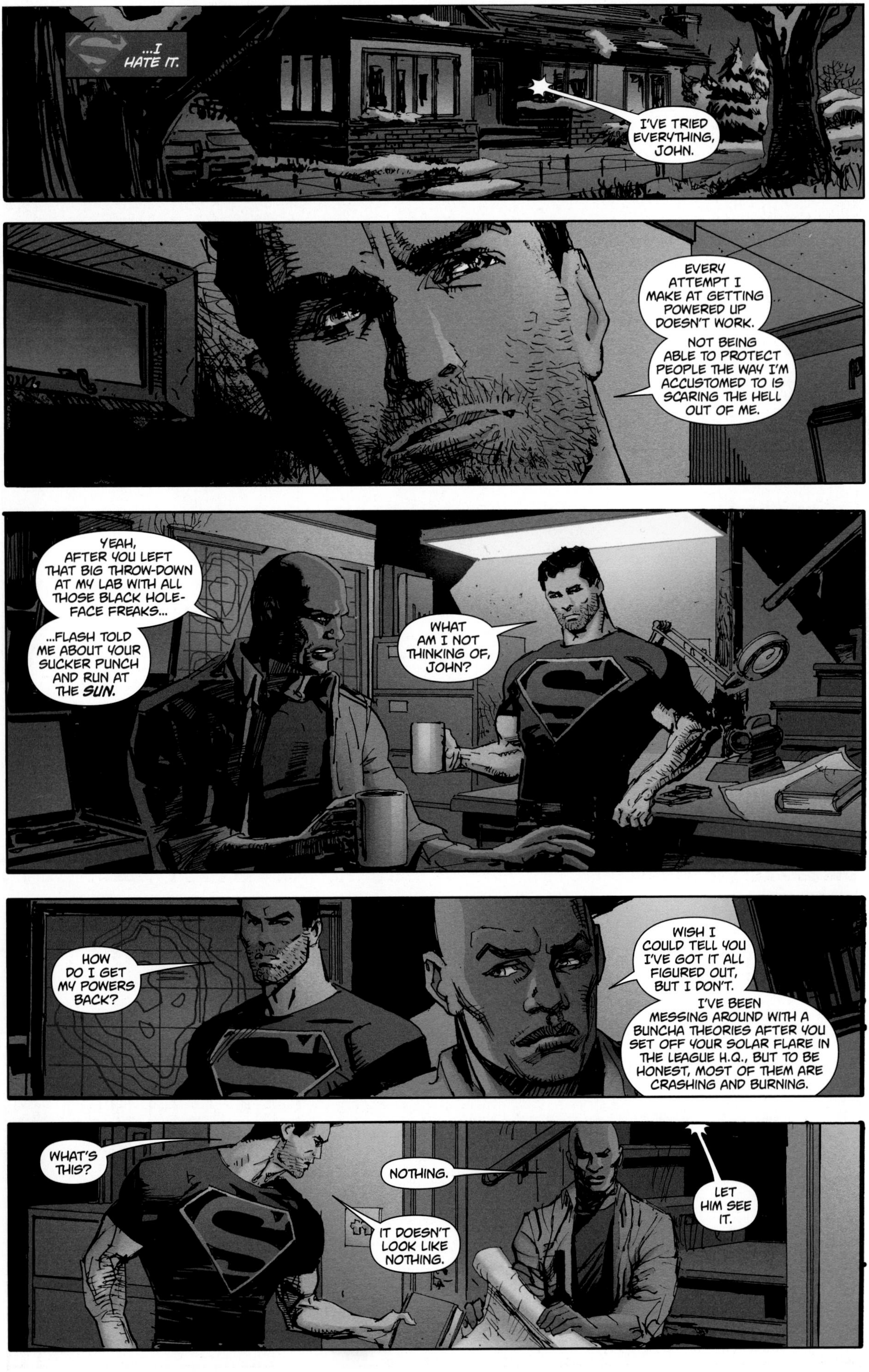
...I HATE IT.
I'VE TRIED EVERYTHING, JOHN.
EVERY ATTEMPT I MAKE AT GETTING POWERED UP DOESN'T WORK.
NOT BEING ABLE TO PROTECT PEOPLE THE WAY I'M ACCUSTOMED TO IS SCARING THE HELL OUT OF ME.
YEAH, AFTER YOU LEFT THAT BIG THROW-DOWN AT MY LAB WITH ALL THOSE BLACK HOLE-FACE FREAKS...
...FLASH TOLD ME ABOUT YOUR SUCKER PUNCH AND RUN AT THE SUN.
WHAT AM I NOT THINKING OF, JOHN?
HOW DO I GET MY POWERS BACK?
WISH I COULD TELL YOU I'VE GOT IT ALL FIGURED OUT, BUT I DON'T.
I'VE BEEN MESSING AROUND WITH A BUNCHA THEORIES AFTER YOU SET OFF YOUR SOLAR FLARE IN THE LEAGUE H.Q., BUT TO BE HONEST, MOST OF THEM ARE CRASHING AND BURNING.
WHAT'S THIS?
NOTHING.
IT DOESN'T LOOK LIKE NOTHING.
LET HIM SEE IT.

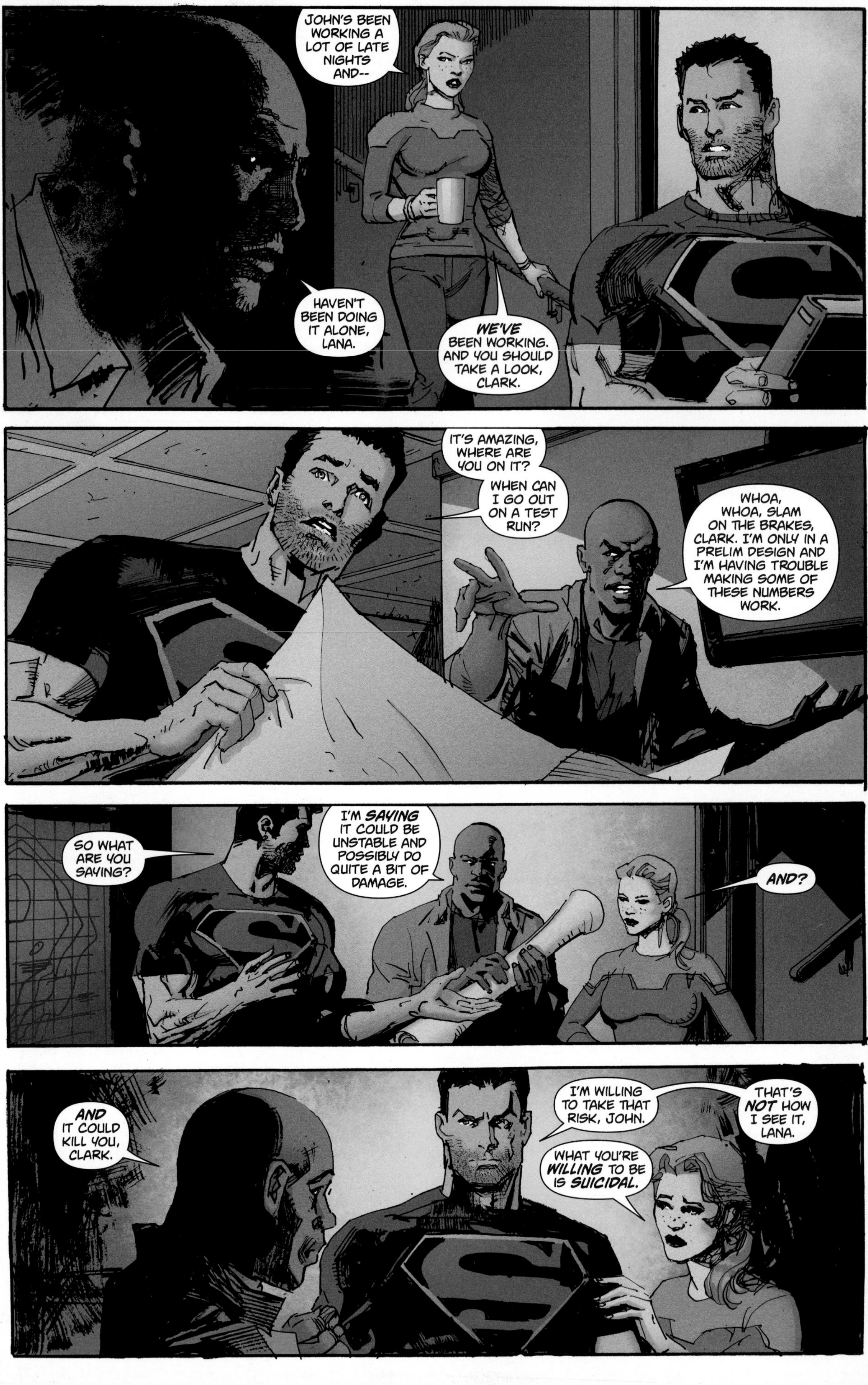
JOHN'S BEEN WORKING A LOT OF LATE NIGHTS AND--
HAVEN'T BEEN DOING IT ALONE, LANA.
WE'VE BEEN WORKING. AND YOU SHOULD TAKE A LOOK, CLARK.
IT'S AMAZING, WHERE ARE YOU ON IT?
WHEN CAN I GO OUT ON A TEST RUN?
WHOA, WHOA, SLAM ON THE BRAKES, CLARK. I'M ONLY IN A PRELIM DESIGN AND I'M HAVING TROUBLE MAKING SOME OF THESE NUMBERS WORK.
SO WHAT ARE YOU SAYING?
I'M SAYING IT COULD BE UNSTABLE AND POSSIBLY DO QUITE A BIT OF DAMAGE.
AND?
AND IT COULD KILL YOU, CLARK.
I'M WILLING TO TAKE THAT RISK, JOHN.
THAT'S NOT HOW I SEE IT, LANA.
WHAT YOU'RE WILLING TO BE IS SUICIDAL.

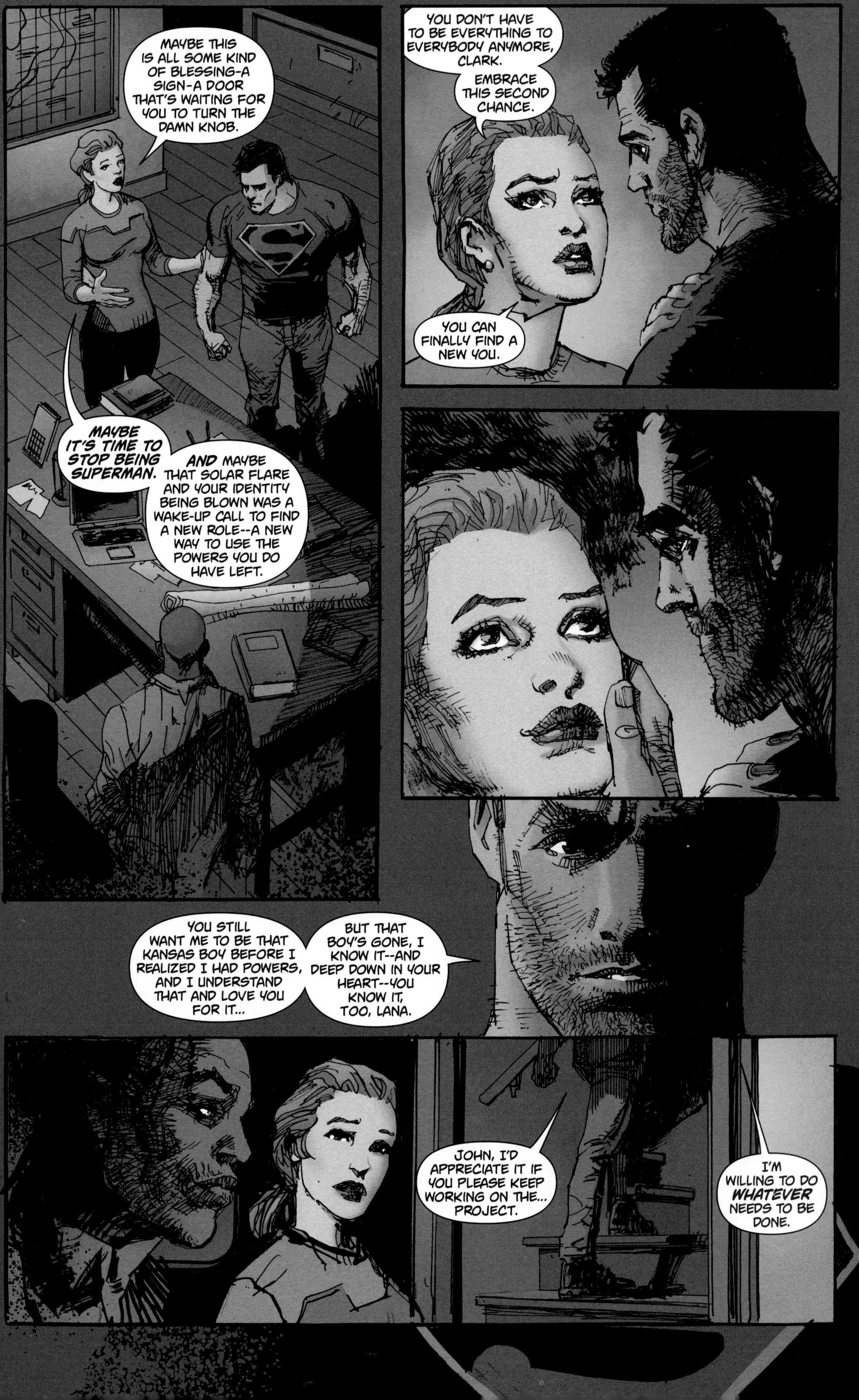

MAYBE THIS IS ALL SOME KIND OF BLESSING--A SIGN--A DOOR THAT'S WAITING FOR YOU TO TURN THE DAMN KNOB.
MAYBE IT'S TIME TO STOP BEING SUPERMAN.
AND MAYBE THAT SOLAR FLARE AND YOUR IDENTITY BEING BLOWN WAS A WAKE-UP CALL TO FIND A NEW ROLE--A NEW WAY TO USE THE POWERS YOU DO HAVE LEFT.
YOU DON'T HAVE TO BE EVERYTHING TO EVERYBODY ANYMORE, CLARK.
EMBRACE THIS SECOND CHANCE.
YOU CAN FINALLY FIND A NEW YOU.
YOU STILL WANT ME TO BE THAT KANSAS BOY BEFORE I REALIZED I HAD POWERS, AND I UNDERSTAND THAT AND LOVE YOU FOR IT...
BUT THAT BOY'S GONE, I KNOW IT--AND DEEP DOWN IN YOUR HEART--YOU KNOW IT, TOO, LANA.
JOHN, I'D APPRECIATE IT IF YOU PLEASE KEEP WORKING ON THE... PROJECT.
I'M WILLING TO DO WHATEVER NEEDS TO BE DONE.

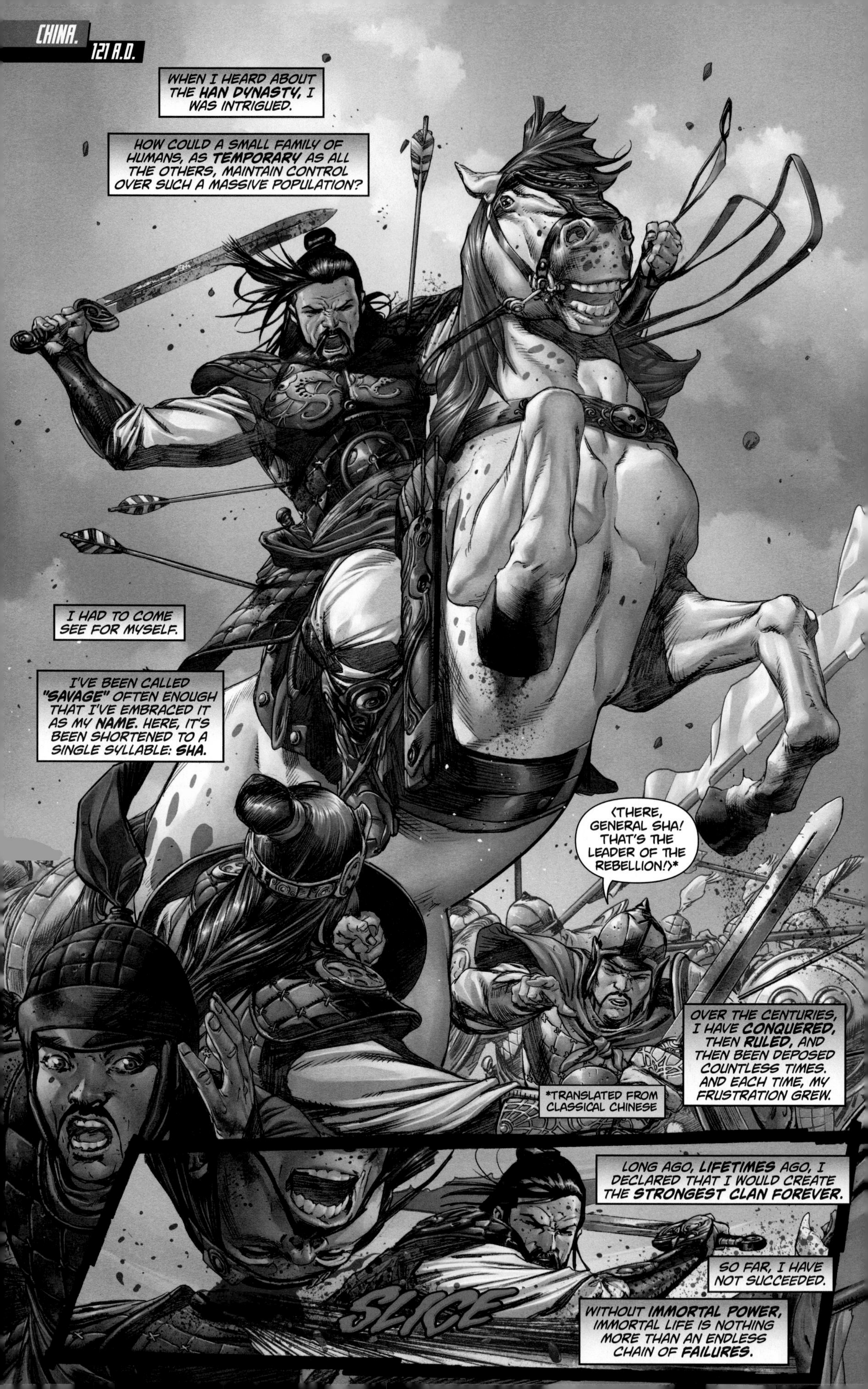
CHINA.
121 A.D.
WHEN I HEARD ABOUT THE HAN DYNASTY, I WAS INTRIGUED.
HOW COULD A SMALL FAMILY OF HUMANS, AS TEMPORARY AS ALL THE OTHERS, MAINTAIN CONTROL OVER SUCH A MASSIVE POPULATION?
I HAD TO COME SEE FOR MYSELF.
I'VE BEEN CALLED "SAVAGE" OFTEN ENOUGH THAT I'VE EMBRACED IT AS MY NAME. HERE, IT'S BEEN SHORTENED TO A SINGLE SYLLABLE: SHA.
⟨THERE, GENERAL SHA! THAT'S THE LEADER OF THE REBELLION!⟩*
OVER THE CENTURIES, I HAVE CONQUERED, THEN RULED, AND THEN BEEN DEPOSED COUNTLESS TIMES. AND EACH TIME, MY FRUSTRATION GREW.
*TRANSLATED FROM CLASSICAL CHINESE
LONG AGO, LIFETIMES AGO, I DECLARED THAT I WOULD CREATE THE STRONGEST CLAN FOREVER.
SO FAR, I HAVE NOT SUCCEEDED.
SLICE
WITHOUT IMMORTAL POWER, IMMORTAL LIFE IS NOTHING MORE THAN AN ENDLESS CHAIN OF FAILURES.

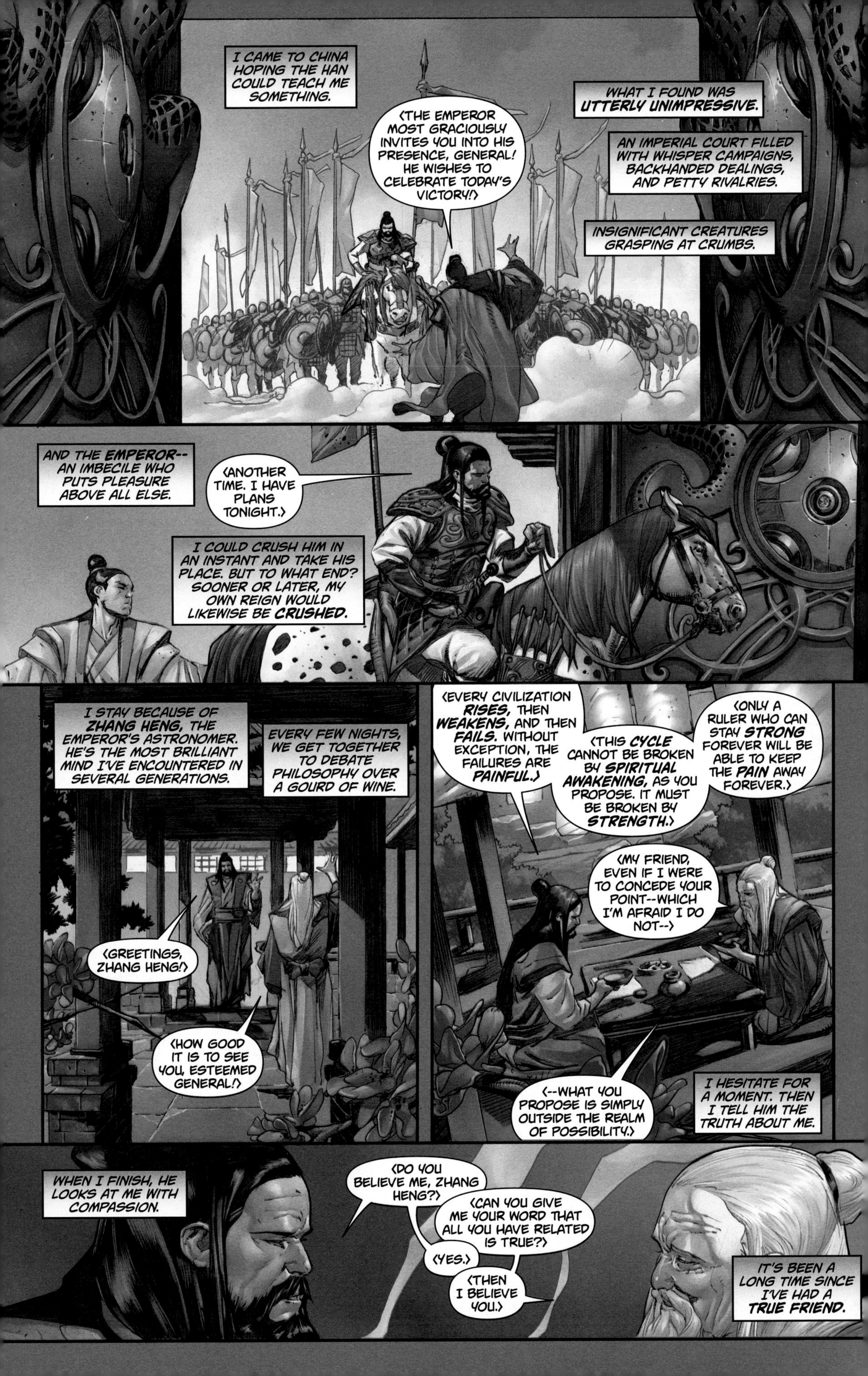
I CAME TO CHINA HOPING THE HAN COULD TEACH ME SOMETHING.
(THE EMPEROR MOST GRACIOUSLY INVITES YOU INTO HIS PRESENCE, GENERAL! HE WISHES TO CELEBRATE TODAY'S VICTORY!)
WHAT I FOUND WAS UTTERLY UNIMPRESSIVE.
AN IMPERIAL COURT FILLED WITH WHISPER CAMPAIGNS, BACKHANDED DEALINGS, AND PETTY RIVALRIES.
INSIGNIFICANT CREATURES GRASPING AT CRUMBS.
AND THE EMPEROR-- AN IMBECILE WHO PUTS PLEASURE ABOVE ALL ELSE.
(ANOTHER TIME. I HAVE PLANS TONIGHT.)
I COULD CRUSH HIM IN AN INSTANT AND TAKE HIS PLACE. BUT TO WHAT END? SOONER OR LATER, MY OWN REIGN WOULD LIKEWISE BE CRUSHED.
I STAY BECAUSE OF ZHANG HENG, THE EMPEROR'S ASTRONOMER. HE'S THE MOST BRILLIANT MIND I'VE ENCOUNTERED IN SEVERAL GENERATIONS.
EVERY FEW NIGHTS, WE GET TOGETHER TO DEBATE PHILOSOPHY OVER A GOURD OF WINE.
(GREETINGS, ZHANG HENG!)
(HOW GOOD IT IS TO SEE YOU, ESTEEMED GENERAL!)
(EVERY CIVILIZATION RISES, THEN WEAKENS, AND THEN FAILS. WITHOUT EXCEPTION, THE FAILURES ARE PAINFUL.)
(THIS CYCLE CANNOT BE BROKEN BY SPIRITUAL AWAKENING, AS YOU PROPOSE. IT MUST BE BROKEN BY STRENGTH.)
(ONLY A RULER WHO CAN STAY STRONG FOREVER WILL BE ABLE TO KEEP THE PAIN AWAY FOREVER.)
(MY FRIEND, EVEN IF I WERE TO CONCEDE YOUR POINT--WHICH I'M AFRAID I DO NOT--)
(--WHAT YOU PROPOSE IS SIMPLY OUTSIDE THE REALM OF POSSIBILITY.)
I HESITATE FOR A MOMENT. THEN I TELL HIM THE TRUTH ABOUT ME.
WHEN I FINISH, HE LOOKS AT ME WITH COMPASSION.
(DO YOU BELIEVE ME, ZHANG HENG?)
(CAN YOU GIVE ME YOUR WORD THAT ALL YOU HAVE RELATED IS TRUE?)
(YES.)
(THEN I BELIEVE YOU.)
IT'S BEEN A LONG TIME SINCE I'VE HAD A TRUE FRIEND.

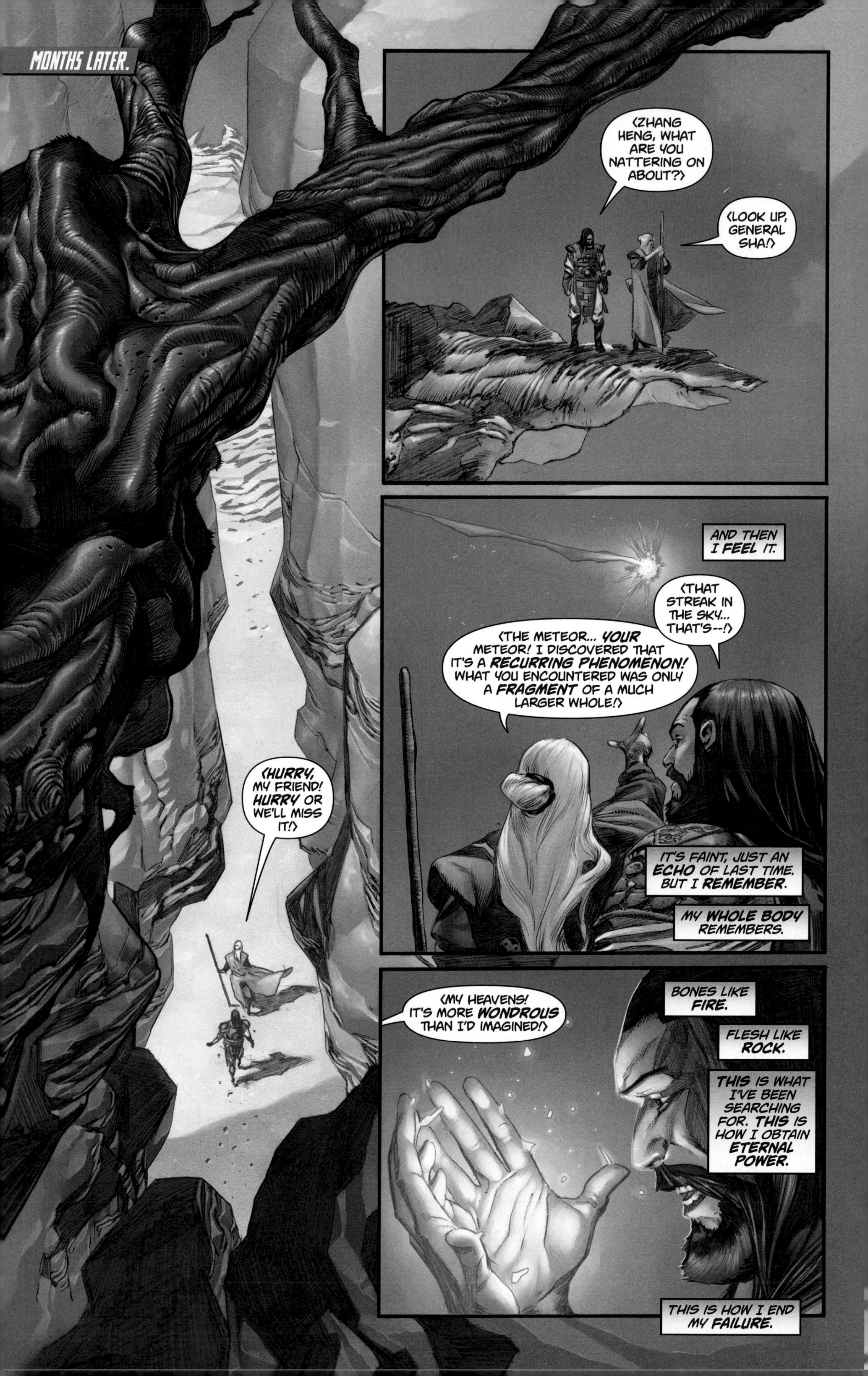
MONTHS LATER.
<ZHANG HENG, WHAT ARE YOU NATTERING ON ABOUT?>
<LOOK UP, GENERAL SHA!>
<HURRY, MY FRIEND! HURRY OR WE'LL MISS IT!>
AND THEN I FEEL IT.
<THAT STREAK IN THE SKY... THAT'S--!>
<THE METEOR... YOUR METEOR! I DISCOVERED THAT IT'S A RECURRING PHENOMENON! WHAT YOU ENCOUNTERED WAS ONLY A FRAGMENT OF A MUCH LARGER WHOLE!>
IT'S FAINT, JUST AN ECHO OF LAST TIME. BUT I REMEMBER.
MY WHOLE BODY REMEMBERS.
<MY HEAVENS! IT'S MORE WONDROUS THAN I'D IMAGINED!>
BONES LIKE FIRE.
FLESH LIKE ROCK.
THIS IS WHAT I'VE BEEN SEARCHING FOR. THIS IS HOW I OBTAIN ETERNAL POWER.
THIS IS HOW I END MY FAILURE.

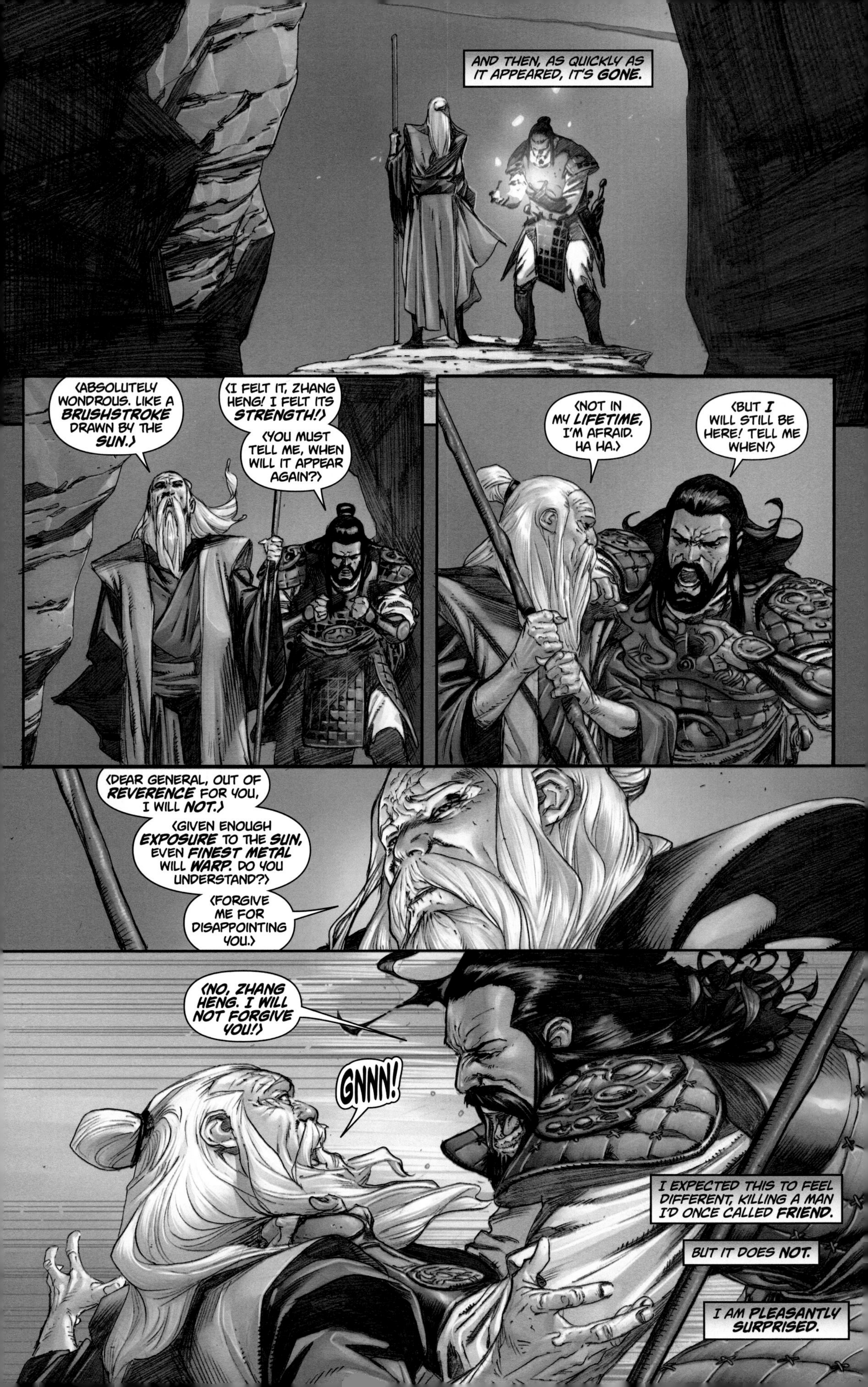
AND THEN, AS QUICKLY AS IT APPEARED, IT'S GONE.
‹ABSOLUTELY WONDROUS. LIKE A BRUSHSTROKE DRAWN BY THE SUN.›
‹I FELT IT, ZHANG HENG! I FELT ITS STRENGTH!›
‹YOU MUST TELL ME, WHEN WILL IT APPEAR AGAIN?›
‹NOT IN MY LIFETIME, I'M AFRAID. HA HA.›
‹BUT I WILL STILL BE HERE! TELL ME WHEN!›
‹DEAR GENERAL, OUT OF REVERENCE FOR YOU, I WILL NOT.›
‹GIVEN ENOUGH EXPOSURE TO THE SUN, EVEN FINEST METAL WILL WARP. DO YOU UNDERSTAND?›
‹FORGIVE ME FOR DISAPPOINTING YOU.›
‹NO, ZHANG HENG. I WILL NOT FORGIVE YOU!›
GNNN!
I EXPECTED THIS TO FEEL DIFFERENT, KILLING A MAN I'D ONCE CALLED FRIEND.
BUT IT DOES NOT.
I AM PLEASANTLY SURPRISED.

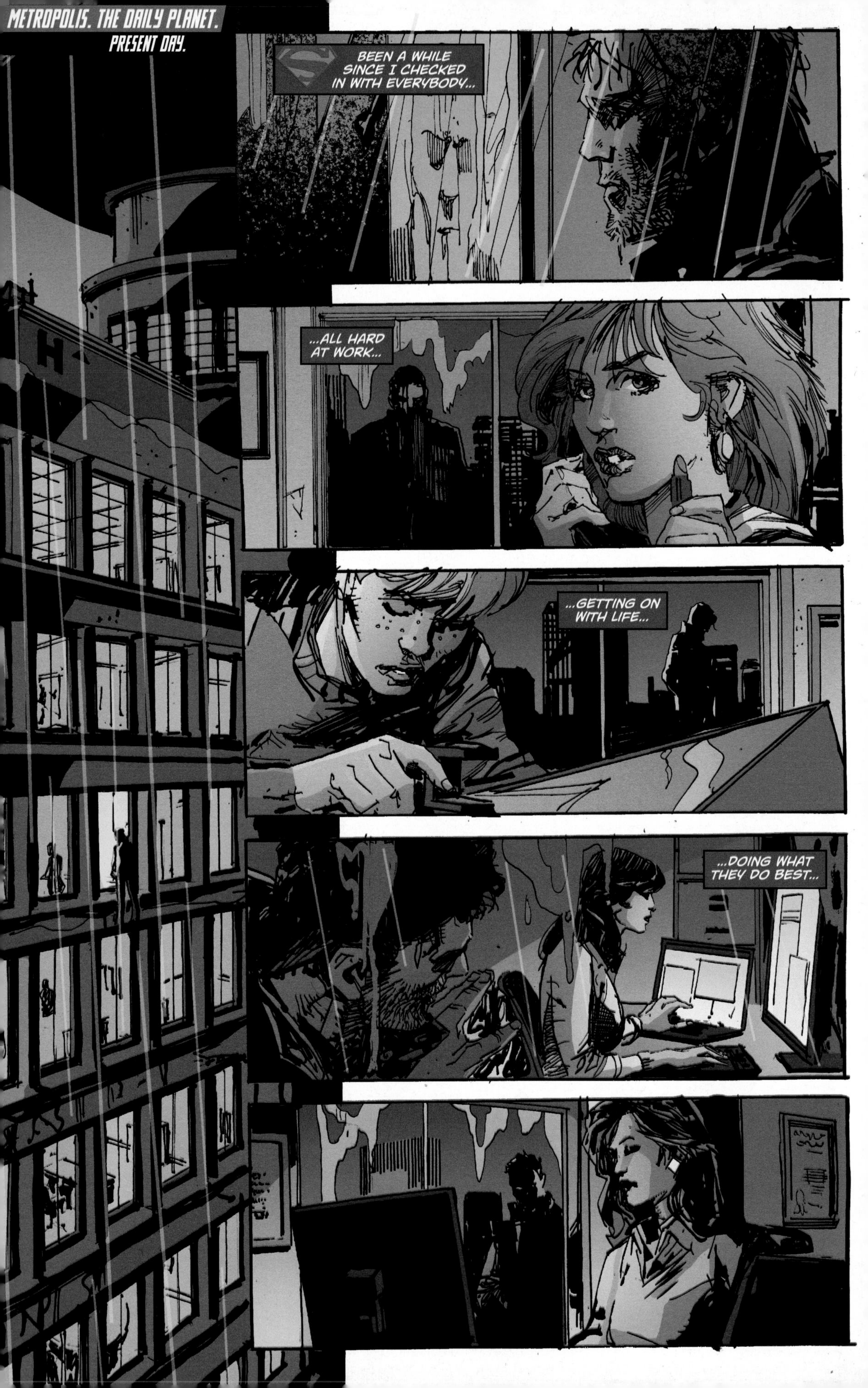
METROPOLIS. THE DAILY PLANET.
PRESENT DAY.
BEEN A WHILE SINCE I CHECKED IN WITH EVERYBODY...
...ALL HARD AT WORK...
...GETTING ON WITH LIFE...
...DOING WHAT THEY DO BEST...

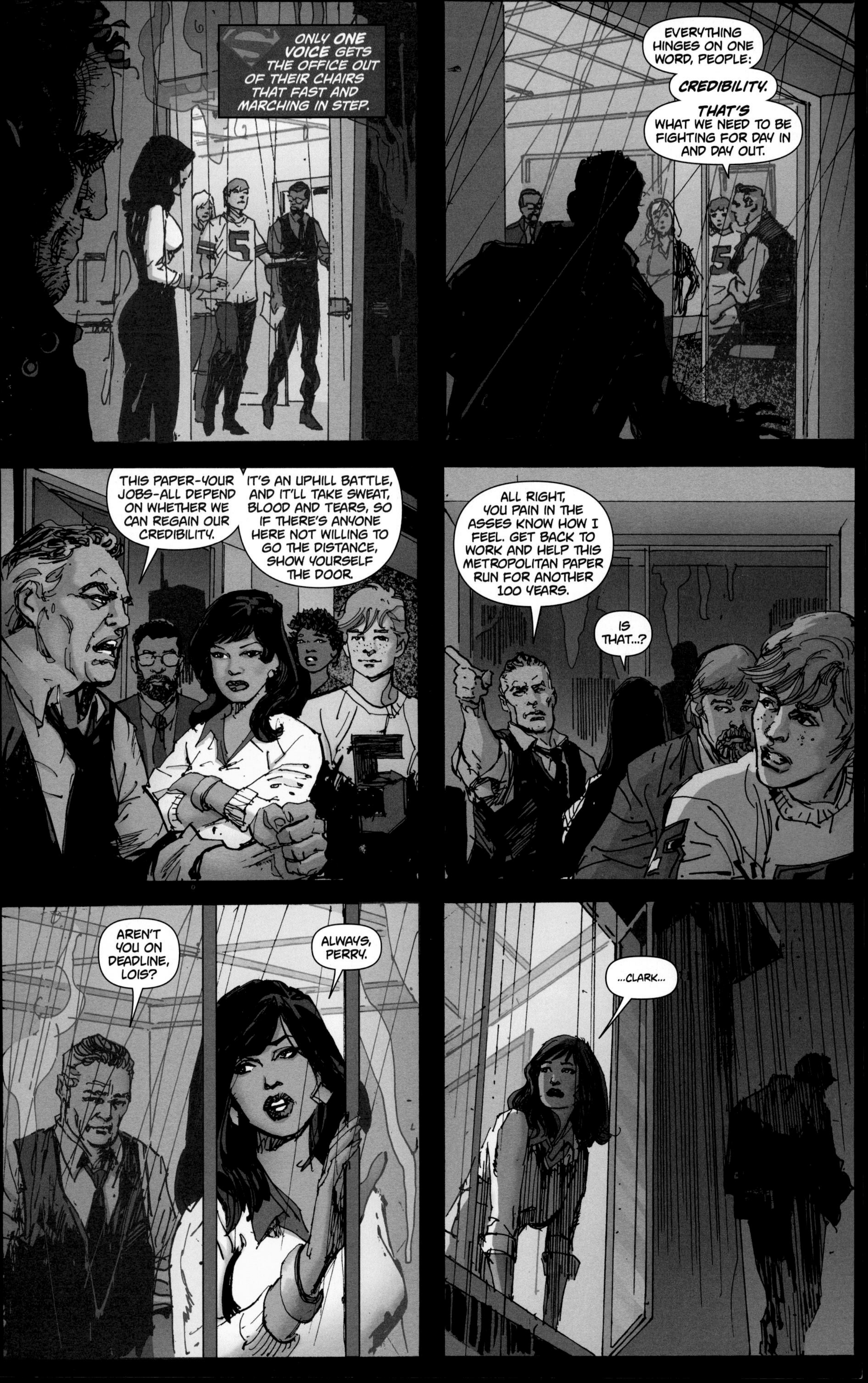
ONLY ONE VOICE GETS THE OFFICE OUT OF THEIR CHAIRS THAT FAST AND MARCHING IN STEP.
EVERYTHING HINGES ON ONE WORD, PEOPLE:
CREDIBILITY.
THAT'S WHAT WE NEED TO BE FIGHTING FOR DAY IN AND DAY OUT.
THIS PAPER-YOUR JOBS-ALL DEPEND ON WHETHER WE CAN REGAIN OUR CREDIBILITY.
IT'S AN UPHILL BATTLE, AND IT'LL TAKE SWEAT, BLOOD AND TEARS, SO IF THERE'S ANYONE HERE NOT WILLING TO GO THE DISTANCE, SHOW YOURSELF THE DOOR.
ALL RIGHT, YOU PAIN IN THE ASSES KNOW HOW I FEEL. GET BACK TO WORK AND HELP THIS METROPOLITAN PAPER RUN FOR ANOTHER 100 YEARS.
IS THAT...?
AREN'T YOU ON DEADLINE, LOIS?
ALWAYS, PERRY.
...CLARK...

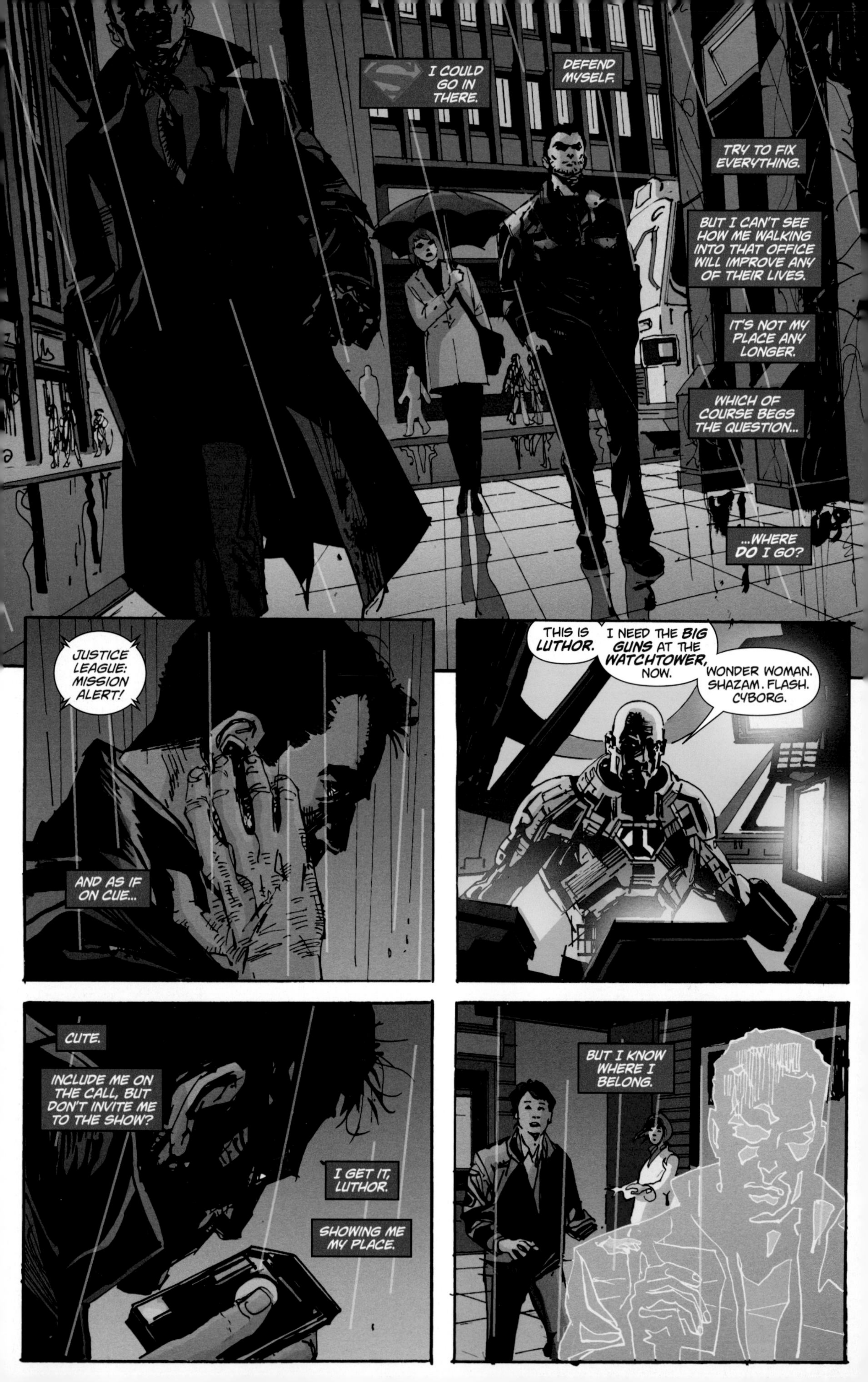

I COULD GO IN THERE.
DEFEND MYSELF.
TRY TO FIX EVERYTHING.
BUT I CAN'T SEE HOW ME WALKING INTO THAT OFFICE WILL IMPROVE ANY OF THEIR LIVES.
IT'S NOT MY PLACE ANY LONGER.
WHICH OF COURSE BEGS THE QUESTION...
...WHERE DO I GO?
JUSTICE LEAGUE: MISSION ALERT!
AND AS IF ON CUE...
THIS IS LUTHOR.
I NEED THE BIG GUNS AT THE WATCHTOWER, NOW.
WONDER WOMAN. SHAZAM. FLASH. CYBORG.
CUTE.
INCLUDE ME ON THE CALL, BUT DON'T INVITE ME TO THE SHOW?
I GET IT, LUTHOR.
SHOWING ME MY PLACE.
BUT I KNOW WHERE I BELONG.

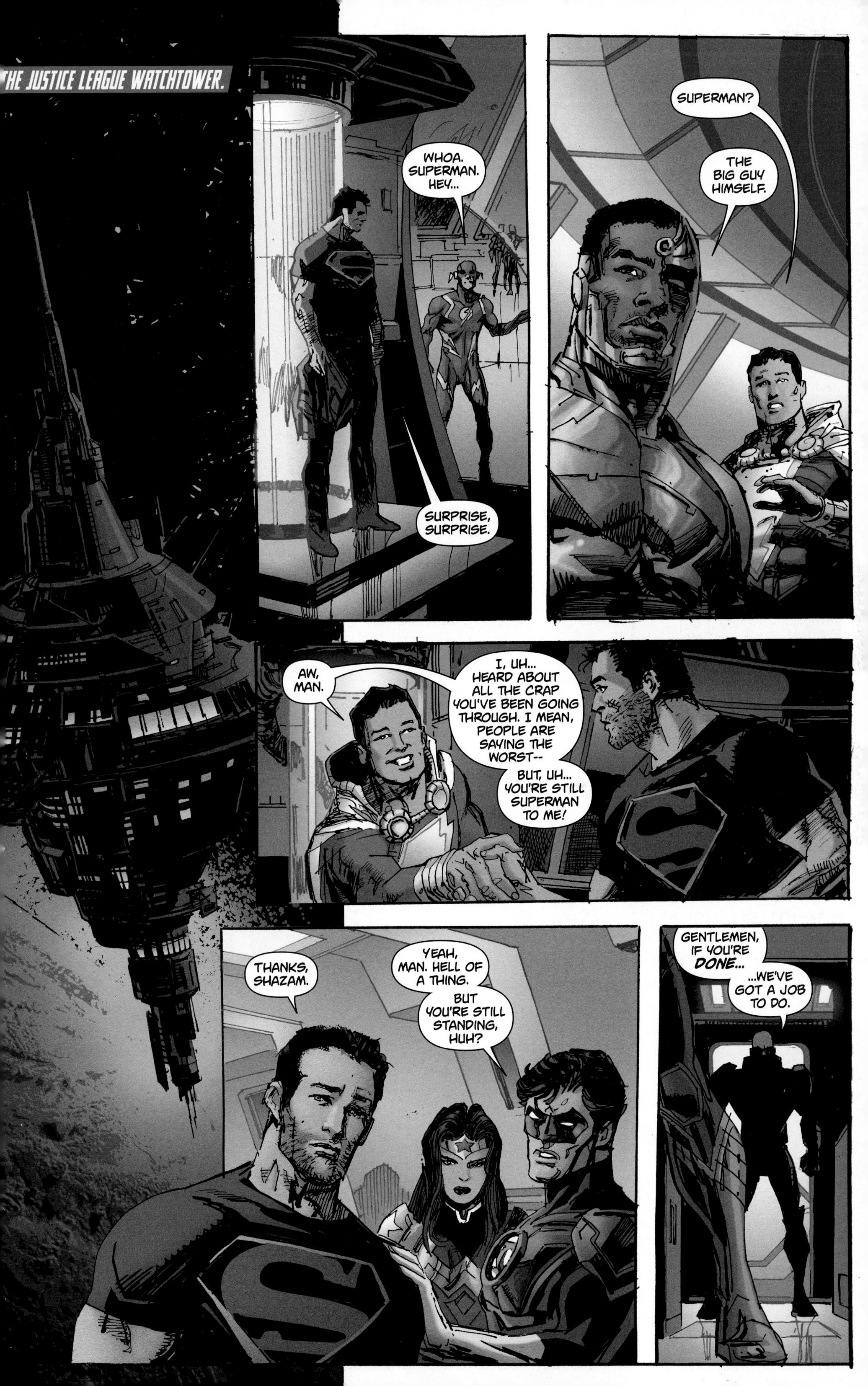
THE JUSTICE LEAGUE WATCHTOWER.
WHOA. SUPERMAN. HEY...
SURPRISE, SURPRISE.
SUPERMAN?
THE BIG GUY HIMSELF.
AW, MAN.
I, UH... HEARD ABOUT ALL THE CRAP YOU'VE BEEN GOING THROUGH. I MEAN, PEOPLE ARE SAYING THE WORST--
BUT, UH... YOU'RE STILL SUPERMAN TO ME!
THANKS, SHAZAM.
YEAH, MAN. HELL OF A THING.
BUT YOU'RE STILL STANDING, HUH?
GENTLEMEN, IF YOU'RE *DONE*...
...WE'VE GOT A JOB TO DO.

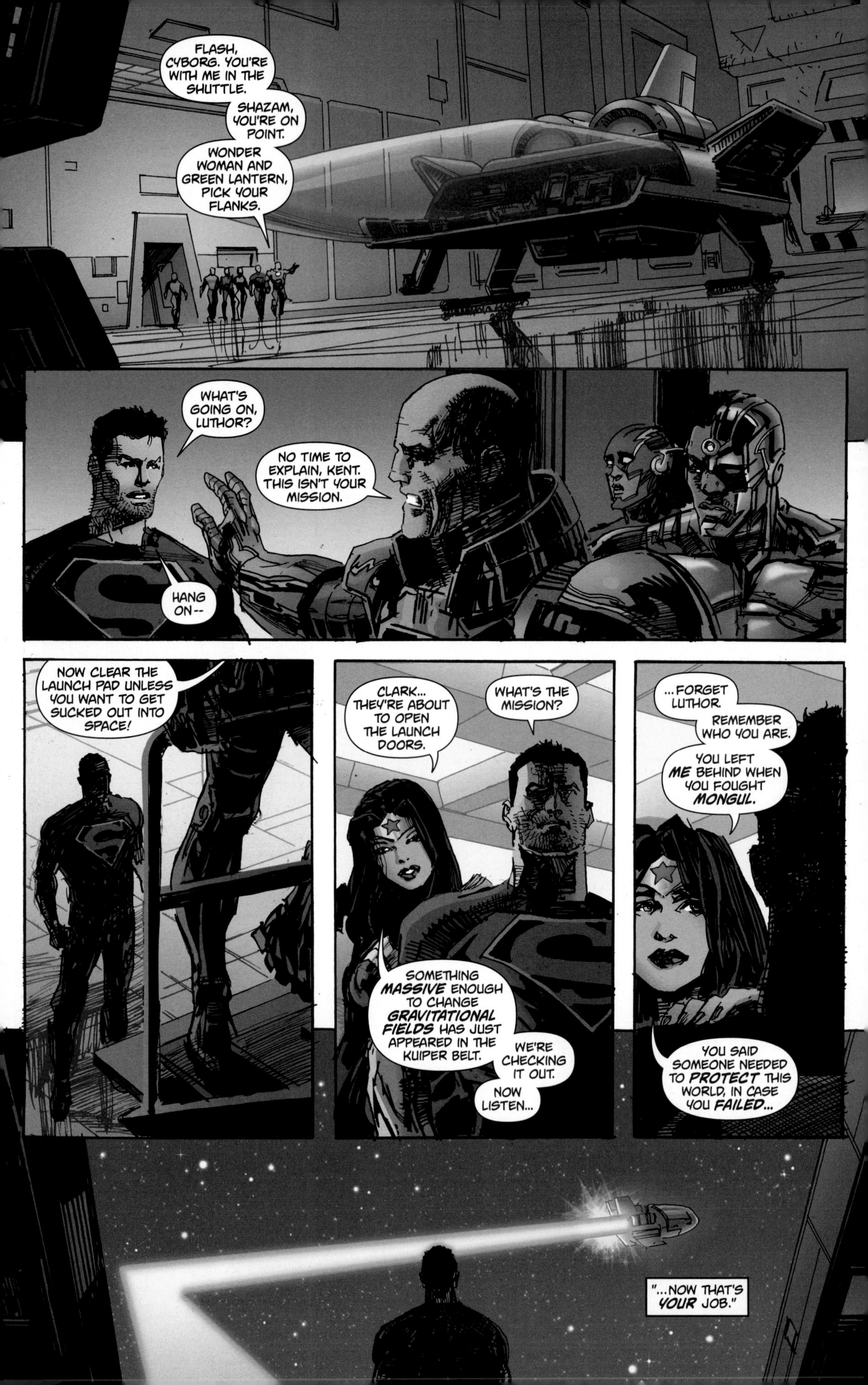
FLASH, CYBORG. YOU'RE WITH ME IN THE SHUTTLE.
SHAZAM, YOU'RE ON POINT.
WONDER WOMAN AND GREEN LANTERN, PICK YOUR FLANKS.
WHAT'S GOING ON, LUTHOR?
NO TIME TO EXPLAIN, KENT. THIS ISN'T YOUR MISSION.
HANG ON--
NOW CLEAR THE LAUNCH PAD UNLESS YOU WANT TO GET SUCKED OUT INTO SPACE!
CLARK... THEY'RE ABOUT TO OPEN THE LAUNCH DOORS.
WHAT'S THE MISSION?
SOMETHING **MASSIVE** ENOUGH TO CHANGE **GRAVITATIONAL FIELDS** HAS JUST APPEARED IN THE KUIPER BELT.
WE'RE CHECKING IT OUT.
NOW LISTEN...
...FORGET LUTHOR.
REMEMBER WHO YOU ARE.
YOU LEFT **ME** BEHIND WHEN YOU FOUGHT **MONGUL.**
YOU SAID SOMEONE NEEDED TO **PROTECT** THIS WORLD, IN CASE YOU **FAILED...**
"...NOW THAT'S **YOUR** JOB."

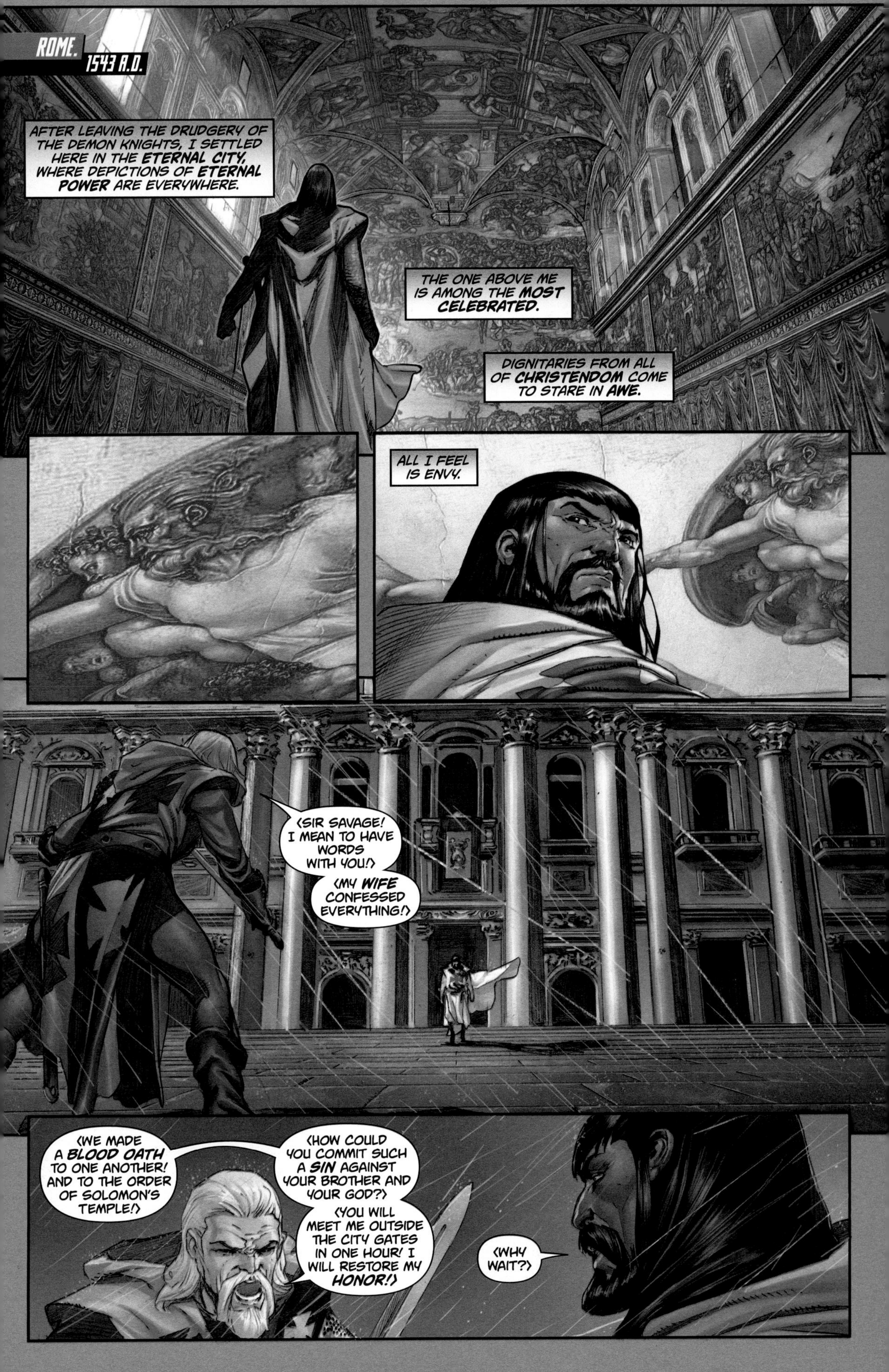
ROME.
1543 A.D.
AFTER LEAVING THE DRUDGERY OF THE DEMON KNIGHTS, I SETTLED HERE IN THE ETERNAL CITY, WHERE DEPICTIONS OF ETERNAL POWER ARE EVERYWHERE.
THE ONE ABOVE ME IS AMONG THE MOST CELEBRATED.
DIGNITARIES FROM ALL OF CHRISTENDOM COME TO STARE IN AWE.
ALL I FEEL IS ENVY.
‹SIR SAVAGE! I MEAN TO HAVE WORDS WITH YOU!›
‹MY WIFE CONFESSED EVERYTHING!›
‹WE MADE A BLOOD OATH TO ONE ANOTHER! AND TO THE ORDER OF SOLOMON'S TEMPLE!›
‹HOW COULD YOU COMMIT SUCH A SIN AGAINST YOUR BROTHER AND YOUR GOD?›
‹YOU WILL MEET ME OUTSIDE THE CITY GATES IN ONE HOUR! I WILL RESTORE MY HONOR!›
‹WHY WAIT?›

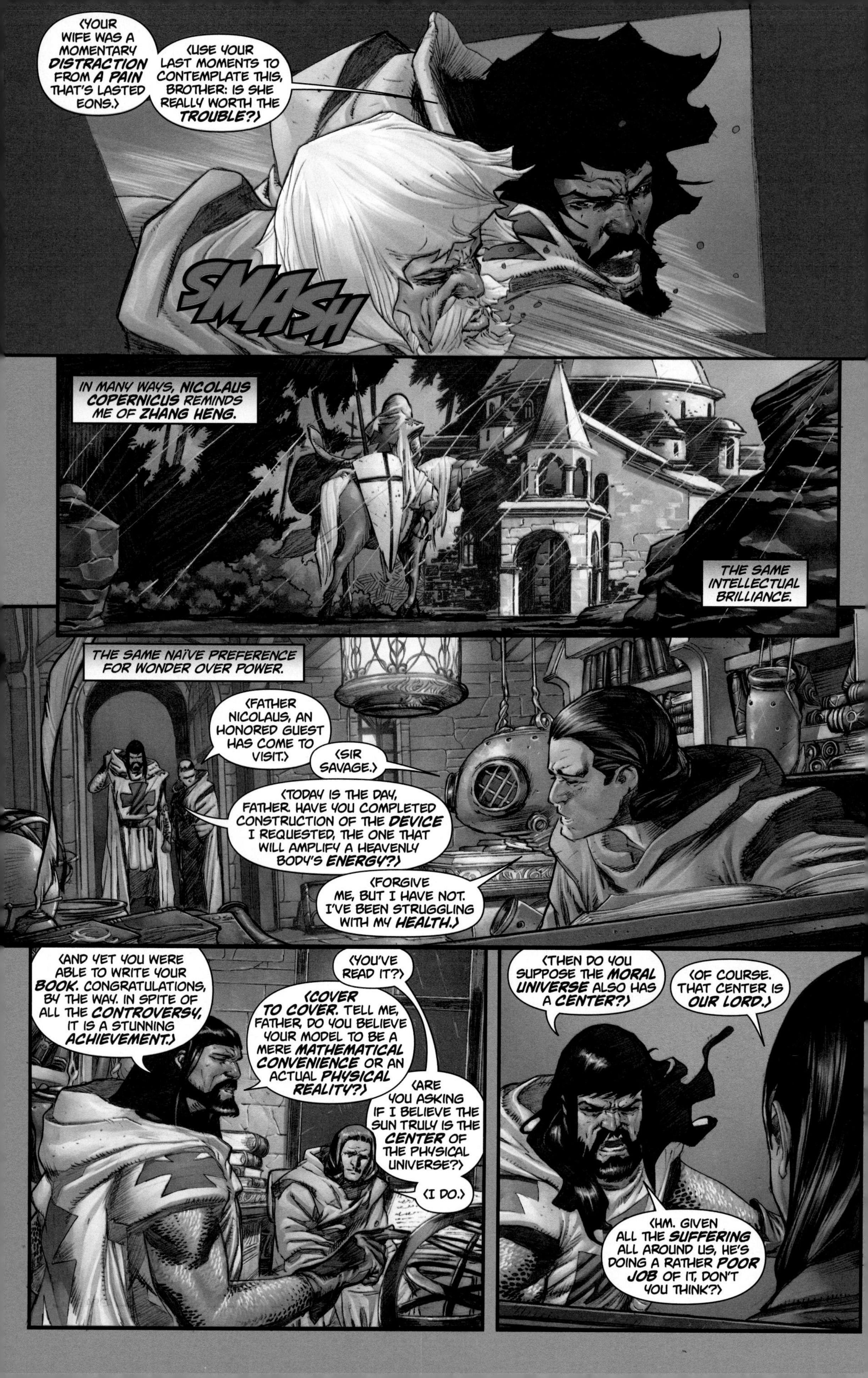

‹YOUR WIFE WAS A MOMENTARY DISTRACTION FROM A PAIN THAT'S LASTED EONS.›
‹USE YOUR LAST MOMENTS TO CONTEMPLATE THIS, BROTHER: IS SHE REALLY WORTH THE TROUBLE?›
SMASH
IN MANY WAYS, NICOLAUS COPERNICUS REMINDS ME OF ZHANG HENG.
THE SAME INTELLECTUAL BRILLIANCE.
THE SAME NAÏVE PREFERENCE FOR WONDER OVER POWER.
‹FATHER NICOLAUS, AN HONORED GUEST HAS COME TO VISIT.›
‹SIR SAVAGE.›
‹TODAY IS THE DAY, FATHER. HAVE YOU COMPLETED CONSTRUCTION OF THE DEVICE I REQUESTED, THE ONE THAT WILL AMPLIFY A HEAVENLY BODY'S ENERGY?›
‹FORGIVE ME, BUT I HAVE NOT. I'VE BEEN STRUGGLING WITH MY HEALTH.›
‹AND YET YOU WERE ABLE TO WRITE YOUR BOOK. CONGRATULATIONS, BY THE WAY. IN SPITE OF ALL THE CONTROVERSY, IT IS A STUNNING ACHIEVEMENT.›
‹YOU'VE READ IT?›
‹COVER TO COVER. TELL ME, FATHER, DO YOU BELIEVE YOUR MODEL TO BE A MERE MATHEMATICAL CONVENIENCE OR AN ACTUAL PHYSICAL REALITY?›
‹ARE YOU ASKING IF I BELIEVE THE SUN TRULY IS THE CENTER OF THE PHYSICAL UNIVERSE?›
‹I DO.›
‹THEN DO YOU SUPPOSE THE MORAL UNIVERSE ALSO HAS A CENTER?›
‹OF COURSE. THAT CENTER IS OUR LORD.›
‹HM. GIVEN ALL THE SUFFERING ALL AROUND US, HE'S DOING A RATHER POOR JOB OF IT, DON'T YOU THINK?›

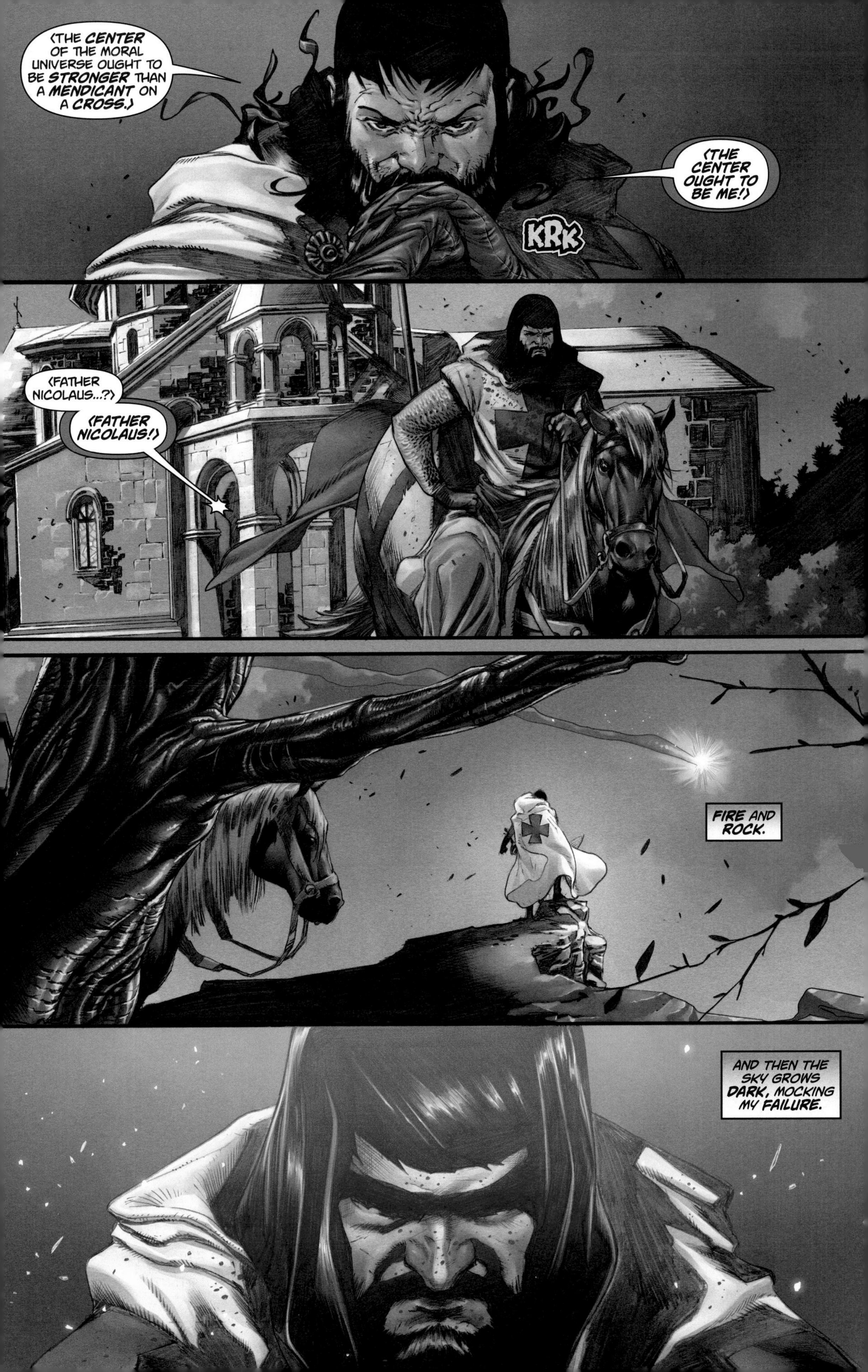
‹THE CENTER OF THE MORAL UNIVERSE OUGHT TO BE STRONGER THAN A MENDICANT ON A CROSS.›
‹THE CENTER OUGHT TO BE ME!›
KRK
‹FATHER NICOLAUS...?›
‹FATHER NICOLAUS!›
FIRE AND ROCK.
AND THEN THE SKY GROWS DARK, MOCKING MY FAILURE.

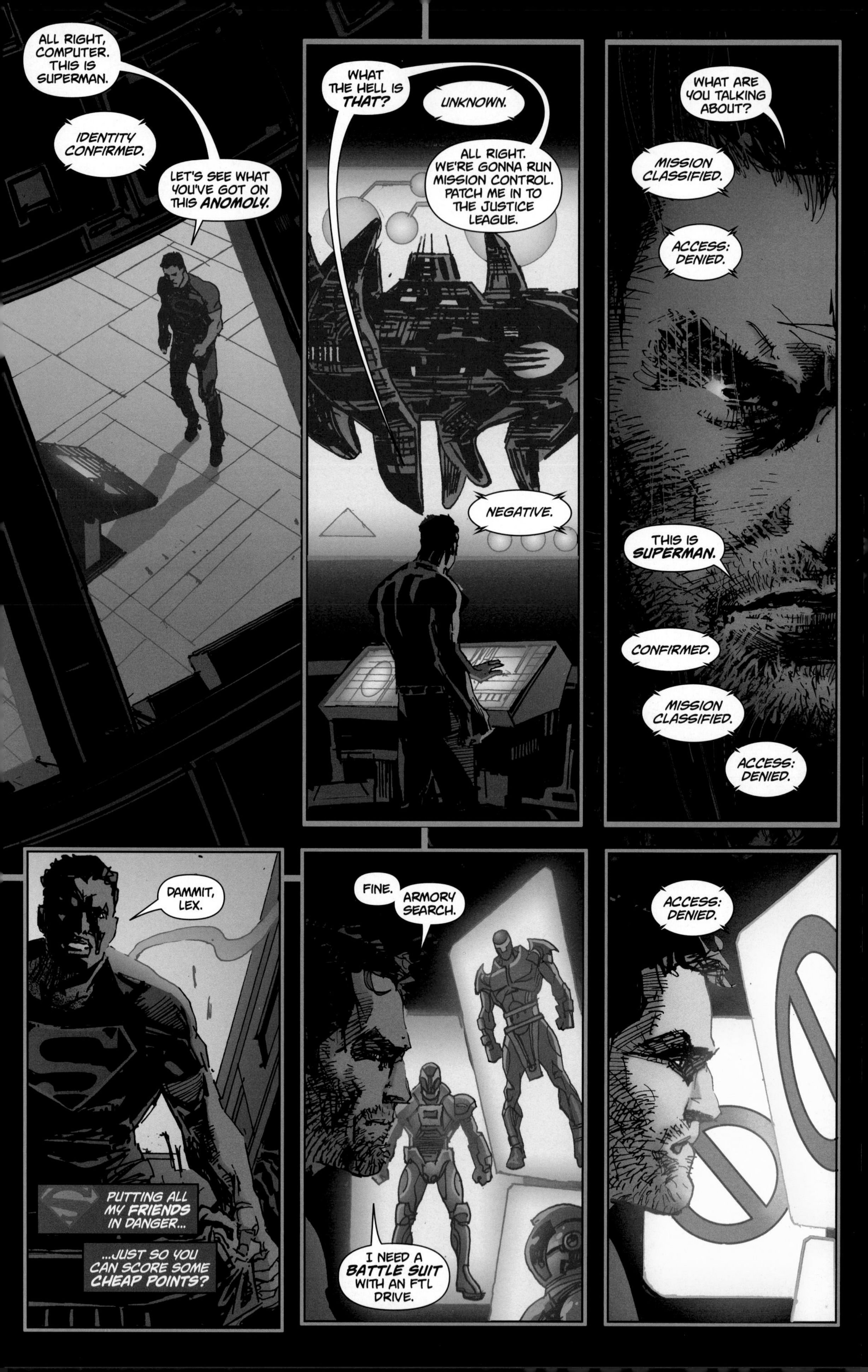
ALL RIGHT, COMPUTER. THIS IS SUPERMAN.
IDENTITY CONFIRMED.
LET'S SEE WHAT YOU'VE GOT ON THIS ANOMOLY.
WHAT THE HELL IS THAT?
UNKNOWN.
ALL RIGHT. WE'RE GONNA RUN MISSION CONTROL. PATCH ME IN TO THE JUSTICE LEAGUE.
NEGATIVE.
WHAT ARE YOU TALKING ABOUT?
MISSION CLASSIFIED.
ACCESS: DENIED.
THIS IS SUPERMAN.
CONFIRMED.
MISSION CLASSIFIED.
ACCESS: DENIED.
DAMMIT, LEX.
PUTTING ALL MY FRIENDS IN DANGER...
...JUST SO YOU CAN SCORE SOME CHEAP POINTS?
FINE.
ARMORY SEARCH.
I NEED A BATTLE SUIT WITH AN FTL DRIVE.
ACCESS: DENIED.

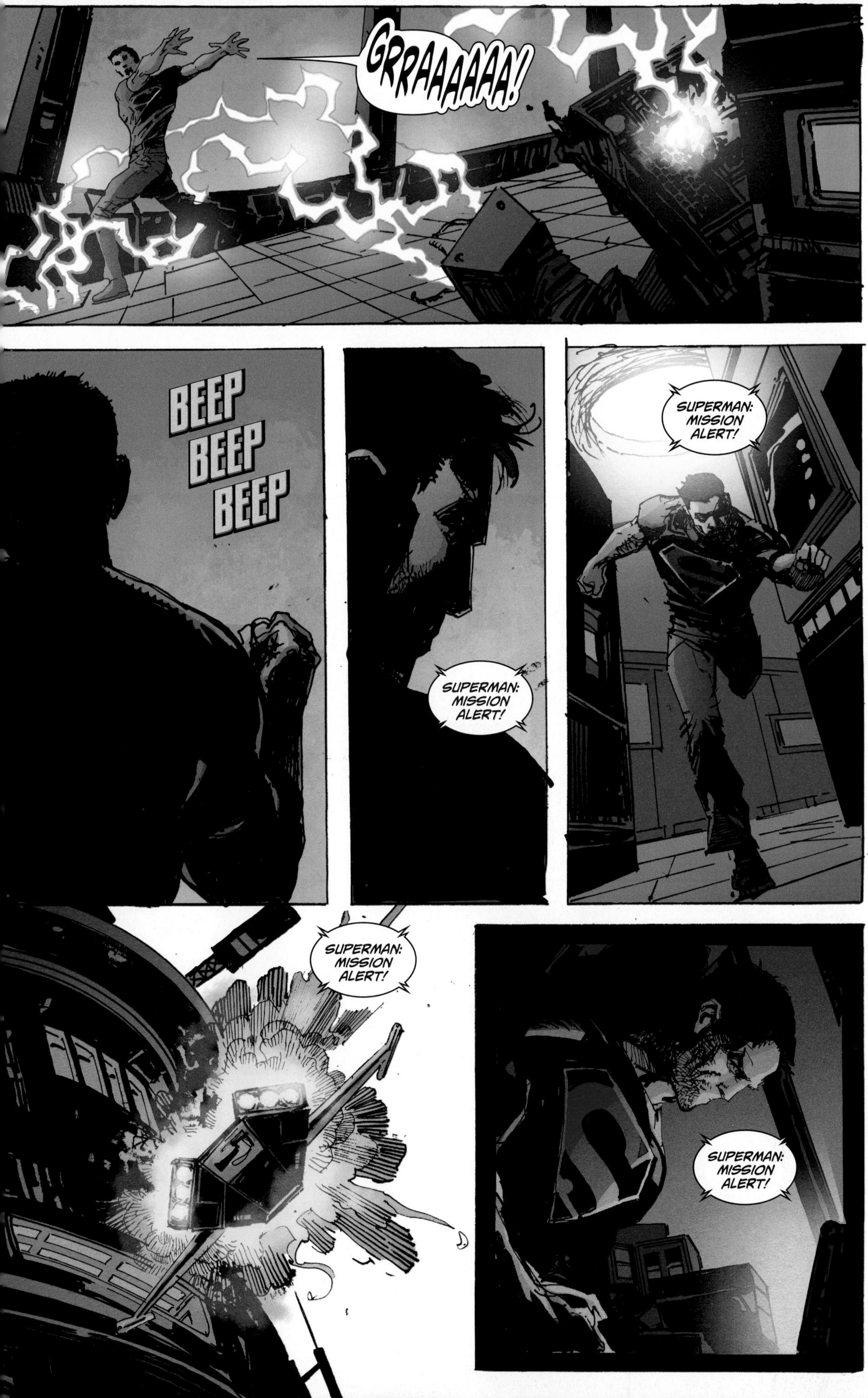
GRRAAAAAA!
BEEP
BEEP
BEEP
SUPERMAN: MISSION ALERT!
SUPERMAN: MISSION ALERT!
SUPERMAN: MISSION ALERT!
SUPERMAN: MISSION ALERT!

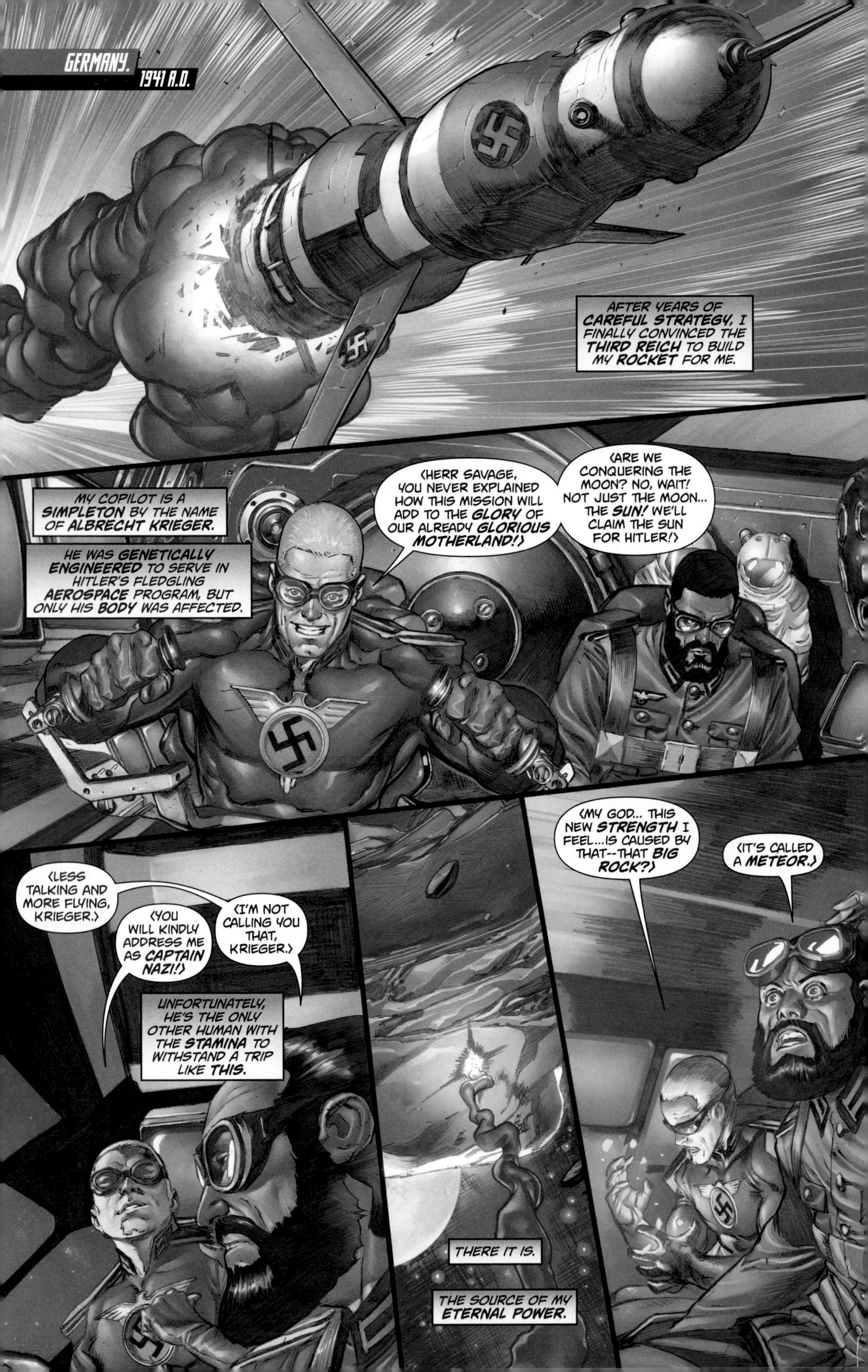
GERMANY.
1941 A.D.
AFTER YEARS OF CAREFUL STRATEGY, I FINALLY CONVINCED THE THIRD REICH TO BUILD MY ROCKET FOR ME.
MY COPILOT IS A SIMPLETON BY THE NAME OF ALBRECHT KRIEGER.
HE WAS GENETICALLY ENGINEERED TO SERVE IN HITLER'S FLEDGLING AEROSPACE PROGRAM, BUT ONLY HIS BODY WAS AFFECTED.
‹HERR SAVAGE, YOU NEVER EXPLAINED HOW THIS MISSION WILL ADD TO THE GLORY OF OUR ALREADY GLORIOUS MOTHERLAND!›
‹ARE WE CONQUERING THE MOON? NO, WAIT! NOT JUST THE MOON... THE SUN! WE'LL CLAIM THE SUN FOR HITLER!›
‹LESS TALKING AND MORE FLYING, KRIEGER.›
‹YOU WILL KINDLY ADDRESS ME AS CAPTAIN NAZI!›
‹I'M NOT CALLING YOU THAT, KRIEGER.›
UNFORTUNATELY, HE'S THE ONLY OTHER HUMAN WITH THE STAMINA TO WITHSTAND A TRIP LIKE THIS.
THERE IT IS.
THE SOURCE OF MY ETERNAL POWER.
‹MY GOD... THIS NEW STRENGTH I FEEL...IS CAUSED BY THAT--THAT BIG ROCK?›
‹IT'S CALLED A METEOR.›

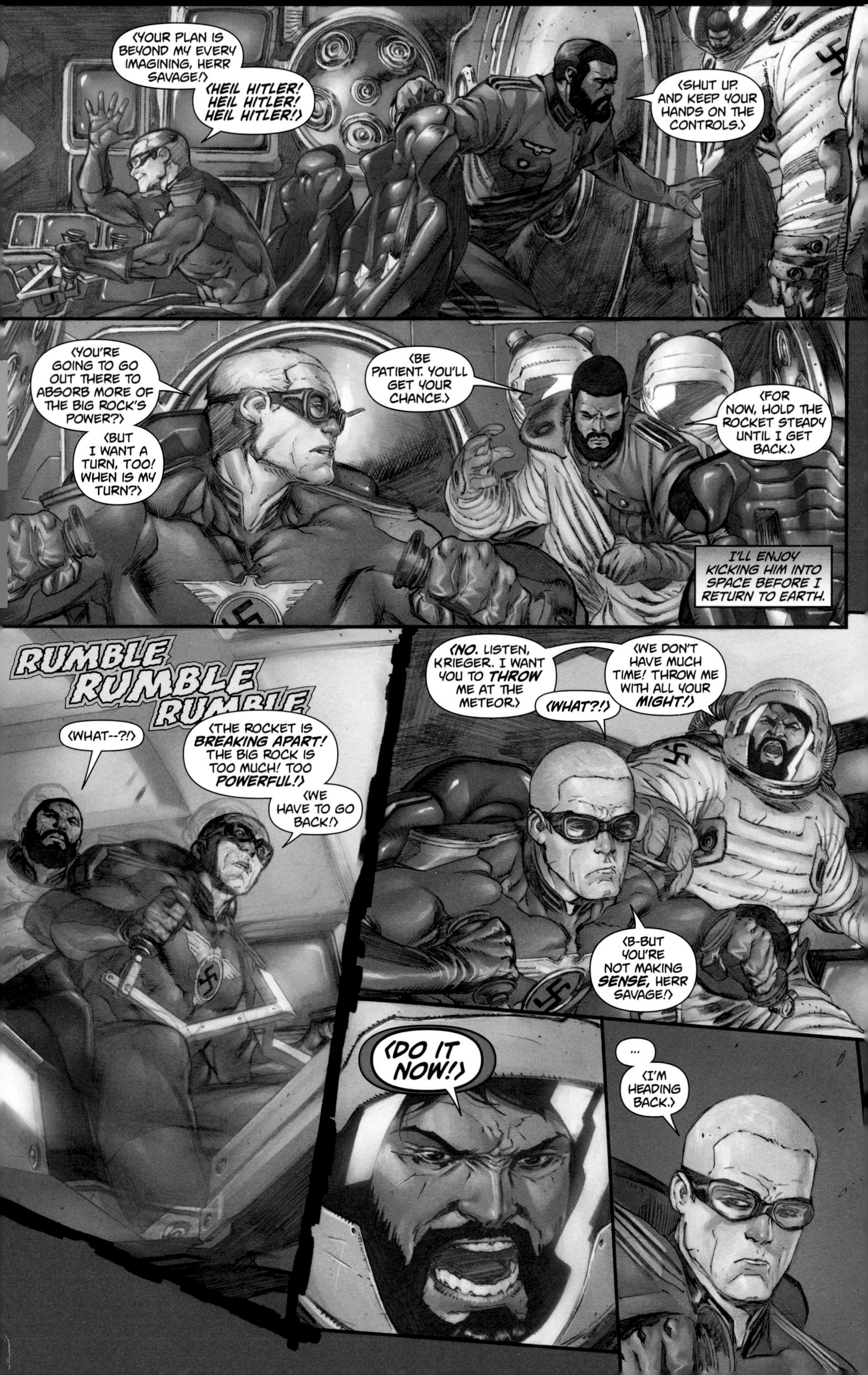

‹YOUR PLAN IS BEYOND MY EVERY IMAGINING, HERR SAVAGE!›
‹HEIL HITLER! HEIL HITLER! HEIL HITLER!›
‹SHUT UP. AND KEEP YOUR HANDS ON THE CONTROLS.›
‹YOU'RE GOING TO GO OUT THERE TO ABSORB MORE OF THE BIG ROCK'S POWER?›
‹BUT I WANT A TURN, TOO! WHEN IS MY TURN?›
‹BE PATIENT. YOU'LL GET YOUR CHANCE.›
‹FOR NOW, HOLD THE ROCKET STEADY UNTIL I GET BACK.›
I'LL ENJOY KICKING HIM INTO SPACE BEFORE I RETURN TO EARTH.
RUMBLE RUMBLE RUMBLE
‹WHAT--?!›
‹THE ROCKET IS BREAKING APART! THE BIG ROCK IS TOO MUCH! TOO POWERFUL!›
‹WE HAVE TO GO BACK!›
‹NO. LISTEN, KRIEGER. I WANT YOU TO THROW ME AT THE METEOR.›
‹WHAT?!›
‹WE DON'T HAVE MUCH TIME! THROW ME WITH ALL YOUR MIGHT!›
‹B-BUT YOU'RE NOT MAKING SENSE, HERR SAVAGE!›
‹DO IT NOW!›
...
‹I'M HEADING BACK.›

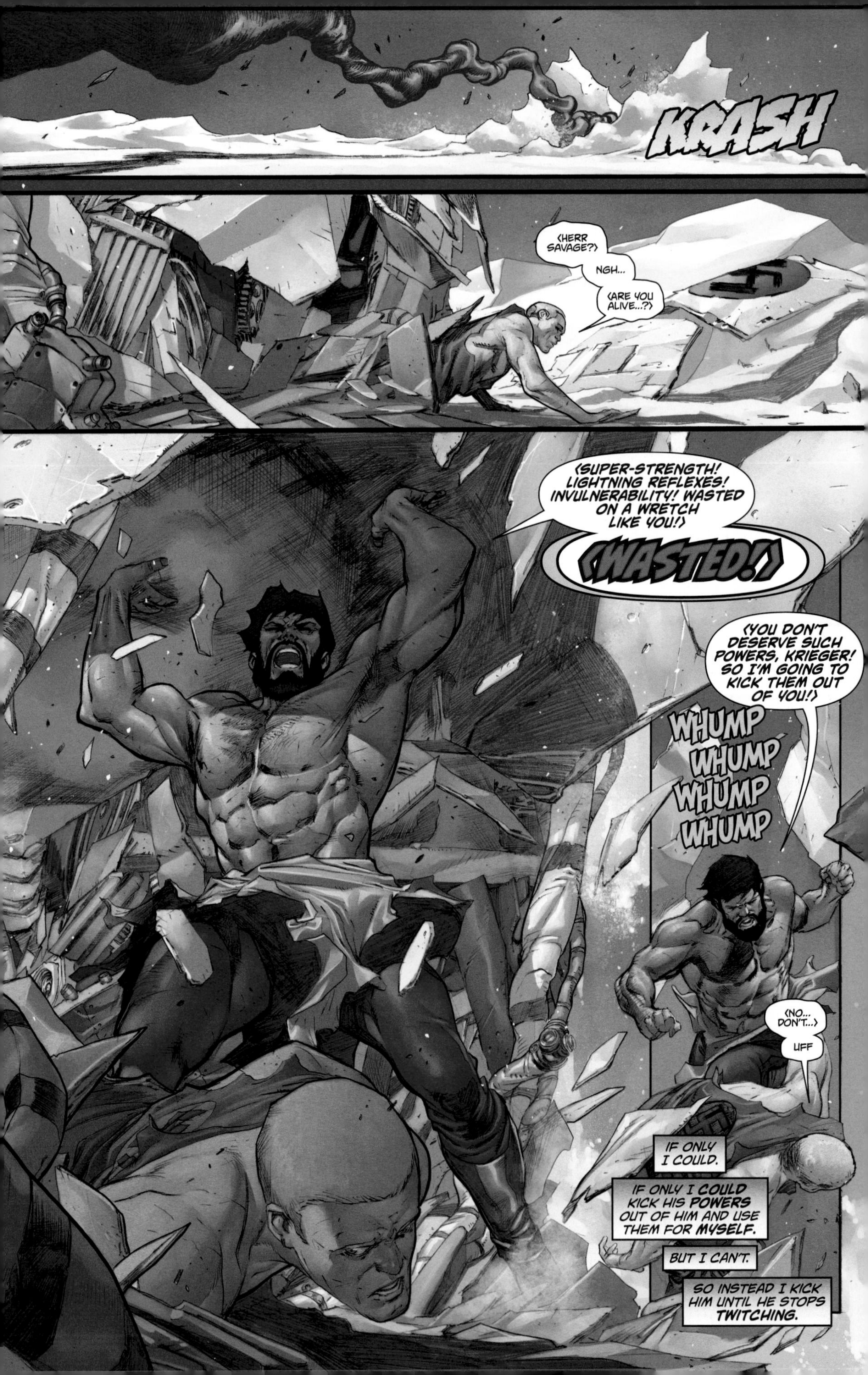
KRASH
⟨HERR SAVAGE?⟩
NGH...
⟨ARE YOU ALIVE...?⟩
⟨SUPER-STRENGTH! LIGHTNING REFLEXES! INVULNERABILITY! WASTED ON A WRETCH LIKE YOU!⟩
⟨WASTED!⟩
⟨YOU DON'T DESERVE SUCH POWERS, KRIEGER! SO I'M GOING TO KICK THEM OUT OF YOU!⟩
WHUMP
WHUMP
WHUMP
WHUMP
⟨NO... DON'T...⟩
UFF
IF ONLY I COULD.
IF ONLY I COULD KICK HIS POWERS OUT OF HIM AND USE THEM FOR MYSELF.
BUT I CAN'T.
SO INSTEAD I KICK HIM UNTIL HE STOPS TWITCHING.

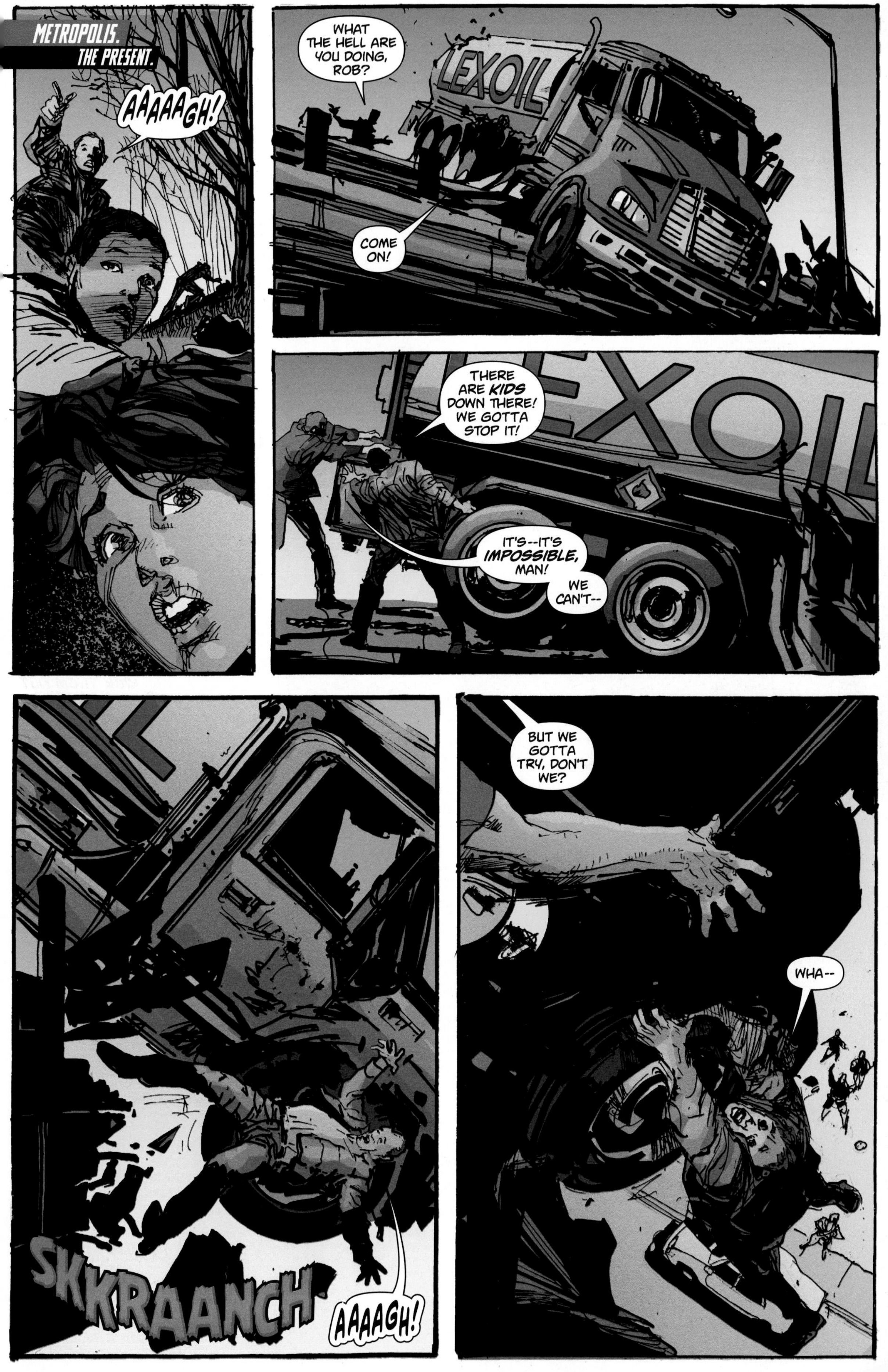
METROPOLIS. THE PRESENT.
AAAAAGH!
WHAT THE HELL ARE YOU DOING, ROB?
COME ON!
THERE ARE KIDS DOWN THERE! WE GOTTA STOP IT!
IT'S--IT'S IMPOSSIBLE, MAN!
WE CAN'T--
SKKRAANCH
AAAAGH!
BUT WE GOTTA TRY, DON'T WE?
WHA--

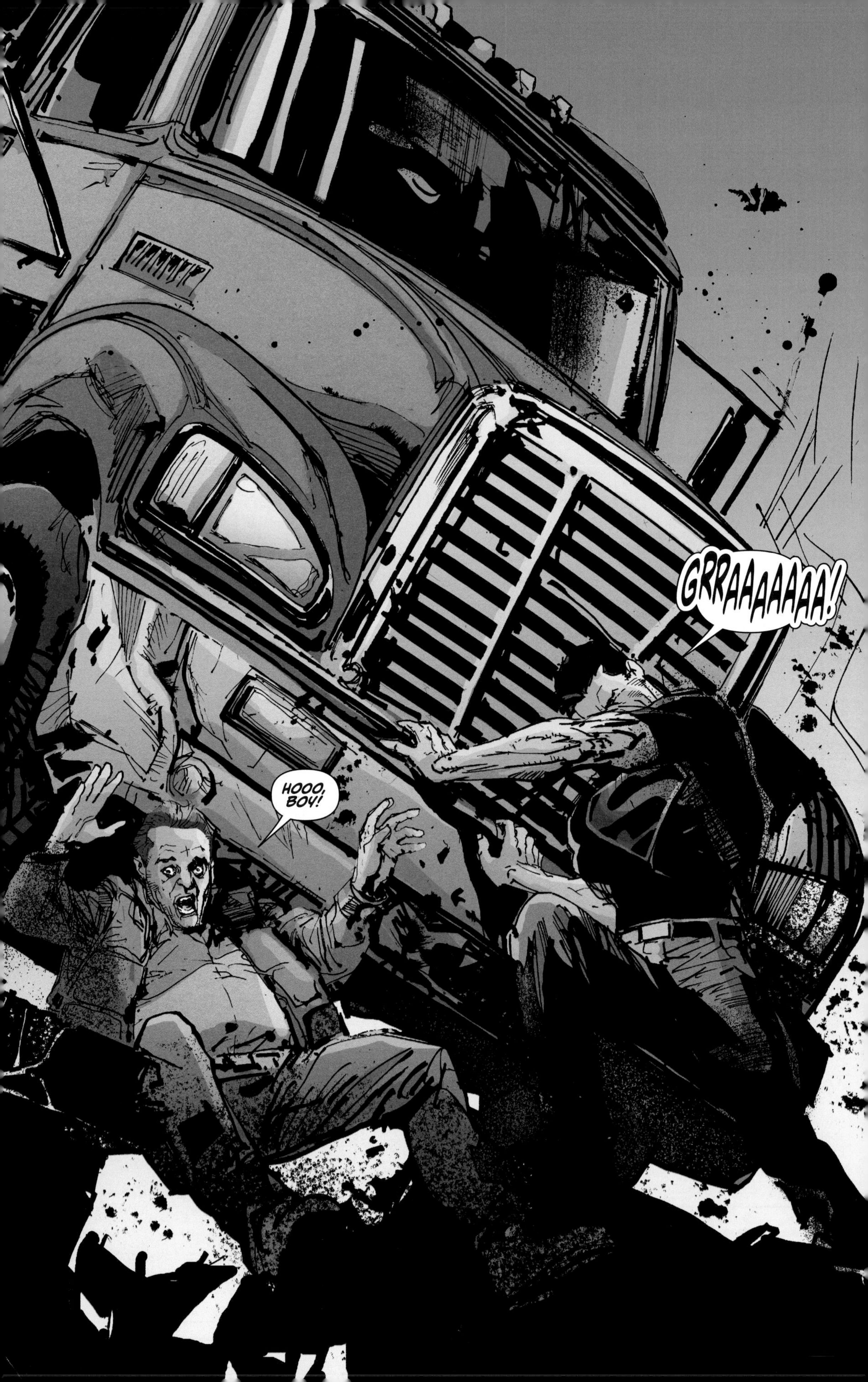
GRRAAAAAAA!
HOOO, BOY!

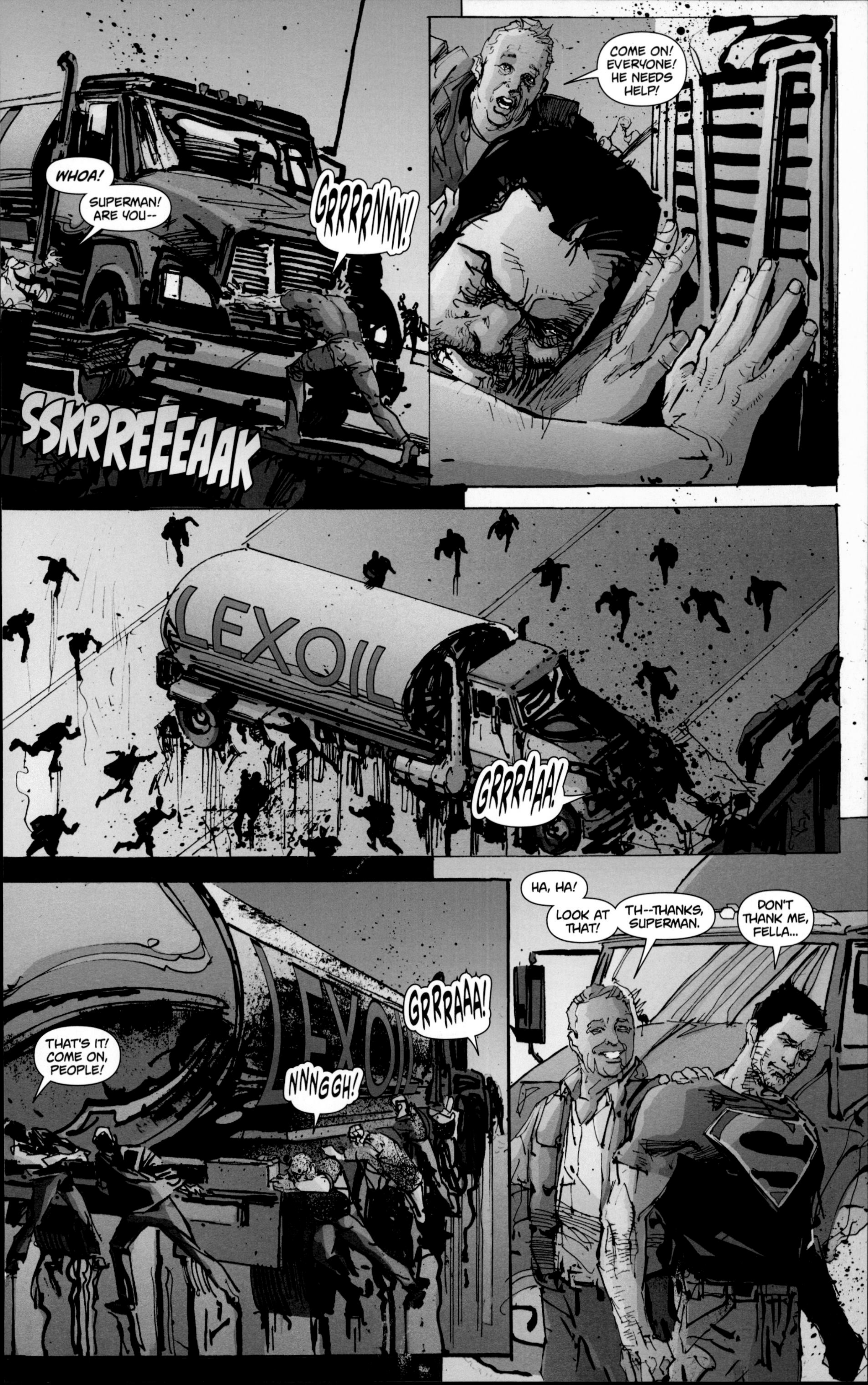
WHOA!
SUPERMAN! ARE YOU--
GRRRRNNN!
SSKRREEEAAK
COME ON! EVERYONE! HE NEEDS HELP!
LEXOIL
GRRRAAA!
THAT'S IT! COME ON, PEOPLE!
LEXOIL
GRRRAAA!
NNNGGH!
HA, HA!
LOOK AT THAT!
TH--THANKS, SUPERMAN.
DON'T THANK ME, FELLA...

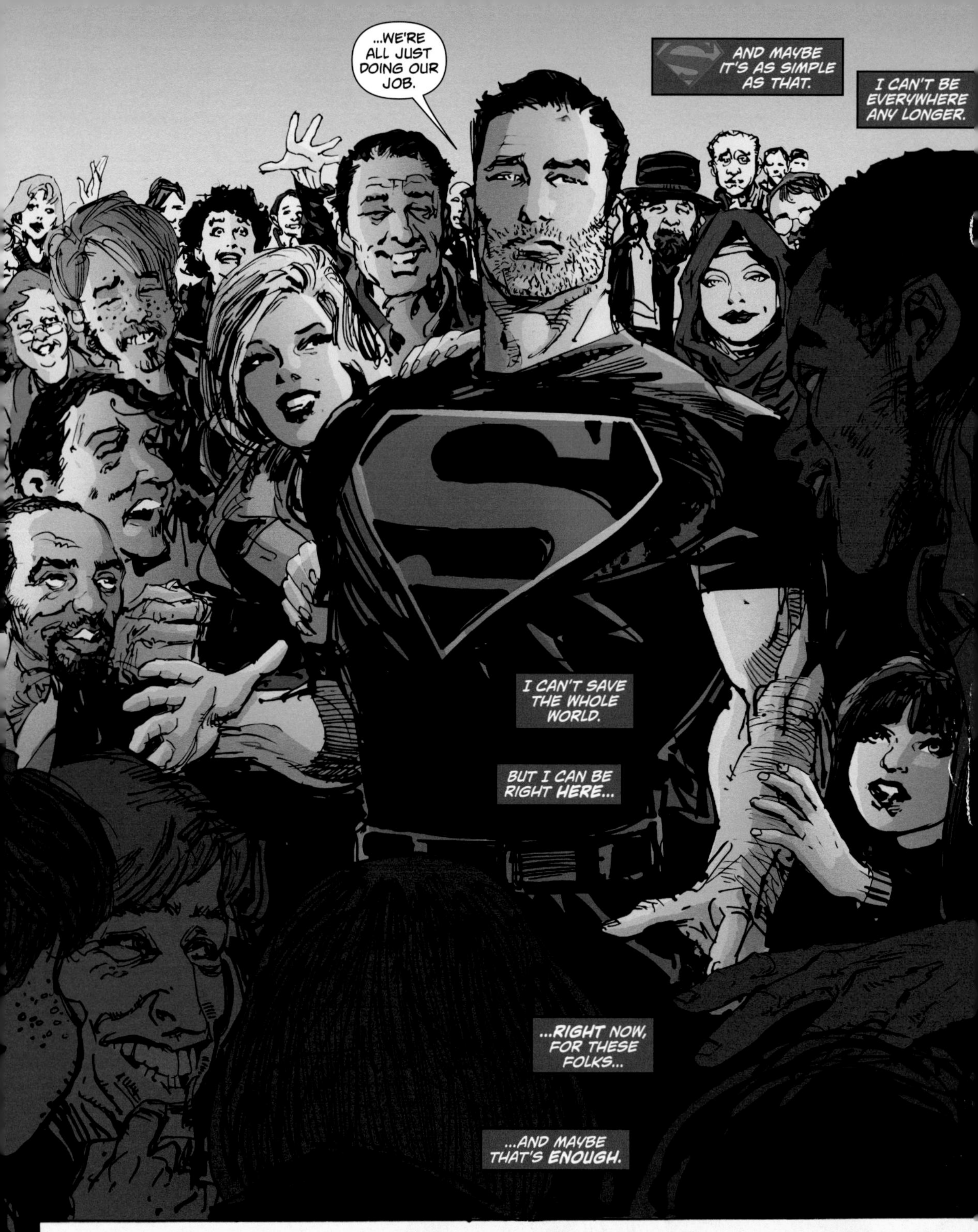
...WE'RE ALL JUST DOING OUR JOB.
AND MAYBE IT'S AS SIMPLE AS THAT.
I CAN'T BE EVERYWHERE ANY LONGER.
I CAN'T SAVE THE WHOLE WORLD.
BUT I CAN BE RIGHT HERE...
...RIGHT NOW, FOR THESE FOLKS...
...AND MAYBE THAT'S ENOUGH.
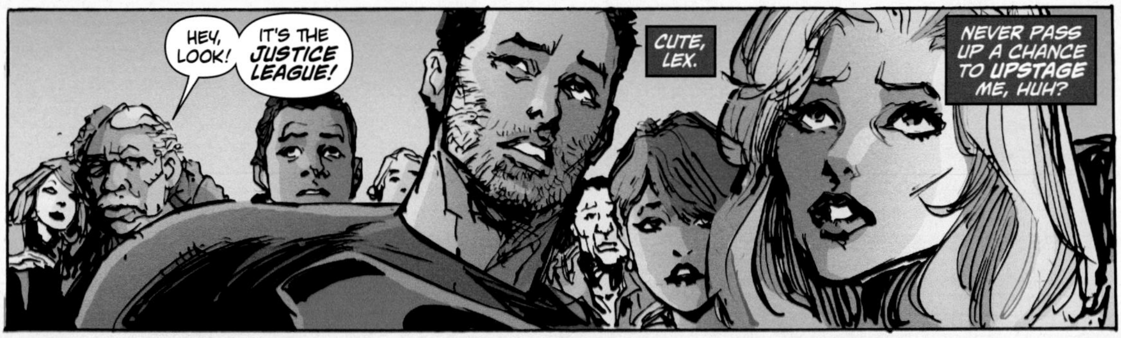
HEY, LOOK!
IT'S THE JUSTICE LEAGUE!
CUTE, LEX.
NEVER PASS UP A CHANCE TO UPSTAGE ME, HUH?

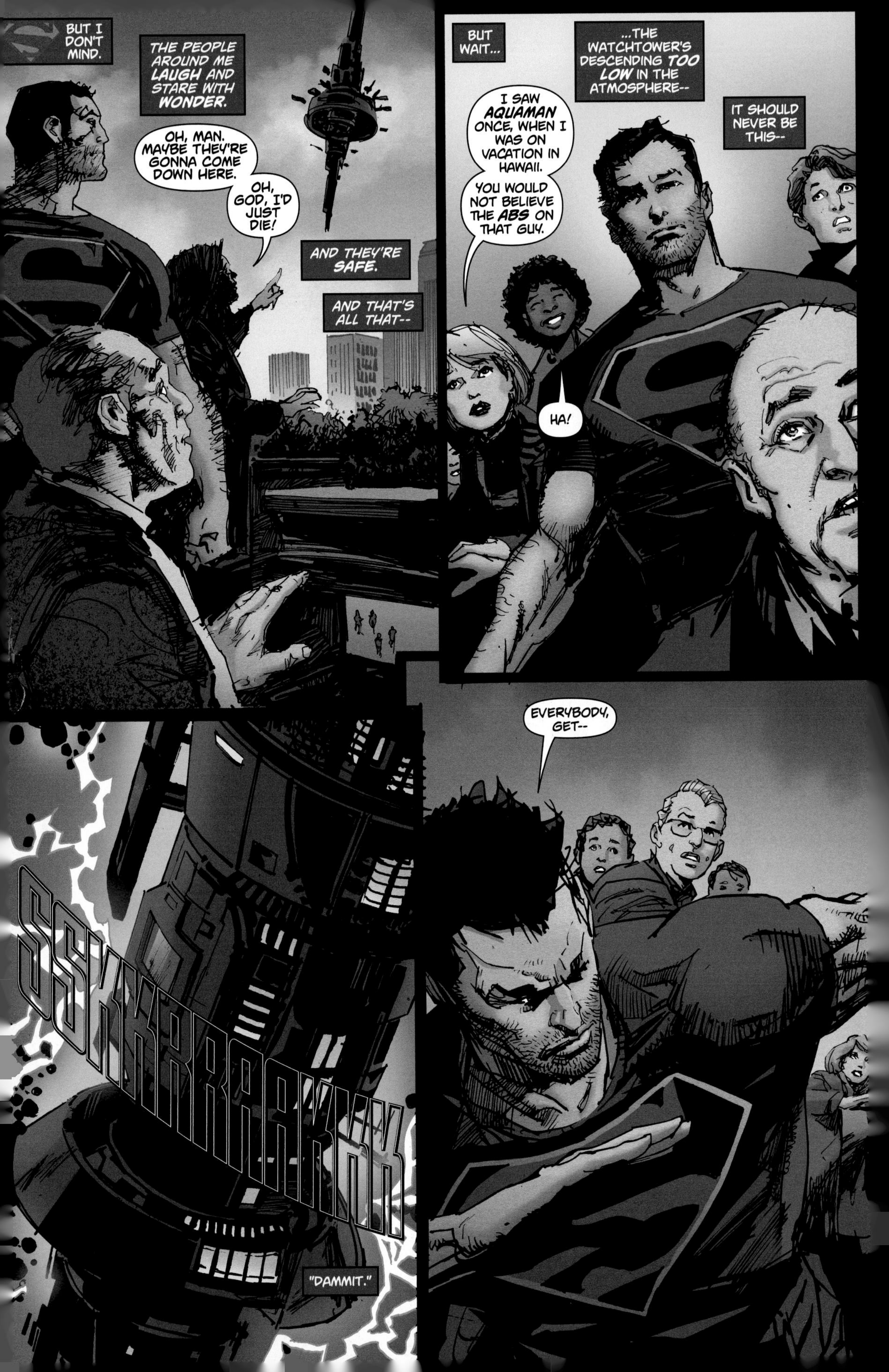
BUT I DON'T MIND.
THE PEOPLE AROUND ME LAUGH AND STARE WITH WONDER.
OH, MAN. MAYBE THEY'RE GONNA COME DOWN HERE.
OH, GOD, I'D JUST DIE!
AND THEY'RE SAFE.
AND THAT'S ALL THAT--
BUT WAIT...
...THE WATCHTOWER'S DESCENDING TOO LOW IN THE ATMOSPHERE--
I SAW AQUAMAN ONCE, WHEN I WAS ON VACATION IN HAWAII.
YOU WOULD NOT BELIEVE THE ABS ON THAT GUY.
IT SHOULD NEVER BE THIS--
HA!
SSKRRRAKKKK
"DAMMIT."
EVERYBODY, GET--

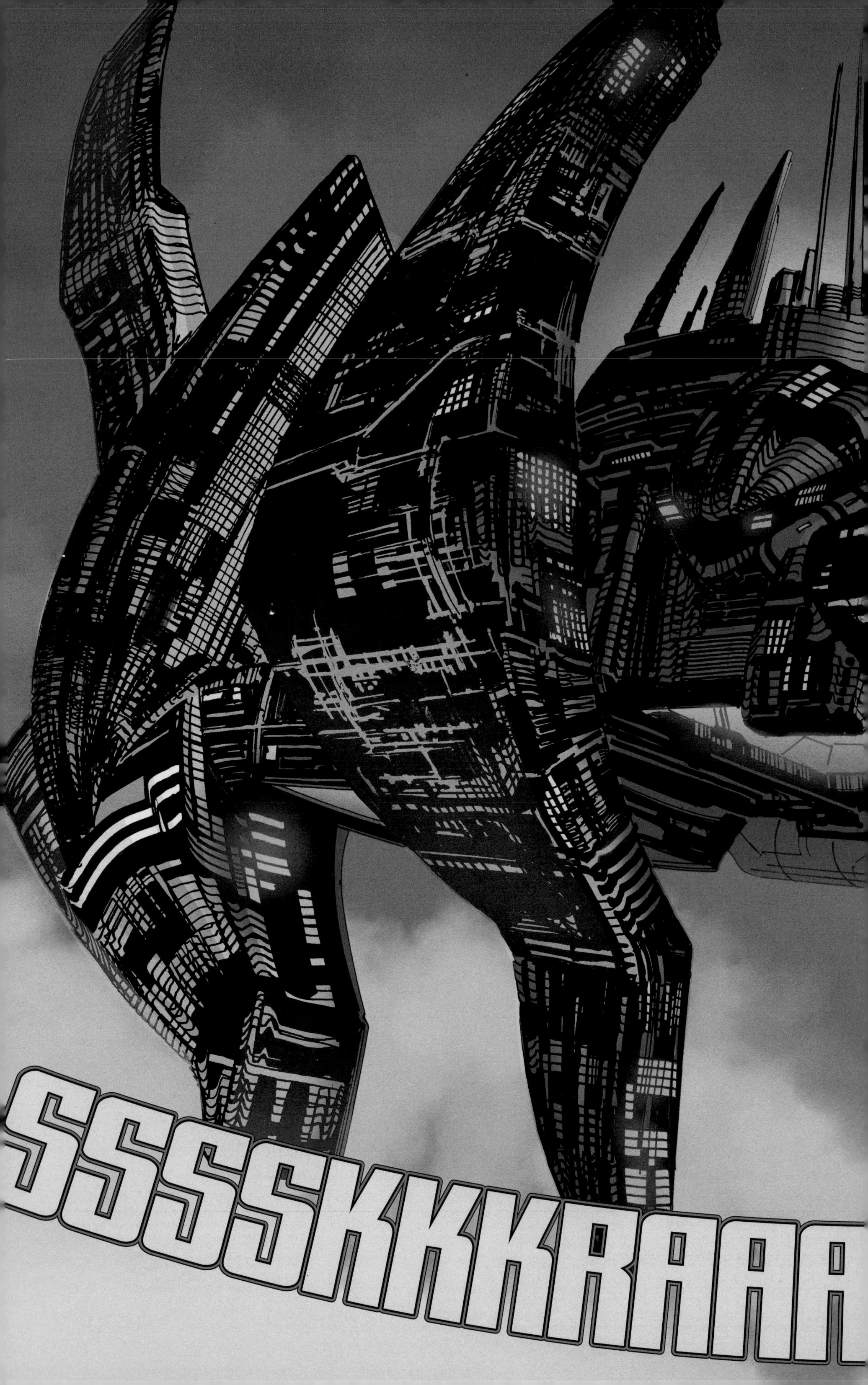
SSSSKKKRAAA

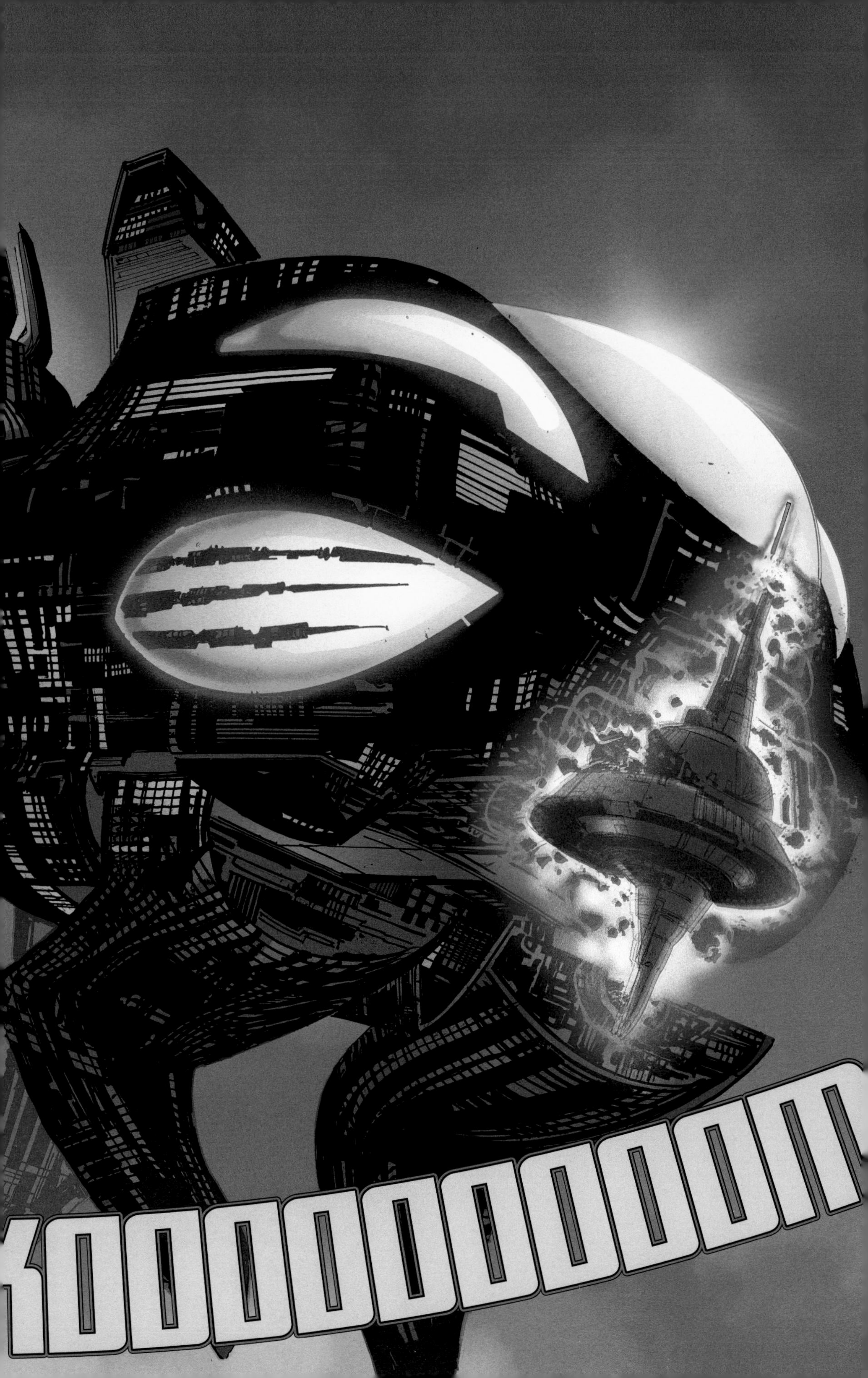
OOOOOOOOOM

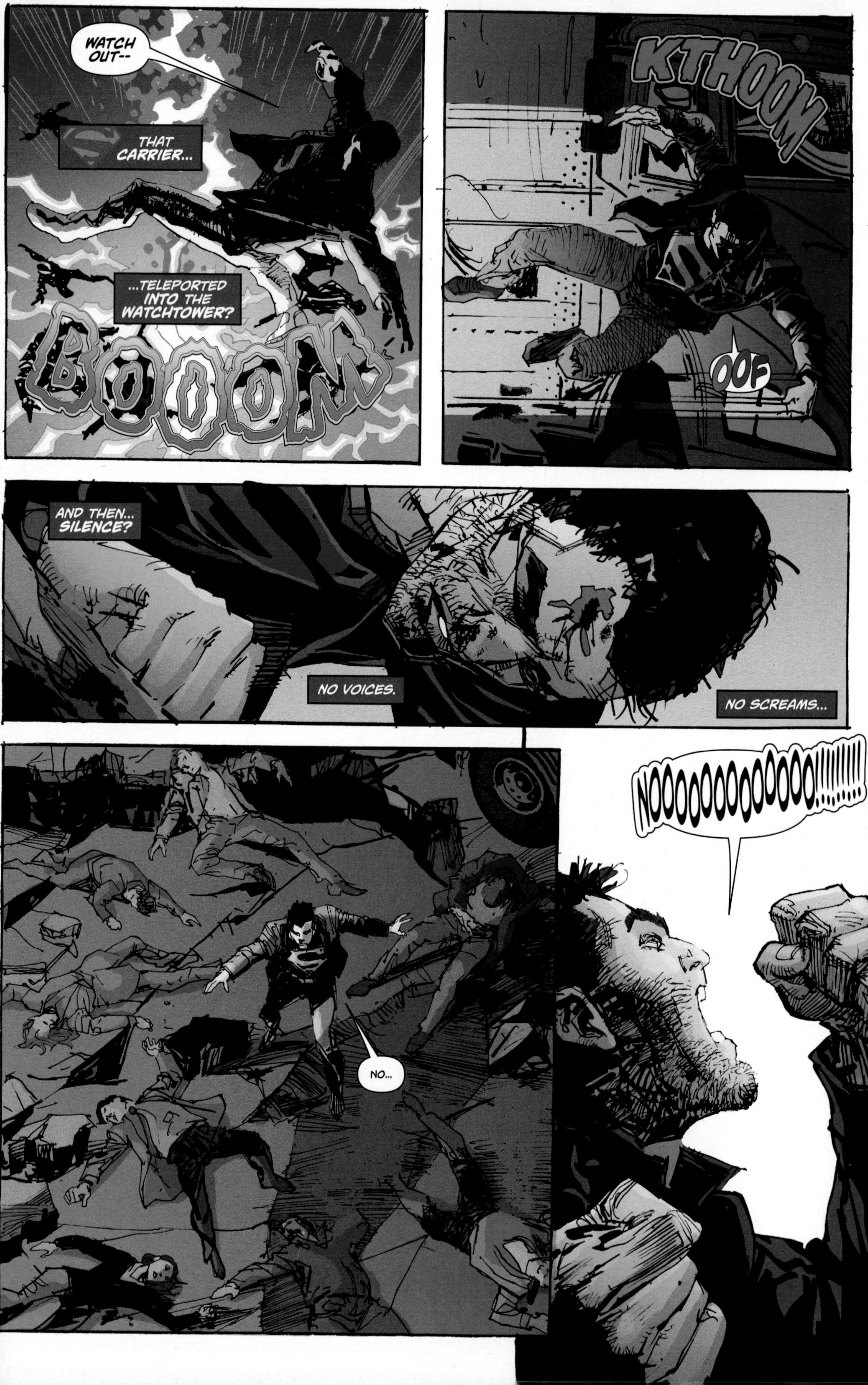
WATCH OUT--
THAT CARRIER...
...TELEPORTED INTO THE WATCHTOWER?
BOOOM
KTHOOM
OOF
AND THEN... SILENCE?
NO VOICES.
NO SCREAMS...
NO...
NOOOOOOOOOOOO!!!!!!!!!

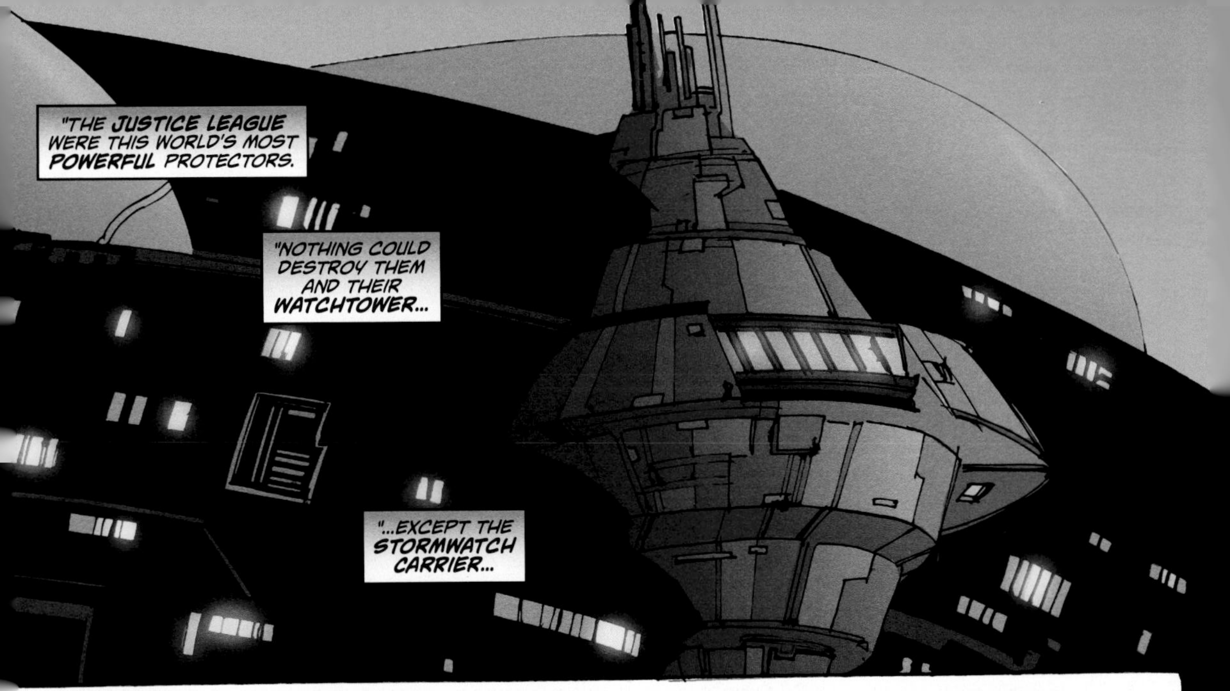
"THE JUSTICE LEAGUE WERE THIS WORLD'S MOST POWERFUL PROTECTORS.
"NOTHING COULD DESTROY THEM AND THEIR WATCHTOWER...
"...EXCEPT THE STORMWATCH CARRIER...

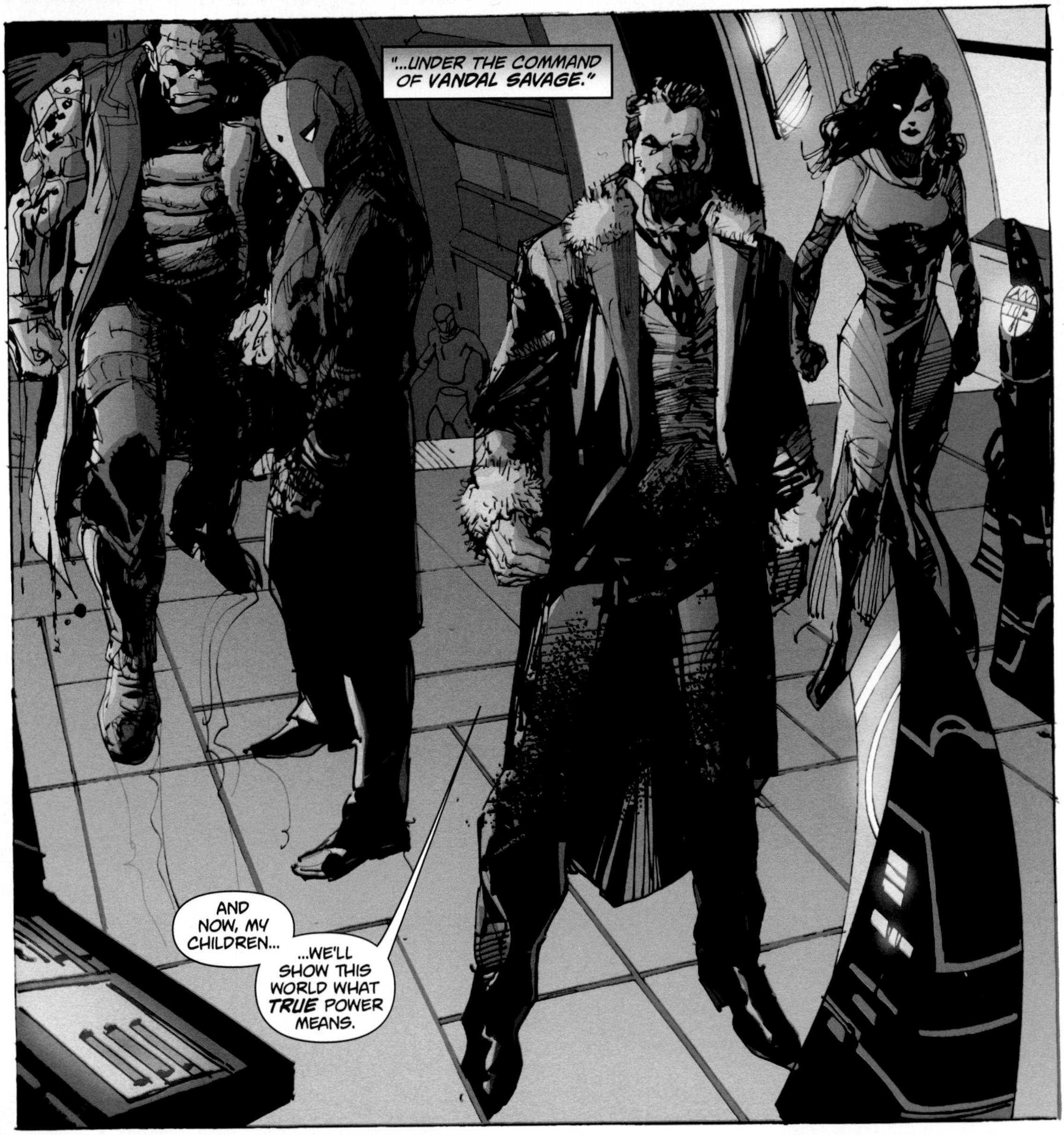
"...UNDER THE COMMAND OF VANDAL SAVAGE."
AND NOW, MY CHILDREN...
...WE'LL SHOW THIS WORLD WHAT TRUE POWER MEANS.

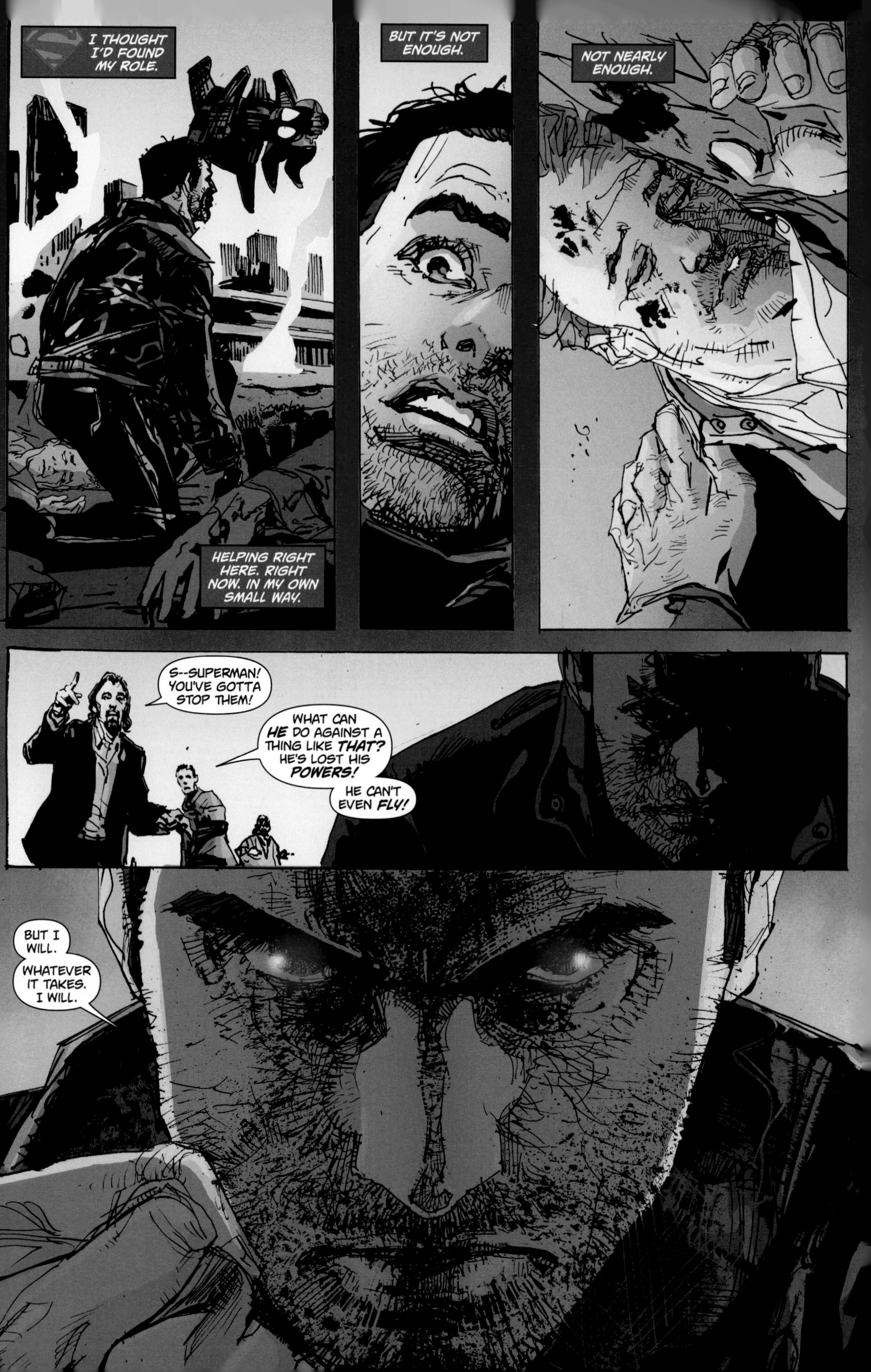
I THOUGHT I'D FOUND MY ROLE.
HELPING RIGHT HERE. RIGHT NOW. IN MY OWN SMALL WAY.
BUT IT'S NOT ENOUGH.
NOT NEARLY ENOUGH.
S--SUPERMAN! YOU'VE GOTTA STOP THEM!
WHAT CAN HE DO AGAINST A THING LIKE THAT? HE'S LOST HIS POWERS!
HE CAN'T EVEN FLY!
BUT I WILL.
WHATEVER IT TAKES. I WILL.

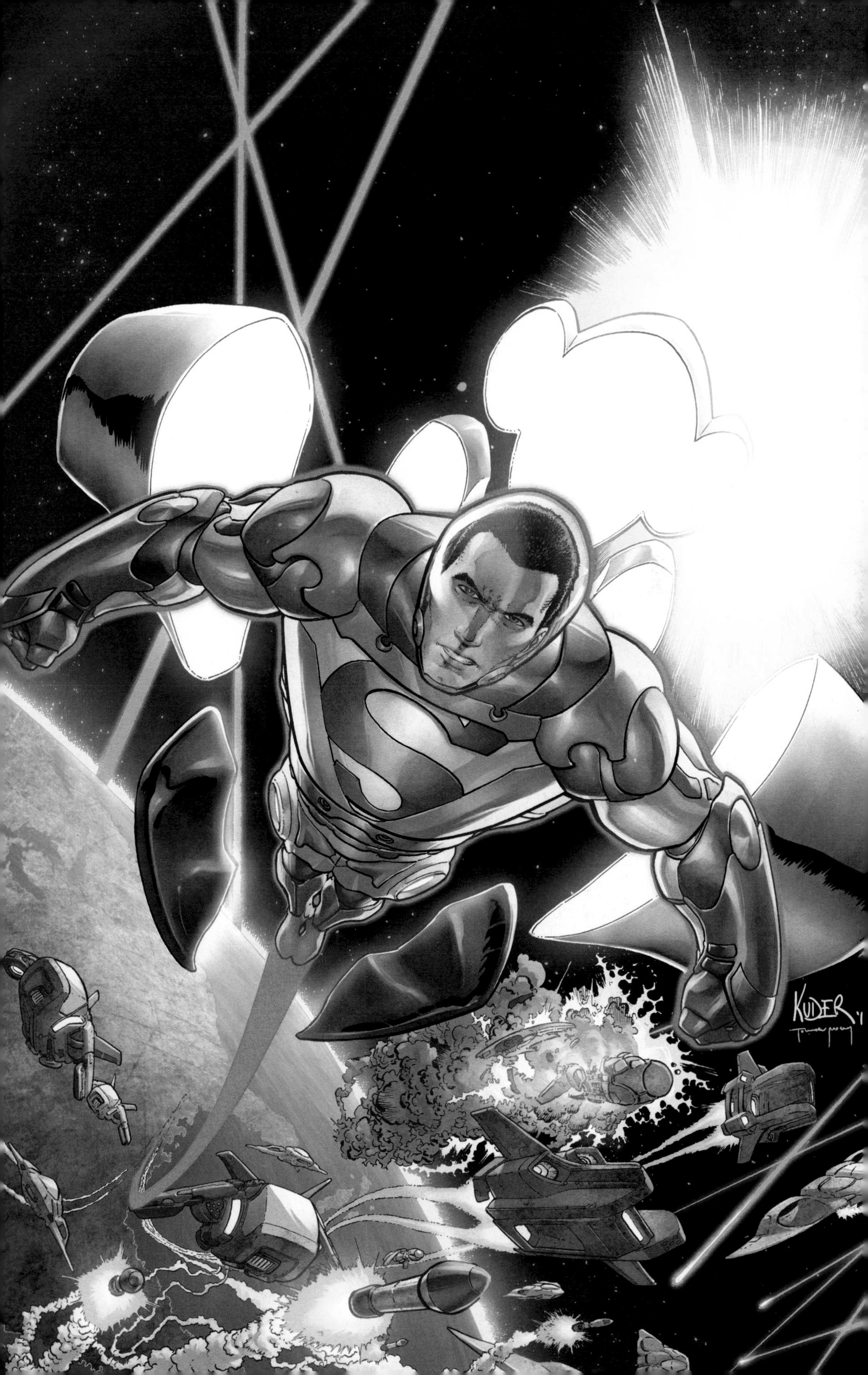

SAVAGE DAWN: ASSAULT

GREK PAK AARON KUDER writers **AARON KUDER RAFA SANDOVAL** pencillers **AARON KUDER JORDI TARRAGONA** inkers **TOMEU MOREY** colorist **STEVE WANDS** letterer
AARON KUDER TOMEU MOREY cover

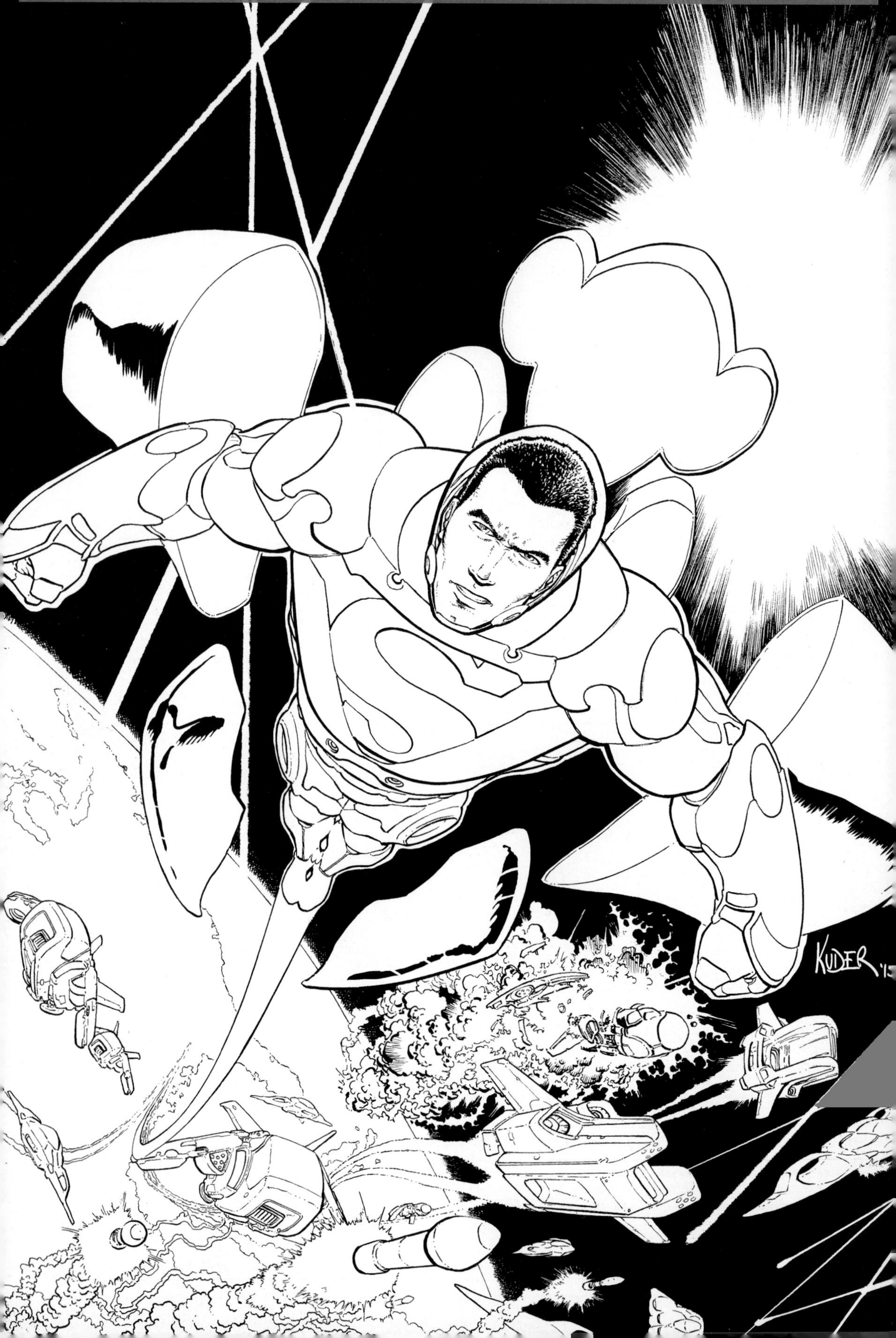
KUDER

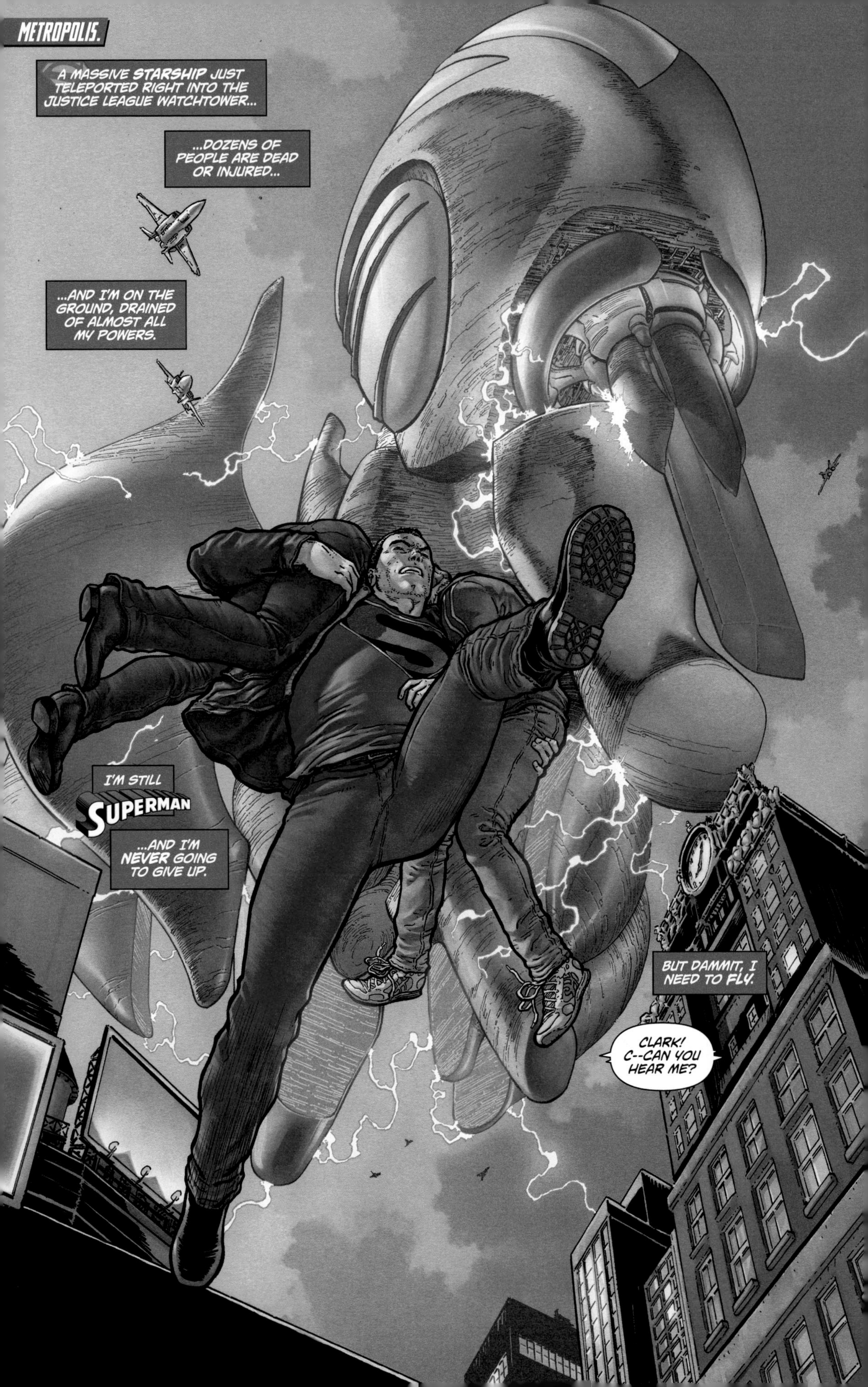
METROPOLIS.
A MASSIVE STARSHIP JUST TELEPORTED RIGHT INTO THE JUSTICE LEAGUE WATCHTOWER...
...DOZENS OF PEOPLE ARE DEAD OR INJURED...
...AND I'M ON THE GROUND, DRAINED OF ALMOST ALL MY POWERS.
I'M STILL SUPERMAN
...AND I'M NEVER GOING TO GIVE UP.
BUT DAMMIT, I NEED TO FLY.
CLARK! C--CAN YOU HEAR ME?

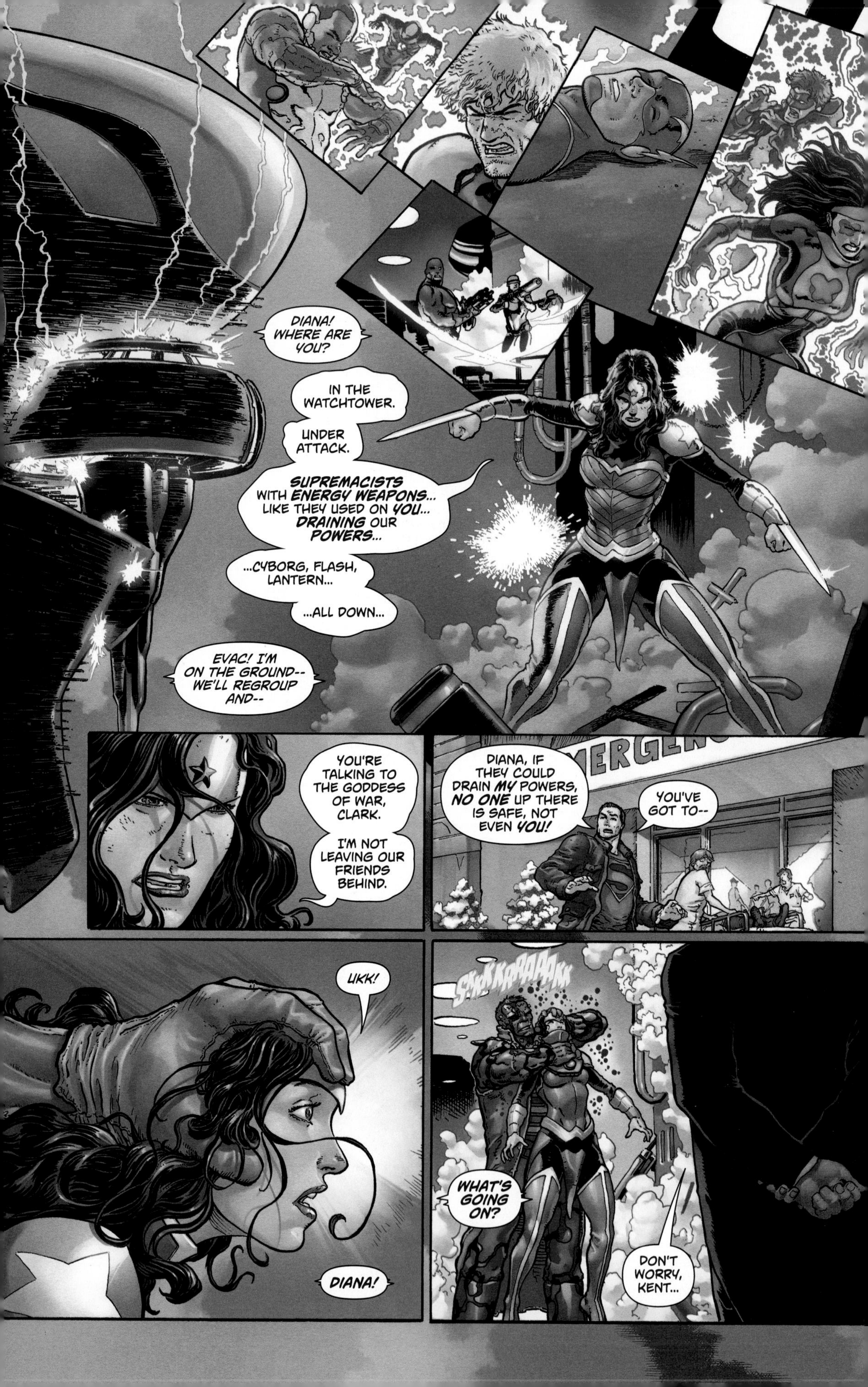
DIANA! WHERE ARE YOU?
IN THE WATCHTOWER.
UNDER ATTACK.
SUPREMACISTS WITH ENERGY WEAPONS... LIKE THEY USED ON YOU... DRAINING OUR POWERS...
...CYBORG, FLASH, LANTERN...
...ALL DOWN...
EVAC! I'M ON THE GROUND-- WE'LL REGROUP AND--
YOU'RE TALKING TO THE GODDESS OF WAR, CLARK.
I'M NOT LEAVING OUR FRIENDS BEHIND.
DIANA, IF THEY COULD DRAIN MY POWERS, NO ONE UP THERE IS SAFE, NOT EVEN YOU!
YOU'VE GOT TO--
UKK!
DIANA!
SKKKRRAAAKK
WHAT'S GOING ON?
DON'T WORRY, KENT...

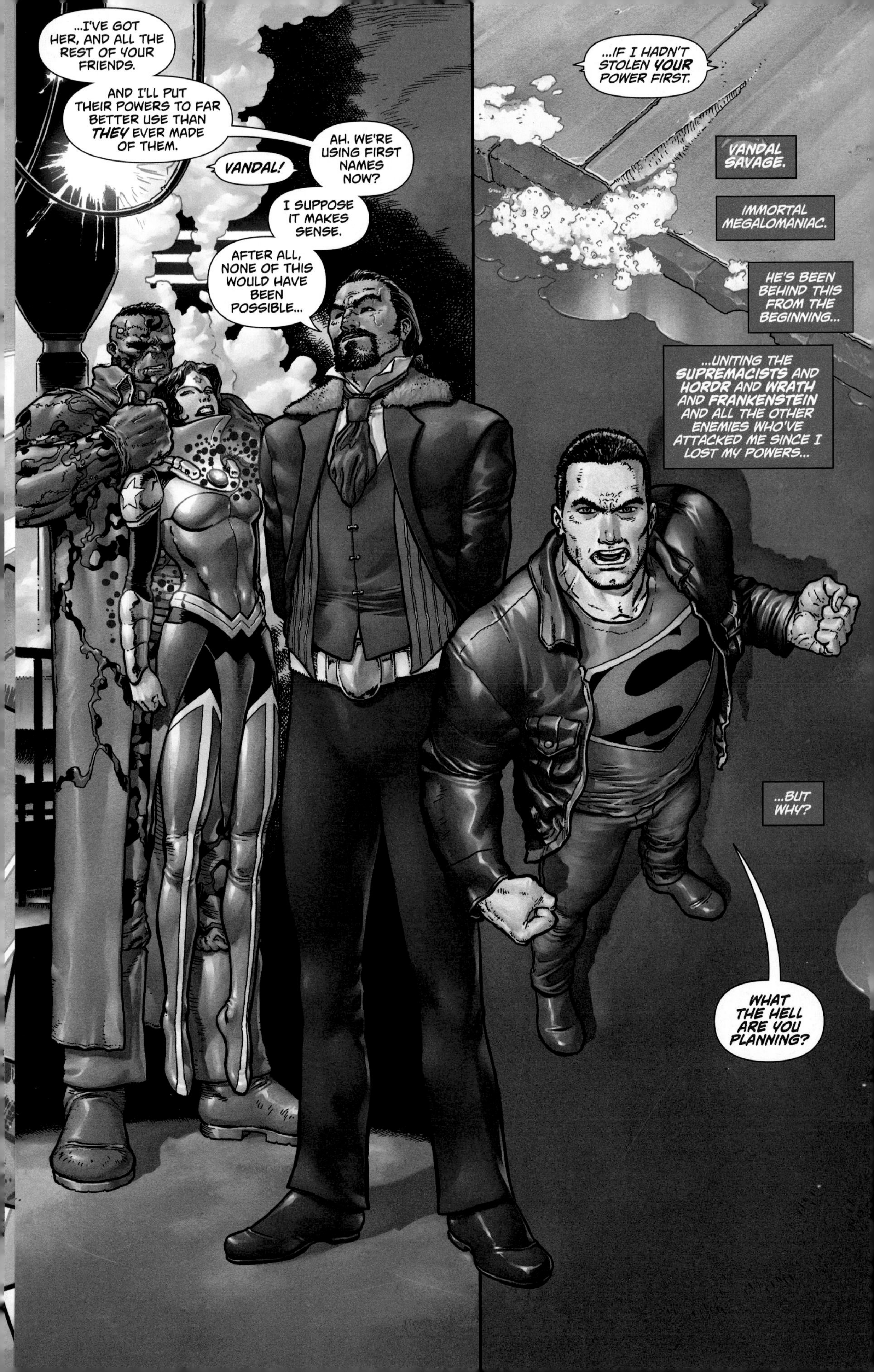
...I'VE GOT HER, AND ALL THE REST OF YOUR FRIENDS.
AND I'LL PUT THEIR POWERS TO FAR BETTER USE THAN *THEY* EVER MADE OF THEM.
VANDAL!
AH. WE'RE USING FIRST NAMES NOW?
I SUPPOSE IT MAKES SENSE.
AFTER ALL, NONE OF THIS WOULD HAVE BEEN POSSIBLE...
...IF I HADN'T STOLEN *YOUR* POWER FIRST.
VANDAL SAVAGE.
IMMORTAL MEGALOMANIAC.
HE'S BEEN BEHIND THIS FROM THE BEGINNING...
...UNITING THE **SUPREMACISTS** AND **HORDR** AND **WRATH** AND **FRANKENSTEIN** AND ALL THE OTHER ENEMIES WHO'VE ATTACKED ME SINCE I LOST MY POWERS...
...BUT WHY?
WHAT THE HELL ARE YOU PLANNING?

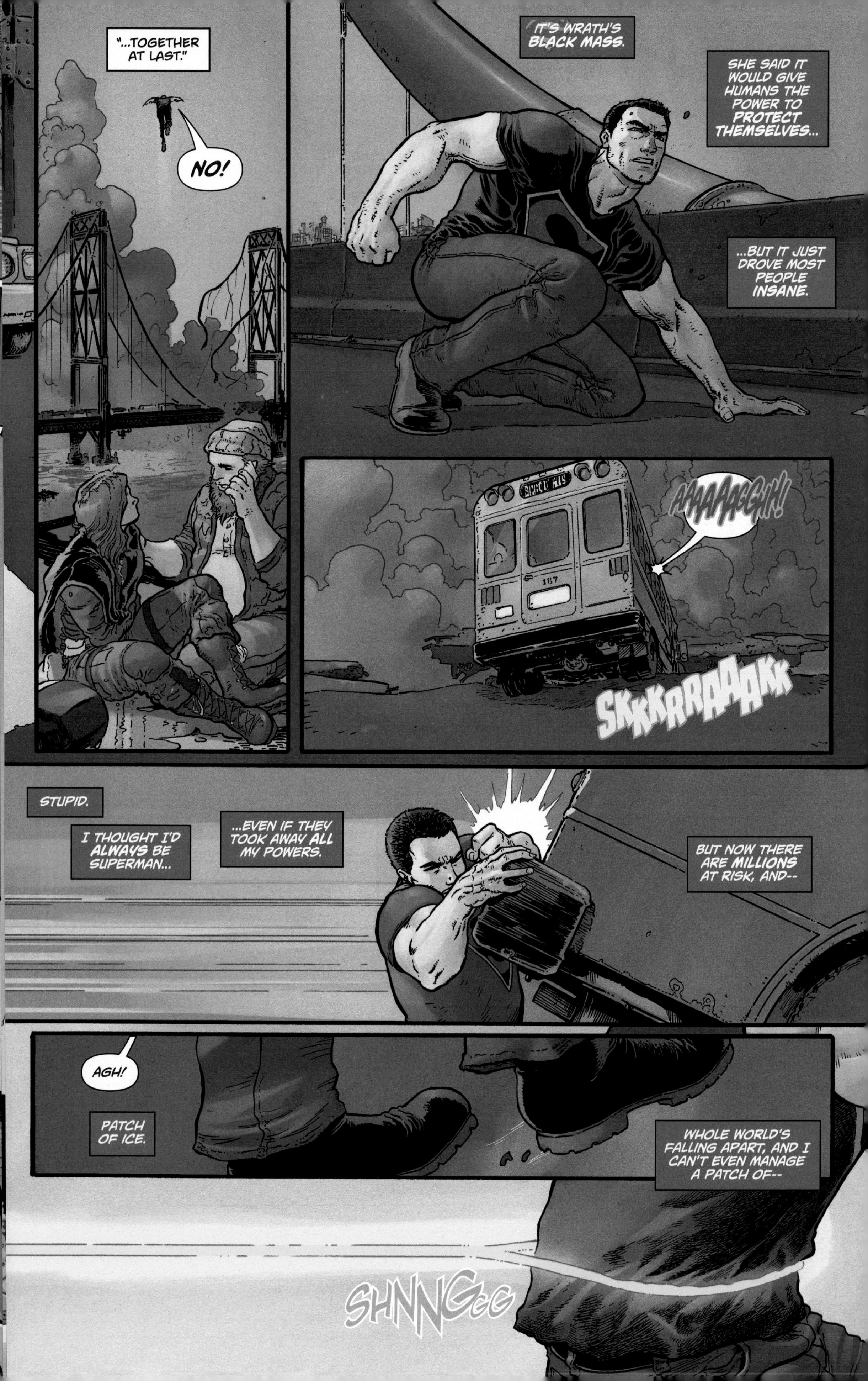
"...TOGETHER AT LAST."
NO!
IT'S WRATH'S BLACK MASS.
SHE SAID IT WOULD GIVE HUMANS THE POWER TO PROTECT THEMSELVES...
...BUT IT JUST DROVE MOST PEOPLE INSANE.
AAAAAAGGHH!
SKKRRAAAKK
STUPID.
I THOUGHT I'D ALWAYS BE SUPERMAN...
...EVEN IF THEY TOOK AWAY ALL MY POWERS.
BUT NOW THERE ARE MILLIONS AT RISK, AND--
AGH!
PATCH OF ICE.
WHOLE WORLD'S FALLING APART, AND I CAN'T EVEN MANAGE A PATCH OF--
SHNNGGG

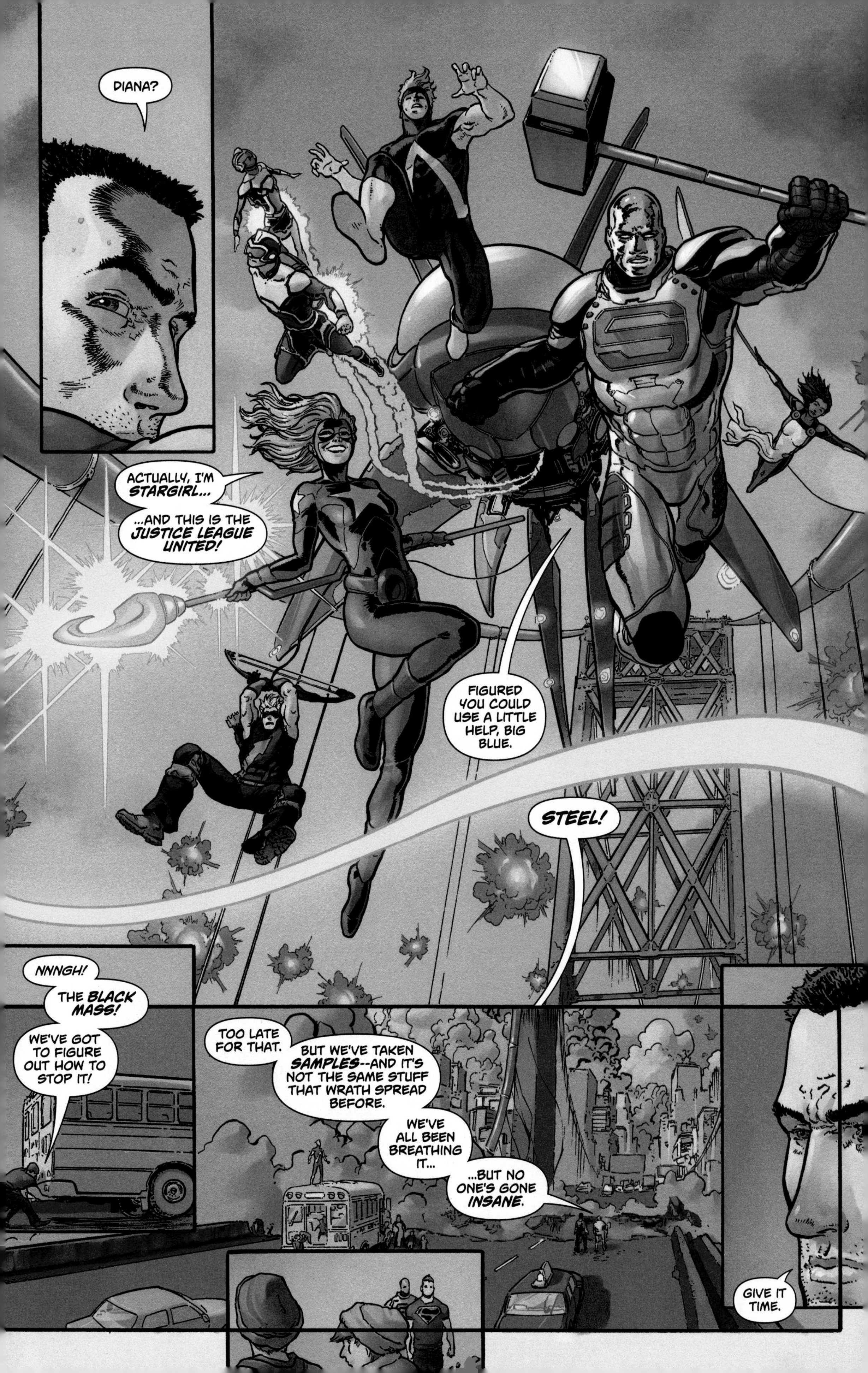

DIANA?
ACTUALLY, I'M STARGIRL...
...AND THIS IS THE JUSTICE LEAGUE UNITED!
FIGURED YOU COULD USE A LITTLE HELP, BIG BLUE.
STEEL!
NNNGH!
THE BLACK MASS!
WE'VE GOT TO FIGURE OUT HOW TO STOP IT!
TOO LATE FOR THAT.
BUT WE'VE TAKEN SAMPLES--AND IT'S NOT THE SAME STUFF THAT WRATH SPREAD BEFORE.
WE'VE ALL BEEN BREATHING IT...
...BUT NO ONE'S GONE INSANE.
GIVE IT TIME.

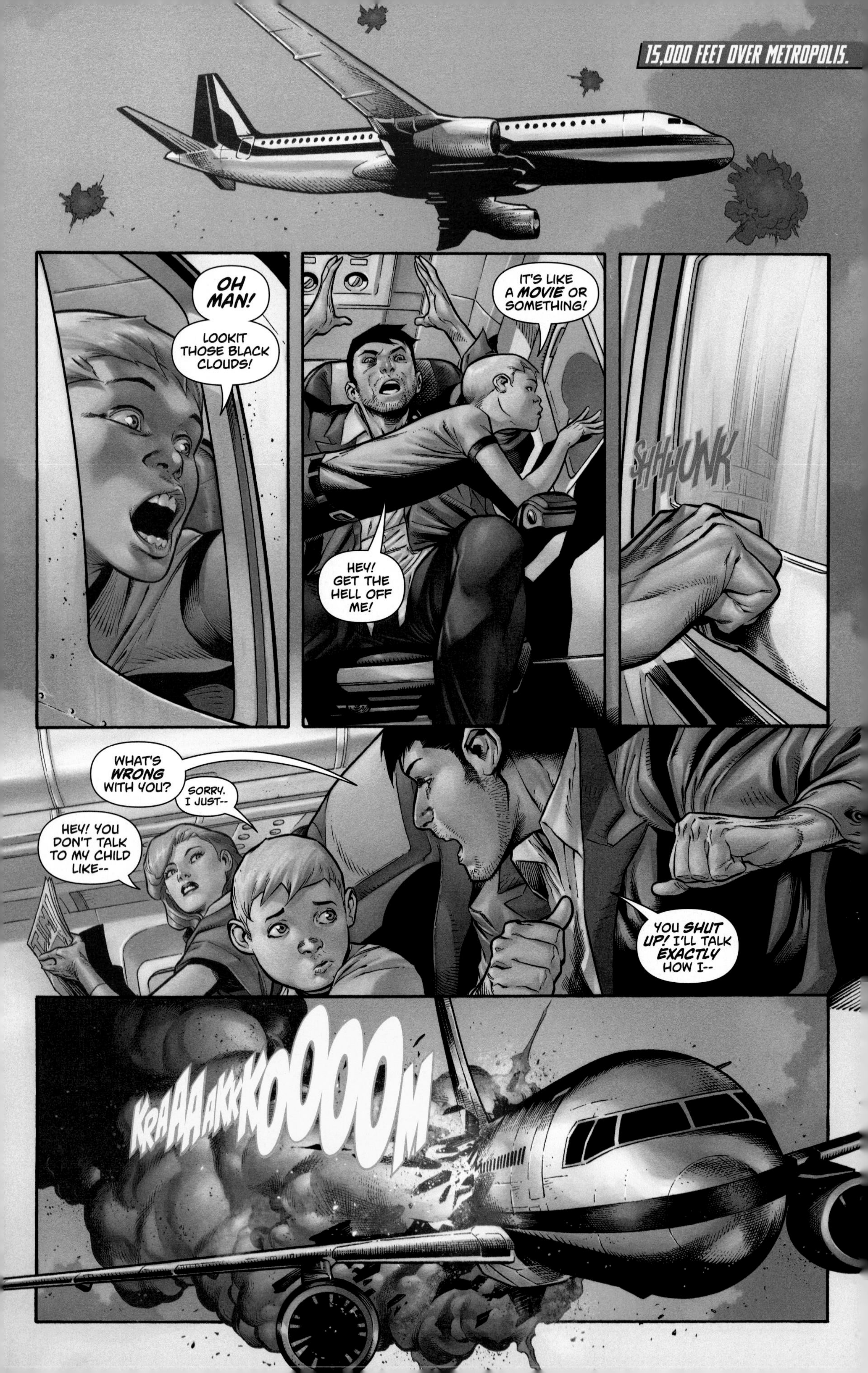
15,000 FEET OVER METROPOLIS.
OH MAN!
LOOKIT THOSE BLACK CLOUDS!
IT'S LIKE A MOVIE OR SOMETHING!
HEY! GET THE HELL OFF ME!
SHHHUNK
WHAT'S WRONG WITH YOU?
SORRY. I JUST--
HEY! YOU DON'T TALK TO MY CHILD LIKE--
YOU SHUT UP! I'LL TALK EXACTLY HOW I--
KRAAAAKKKOOOOM

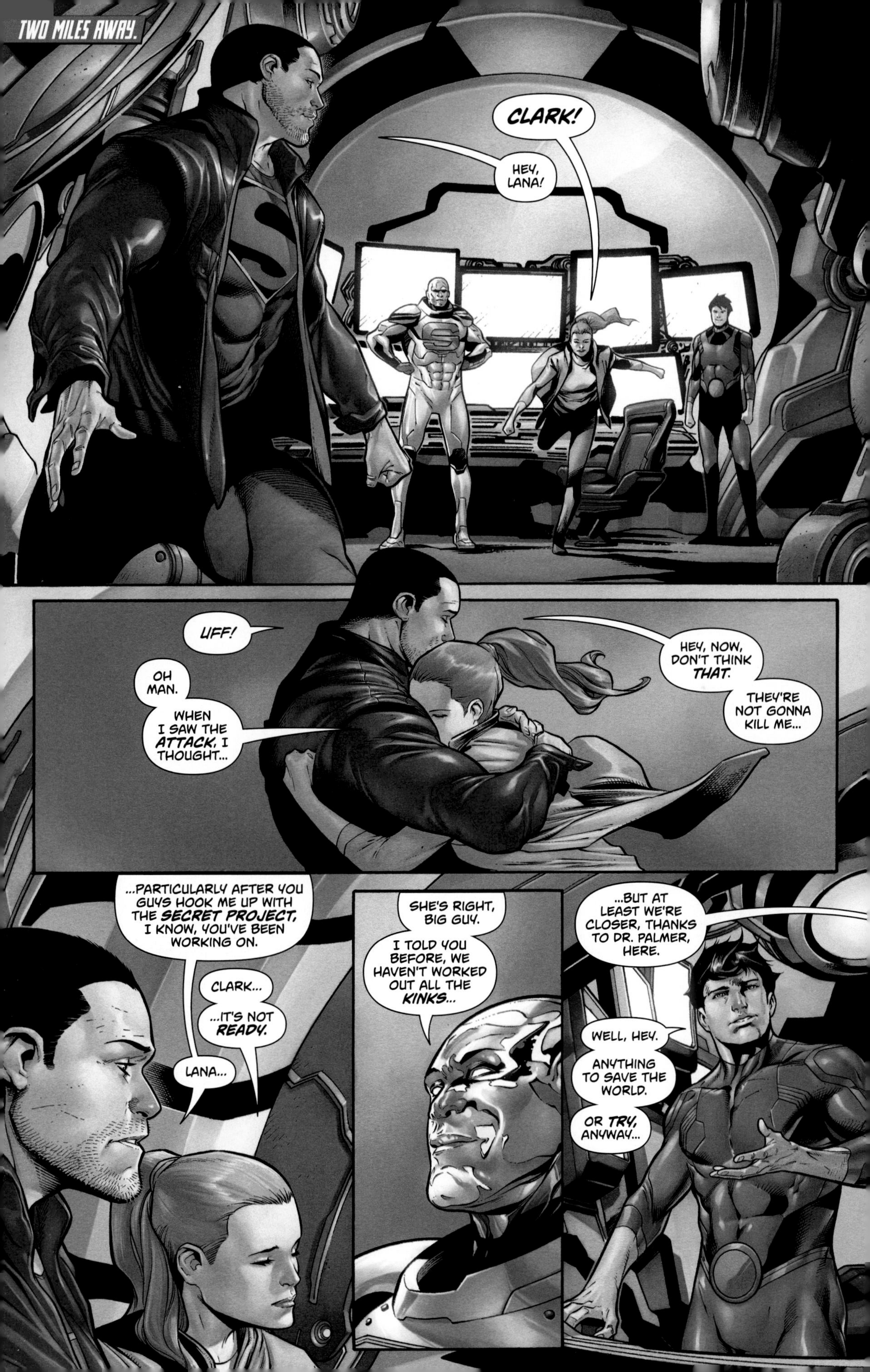
TWO MILES AWAY.
CLARK!
HEY, LANA!
UFF!
OH MAN.
WHEN I SAW THE ATTACK, I THOUGHT...
HEY, NOW, DON'T THINK THAT.
THEY'RE NOT GONNA KILL ME...
...PARTICULARLY AFTER YOU GUYS HOOK ME UP WITH THE SECRET PROJECT, I KNOW, YOU'VE BEEN WORKING ON.
CLARK...
...IT'S NOT READY.
LANA...
SHE'S RIGHT, BIG GUY.
I TOLD YOU BEFORE, WE HAVEN'T WORKED OUT ALL THE KINKS...
...BUT AT LEAST WE'RE CLOSER, THANKS TO DR. PALMER, HERE.
WELL, HEY.
ANYTHING TO SAVE THE WORLD.
OR TRY, ANYWAY...

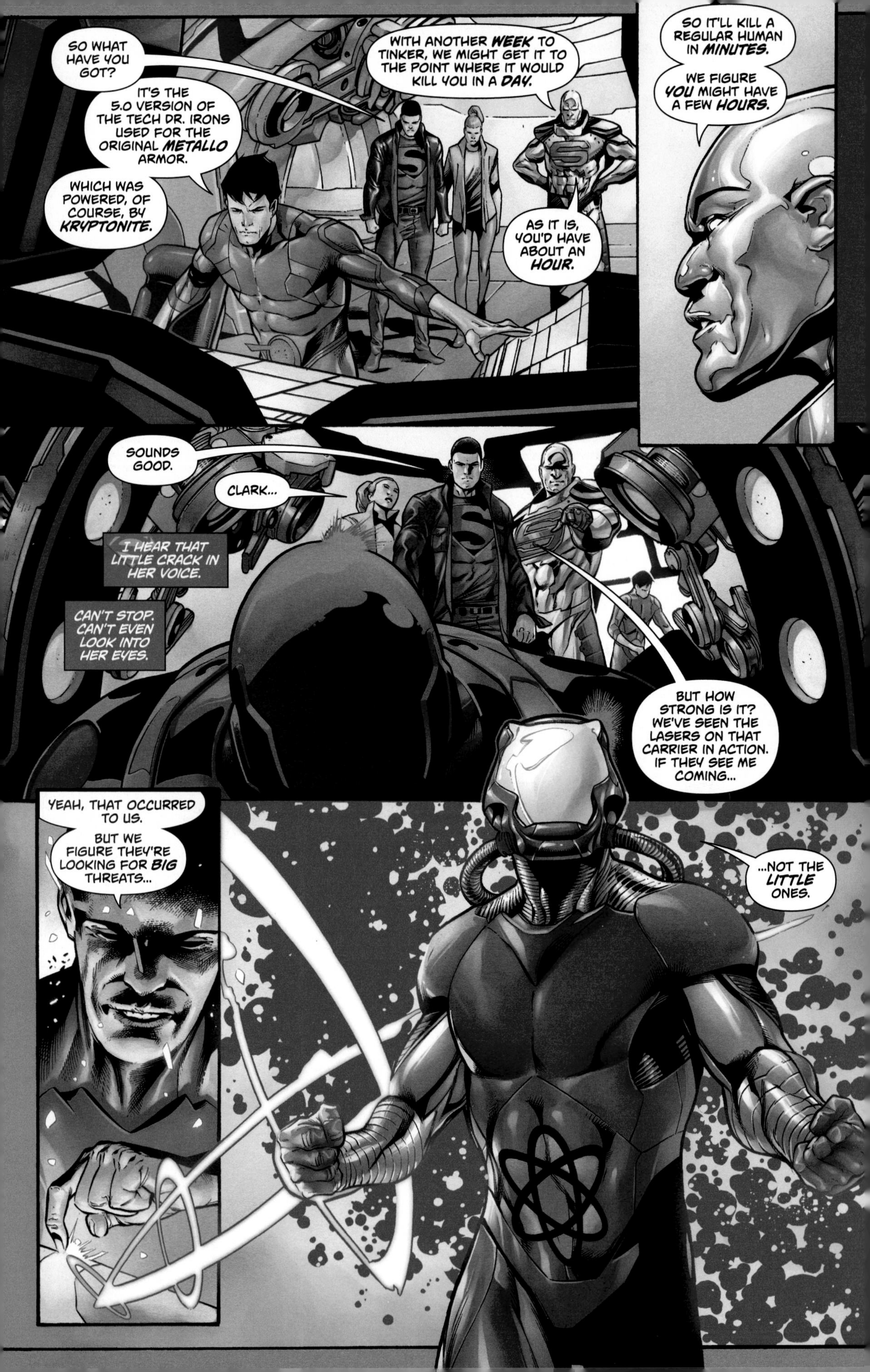
SO WHAT HAVE YOU GOT?
IT'S THE 5.0 VERSION OF THE TECH DR. IRONS USED FOR THE ORIGINAL METALLO ARMOR.
WHICH WAS POWERED, OF COURSE, BY KRYPTONITE.
WITH ANOTHER WEEK TO TINKER, WE MIGHT GET IT TO THE POINT WHERE IT WOULD KILL YOU IN A DAY.
AS IT IS, YOU'D HAVE ABOUT AN HOUR.
SO IT'LL KILL A REGULAR HUMAN IN MINUTES.
WE FIGURE YOU MIGHT HAVE A FEW HOURS.
SOUNDS GOOD.
CLARK...
I HEAR THAT LITTLE CRACK IN HER VOICE.
CAN'T STOP. CAN'T EVEN LOOK INTO HER EYES.
BUT HOW STRONG IS IT? WE'VE SEEN THE LASERS ON THAT CARRIER IN ACTION. IF THEY SEE ME COMING...
YEAH, THAT OCCURRED TO US.
BUT WE FIGURE THEY'RE LOOKING FOR BIG THREATS...
...NOT THE LITTLE ONES.

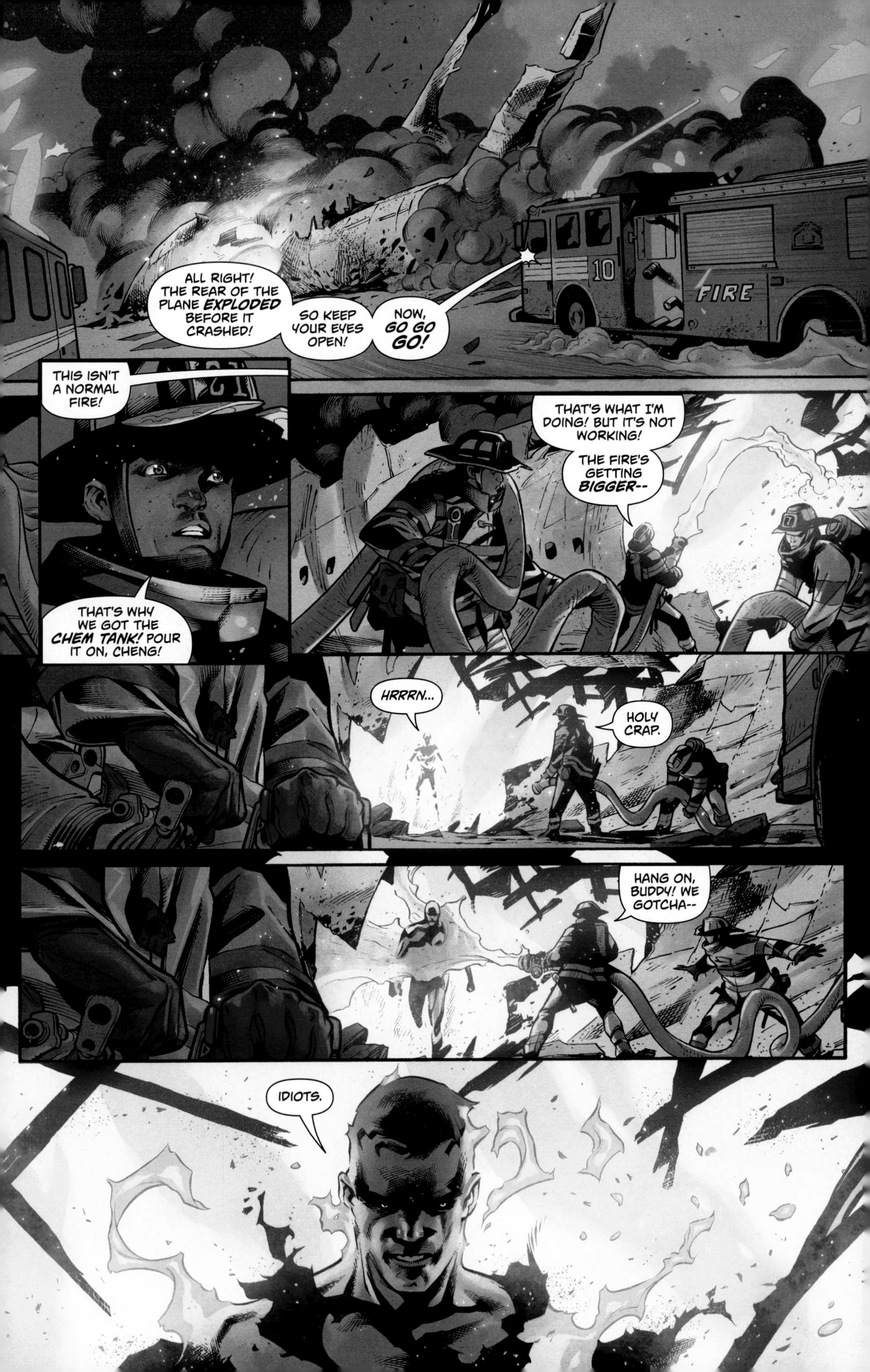
ALL RIGHT! THE REAR OF THE PLANE EXPLODED BEFORE IT CRASHED!
SO KEEP YOUR EYES OPEN!
NOW, GO GO GO!
FIRE
10
THIS ISN'T A NORMAL FIRE!
THAT'S WHY WE GOT THE CHEM TANK! POUR IT ON, CHENG!
THAT'S WHAT I'M DOING! BUT IT'S NOT WORKING!
THE FIRE'S GETTING BIGGER--
HRRRN...
HOLY CRAP.
HANG ON, BUDDY! WE GOTCHA--
IDIOTS.

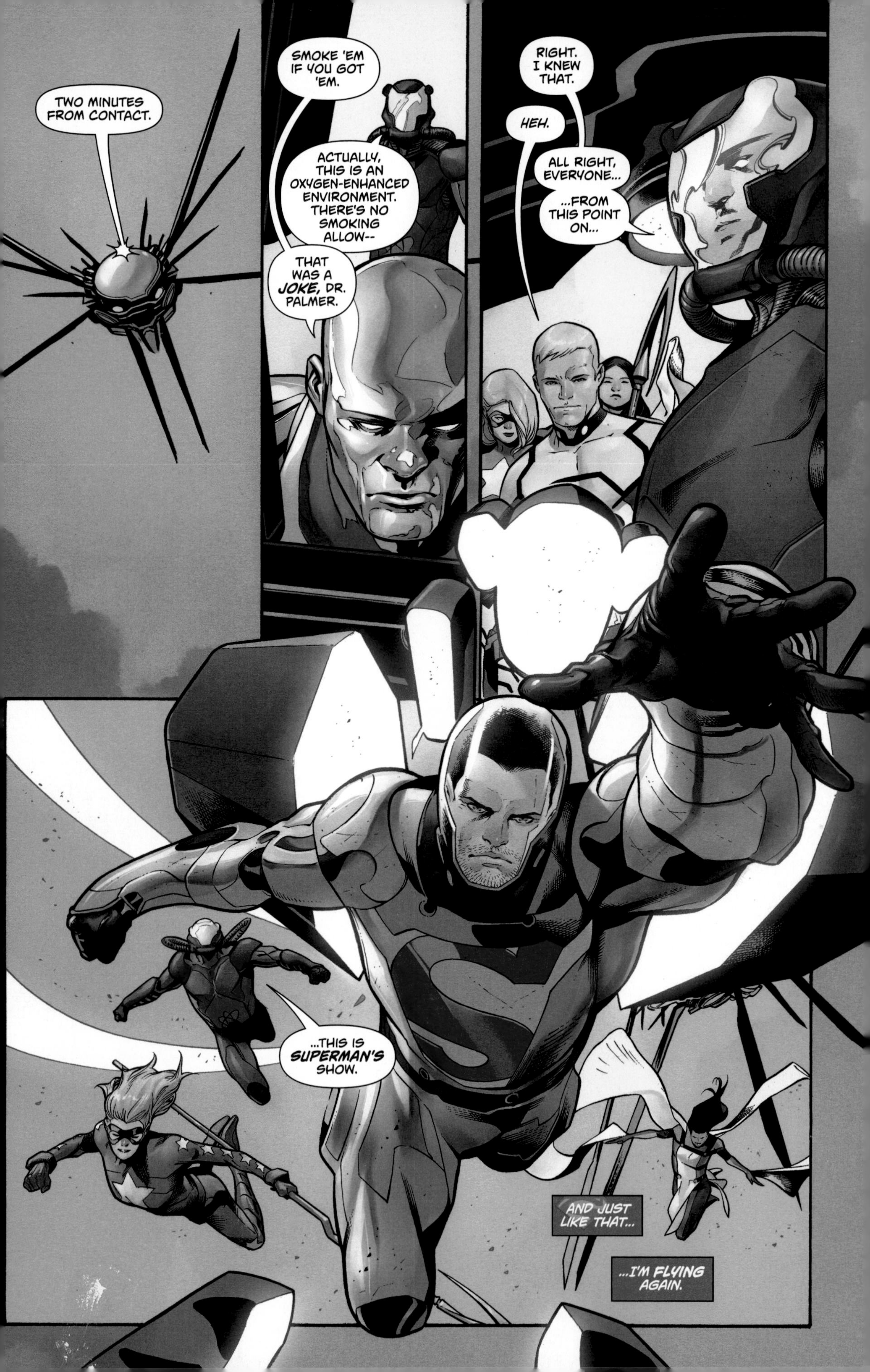
TWO MINUTES FROM CONTACT.
SMOKE 'EM IF YOU GOT 'EM.
ACTUALLY, THIS IS AN OXYGEN-ENHANCED ENVIRONMENT. THERE'S NO SMOKING ALLOW--
THAT WAS A JOKE, DR. PALMER.
RIGHT. I KNEW THAT.
HEH.
ALL RIGHT, EVERYONE...
...FROM THIS POINT ON...
...THIS IS SUPERMAN'S SHOW.
AND JUST LIKE THAT...
...I'M FLYING AGAIN.

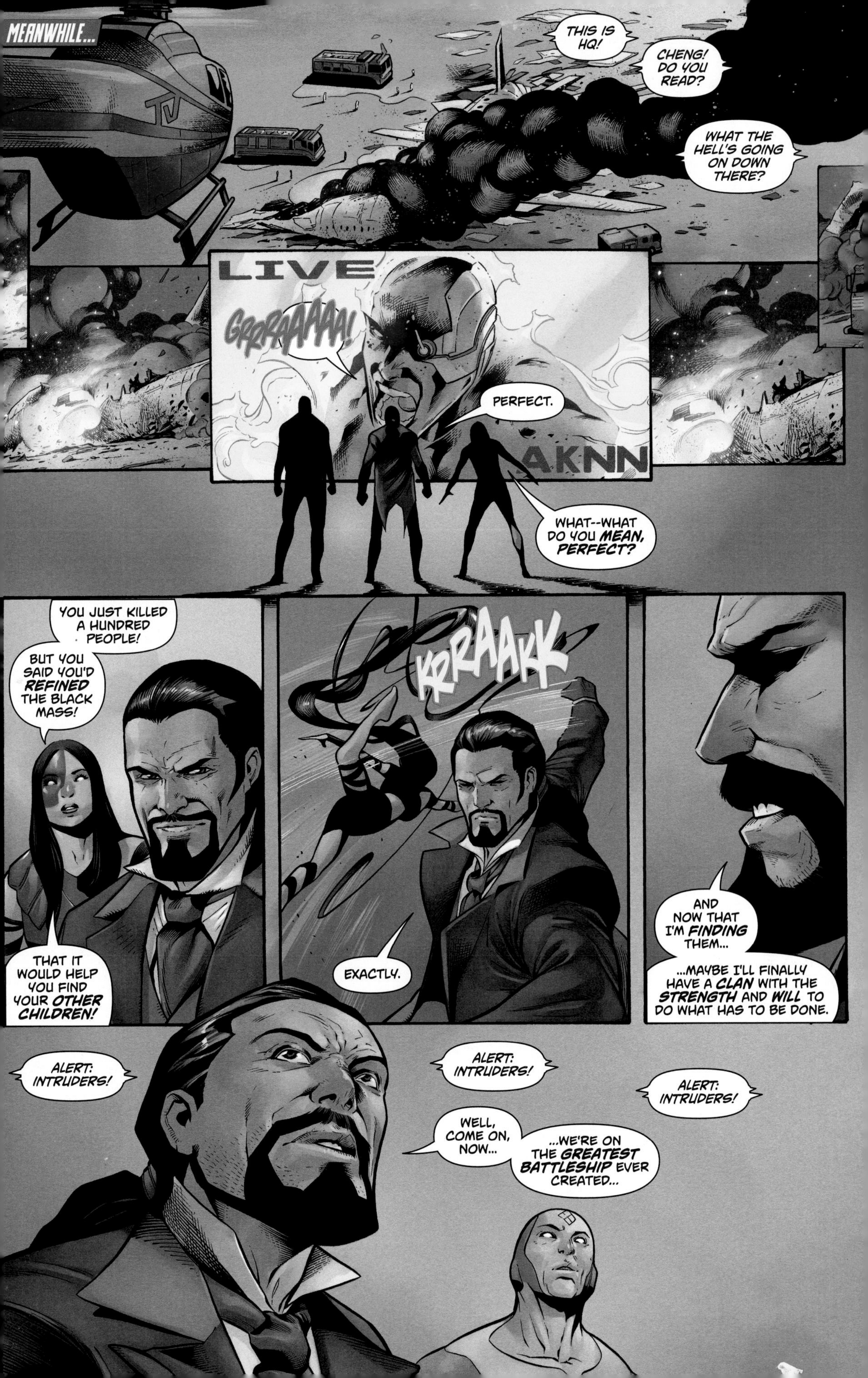
MEANWHILE...
THIS IS HQ!
CHENG! DO YOU READ?
WHAT THE HELL'S GOING ON DOWN THERE?
LIVE
GRRRAAAAAA!
PERFECT.
AKNN
WHAT--WHAT DO YOU MEAN, PERFECT?
YOU JUST KILLED A HUNDRED PEOPLE!
BUT YOU SAID YOU'D REFINED THE BLACK MASS!
THAT IT WOULD HELP YOU FIND YOUR OTHER CHILDREN!
KRRAAKK
EXACTLY.
AND NOW THAT I'M FINDING THEM...
...MAYBE I'LL FINALLY HAVE A CLAN WITH THE STRENGTH AND WILL TO DO WHAT HAS TO BE DONE.
ALERT: INTRUDERS!
ALERT: INTRUDERS!
ALERT: INTRUDERS!
WELL, COME ON, NOW...
...WE'RE ON THE GREATEST BATTLESHIP EVER CREATED...

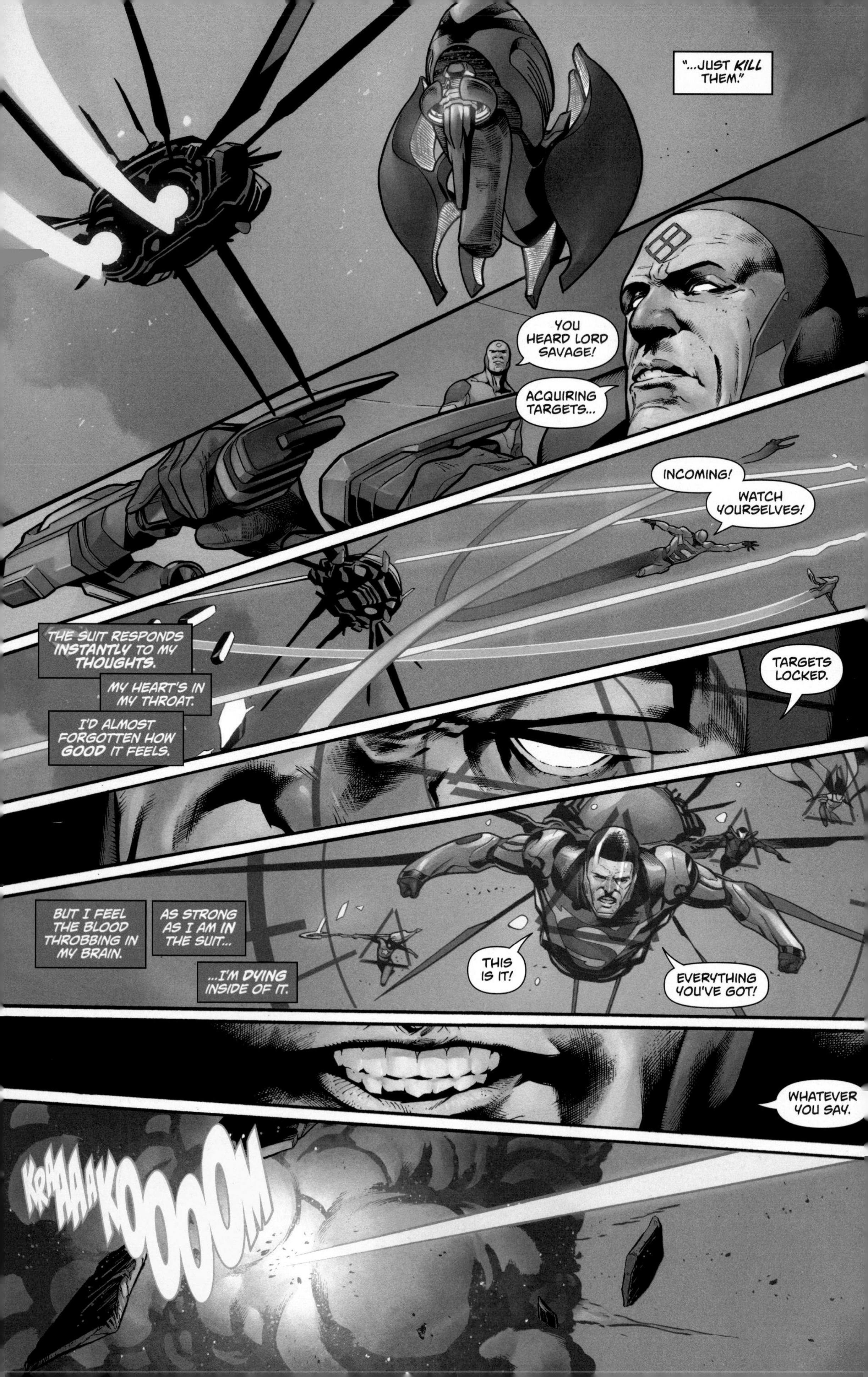
"...JUST KILL THEM."
YOU HEARD LORD SAVAGE!
ACQUIRING TARGETS...
INCOMING!
WATCH YOURSELVES!
THE SUIT RESPONDS INSTANTLY TO MY THOUGHTS.
MY HEART'S IN MY THROAT.
I'D ALMOST FORGOTTEN HOW GOOD IT FEELS.
TARGETS LOCKED.
BUT I FEEL THE BLOOD THROBBING IN MY BRAIN.
AS STRONG AS I AM IN THE SUIT...
...I'M DYING INSIDE OF IT.
THIS IS IT!
EVERYTHING YOU'VE GOT!
WHATEVER YOU SAY.
KRAAAAKOOOOM

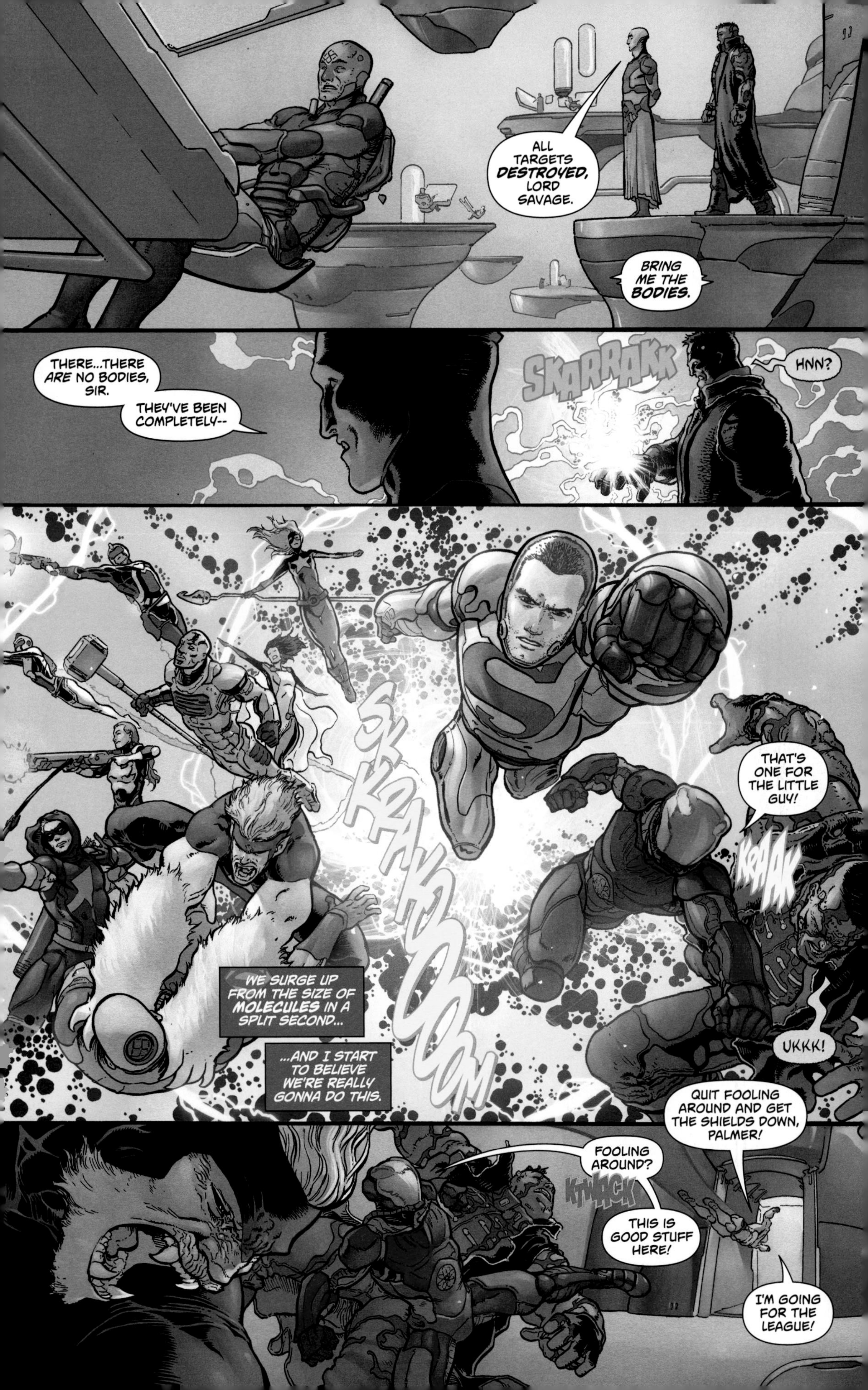
ALL TARGETS DESTROYED, LORD SAVAGE.
BRING ME THE BODIES.
THERE...THERE ARE NO BODIES, SIR.
THEY'VE BEEN COMPLETELY--
SKARRAKK
HNN?
SKRAKOOOOM
THAT'S ONE FOR THE LITTLE GUY!
KRAAK
UKKK!
WE SURGE UP FROM THE SIZE OF MOLECULES IN A SPLIT SECOND...
...AND I START TO BELIEVE WE'RE REALLY GONNA DO THIS.
QUIT FOOLING AROUND AND GET THE SHIELDS DOWN, PALMER!
FOOLING AROUND?
KTWACK
THIS IS GOOD STUFF HERE!
I'M GOING FOR THE LEAGUE!

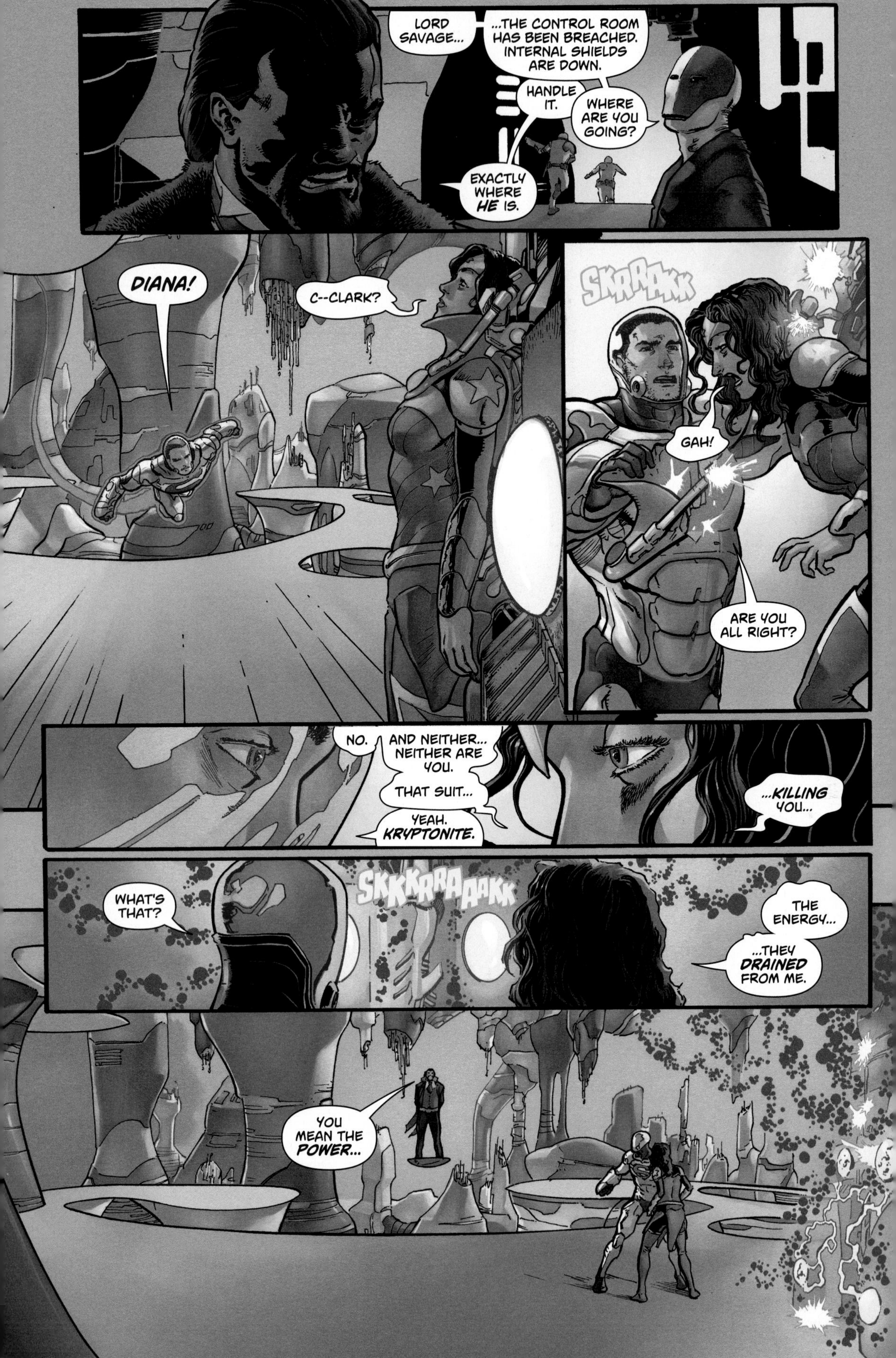
LORD SAVAGE...
...THE CONTROL ROOM HAS BEEN BREACHED. INTERNAL SHIELDS ARE DOWN.
HANDLE IT.
WHERE ARE YOU GOING?
EXACTLY WHERE HE IS.
DIANA!
C--CLARK?
SKRRAAKK
GAH!
ARE YOU ALL RIGHT?
NO.
AND NEITHER... NEITHER ARE YOU.
THAT SUIT...
...KILLING YOU...
YEAH. KRYPTONITE.
WHAT'S THAT?
SKKKRRAAAKK
THE ENERGY...
...THEY DRAINED FROM ME.
YOU MEAN THE POWER...

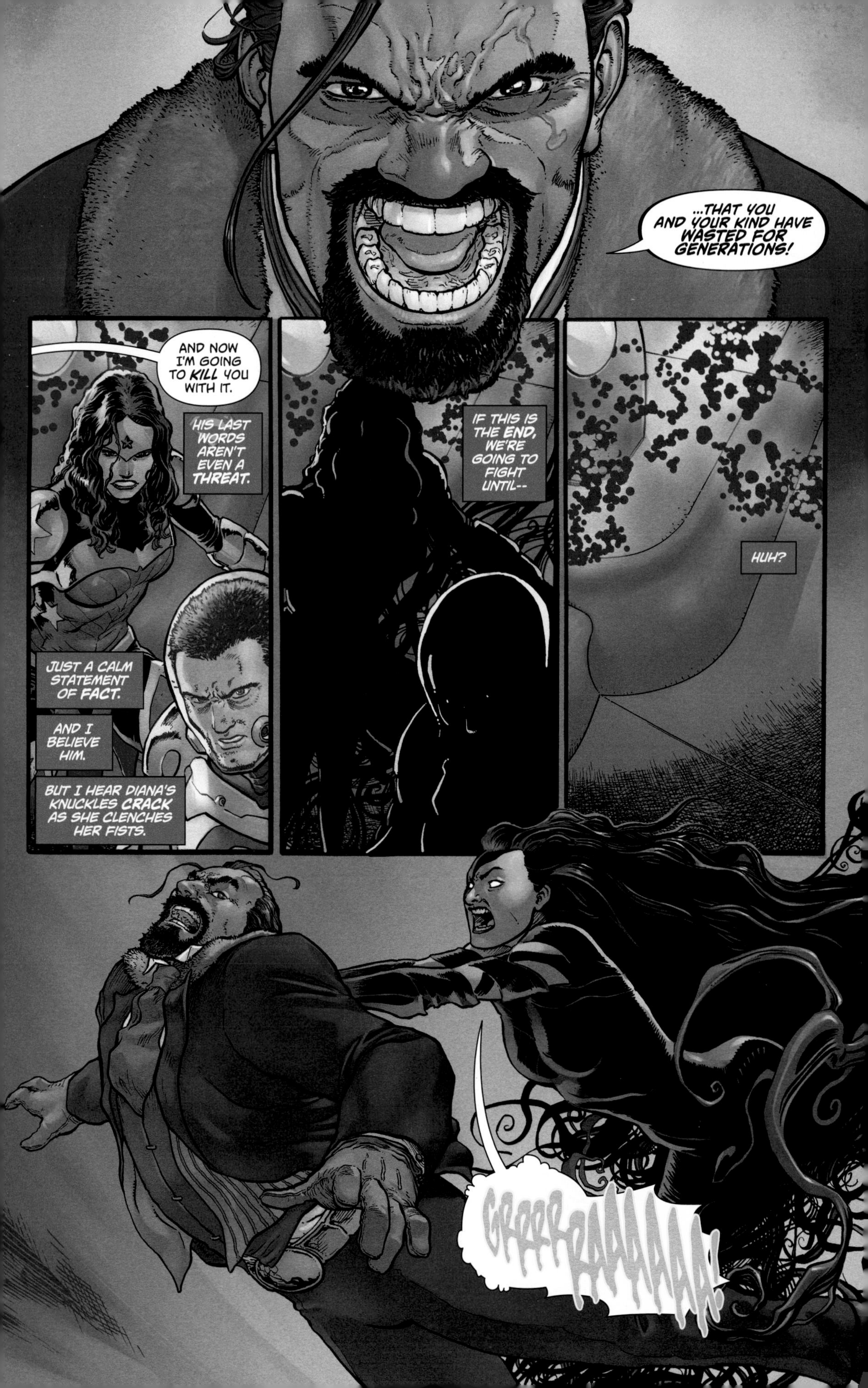
...THAT YOU AND YOUR KIND HAVE WASTED FOR GENERATIONS!
AND NOW I'M GOING TO KILL YOU WITH IT.
HIS LAST WORDS AREN'T EVEN A THREAT.
JUST A CALM STATEMENT OF FACT.
AND I BELIEVE HIM.
BUT I HEAR DIANA'S KNUCKLES CRACK AS SHE CLENCHES HER FISTS.
IF THIS IS THE END, WE'RE GOING TO FIGHT UNTIL--
HUH?
GRRRRAAAAAA!

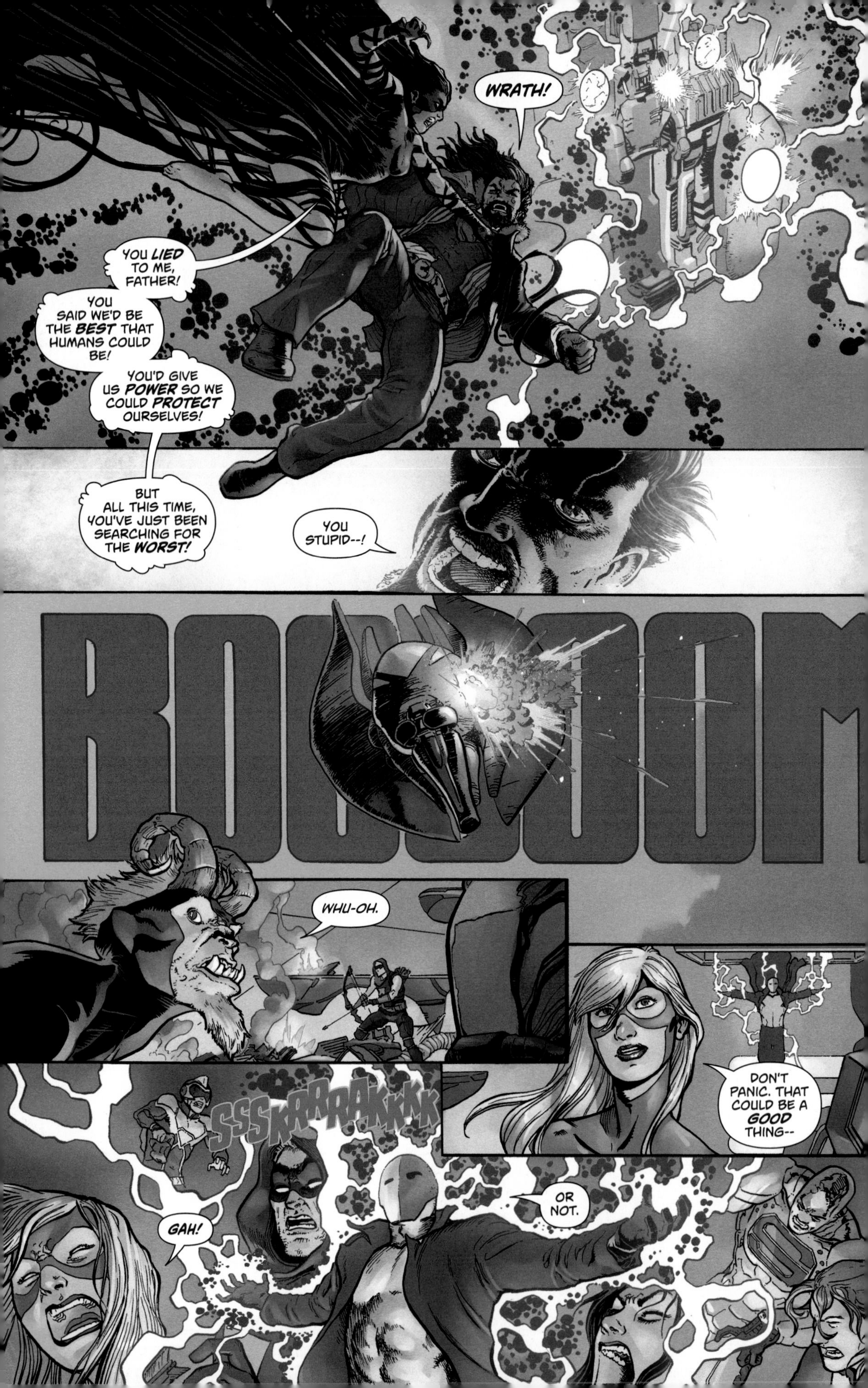
WRATH!
YOU LIED TO ME, FATHER!
YOU SAID WE'D BE THE BEST THAT HUMANS COULD BE!
YOU'D GIVE US POWER SO WE COULD PROTECT OURSELVES!
BUT ALL THIS TIME, YOU'VE JUST BEEN SEARCHING FOR THE WORST!
YOU STUPID--!
WHU-OH.
DON'T PANIC. THAT COULD BE A GOOD THING--
SSSKRRRRAKKKK
GAH!
OR NOT.

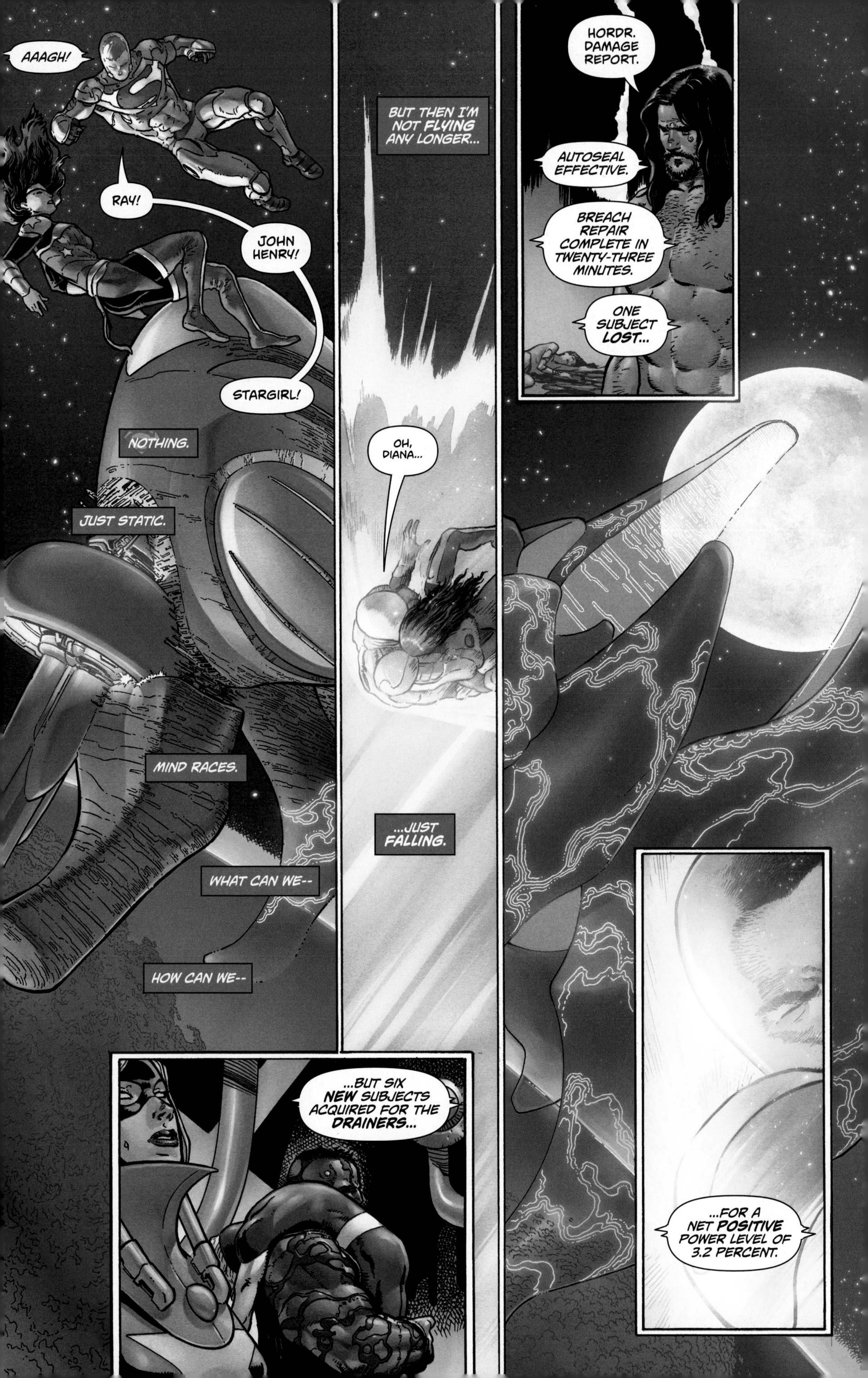
AAAGH!
RAY!
JOHN HENRY!
STARGIRL!
NOTHING.
JUST STATIC.
MIND RACES.
WHAT CAN WE--
HOW CAN WE--
BUT THEN I'M NOT FLYING ANY LONGER...
OH, DIANA...
...JUST FALLING.
HORDR. DAMAGE REPORT.
AUTOSEAL EFFECTIVE.
BREACH REPAIR COMPLETE IN TWENTY-THREE MINUTES.
ONE SUBJECT LOST...
...BUT SIX NEW SUBJECTS ACQUIRED FOR THE DRAINERS...
...FOR A NET POSITIVE POWER LEVEL OF 3.2 PERCENT.

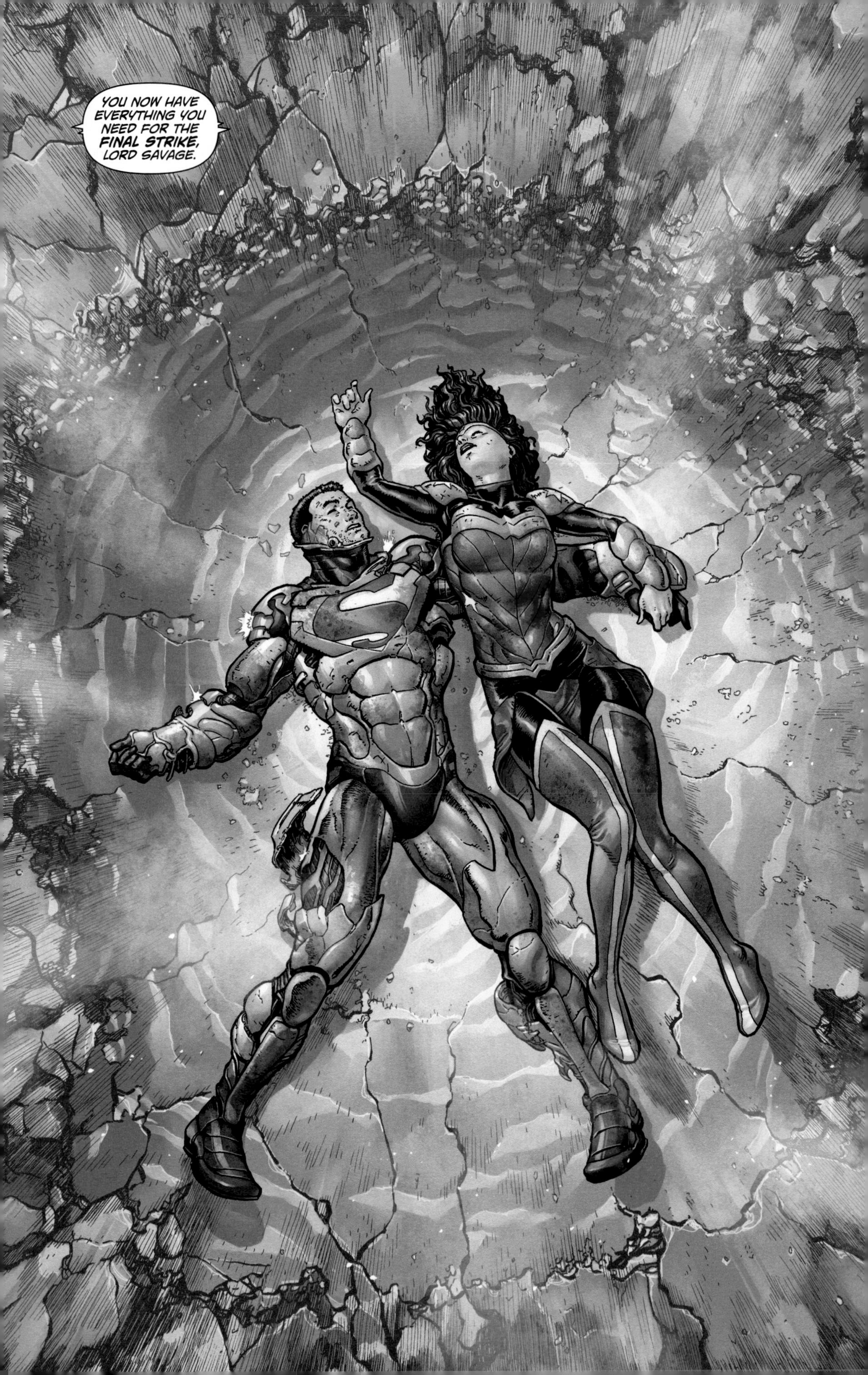
YOU NOW HAVE EVERYTHING YOU NEED FOR THE FINAL STRIKE, LORD SAVAGE.

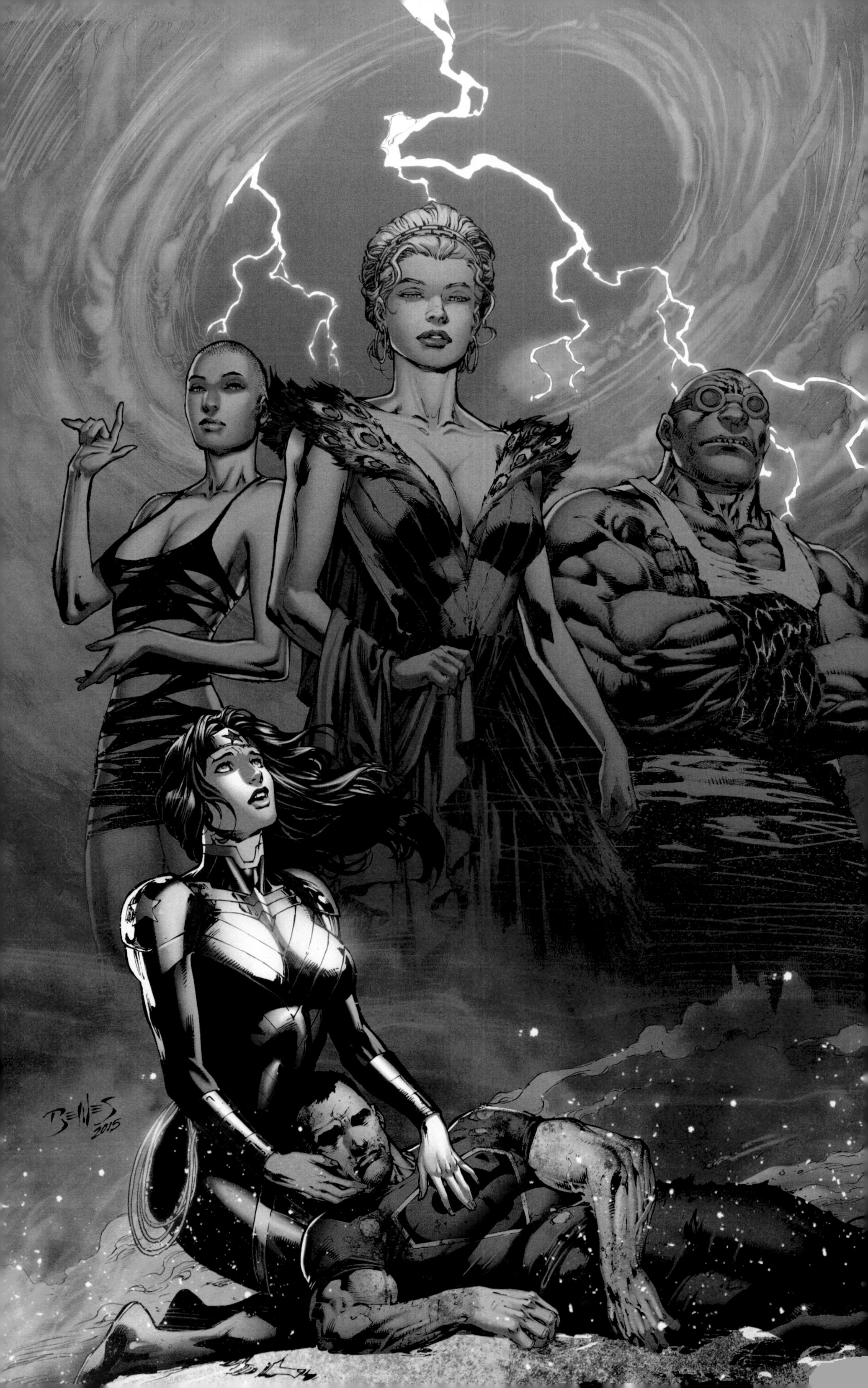

A GOD SOMEWHERE

PETER J. TOMASI writer **DOUG MAHNKE** penciller **JAIME MENDOZA JONATHAN GLAPION SCOTT HANNA** inkers **WIL QUINTANA** colorist **ROB LEIGH** letterer
ED BENES WIL QUINTANA cover

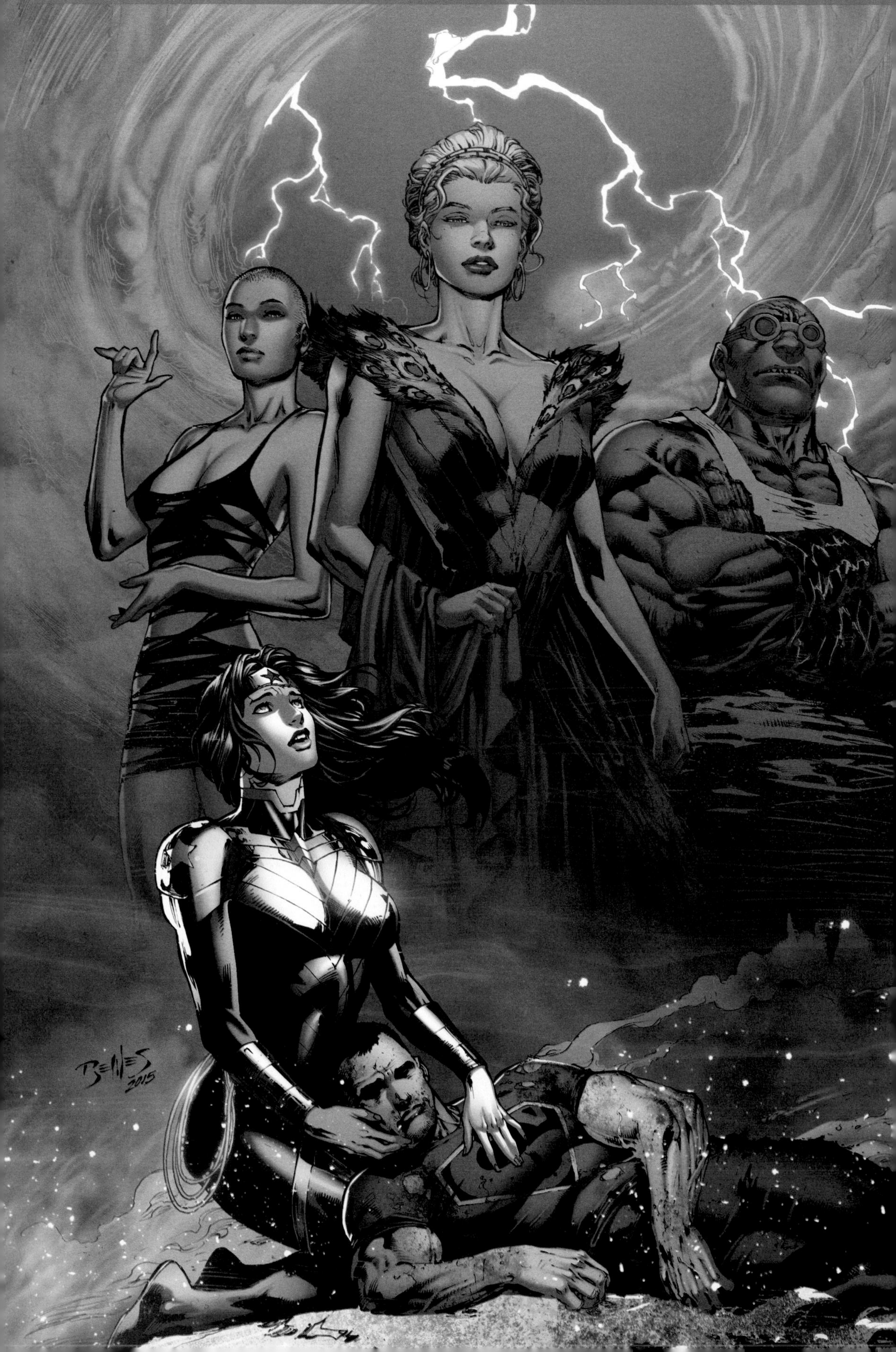
BENES
2015

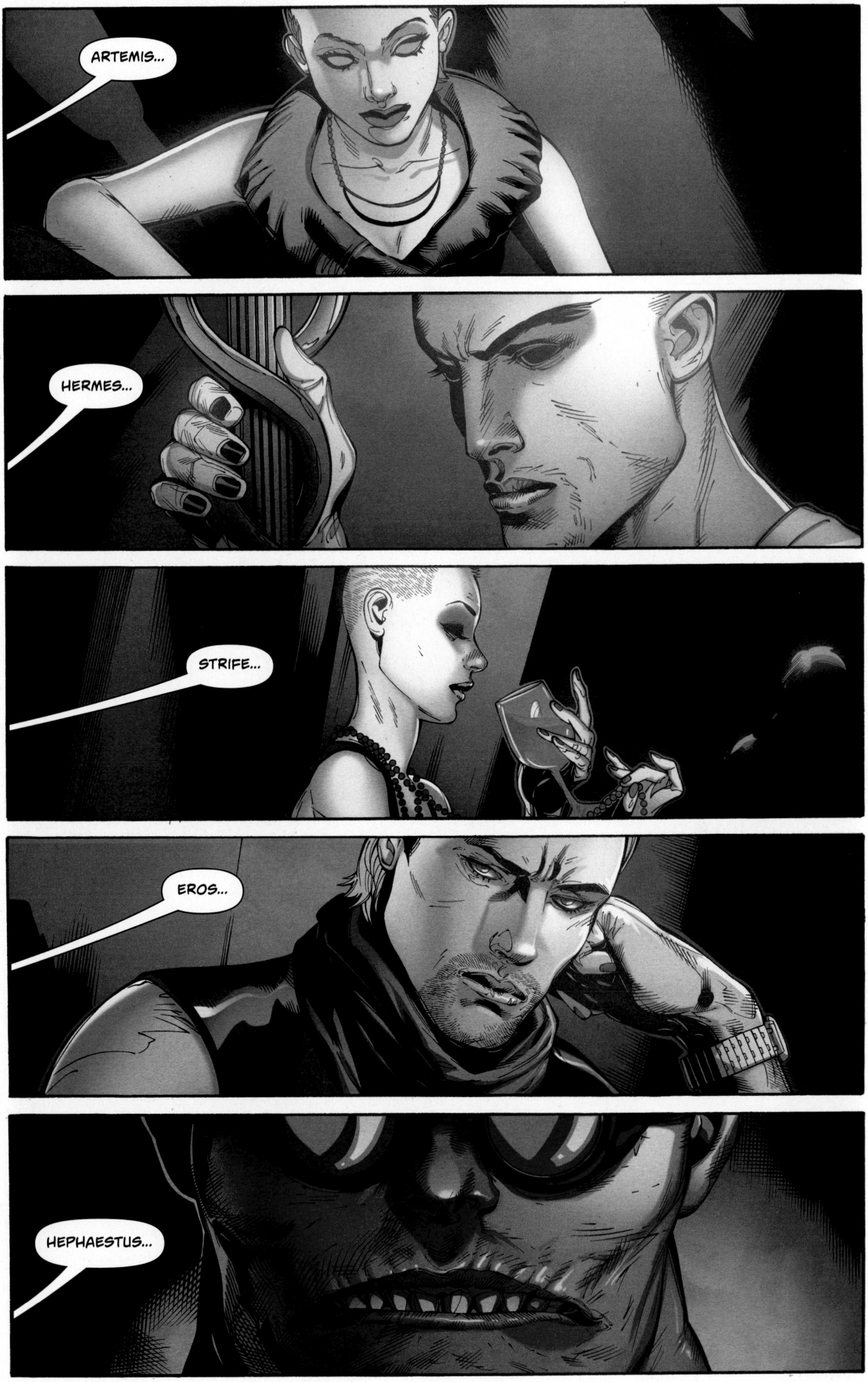
ARTEMIS...
HERMES...
STRIFE...
EROS...
HEPHAESTUS...

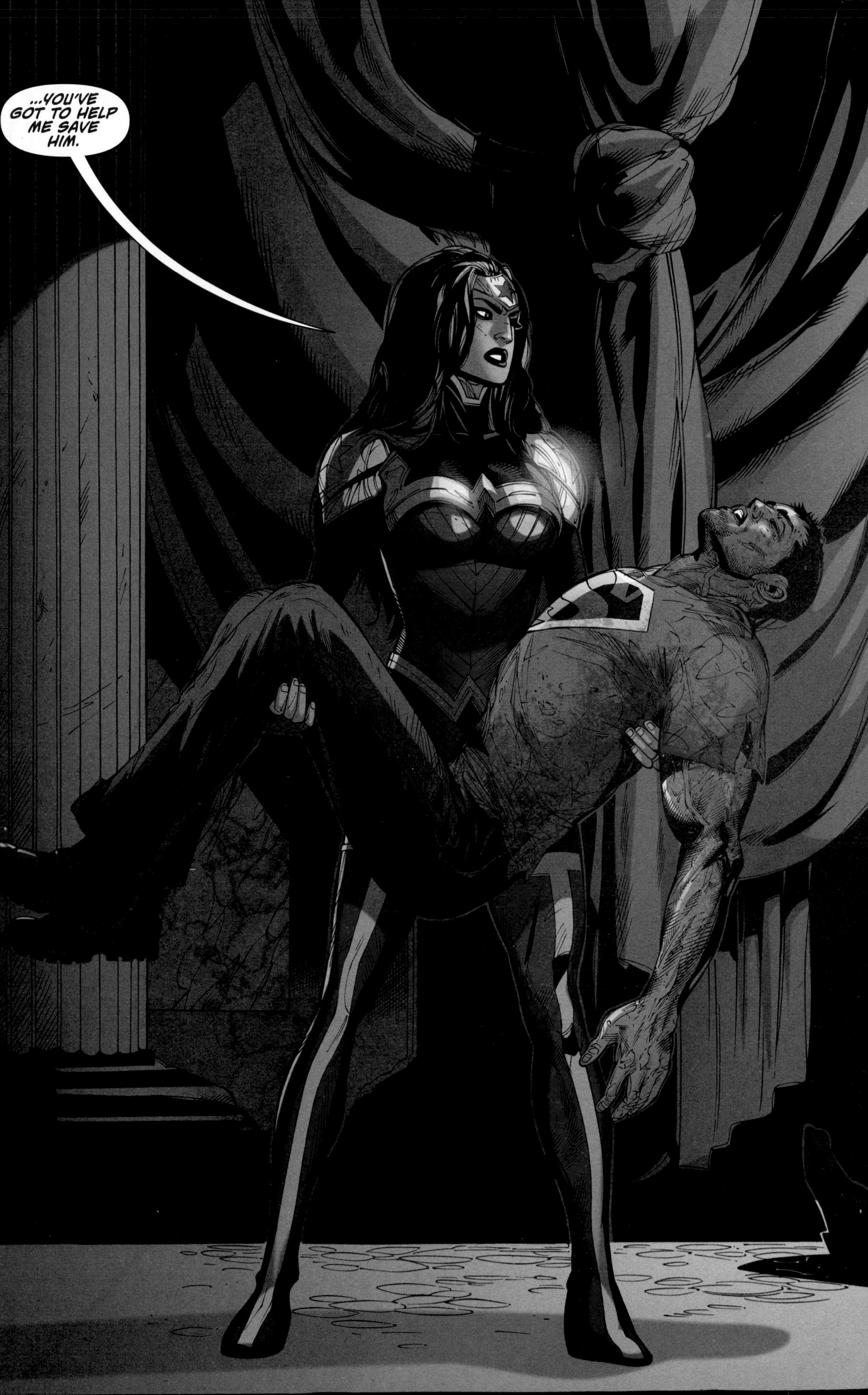
...YOU'VE GOT TO HELP ME SAVE HIM.

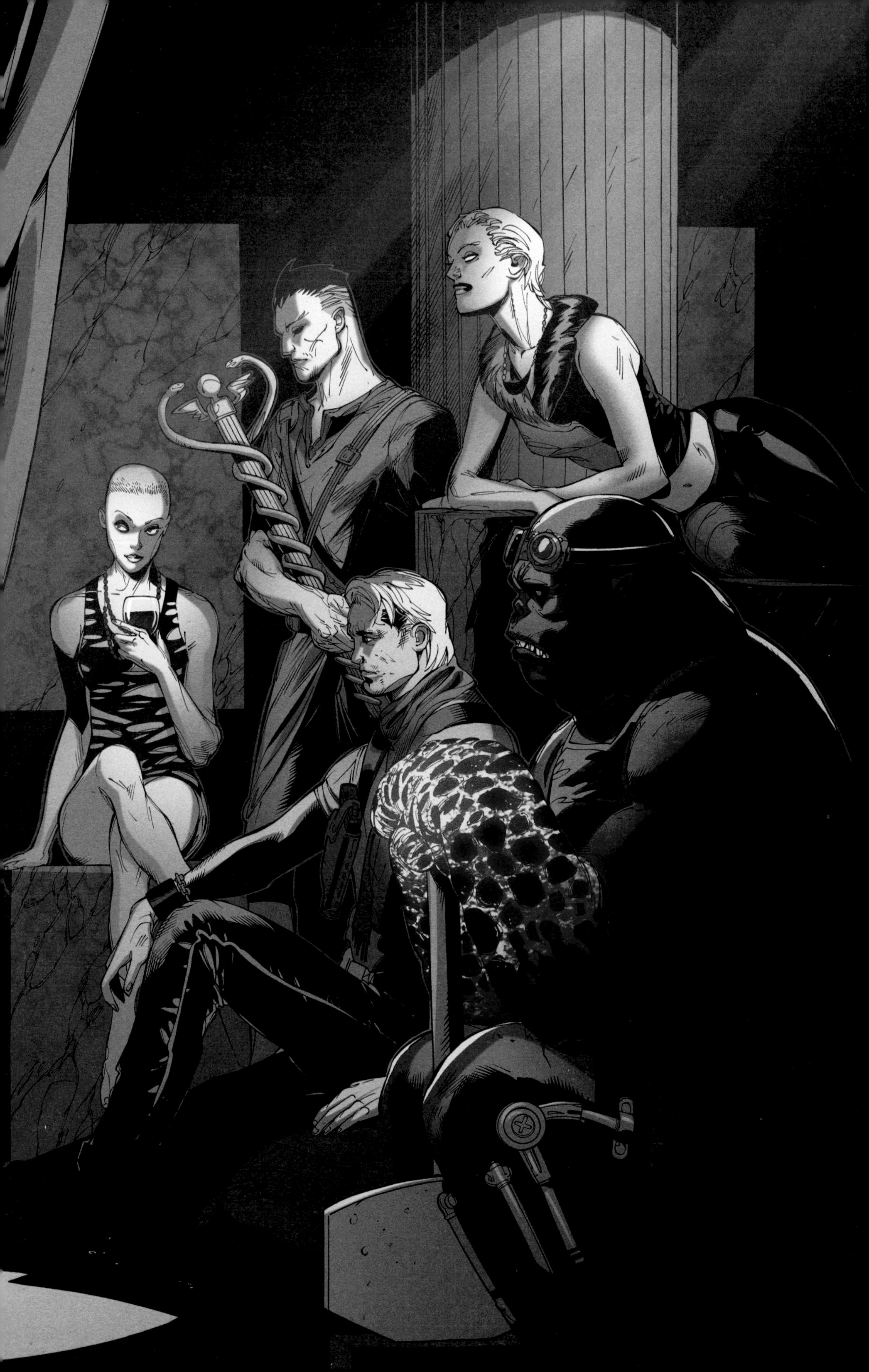

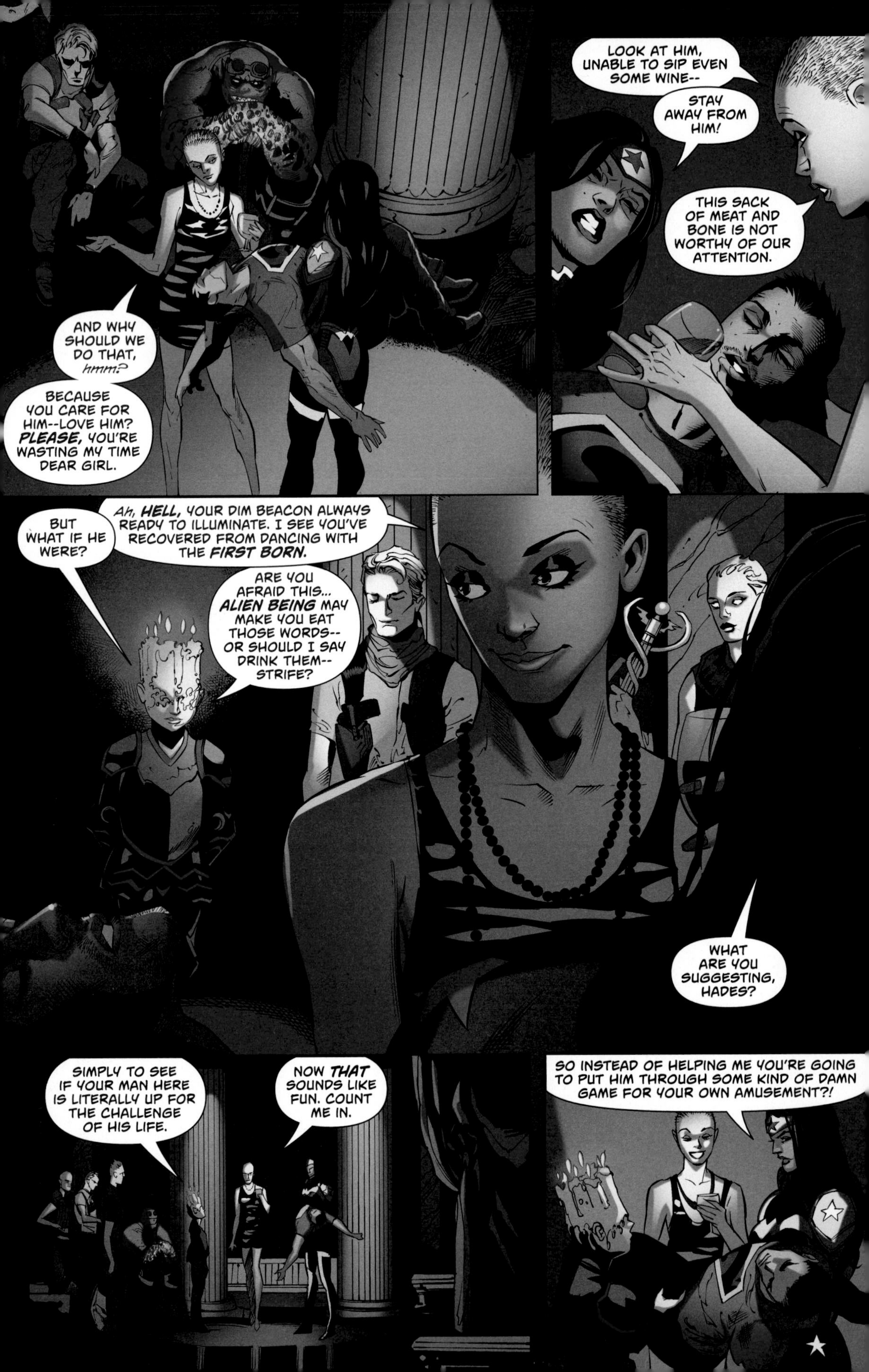

AND WHY SHOULD WE DO THAT, *hmm?*
BECAUSE YOU CARE FOR HIM--LOVE HIM? ***PLEASE,*** YOU'RE WASTING MY TIME DEAR GIRL.
LOOK AT HIM, UNABLE TO SIP EVEN SOME WINE--
STAY AWAY FROM HIM!
THIS SACK OF MEAT AND BONE IS NOT WORTHY OF OUR ATTENTION.
BUT WHAT IF HE WERE?
Ah, ***HELL,*** YOUR DIM BEACON ALWAYS READY TO ILLUMINATE. I SEE YOU'VE RECOVERED FROM DANCING WITH THE ***FIRST BORN.***
ARE YOU AFRAID THIS... ***ALIEN BEING*** MAY MAKE YOU EAT THOSE WORDS--OR SHOULD I SAY DRINK THEM--STRIFE?
WHAT ARE YOU SUGGESTING, HADES?
SIMPLY TO SEE IF YOUR MAN HERE IS LITERALLY UP FOR THE CHALLENGE OF HIS LIFE.
NOW ***THAT*** SOUNDS LIKE FUN. COUNT ME IN.
SO INSTEAD OF HELPING ME YOU'RE GOING TO PUT HIM THROUGH SOME KIND OF DAMN GAME FOR YOUR OWN AMUSEMENT?!

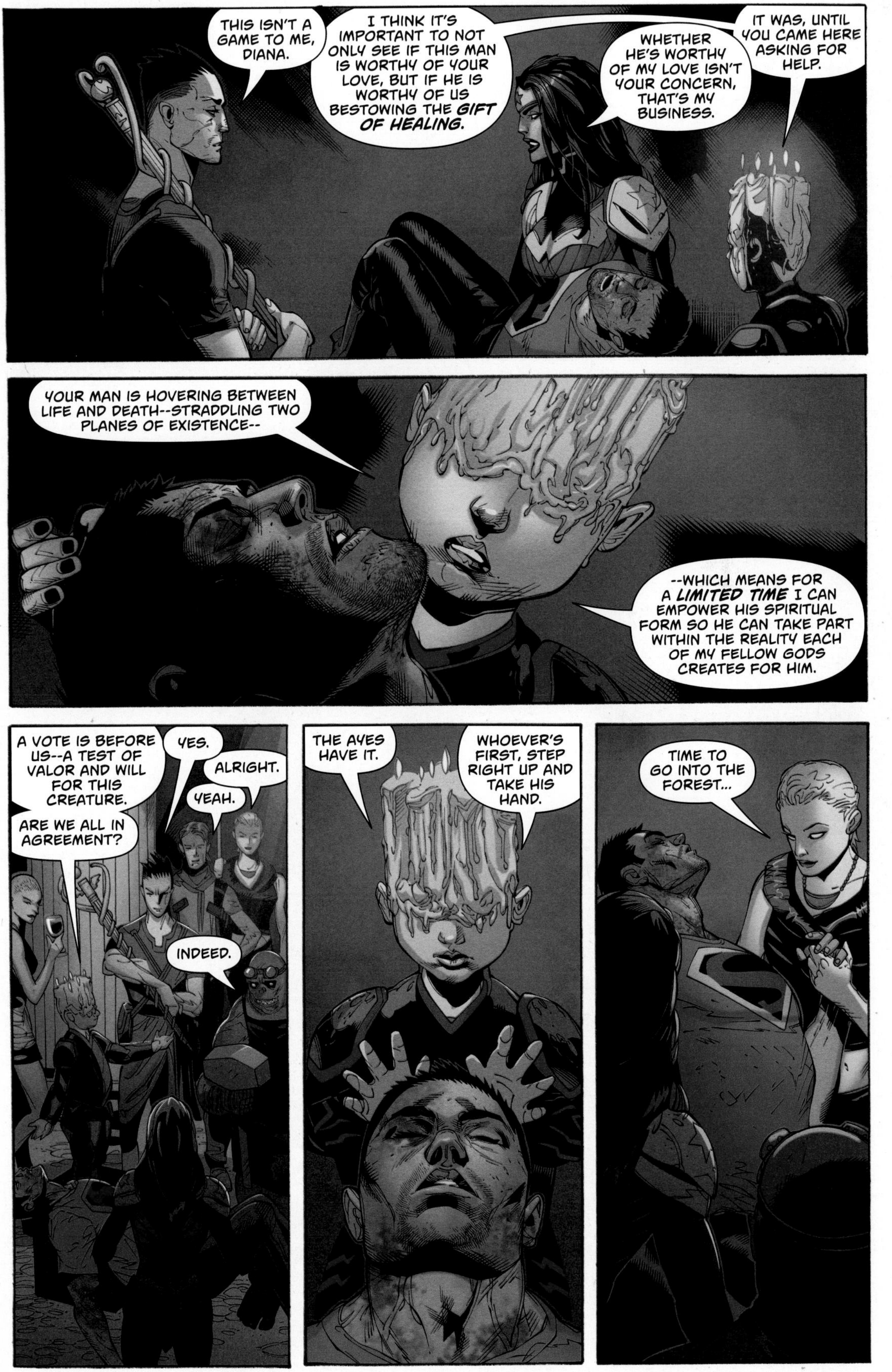
THIS ISN'T A GAME TO ME, DIANA.
I THINK IT'S IMPORTANT TO NOT ONLY SEE IF THIS MAN IS WORTHY OF YOUR LOVE, BUT IF HE IS WORTHY OF US BESTOWING THE GIFT OF HEALING.
WHETHER HE'S WORTHY OF MY LOVE ISN'T YOUR CONCERN, THAT'S MY BUSINESS.
IT WAS, UNTIL YOU CAME HERE ASKING FOR HELP.
YOUR MAN IS HOVERING BETWEEN LIFE AND DEATH--STRADDLING TWO PLANES OF EXISTENCE--
--WHICH MEANS FOR A LIMITED TIME I CAN EMPOWER HIS SPIRITUAL FORM SO HE CAN TAKE PART WITHIN THE REALITY EACH OF MY FELLOW GODS CREATES FOR HIM.
A VOTE IS BEFORE US--A TEST OF VALOR AND WILL FOR THIS CREATURE.
ARE WE ALL IN AGREEMENT?
YES.
ALRIGHT.
YEAH.
INDEED.
THE AYES HAVE IT.
WHOEVER'S FIRST, STEP RIGHT UP AND TAKE HIS HAND.
TIME TO GO INTO THE FOREST...

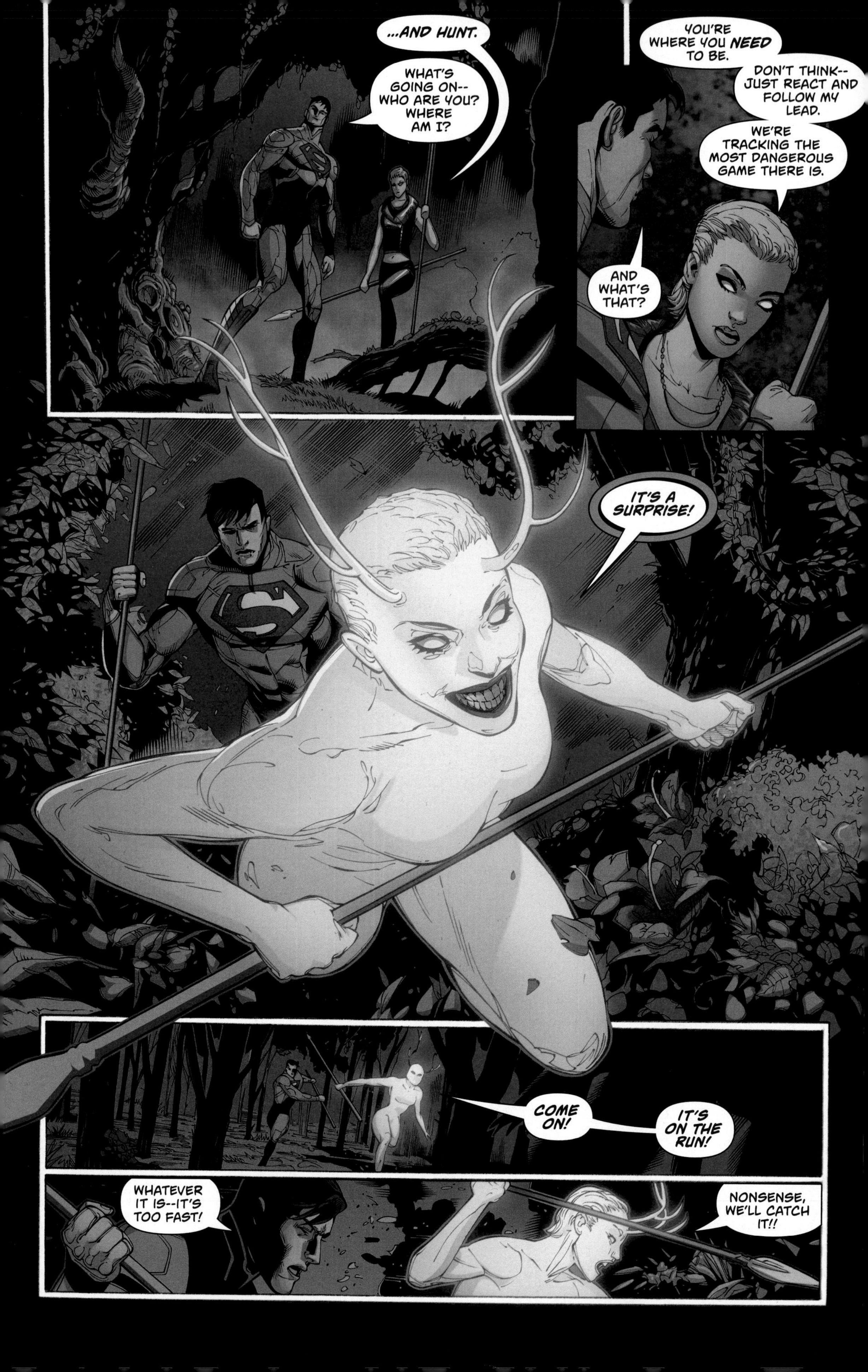
...AND HUNT.
WHAT'S GOING ON-- WHO ARE YOU? WHERE AM I?
YOU'RE WHERE YOU NEED TO BE.
DON'T THINK-- JUST REACT AND FOLLOW MY LEAD.
WE'RE TRACKING THE MOST DANGEROUS GAME THERE IS.
AND WHAT'S THAT?
IT'S A SURPRISE!
COME ON!
IT'S ON THE RUN!
WHATEVER IT IS--IT'S TOO FAST!
NONSENSE, WE'LL CATCH IT!!

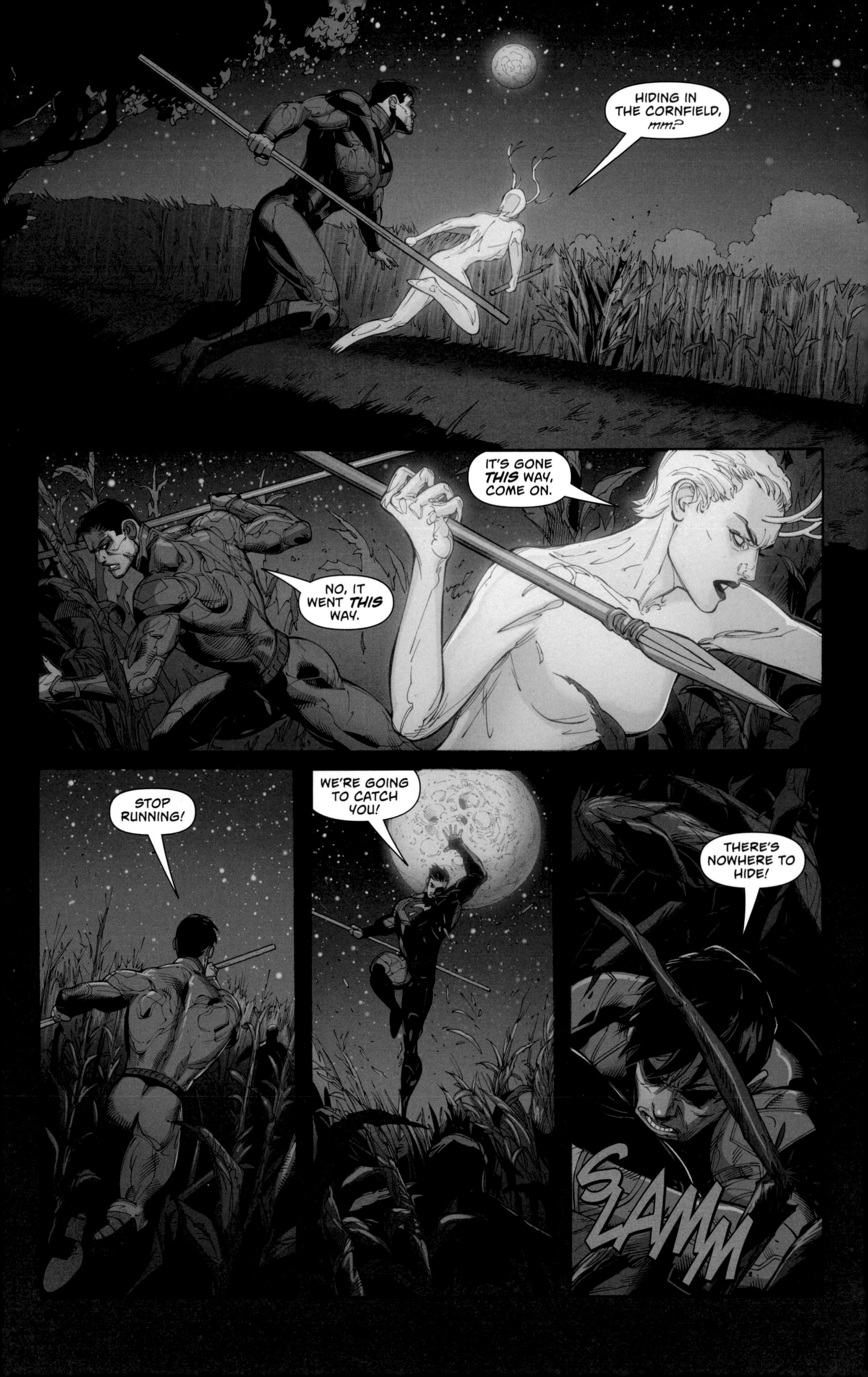
HIDING IN THE CORNFIELD, *mm?*
IT'S GONE ***THIS*** WAY, COME ON.
NO, IT WENT ***THIS*** WAY.
STOP RUNNING!
WE'RE GOING TO CATCH YOU!
THERE'S NOWHERE TO HIDE!
SLAMM

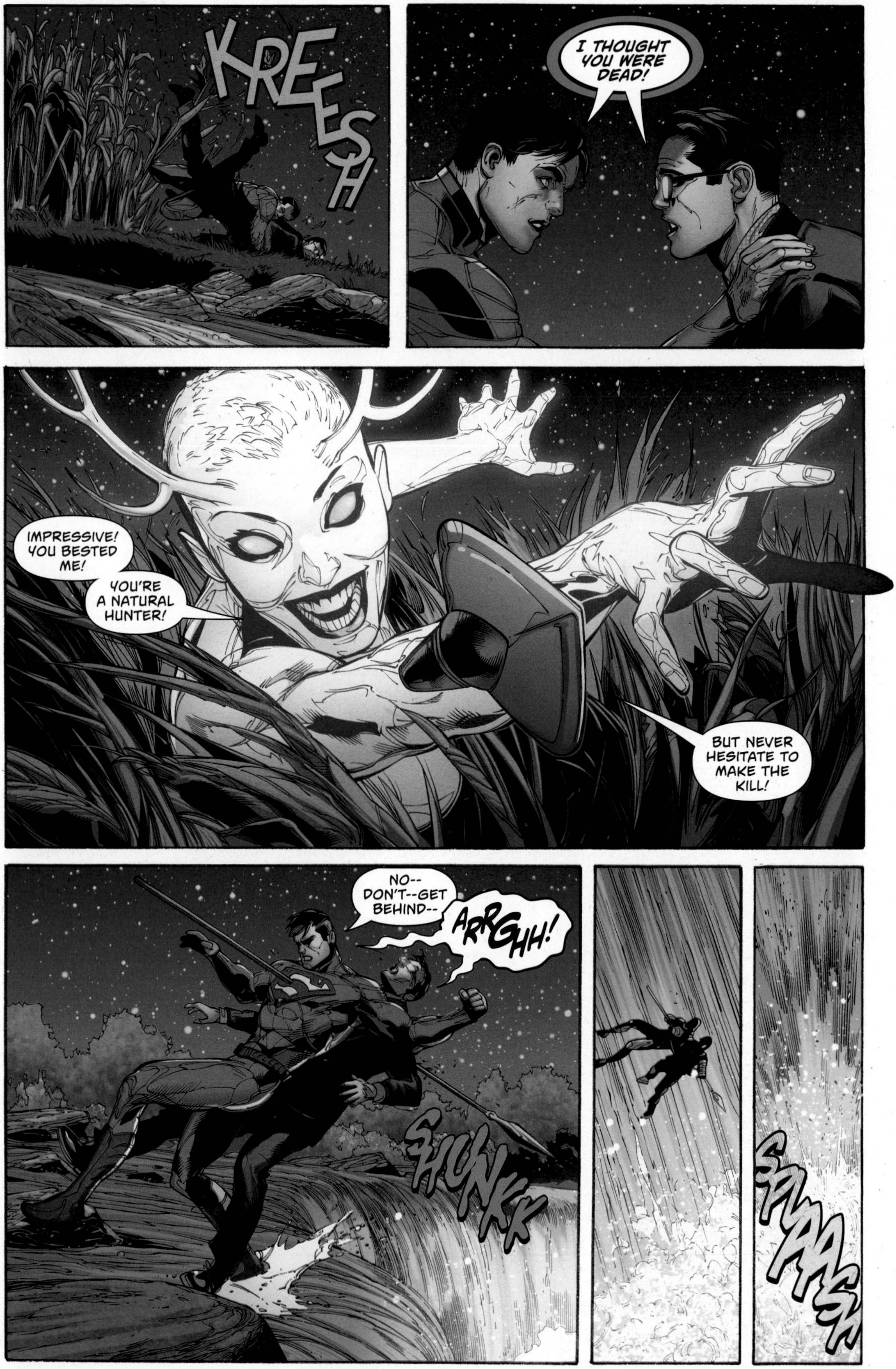
KREESH
I THOUGHT YOU WERE DEAD!
IMPRESSIVE! YOU BESTED ME!
YOU'RE A NATURAL HUNTER!
BUT NEVER HESITATE TO MAKE THE KILL!
NO-- DON'T--GET BEHIND--
ARRGHH!
SHUNKK
SPLAASH

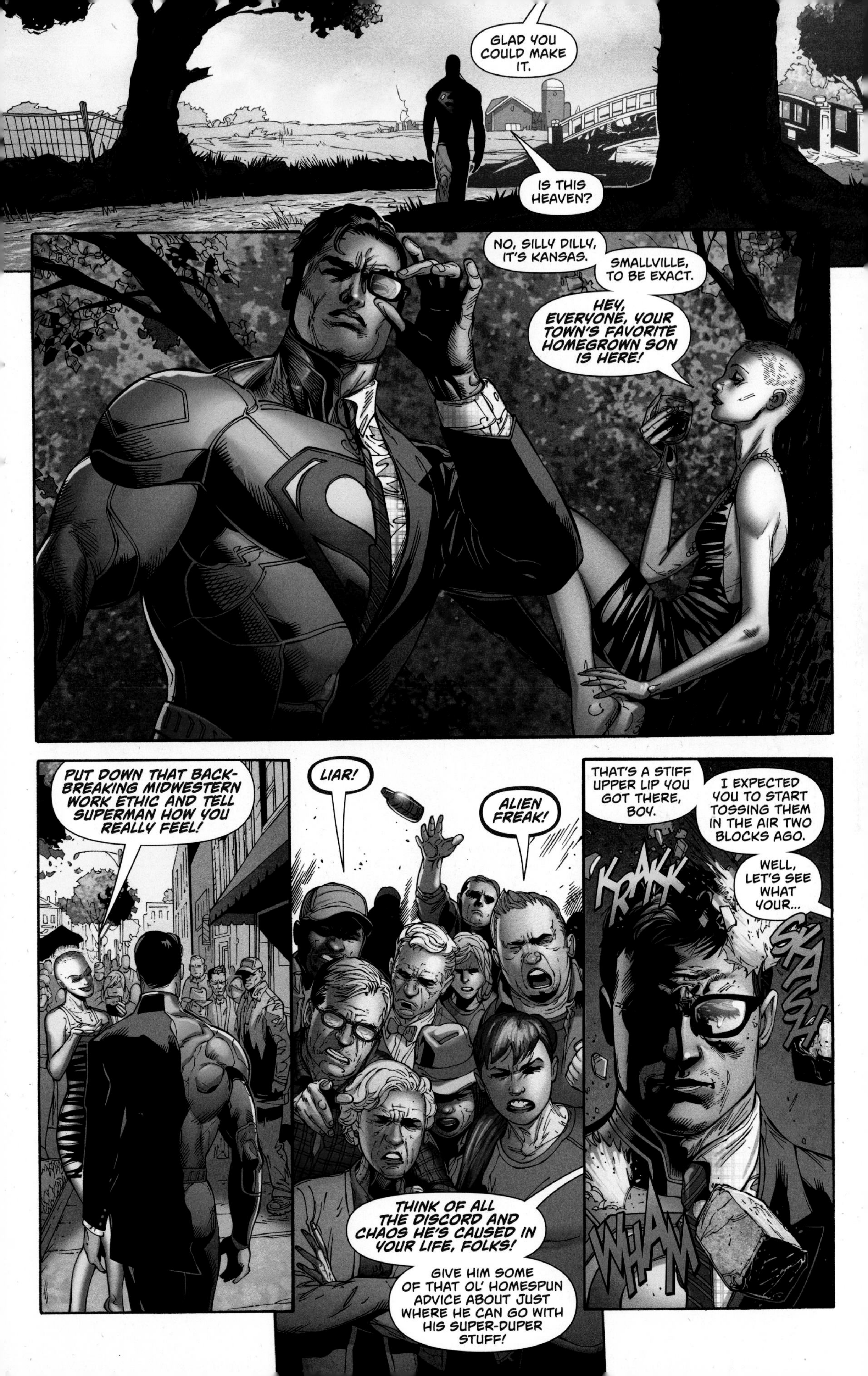
GLAD YOU COULD MAKE IT.
IS THIS HEAVEN?
NO, SILLY DILLY, IT'S KANSAS.
SMALLVILLE, TO BE EXACT.
HEY, EVERYONE, YOUR TOWN'S FAVORITE HOMEGROWN SON IS HERE!
PUT DOWN THAT BACK-BREAKING MIDWESTERN WORK ETHIC AND TELL SUPERMAN HOW YOU REALLY FEEL!
LIAR!
ALIEN FREAK!
THINK OF ALL THE DISCORD AND CHAOS HE'S CAUSED IN YOUR LIFE, FOLKS!
GIVE HIM SOME OF THAT OL' HOMESPUN ADVICE ABOUT JUST WHERE HE CAN GO WITH HIS SUPER-DUPER STUFF!
THAT'S A STIFF UPPER LIP YOU GOT THERE, BOY.
I EXPECTED YOU TO START TOSSING THEM IN THE AIR TWO BLOCKS AGO.
WELL, LET'S SEE WHAT YOUR...
KRAKK
SKASH
WHAM

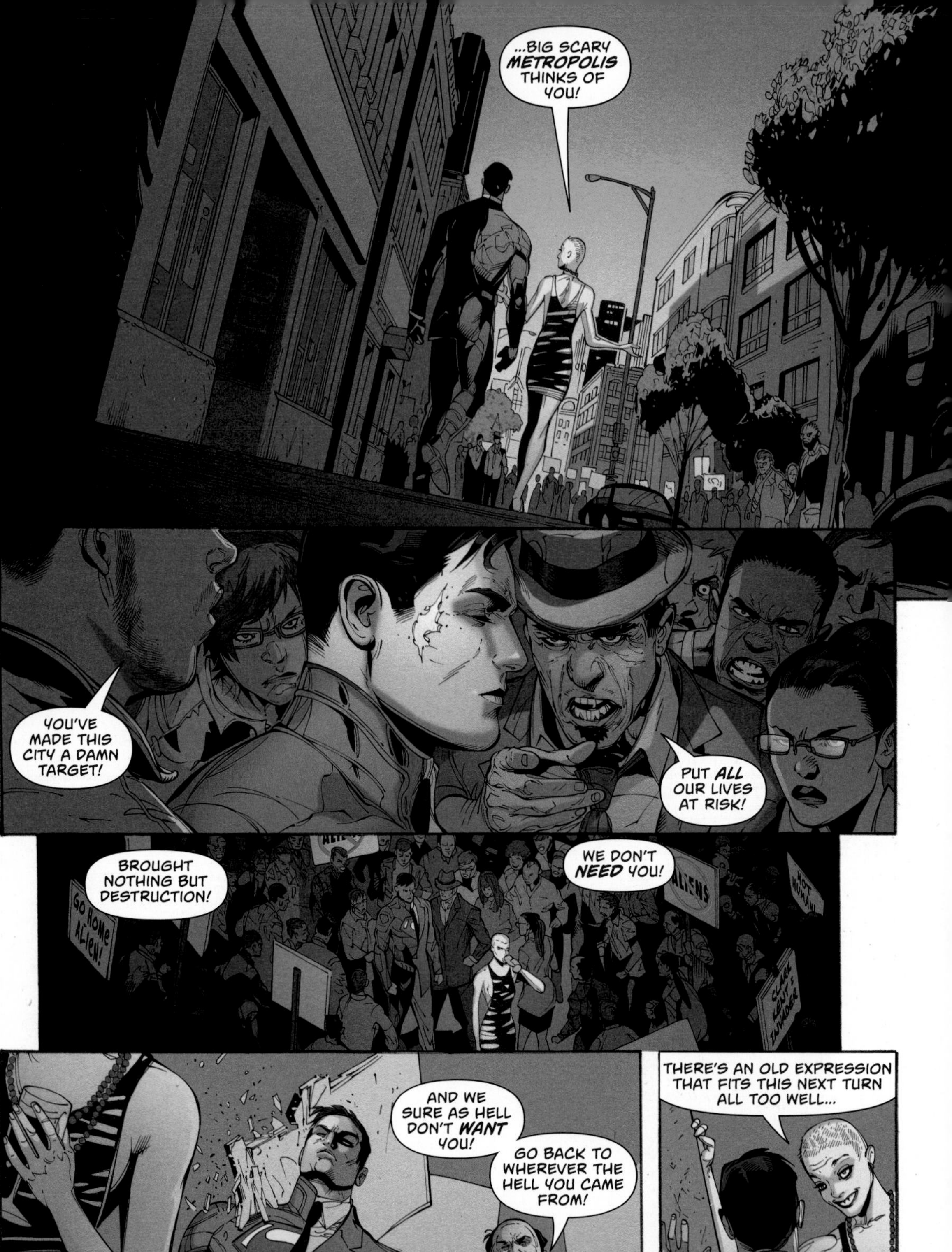
...BIG SCARY *METROPOLIS* THINKS OF YOU!
YOU'VE MADE THIS CITY A DAMN TARGET!
PUT *ALL* OUR LIVES AT RISK!
BROUGHT NOTHING BUT DESTRUCTION!
GO HOME ALIEN!
WE DON'T *NEED* YOU!
NOT HUMAN!
CLARK KENT = INVADER
AND WE SURE AS HELL DON'T *WANT* YOU!
GO BACK TO WHEREVER THE HELL YOU CAME FROM!
THERE'S AN OLD EXPRESSION THAT FITS THIS NEXT TURN ALL TOO WELL...

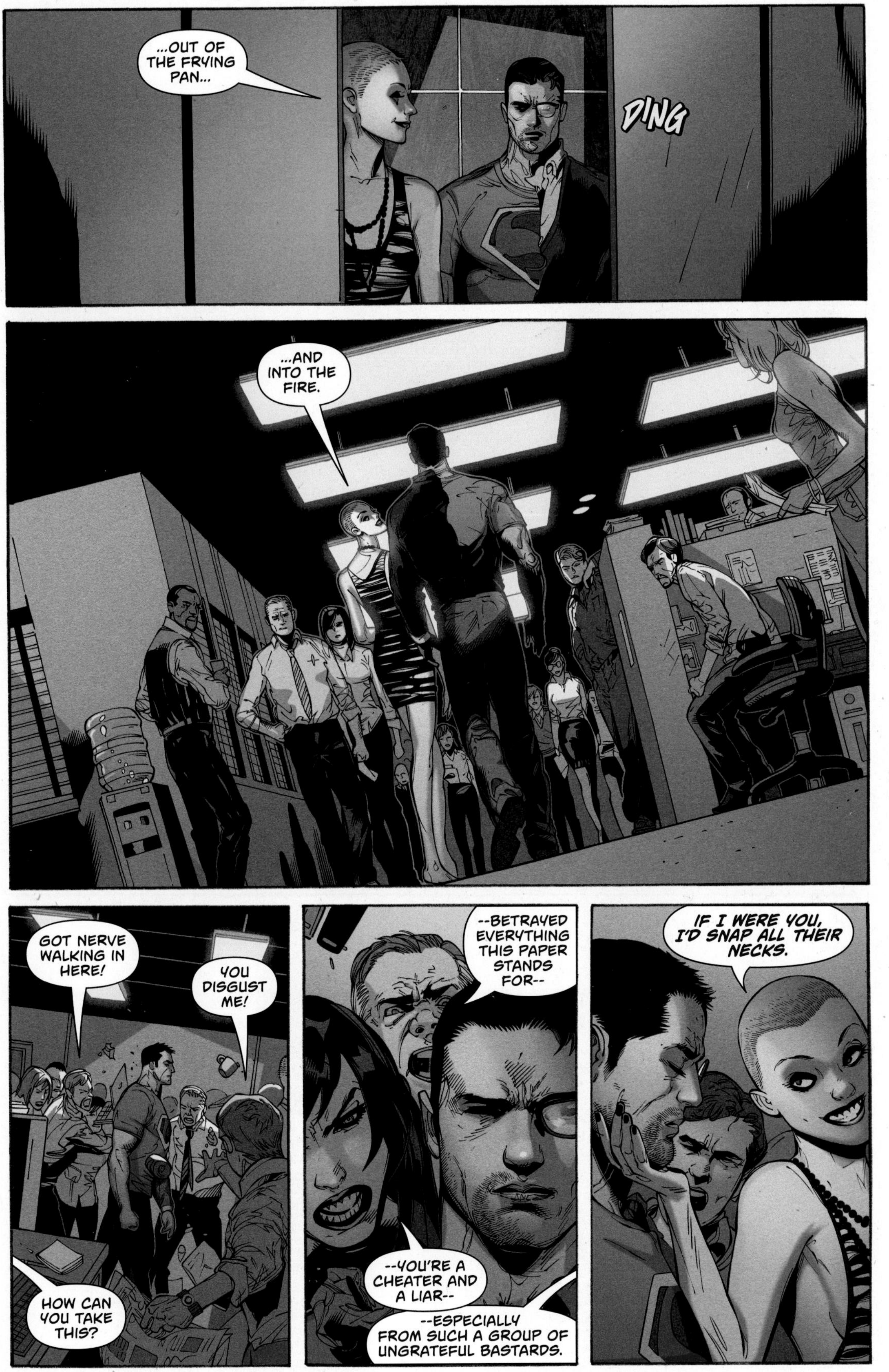
...OUT OF THE FRYING PAN...
DING
...AND INTO THE FIRE.
GOT NERVE WALKING IN HERE!
YOU DISGUST ME!
HOW CAN YOU TAKE THIS?
--BETRAYED EVERYTHING THIS PAPER STANDS FOR--
--YOU'RE A CHEATER AND A LIAR--
--ESPECIALLY FROM SUCH A GROUP OF UNGRATEFUL BASTARDS.
IF I WERE YOU, I'D SNAP ALL THEIR NECKS.

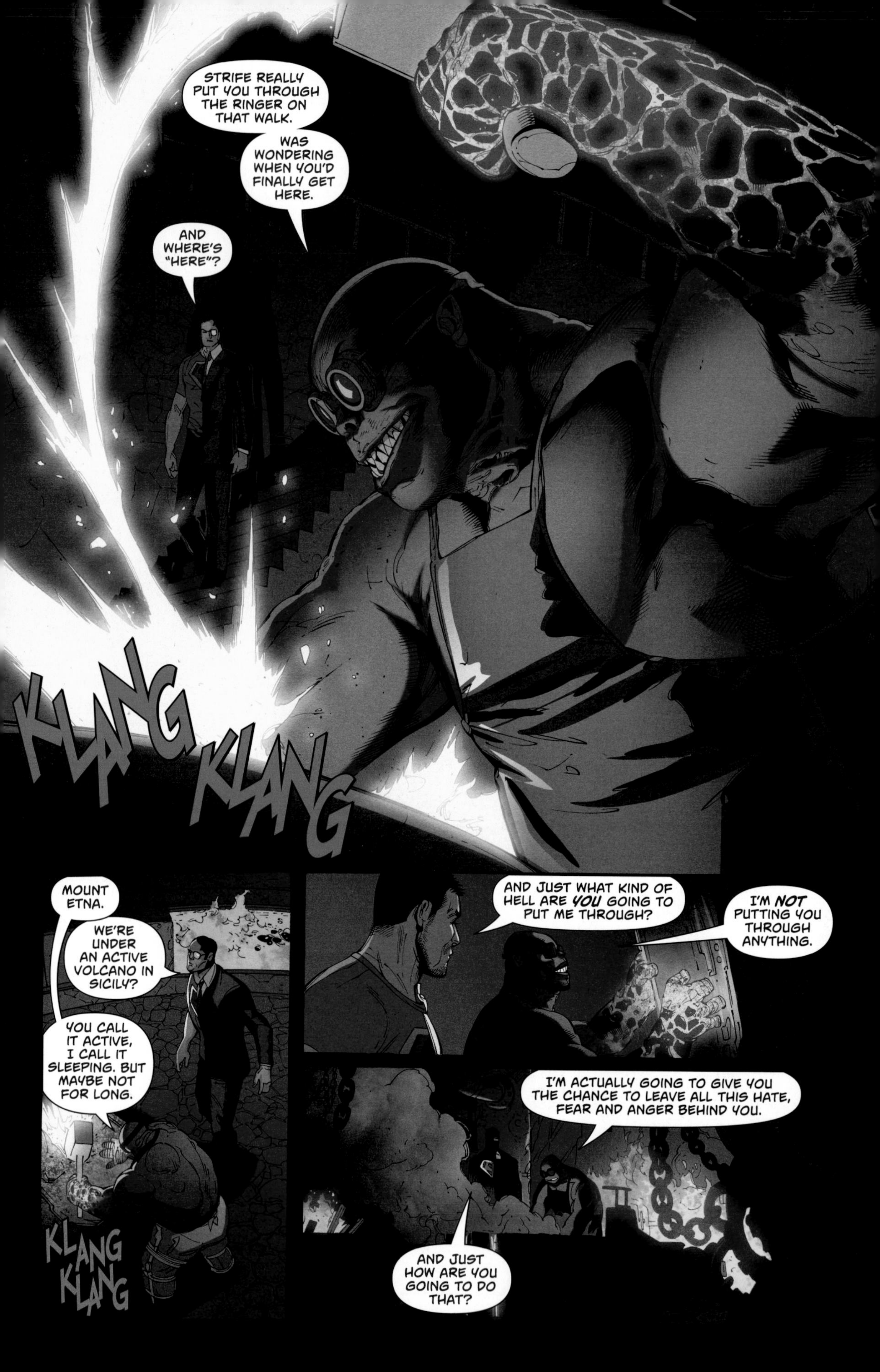
STRIFE REALLY PUT YOU THROUGH THE RINGER ON THAT WALK.
WAS WONDERING WHEN YOU'D FINALLY GET HERE.
AND WHERE'S "HERE"?
KLANG KLANG
MOUNT ETNA.
WE'RE UNDER AN ACTIVE VOLCANO IN SICILY?
YOU CALL IT ACTIVE, I CALL IT SLEEPING. BUT MAYBE NOT FOR LONG.
KLANG KLANG
AND JUST WHAT KIND OF HELL ARE YOU GOING TO PUT ME THROUGH?
I'M NOT PUTTING YOU THROUGH ANYTHING.
I'M ACTUALLY GOING TO GIVE YOU THE CHANCE TO LEAVE ALL THIS HATE, FEAR AND ANGER BEHIND YOU.
AND JUST HOW ARE YOU GOING TO DO THAT?

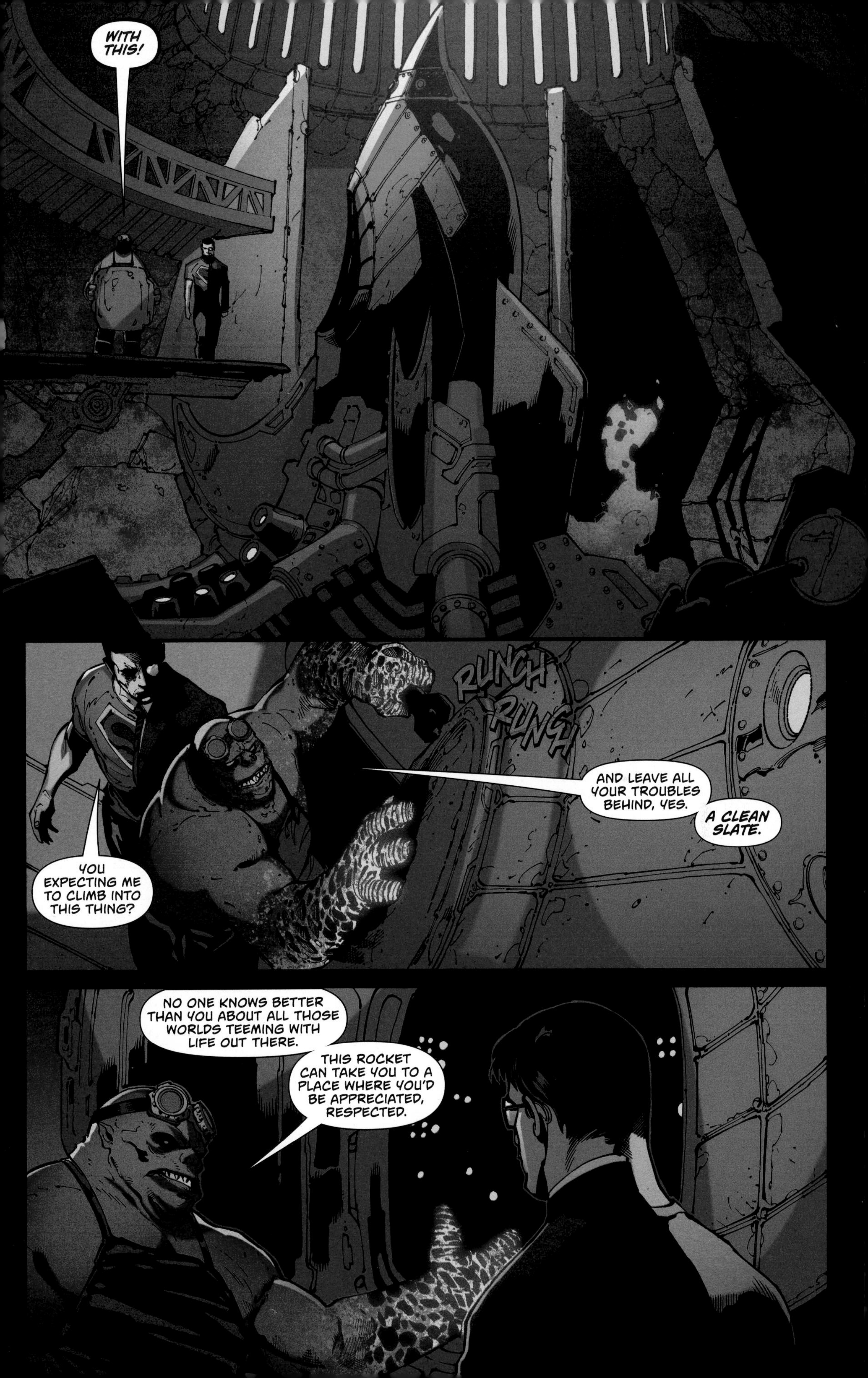
WITH THIS!
RUNCH
RUNCH
YOU EXPECTING ME TO CLIMB INTO THIS THING?
AND LEAVE ALL YOUR TROUBLES BEHIND, YES.
A CLEAN SLATE.
NO ONE KNOWS BETTER THAN YOU ABOUT ALL THOSE WORLDS TEEMING WITH LIFE OUT THERE.
THIS ROCKET CAN TAKE YOU TO A PLACE WHERE YOU'D BE APPRECIATED, RESPECTED.

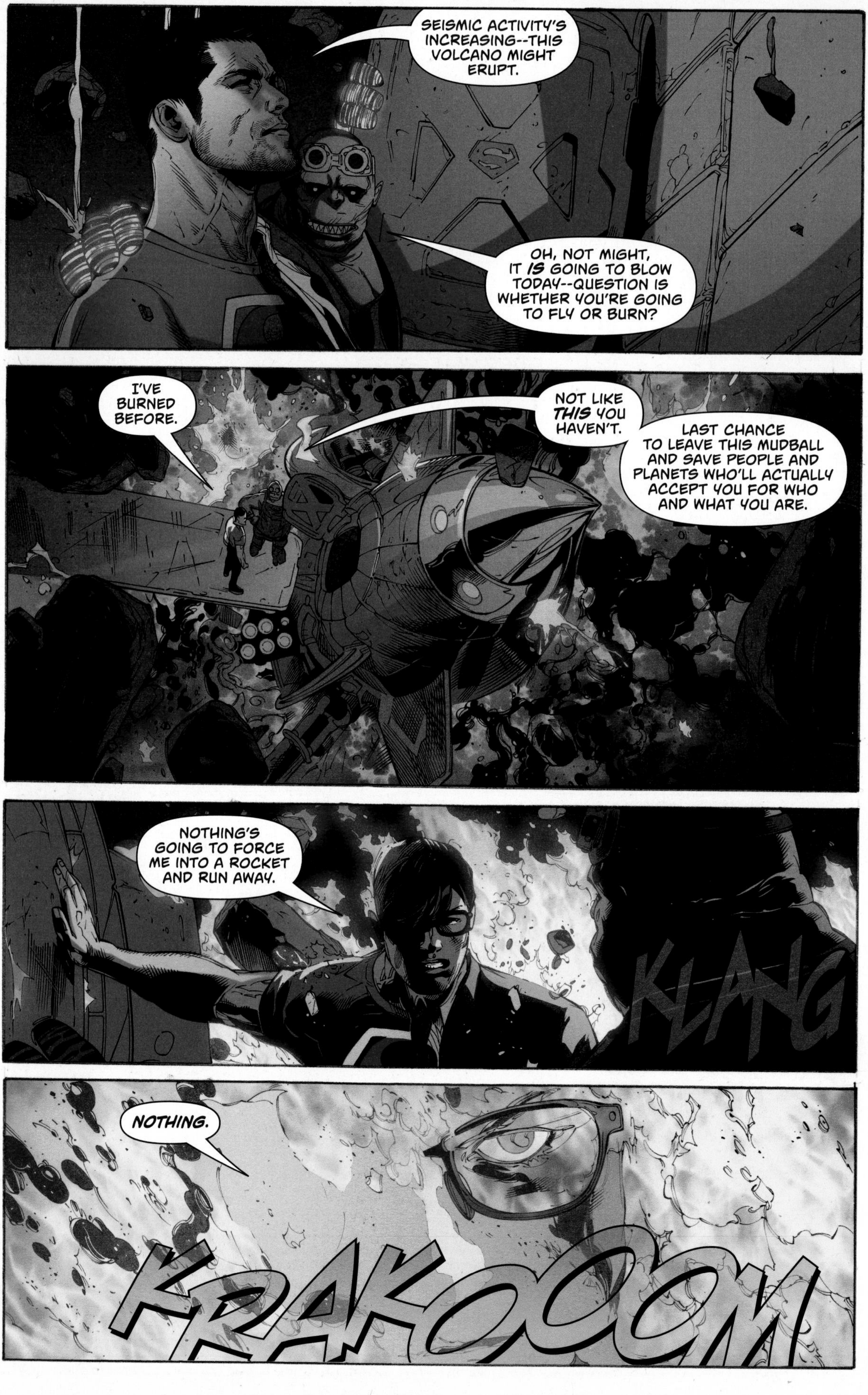
SEISMIC ACTIVITY'S INCREASING--THIS VOLCANO MIGHT ERUPT.
OH, NOT MIGHT, IT *IS* GOING TO BLOW TODAY--QUESTION IS WHETHER YOU'RE GOING TO FLY OR BURN?
I'VE BURNED BEFORE.
NOT LIKE *THIS* YOU HAVEN'T.
LAST CHANCE TO LEAVE THIS MUDBALL AND SAVE PEOPLE AND PLANETS WHO'LL ACTUALLY ACCEPT YOU FOR WHO AND WHAT YOU ARE.
NOTHING'S GOING TO FORCE ME INTO A ROCKET AND RUN AWAY.
KLANG
NOTHING.
KRAKOOOM

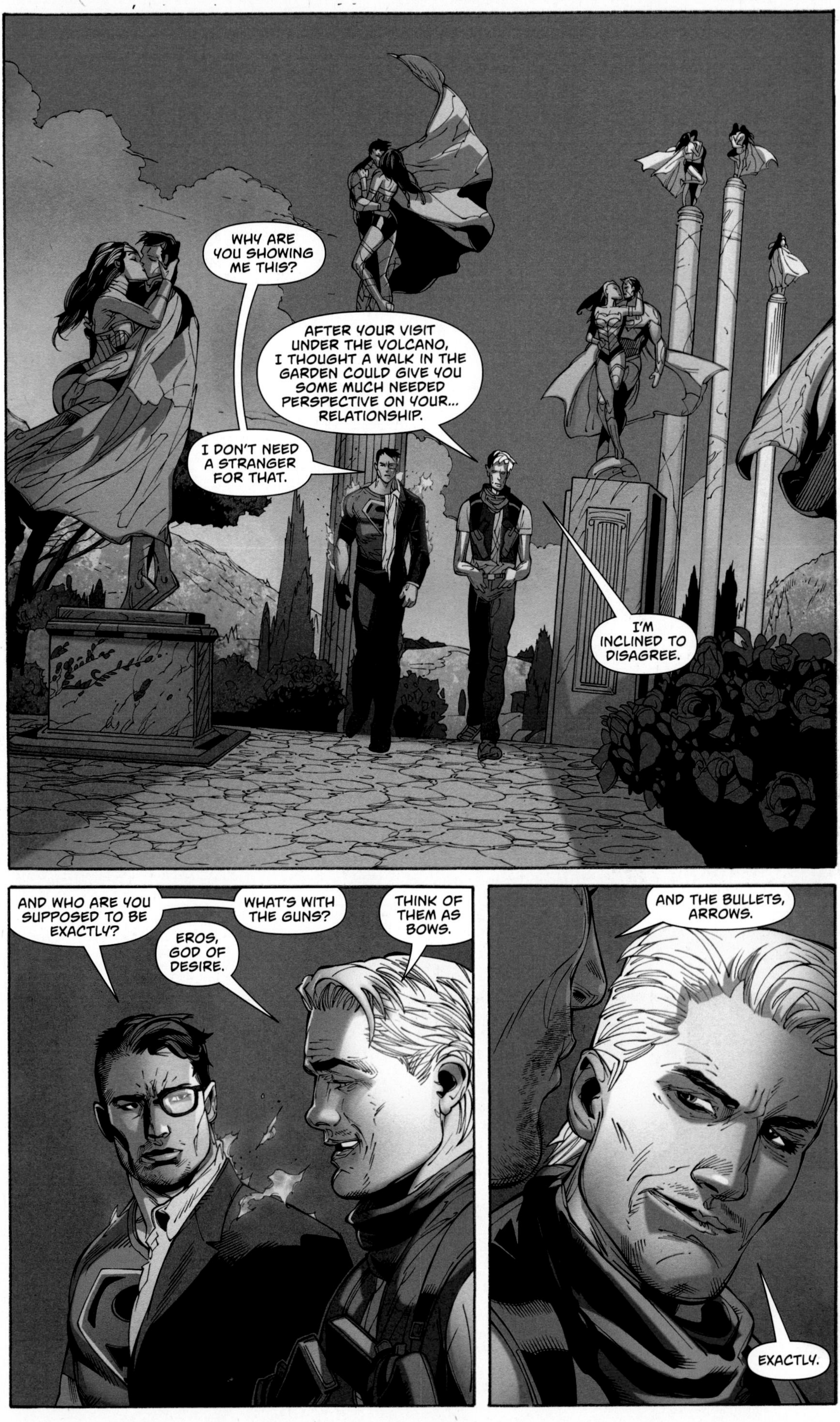
WHY ARE YOU SHOWING ME THIS?
AFTER YOUR VISIT UNDER THE VOLCANO, I THOUGHT A WALK IN THE GARDEN COULD GIVE YOU SOME MUCH NEEDED PERSPECTIVE ON YOUR... RELATIONSHIP.
I DON'T NEED A STRANGER FOR THAT.
I'M INCLINED TO DISAGREE.
AND WHO ARE YOU SUPPOSED TO BE EXACTLY?
EROS, GOD OF DESIRE.
WHAT'S WITH THE GUNS?
THINK OF THEM AS BOWS.
AND THE BULLETS, ARROWS.
EXACTLY.

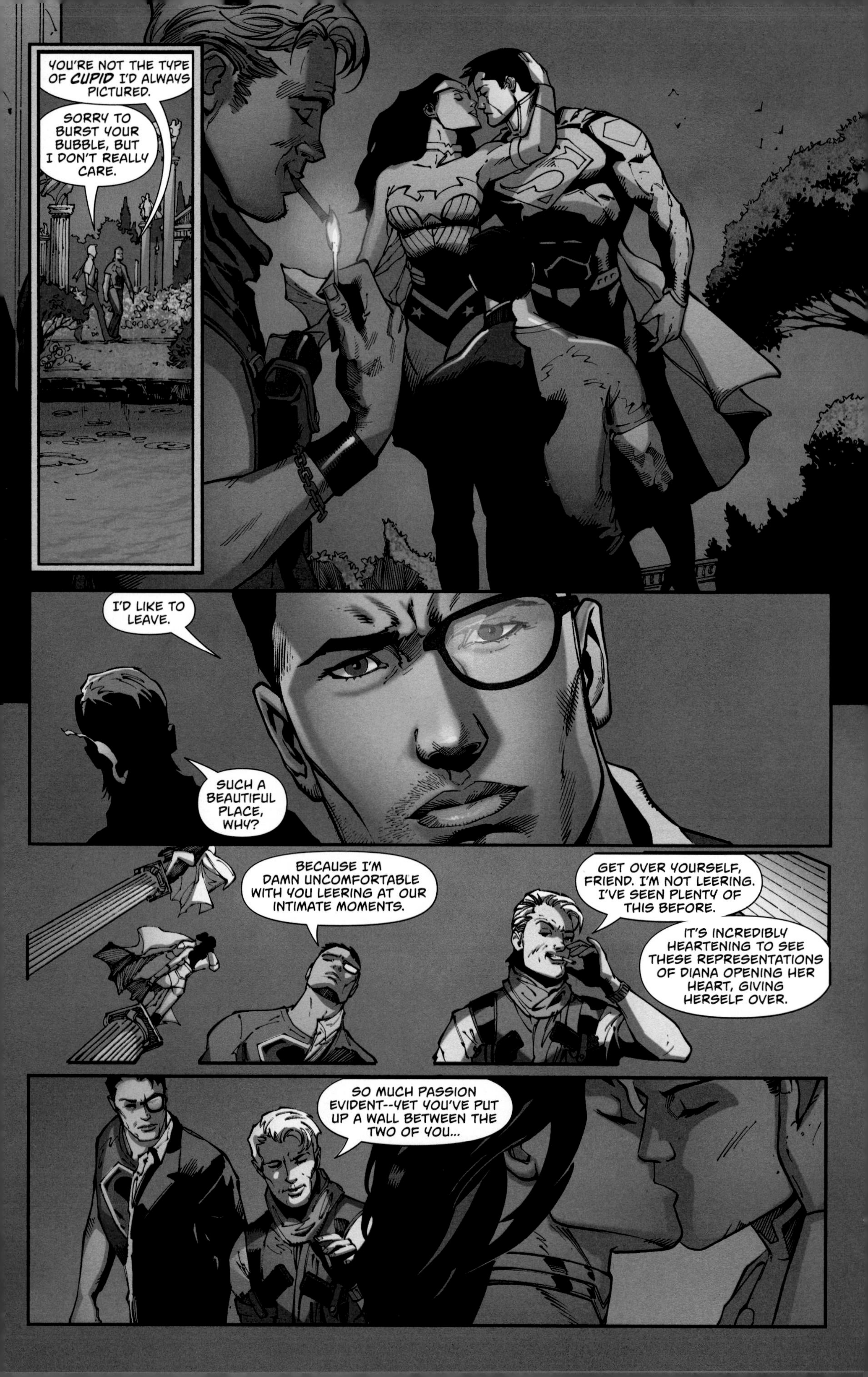

YOU'RE NOT THE TYPE OF **CUPID** I'D ALWAYS PICTURED.
SORRY TO BURST YOUR BUBBLE, BUT I DON'T REALLY CARE.
I'D LIKE TO LEAVE.
SUCH A BEAUTIFUL PLACE, WHY?
BECAUSE I'M DAMN UNCOMFORTABLE WITH YOU LEERING AT OUR INTIMATE MOMENTS.
GET OVER YOURSELF, FRIEND. I'M NOT LEERING. I'VE SEEN PLENTY OF THIS BEFORE.
IT'S INCREDIBLY HEARTENING TO SEE THESE REPRESENTATIONS OF DIANA OPENING HER HEART, GIVING HERSELF OVER.
SO MUCH PASSION EVIDENT--YET YOU'VE PUT UP A WALL BETWEEN THE TWO OF YOU...

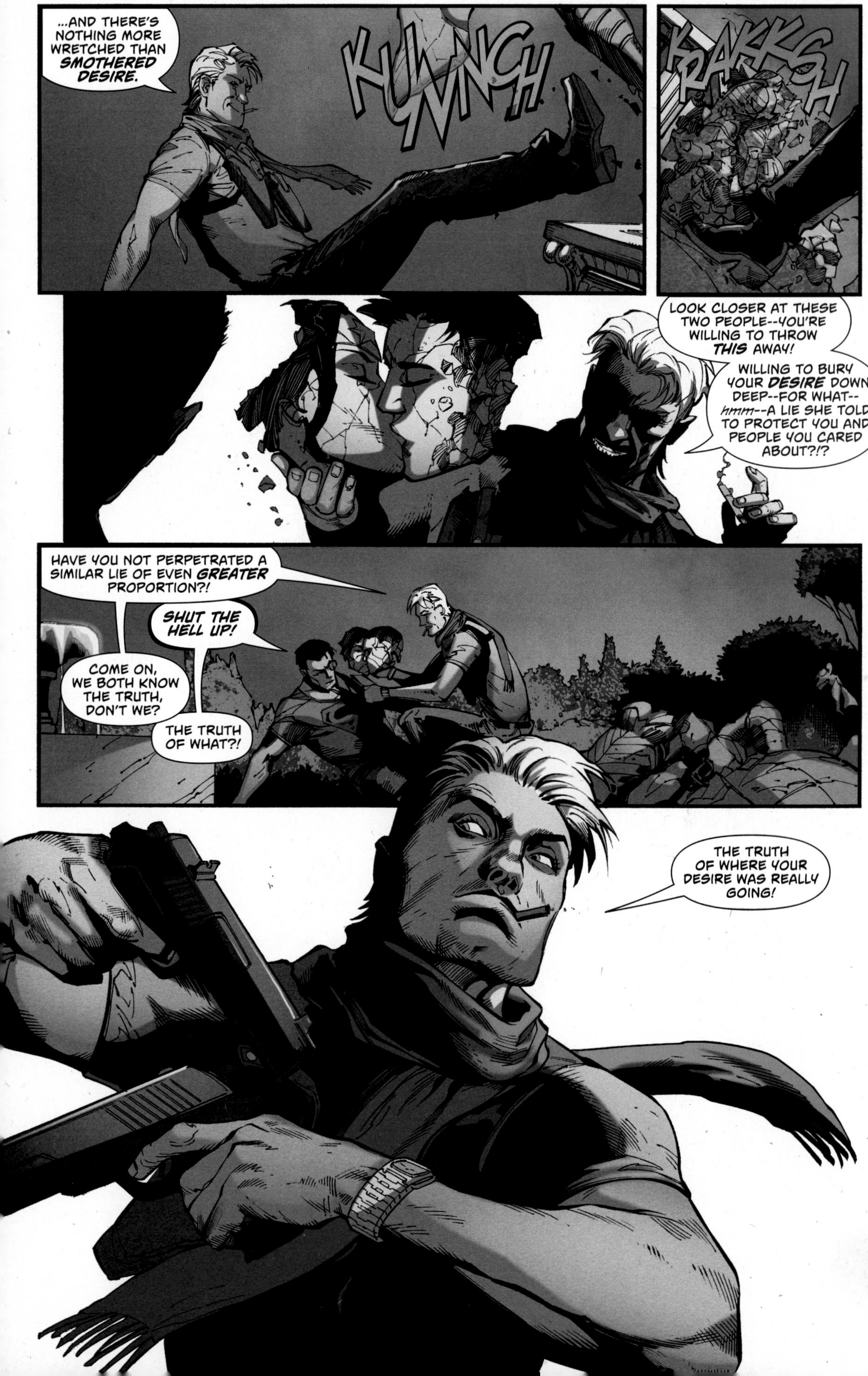
...AND THERE'S NOTHING MORE WRETCHED THAN SMOTHERED DESIRE.
KUNNCH
KRAKKSH
LOOK CLOSER AT THESE TWO PEOPLE--YOU'RE WILLING TO THROW THIS AWAY!
WILLING TO BURY YOUR DESIRE DOWN DEEP--FOR WHAT--hmm--A LIE SHE TOLD TO PROTECT YOU AND PEOPLE YOU CARED ABOUT?!?
HAVE YOU NOT PERPETRATED A SIMILAR LIE OF EVEN GREATER PROPORTION?!
SHUT THE HELL UP!
COME ON, WE BOTH KNOW THE TRUTH, DON'T WE?
THE TRUTH OF WHAT?!
THE TRUTH OF WHERE YOUR DESIRE WAS REALLY GOING!

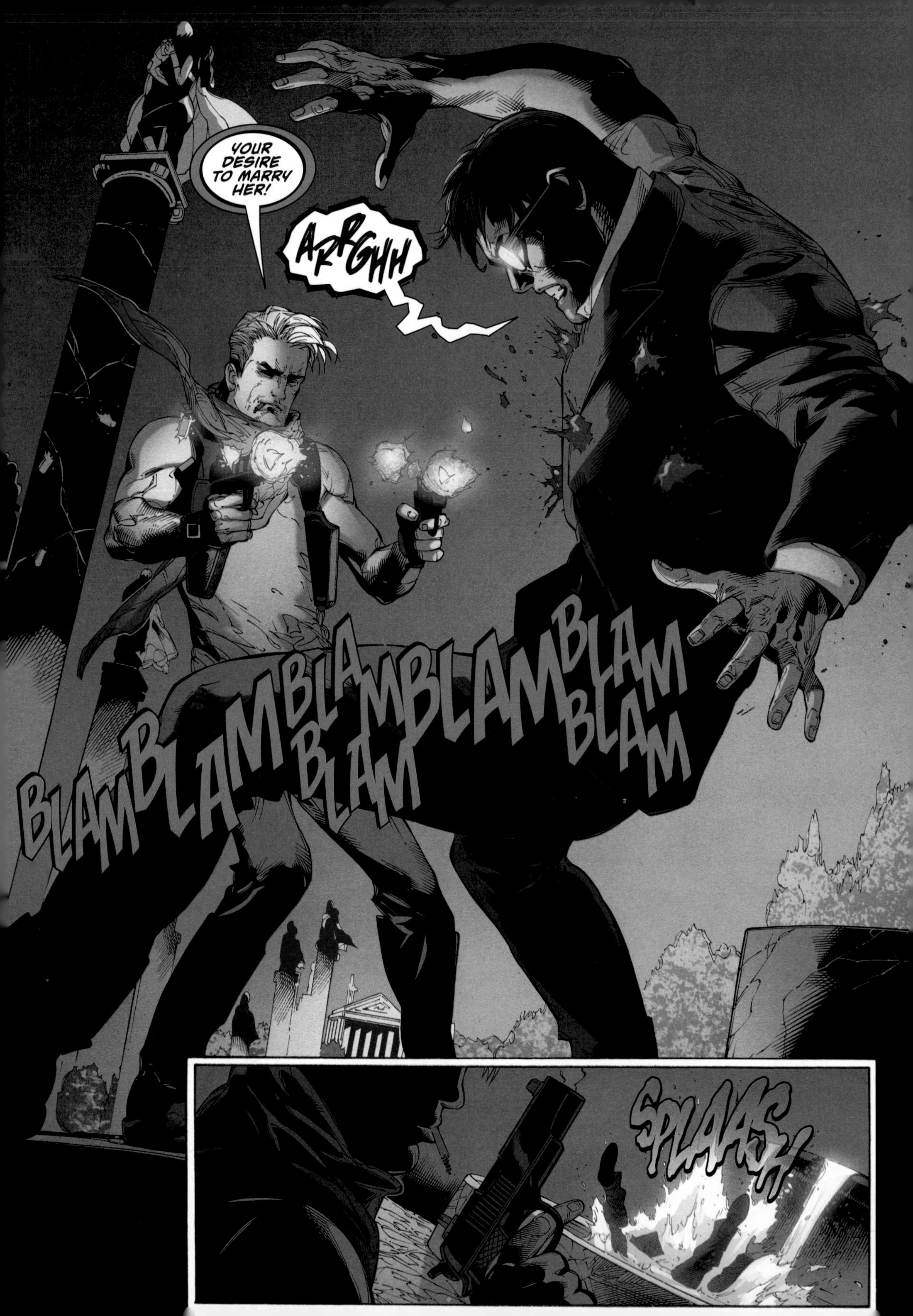
YOUR DESIRE TO MARRY HER!
ARRGHH
BLAM BLAM BLAM BLAM BLAM BLAM BLAM
SPLAASH

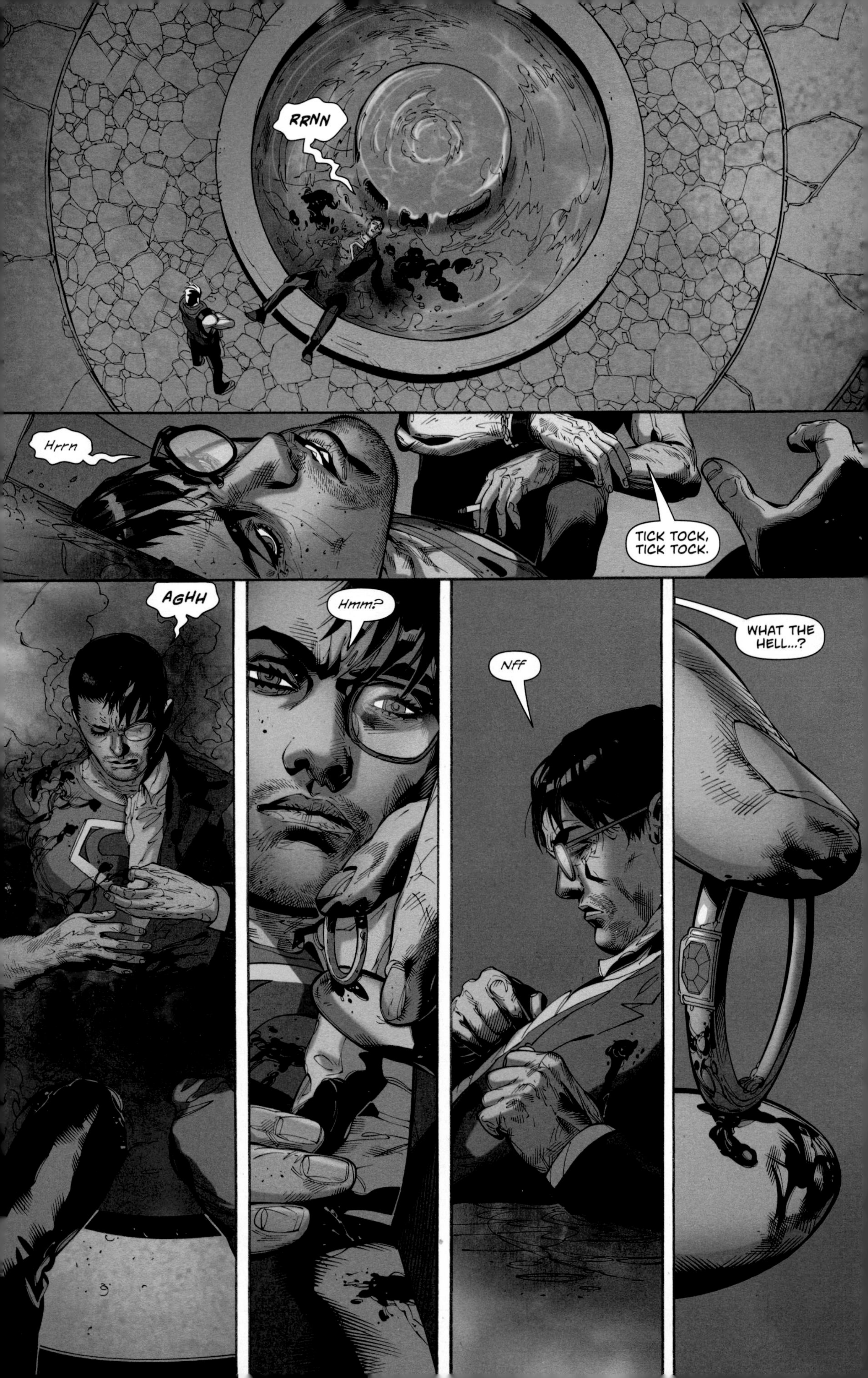
RRNN
Hrrn
TICK TOCK, TICK TOCK.
AGHH
Hmm?
Nff
WHAT THE HELL...?

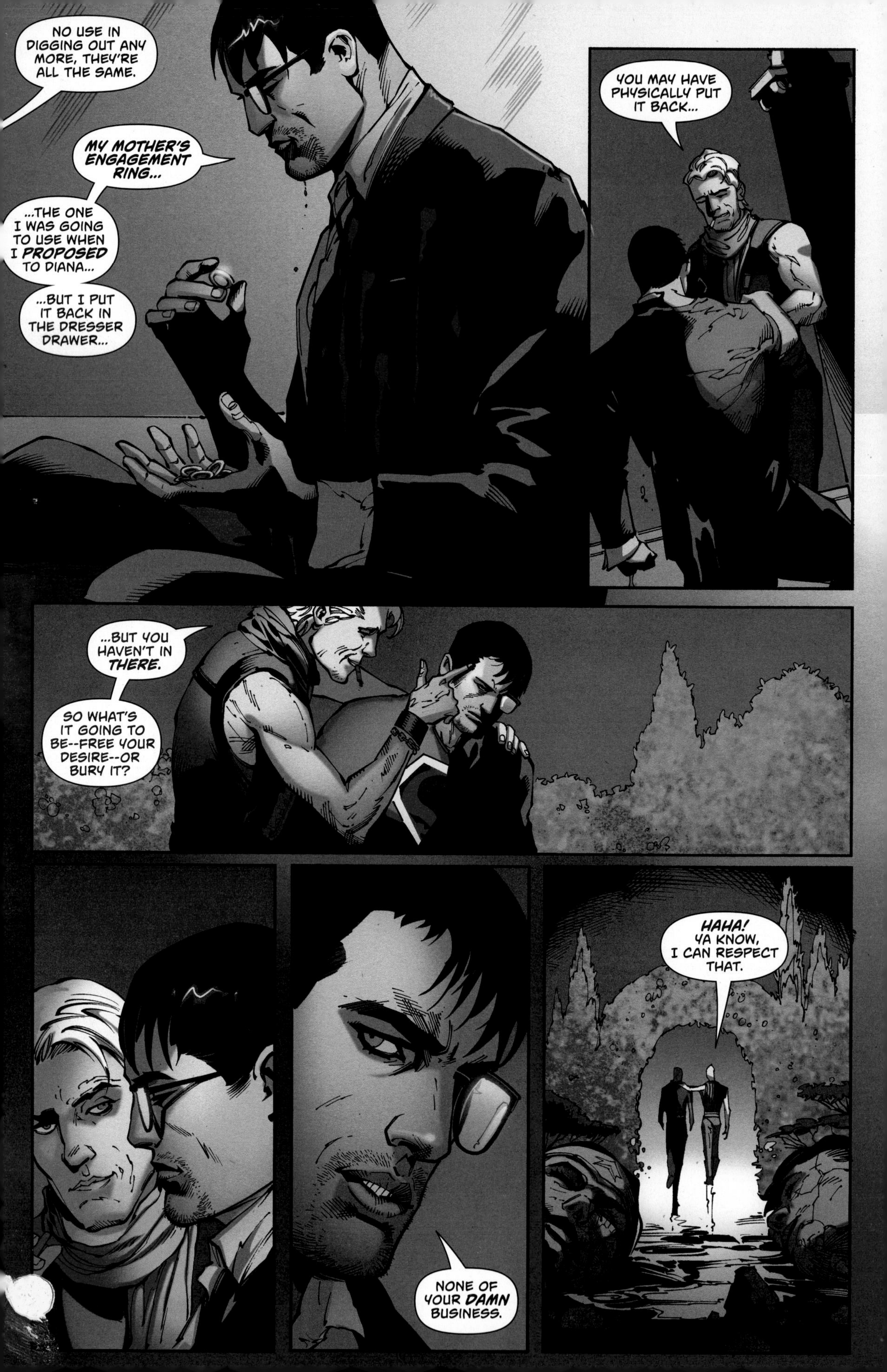
NO USE IN DIGGING OUT ANY MORE, THEY'RE ALL THE SAME.
MY MOTHER'S ENGAGEMENT RING...
...THE ONE I WAS GOING TO USE WHEN I PROPOSED TO DIANA...
...BUT I PUT IT BACK IN THE DRESSER DRAWER...
YOU MAY HAVE PHYSICALLY PUT IT BACK...
...BUT YOU HAVEN'T IN THERE.
SO WHAT'S IT GOING TO BE--FREE YOUR DESIRE--OR BURY IT?
NONE OF YOUR DAMN BUSINESS.
HAHA! YA KNOW, I CAN RESPECT THAT.

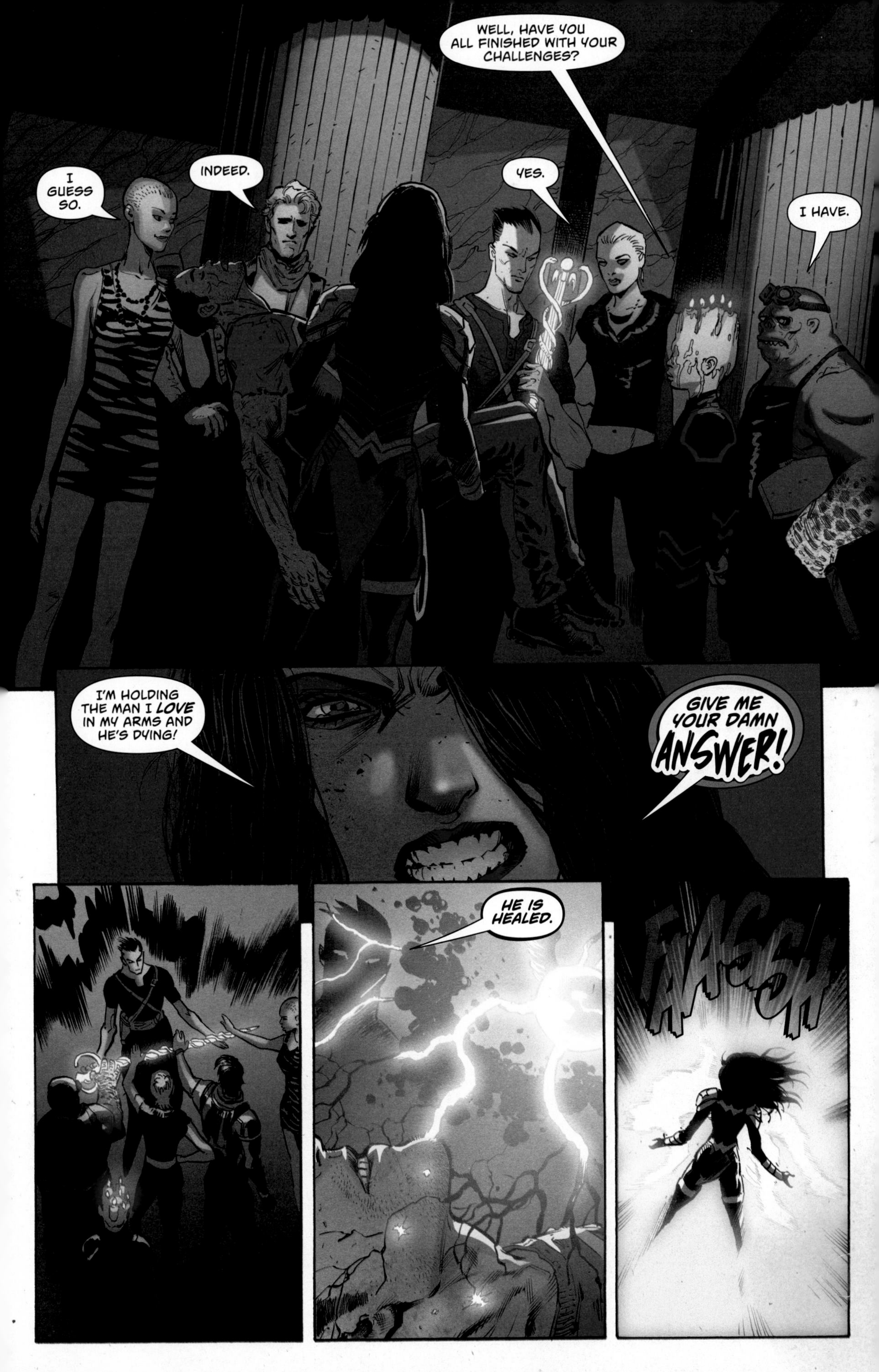
WELL, HAVE YOU ALL FINISHED WITH YOUR CHALLENGES?
I GUESS SO.
INDEED.
YES.
I HAVE.
I'M HOLDING THE MAN I LOVE IN MY ARMS AND HE'S DYING!
GIVE ME YOUR DAMN ANSWER!
HE IS HEALED.
FLASSH

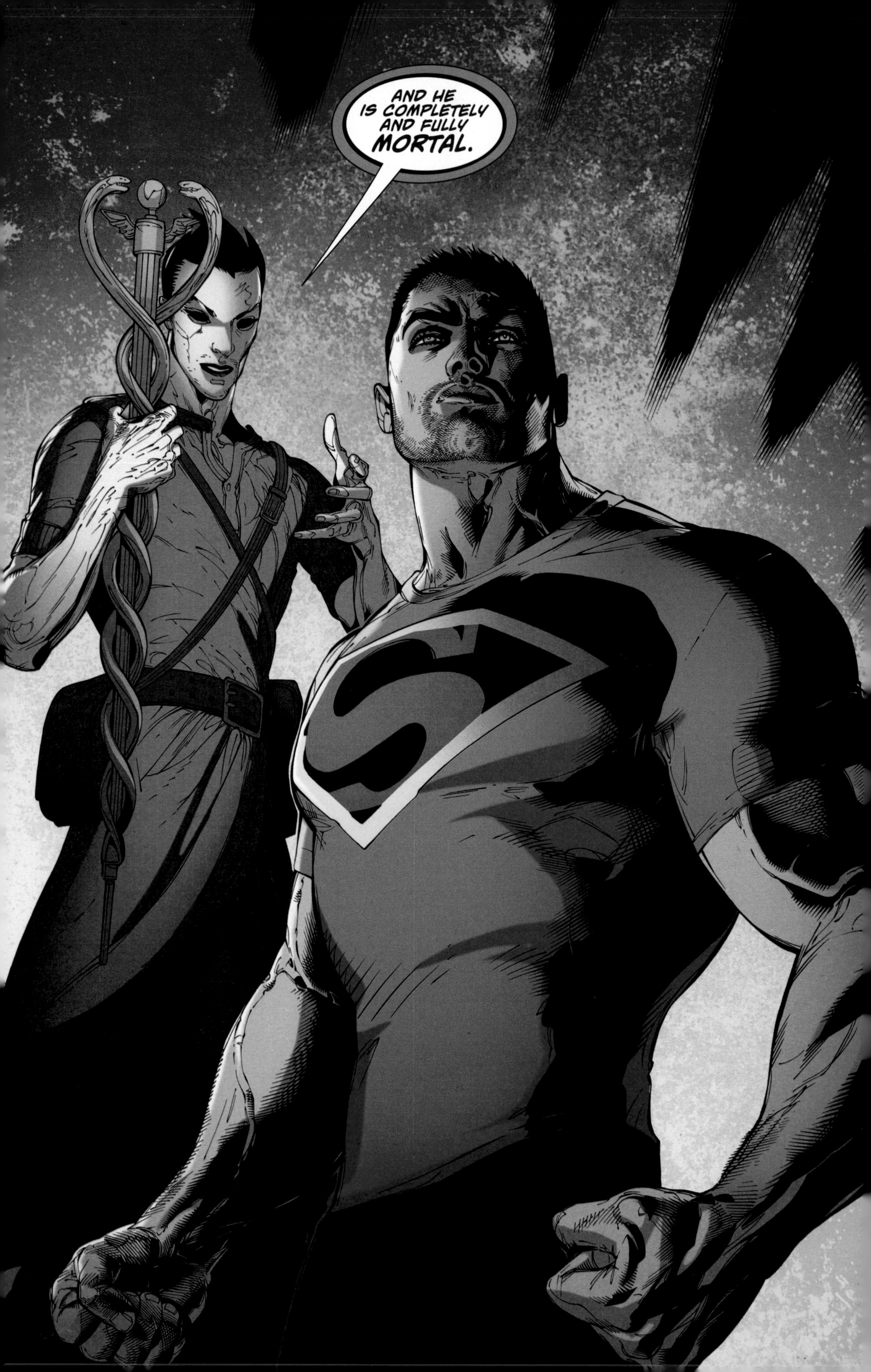
AND HE IS COMPLETELY AND FULLY MORTAL.

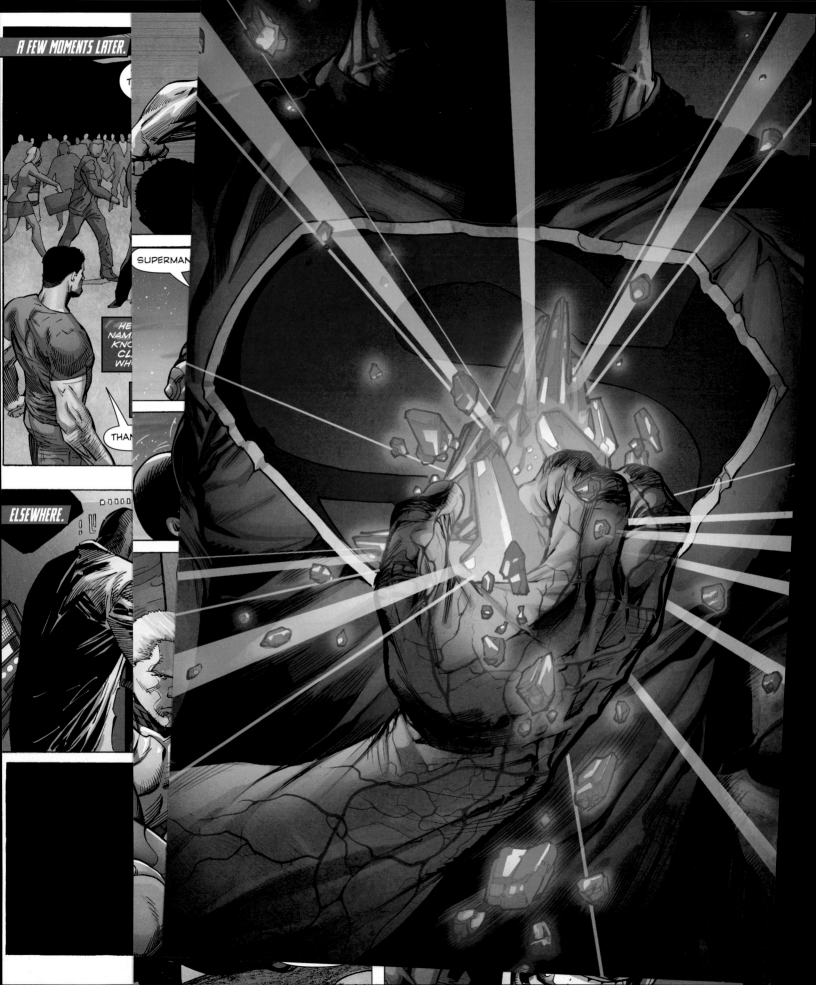

A FEW MOMENTS LATER.

SUPERMAN...

HE
NAM
KNO
CL
WH

THAN

ELSEWHERE.

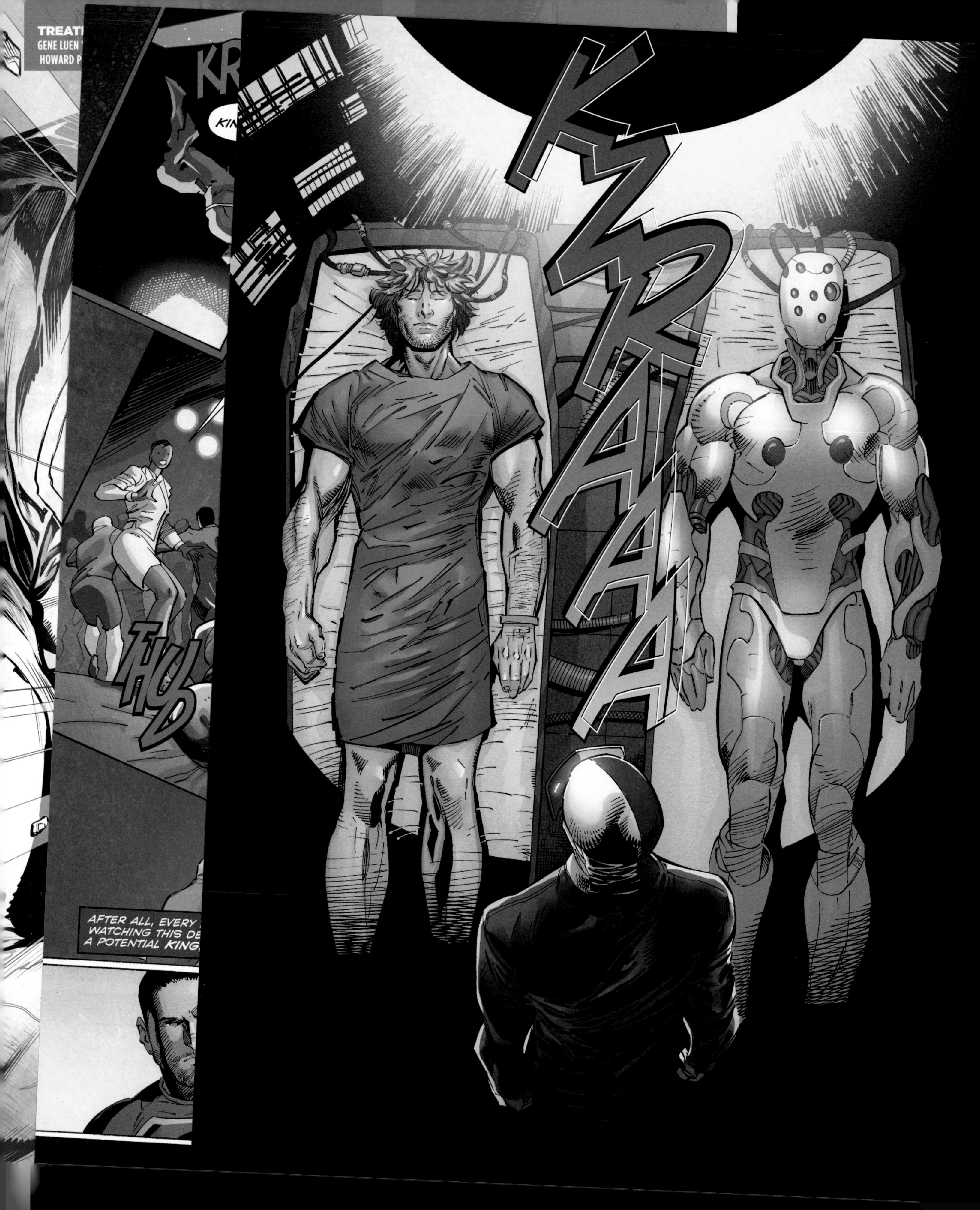
TREATI
GENE LUEN Y
HOWARD P
KR
KIN
THUD
AFTER ALL, EVERY
WATCHING THIS DE
A POTENTIAL KING
KZRAAAAA

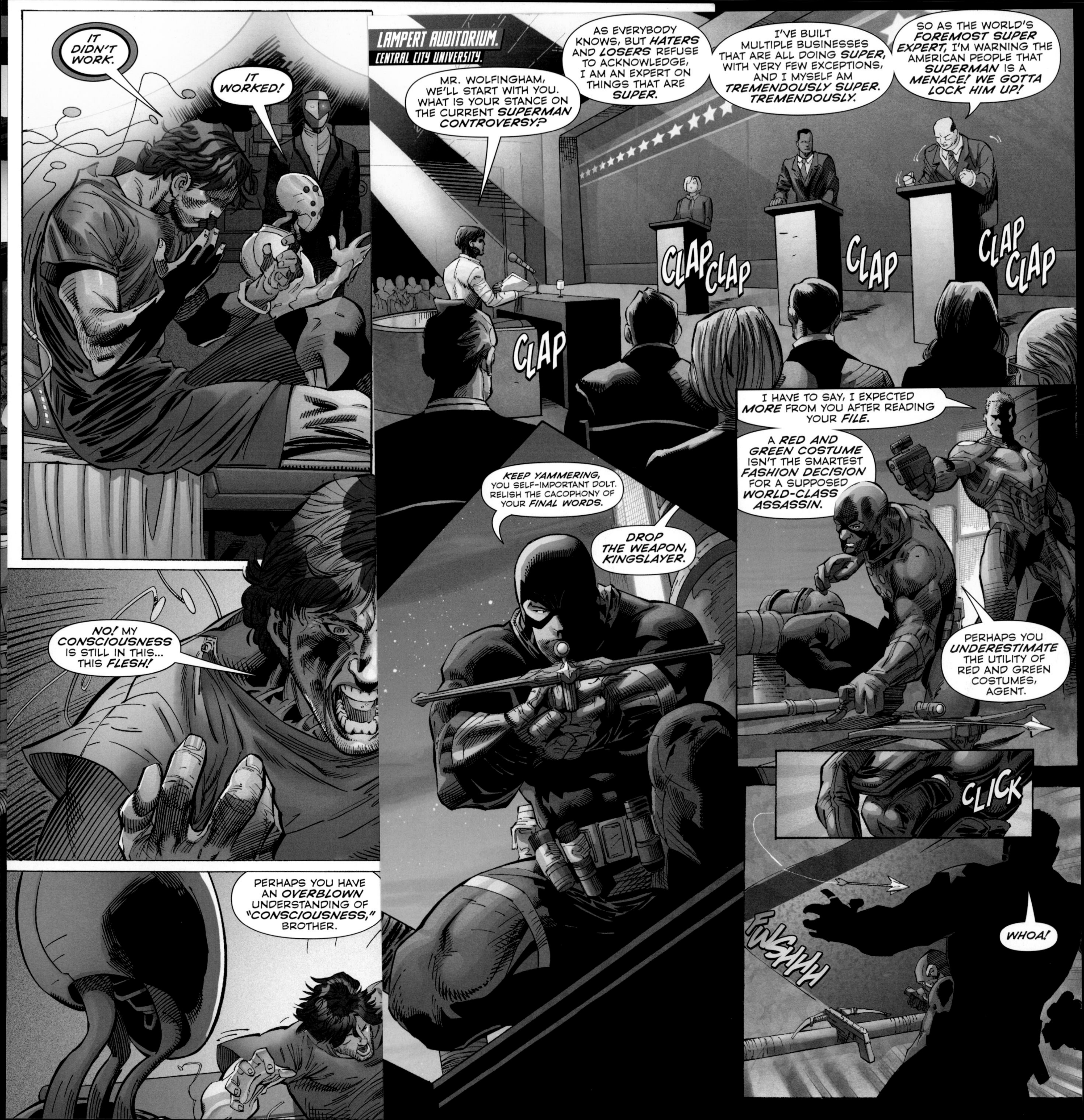
IT DIDN'T WORK.
IT WORKED!
NO! MY CONSCIOUSNESS IS STILL IN THIS... THIS FLESH!
PERHAPS YOU HAVE AN OVERBLOWN UNDERSTANDING OF "CONSCIOUSNESS," BROTHER.
LAMPERT AUDITORIUM.
CENTRAL CITY UNIVERSITY.
MR. WOLFINGHAM, WE'LL START WITH YOU. WHAT IS YOUR STANCE ON THE CURRENT SUPERMAN CONTROVERSY?
AS EVERYBODY KNOWS, BUT HATERS AND LOSERS REFUSE TO ACKNOWLEDGE, I AM AN EXPERT ON THINGS THAT ARE SUPER.
I'VE BUILT MULTIPLE BUSINESSES THAT ARE ALL DOING SUPER, WITH VERY FEW EXCEPTIONS, AND I MYSELF AM TREMENDOUSLY SUPER. TREMENDOUSLY.
SO AS THE WORLD'S FOREMOST SUPER EXPERT, I'M WARNING THE AMERICAN PEOPLE THAT SUPERMAN IS A MENACE! WE GOTTA LOCK HIM UP!
CLAP
CLAP CLAP
CLAP
CLAP CLAP
KEEP YAMMERING, YOU SELF-IMPORTANT DOLT. RELISH THE CACOPHONY OF YOUR FINAL WORDS.
DROP THE WEAPON, KINGSLAYER.
I HAVE TO SAY, I EXPECTED MORE FROM YOU AFTER READING YOUR FILE.
A RED AND GREEN COSTUME ISN'T THE SMARTEST FASHION DECISION FOR A SUPPOSED WORLD-CLASS ASSASSIN.
PERHAPS YOU UNDERESTIMATE THE UTILITY OF RED AND GREEN COSTUMES, AGENT.
CLICK
FWSHHH
WHOA!

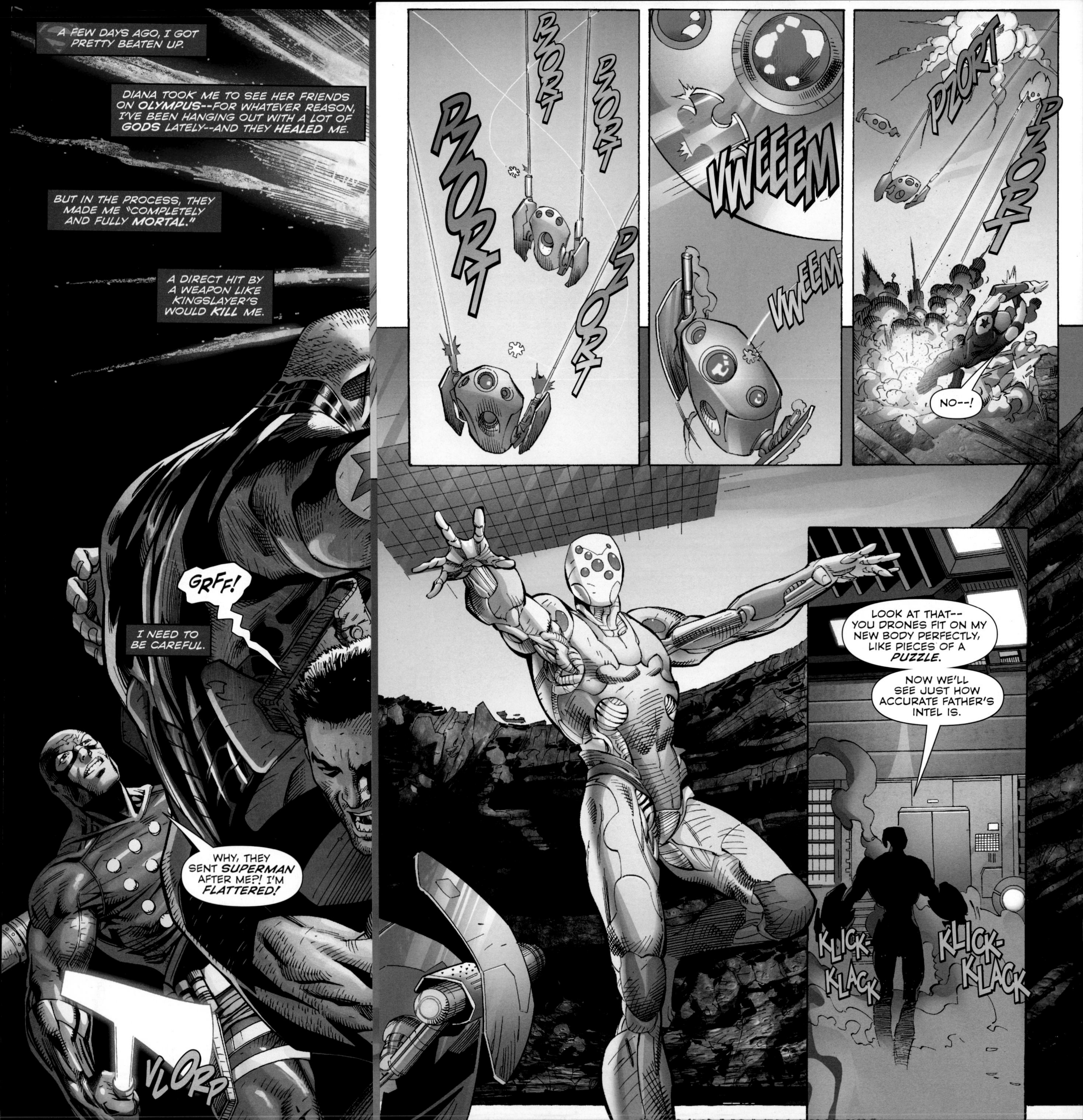
A FEW DAYS AGO, I GOT PRETTY BEATEN UP.
DIANA TOOK ME TO SEE HER FRIENDS ON OLYMPUS--FOR WHATEVER REASON, I'VE BEEN HANGING OUT WITH A LOT OF GODS LATELY--AND THEY HEALED ME.
BUT IN THE PROCESS, THEY MADE ME "COMPLETELY AND FULLY MORTAL."
A DIRECT HIT BY A WEAPON LIKE KINGSLAYER'S WOULD KILL ME.
GRFF!
I NEED TO BE CAREFUL.
WHY, THEY SENT SUPERMAN AFTER ME?! I'M FLATTERED!
VLORP
PZORT
PZORT
PZORT
PZORT
VWEEEM
VWEEM
PZORT
PZORT
NO--!
LOOK AT THAT-- YOU DRONES FIT ON MY NEW BODY PERFECTLY, LIKE PIECES OF A PUZZLE.
NOW WE'LL SEE JUST HOW ACCURATE FATHER'S INTEL IS.
KLICK-KLACK
KLICK-KLACK

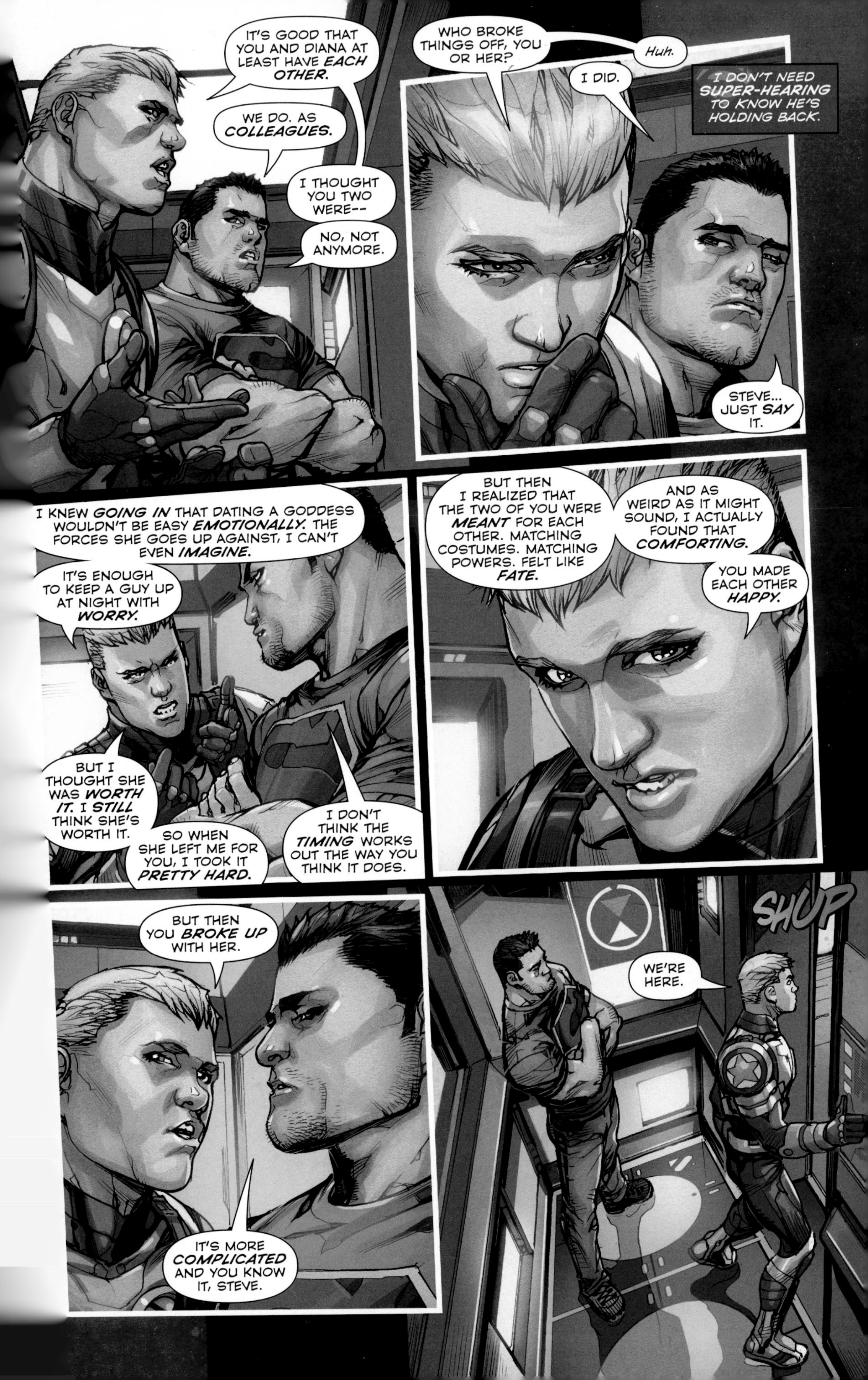
IT'S GOOD THAT YOU AND DIANA AT LEAST HAVE EACH OTHER.
WE DO. AS COLLEAGUES.
I THOUGHT YOU TWO WERE--
NO, NOT ANYMORE.
WHO BROKE THINGS OFF, YOU OR HER?
Huh.
I DID.
I DON'T NEED SUPER-HEARING TO KNOW HE'S HOLDING BACK.
STEVE... JUST SAY IT.
I KNEW GOING IN THAT DATING A GODDESS WOULDN'T BE EASY EMOTIONALLY. THE FORCES SHE GOES UP AGAINST, I CAN'T EVEN IMAGINE.
IT'S ENOUGH TO KEEP A GUY UP AT NIGHT WITH WORRY.
BUT I THOUGHT SHE WAS WORTH IT. I STILL THINK SHE'S WORTH IT.
SO WHEN SHE LEFT ME FOR YOU, I TOOK IT PRETTY HARD.
I DON'T THINK THE TIMING WORKS OUT THE WAY YOU THINK IT DOES.
BUT THEN I REALIZED THAT THE TWO OF YOU WERE MEANT FOR EACH OTHER. MATCHING COSTUMES. MATCHING POWERS. FELT LIKE FATE.
AND AS WEIRD AS IT MIGHT SOUND, I ACTUALLY FOUND THAT COMFORTING.
YOU MADE EACH OTHER HAPPY.
BUT THEN YOU BROKE UP WITH HER.
IT'S MORE COMPLICATED AND YOU KNOW IT, STEVE.
SHUP
WE'RE HERE.

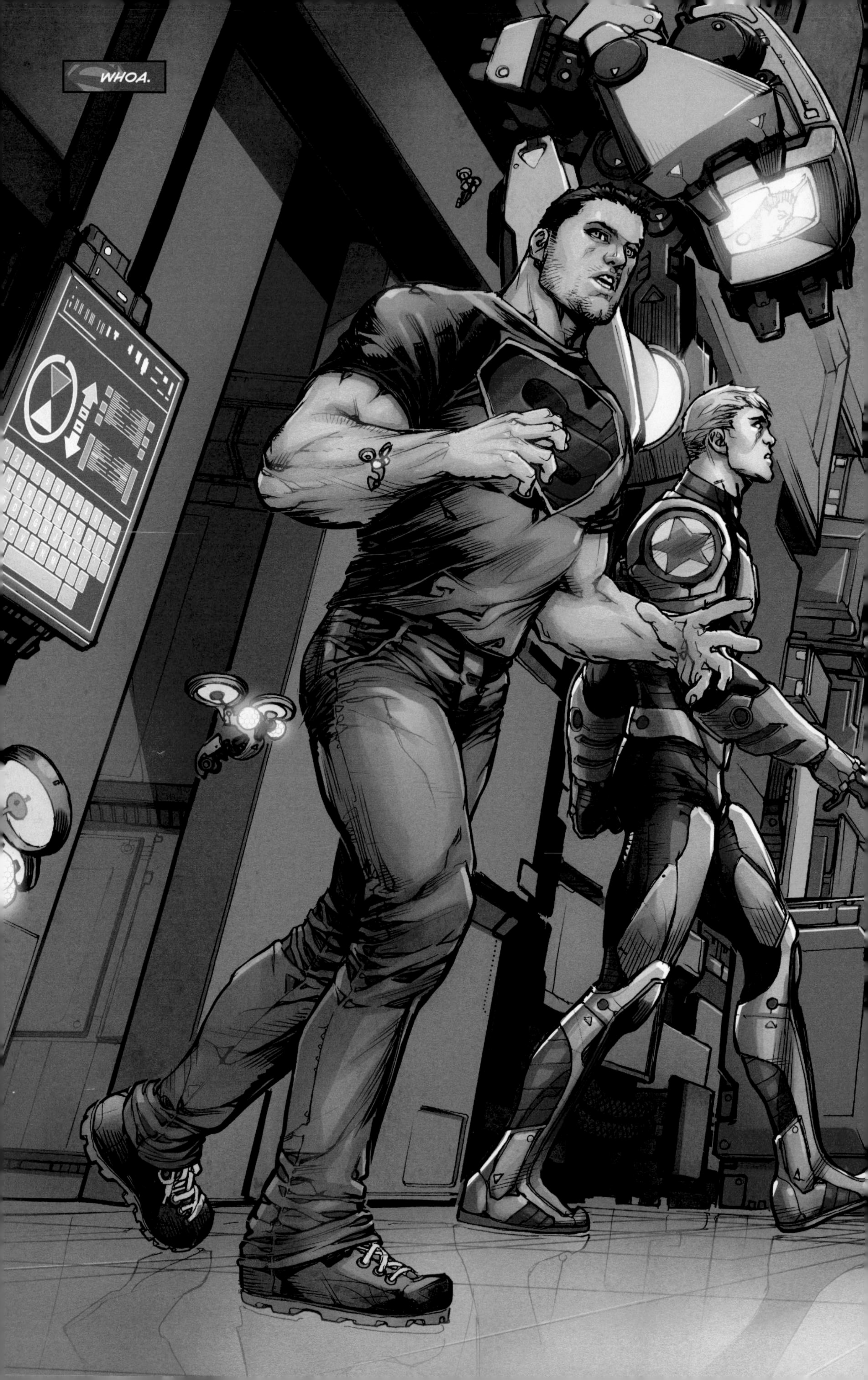
WHOA.

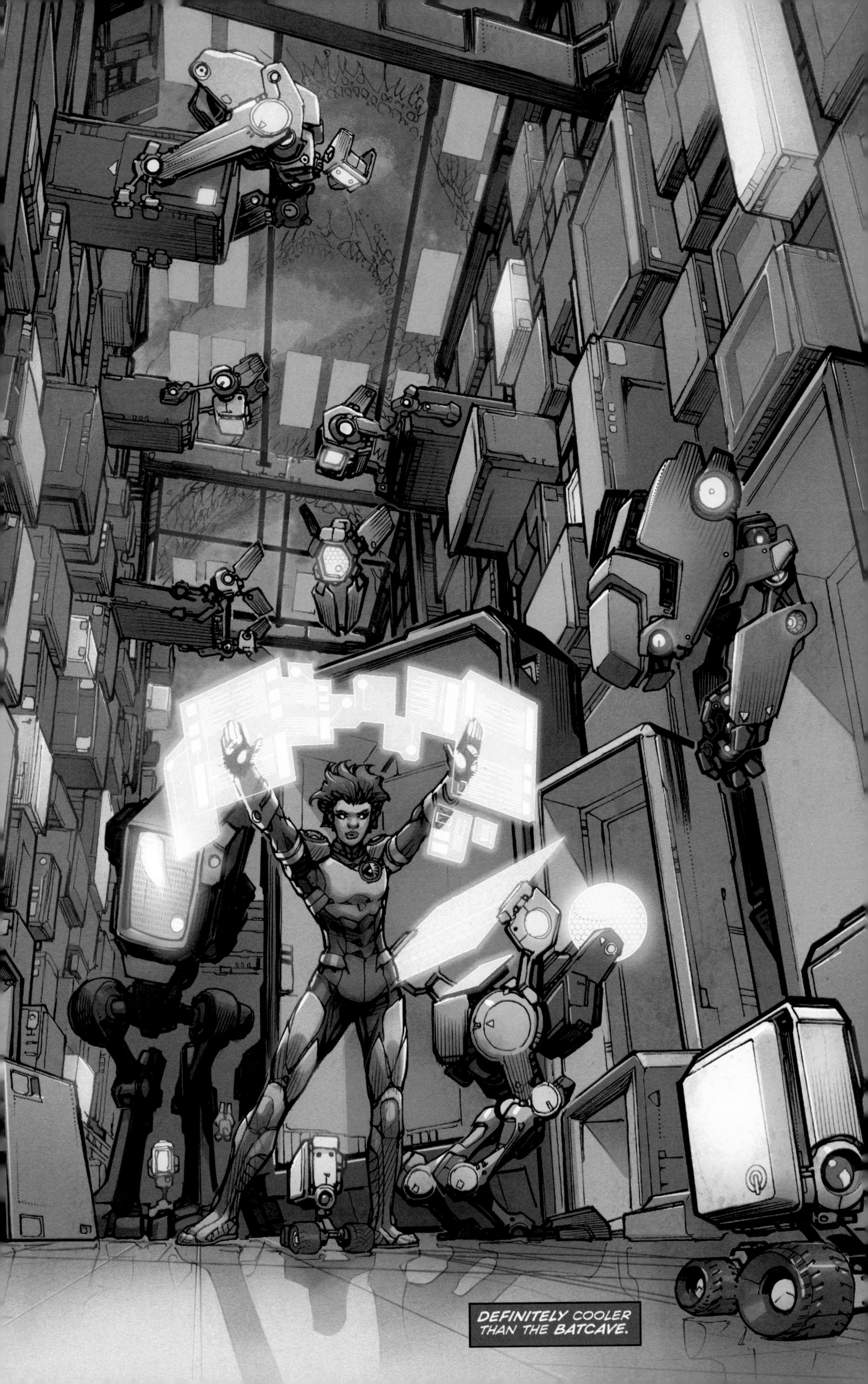
DEFINITELY COOLER THAN THE BATCAVE.

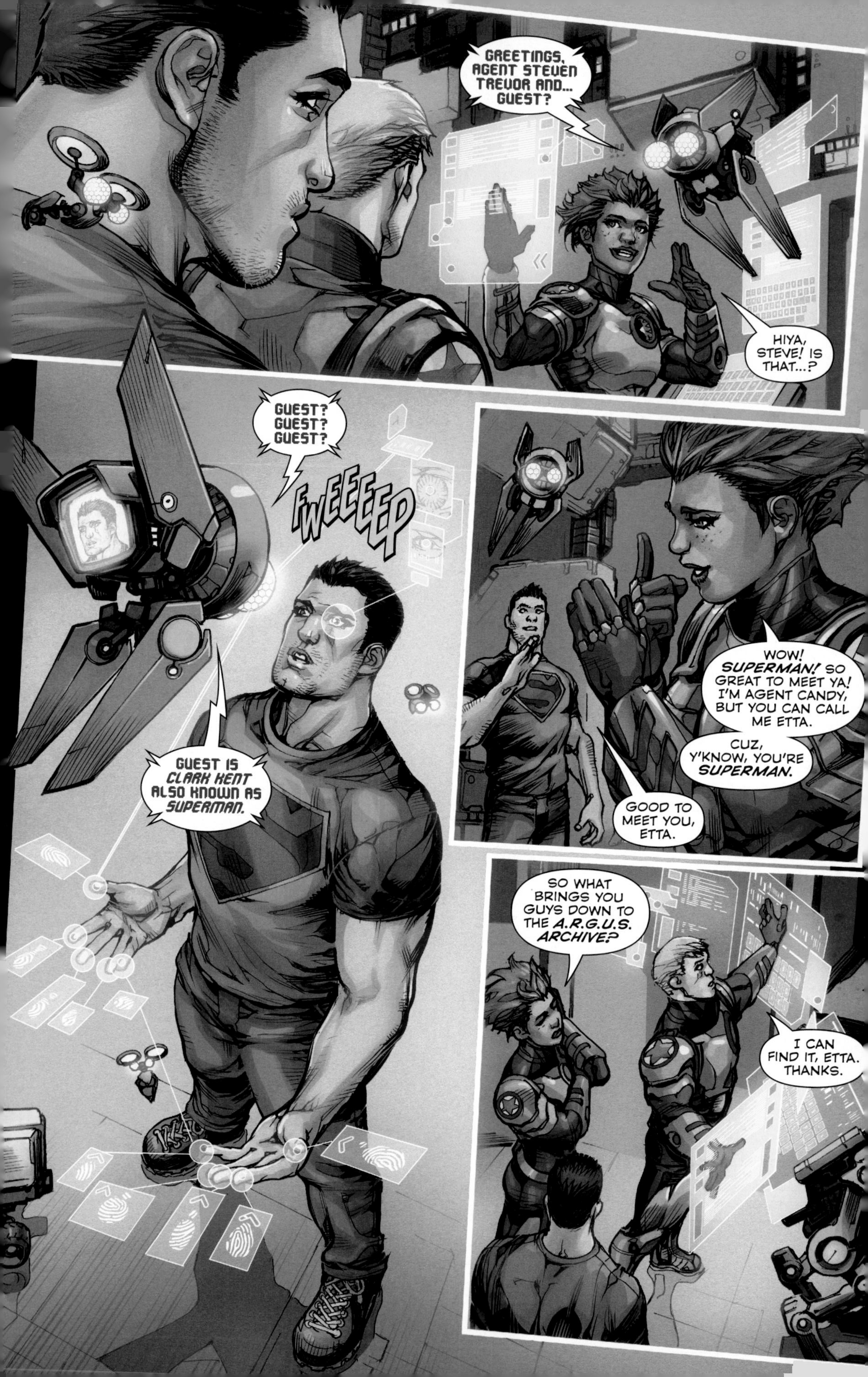
GREETINGS, AGENT STEVEN TREVOR AND... GUEST?
HIYA, STEVE! IS THAT...?
GUEST? GUEST? GUEST?
FWEEEEEP
GUEST IS CLARK KENT ALSO KNOWN AS SUPERMAN.
WOW! SUPERMAN! SO GREAT TO MEET YA! I'M AGENT CANDY, BUT YOU CAN CALL ME ETTA.
CUZ, Y'KNOW, YOU'RE SUPERMAN.
GOOD TO MEET YOU, ETTA.
SO WHAT BRINGS YOU GUYS DOWN TO THE A.R.G.U.S. ARCHIVE?
I CAN FIND IT, ETTA. THANKS.

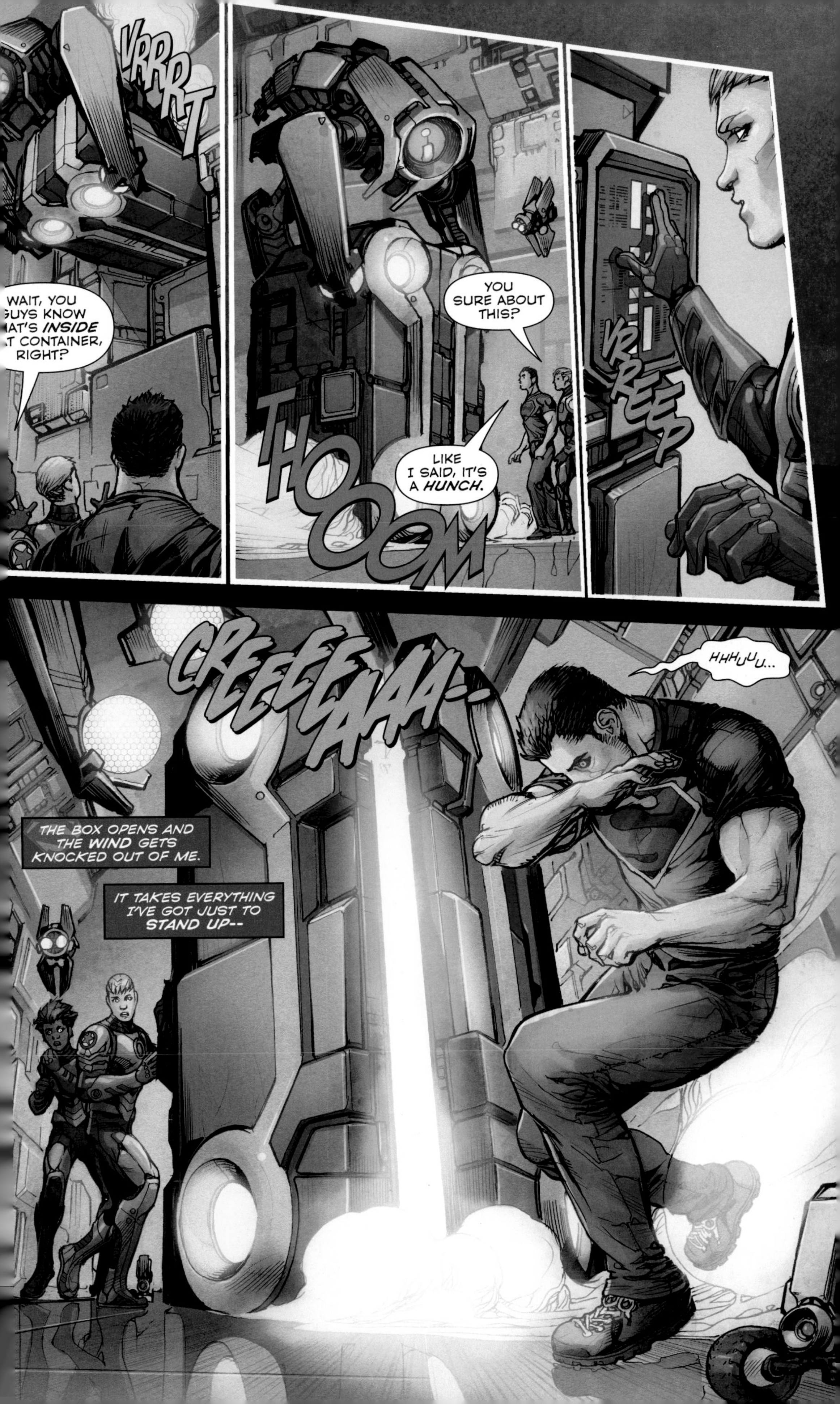
VRRRT
WAIT, YOU GUYS KNOW AT'S INSIDE T CONTAINER, RIGHT?
YOU SURE ABOUT THIS?
LIKE I SAID, IT'S A HUNCH.
THOOOOM
VRREEP
CREEEEAAAA--
HHHUUU...
THE BOX OPENS AND THE WIND GETS KNOCKED OUT OF ME.
IT TAKES EVERYTHING I'VE GOT JUST TO STAND UP--

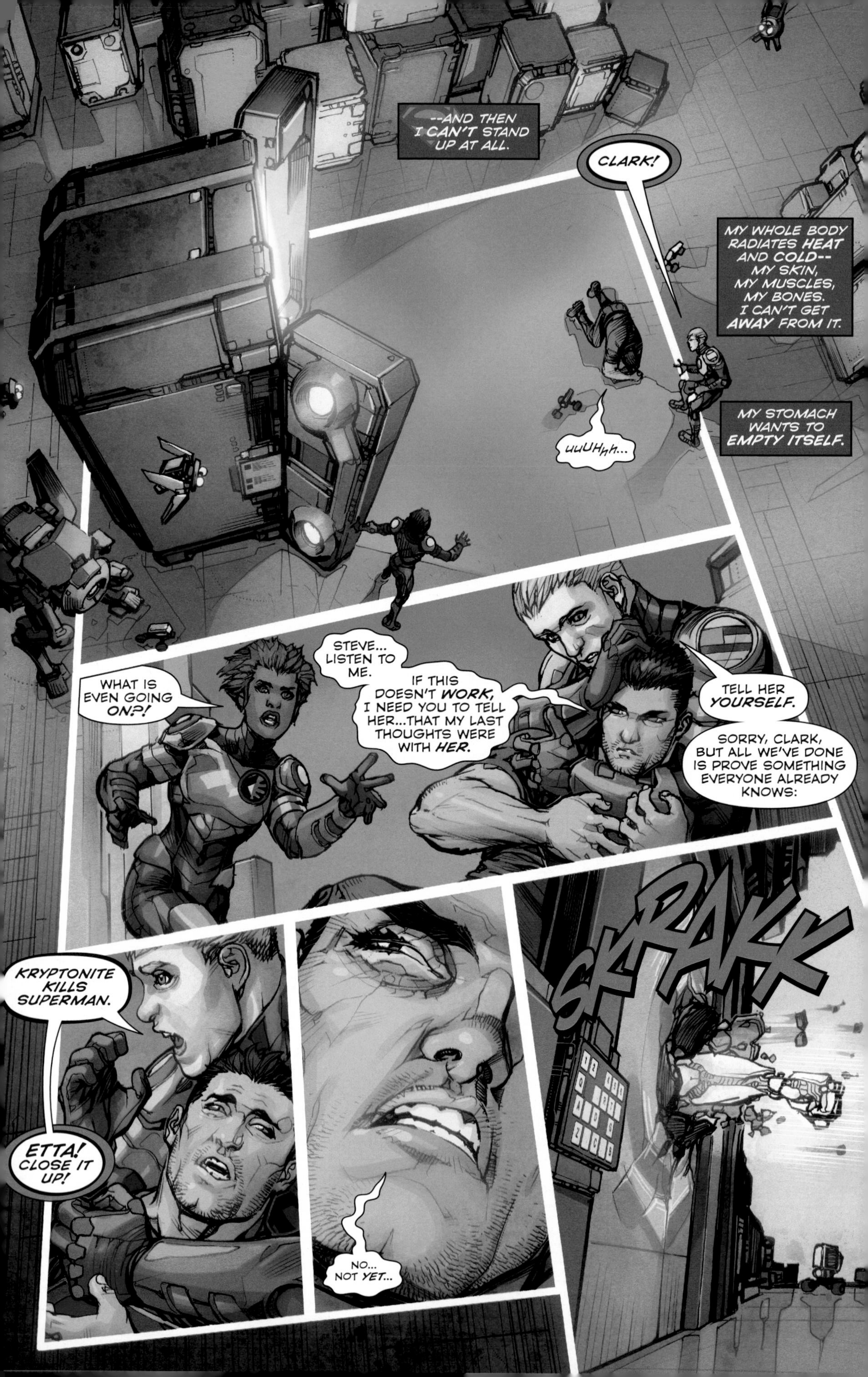
--AND THEN I CAN'T STAND UP AT ALL.
CLARK!
MY WHOLE BODY RADIATES HEAT AND COLD-- MY SKIN, MY MUSCLES, MY BONES. I CAN'T GET AWAY FROM IT.
MY STOMACH WANTS TO EMPTY ITSELF.
uuUHhh...
WHAT IS EVEN GOING ON?!
STEVE... LISTEN TO ME.
IF THIS DOESN'T WORK, I NEED YOU TO TELL HER...THAT MY LAST THOUGHTS WERE WITH HER.
TELL HER YOURSELF.
SORRY, CLARK, BUT ALL WE'VE DONE IS PROVE SOMETHING EVERYONE ALREADY KNOWS:
KRYPTONITE KILLS SUPERMAN.
ETTA! CLOSE IT UP!
NO... NOT YET...
SKRAKK

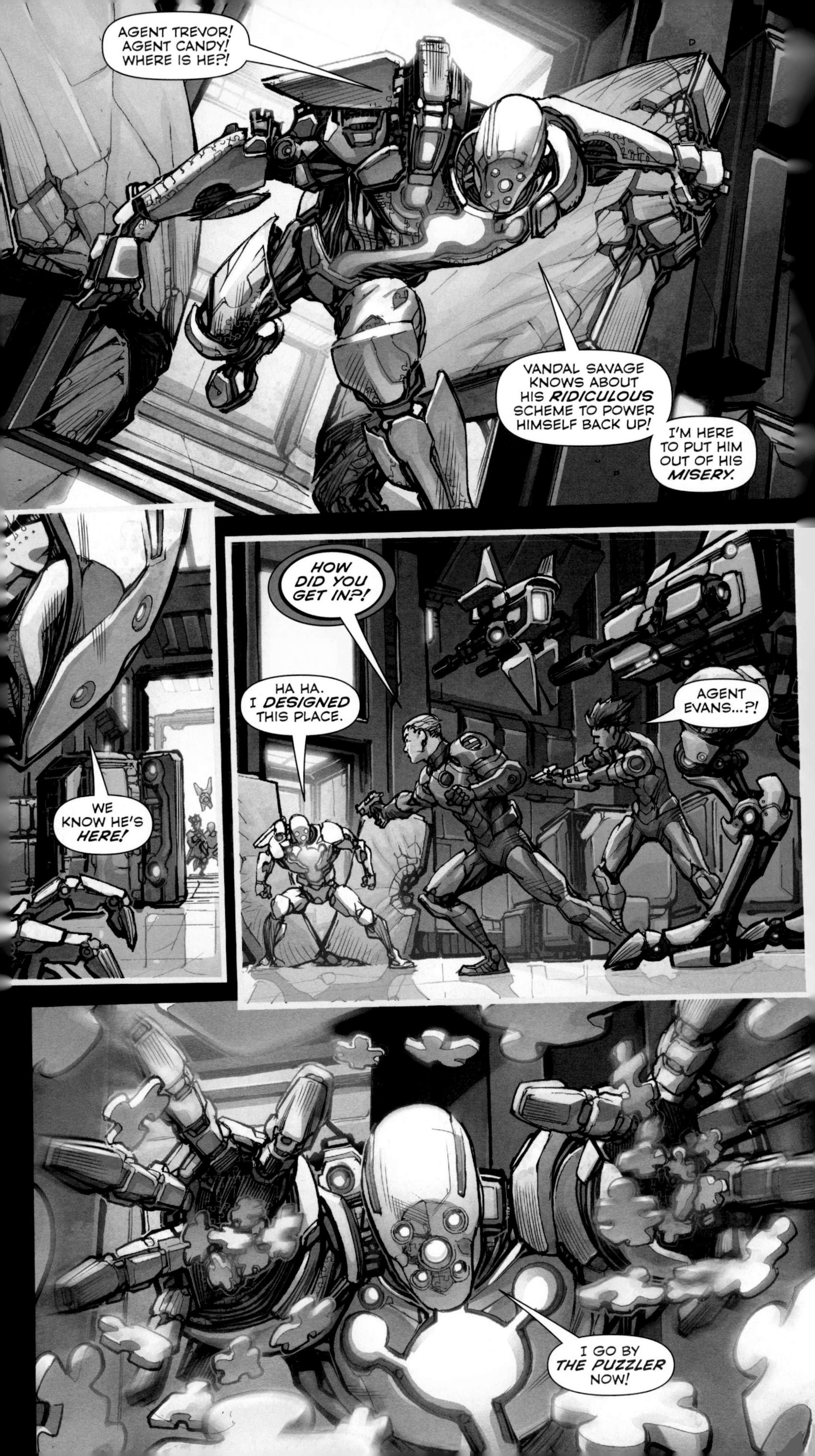
AGENT TREVOR! AGENT CANDY! WHERE IS HE?!
VANDAL SAVAGE KNOWS ABOUT HIS RIDICULOUS SCHEME TO POWER HIMSELF BACK UP!
I'M HERE TO PUT HIM OUT OF HIS MISERY.
WE KNOW HE'S HERE!
HOW DID YOU GET IN?!
HA HA. I DESIGNED THIS PLACE.
AGENT EVANS...?!
I GO BY THE PUZZLER NOW!

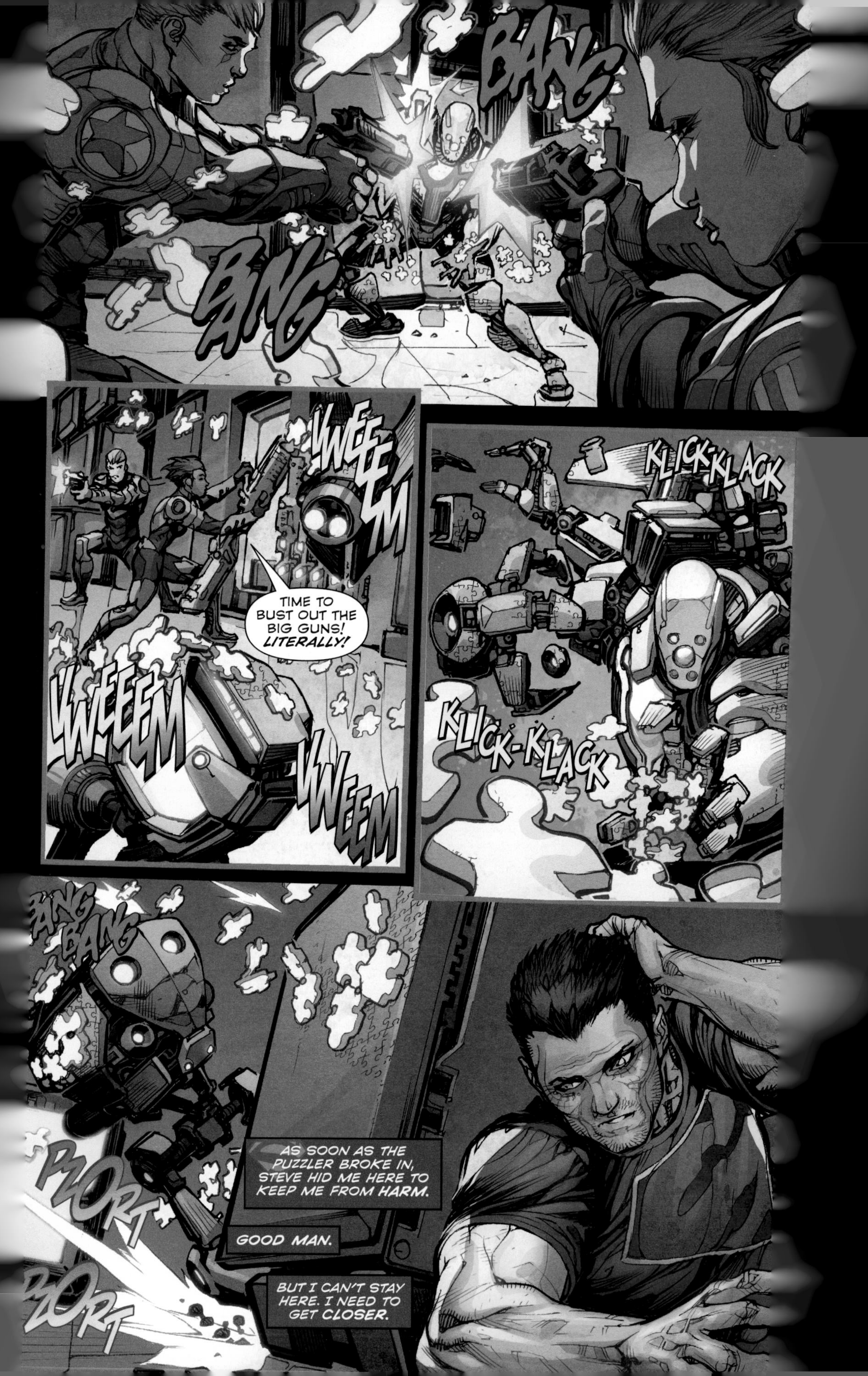
BANG
BANG
VWEEEM
TIME TO BUST OUT THE BIG GUNS! LITERALLY!
VWEEEM
VWEEM
KLICK-KLACK
KLICK-KLACK
BANG BANG
PLORT
AS SOON AS THE PUZZLER BROKE IN, STEVE HID ME HERE TO KEEP ME FROM HARM.
GOOD MAN.
BUT I CAN'T STAY HERE. I NEED TO GET CLOSER.
PLORT

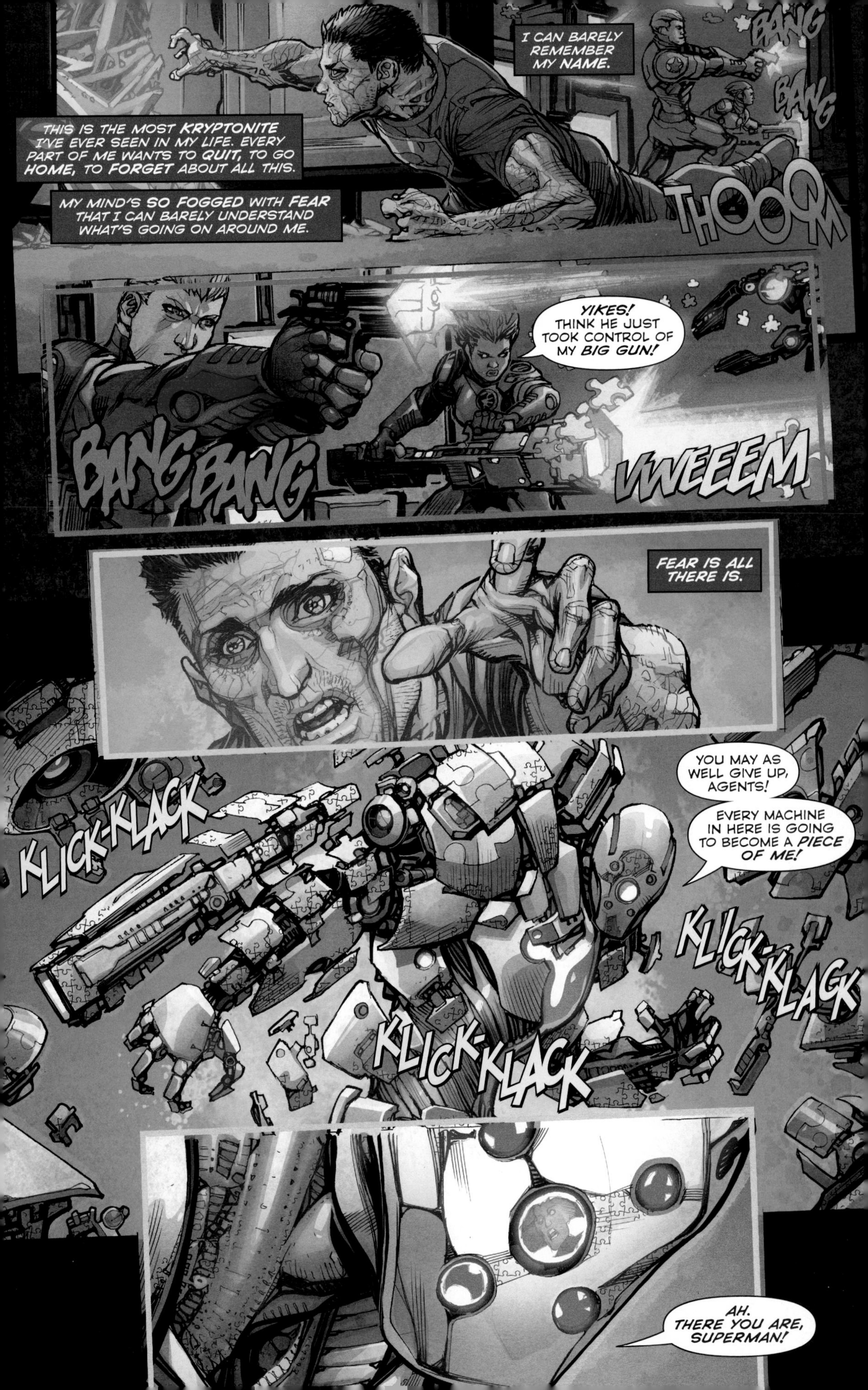
I CAN BARELY REMEMBER MY NAME.
BANG
BANG
THIS IS THE MOST KRYPTONITE I'VE EVER SEEN IN MY LIFE. EVERY PART OF ME WANTS TO QUIT, TO GO HOME, TO FORGET ABOUT ALL THIS.
MY MIND'S SO FOGGED WITH FEAR THAT I CAN BARELY UNDERSTAND WHAT'S GOING ON AROUND ME.
THOOOM
YIKES! THINK HE JUST TOOK CONTROL OF MY BIG GUN!
BANG BANG
VWEEEM
FEAR IS ALL THERE IS.
YOU MAY AS WELL GIVE UP, AGENTS!
EVERY MACHINE IN HERE IS GOING TO BECOME A PIECE OF ME!
KLICK-KLACK
KLICK-KLACK
KLICK-KLACK
AH. THERE YOU ARE, SUPERMAN!

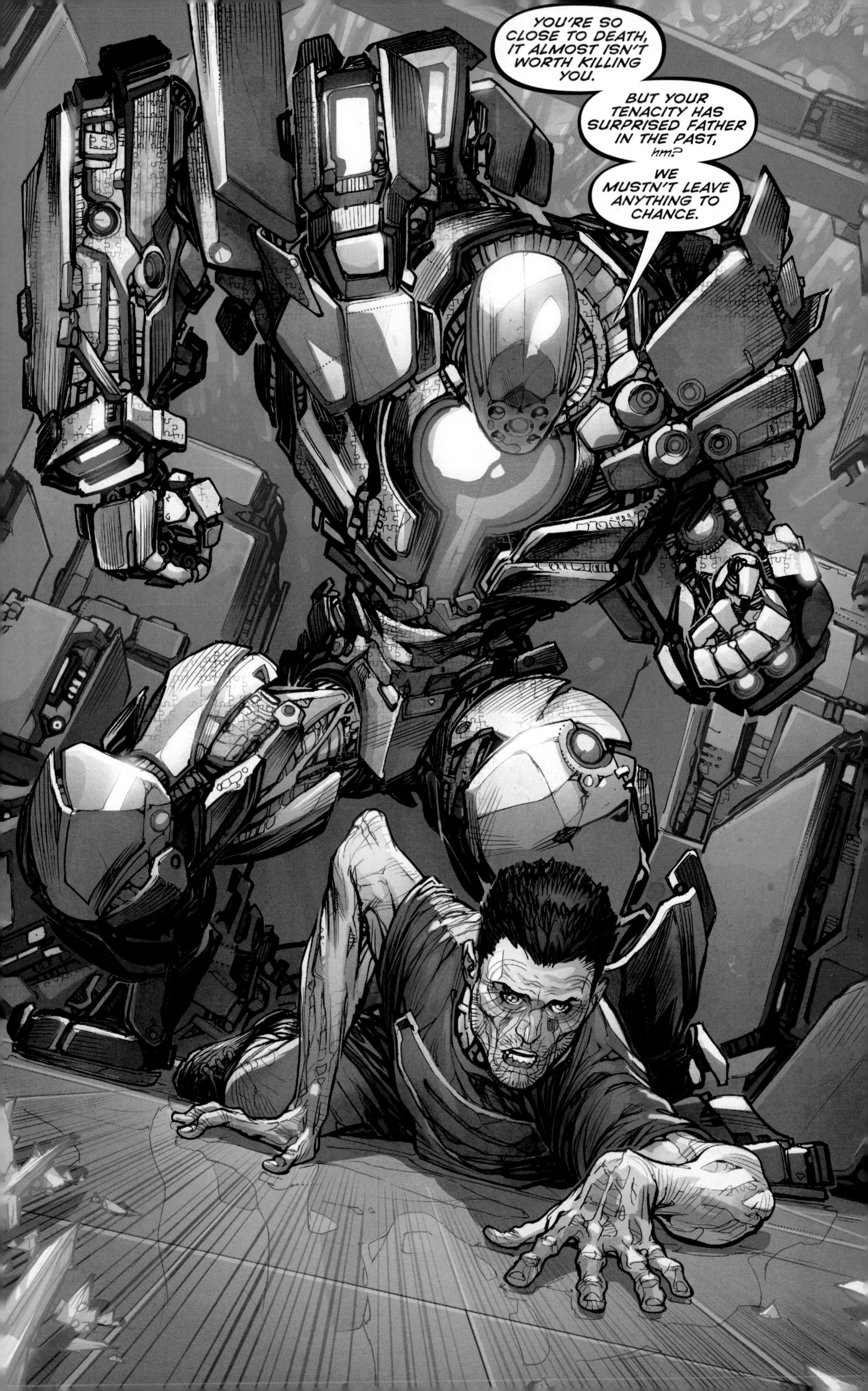
YOU'RE SO CLOSE TO DEATH, IT ALMOST ISN'T WORTH KILLING YOU.
BUT YOUR TENACITY HAS SURPRISED FATHER IN THE PAST, hm?
WE MUSTN'T LEAVE ANYTHING TO CHANCE.

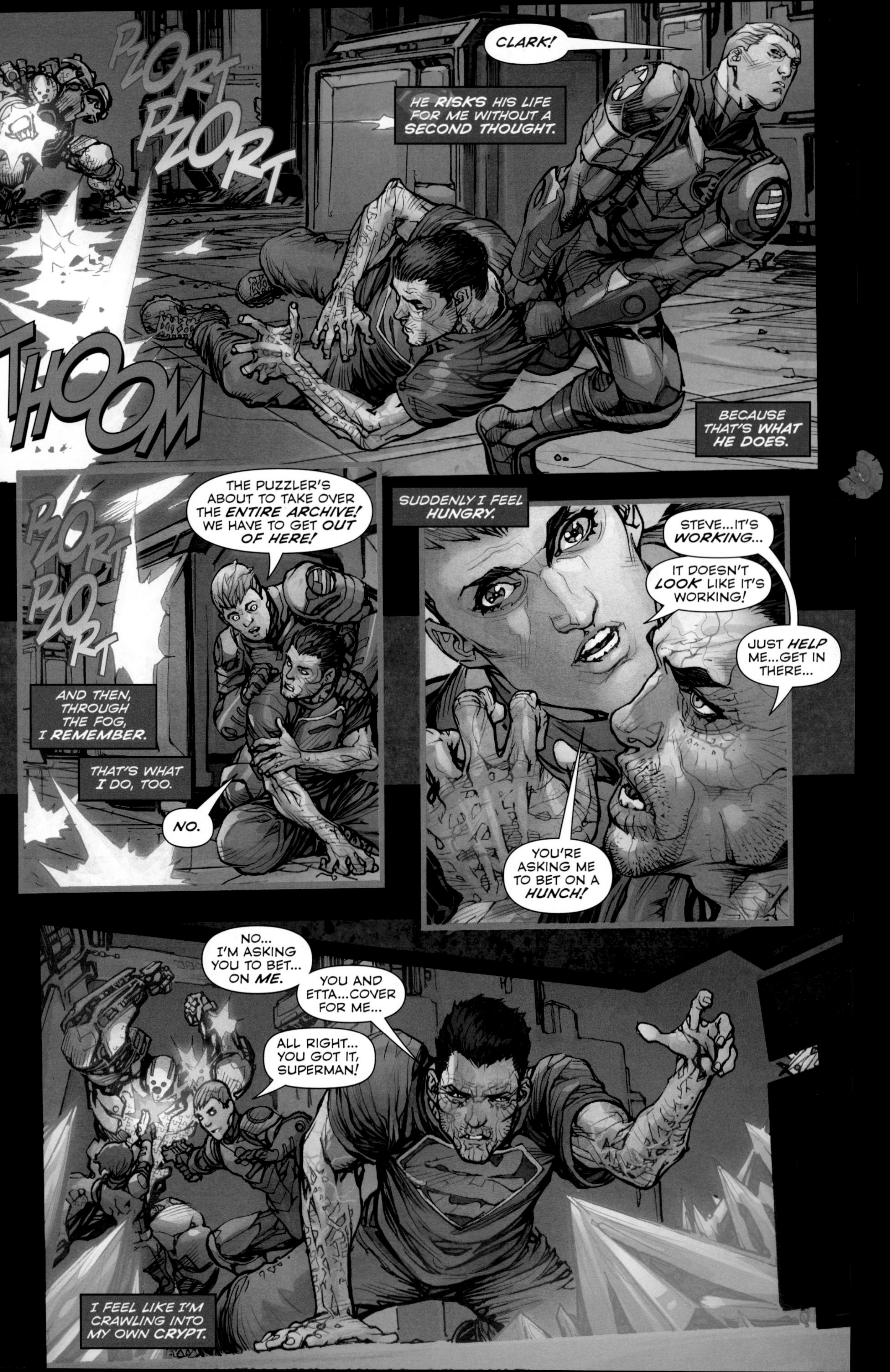
PZORT PZORT PZORT
CLARK!
HE RISKS HIS LIFE FOR ME WITHOUT A SECOND THOUGHT.
THOOM
BECAUSE THAT'S WHAT HE DOES.
PZORT PZORT
THE PUZZLER'S ABOUT TO TAKE OVER THE ENTIRE ARCHIVE! WE HAVE TO GET OUT OF HERE!
AND THEN, THROUGH THE FOG, I REMEMBER.
THAT'S WHAT I DO, TOO.
NO.
SUDDENLY I FEEL HUNGRY.
STEVE...IT'S WORKING...
IT DOESN'T LOOK LIKE IT'S WORKING!
JUST HELP ME...GET IN THERE...
YOU'RE ASKING ME TO BET ON A HUNCH!
NO... I'M ASKING YOU TO BET... ON ME.
YOU AND ETTA...COVER FOR ME...
ALL RIGHT... YOU GOT IT, SUPERMAN!
I FEEL LIKE I'M CRAWLING INTO MY OWN CRYPT.

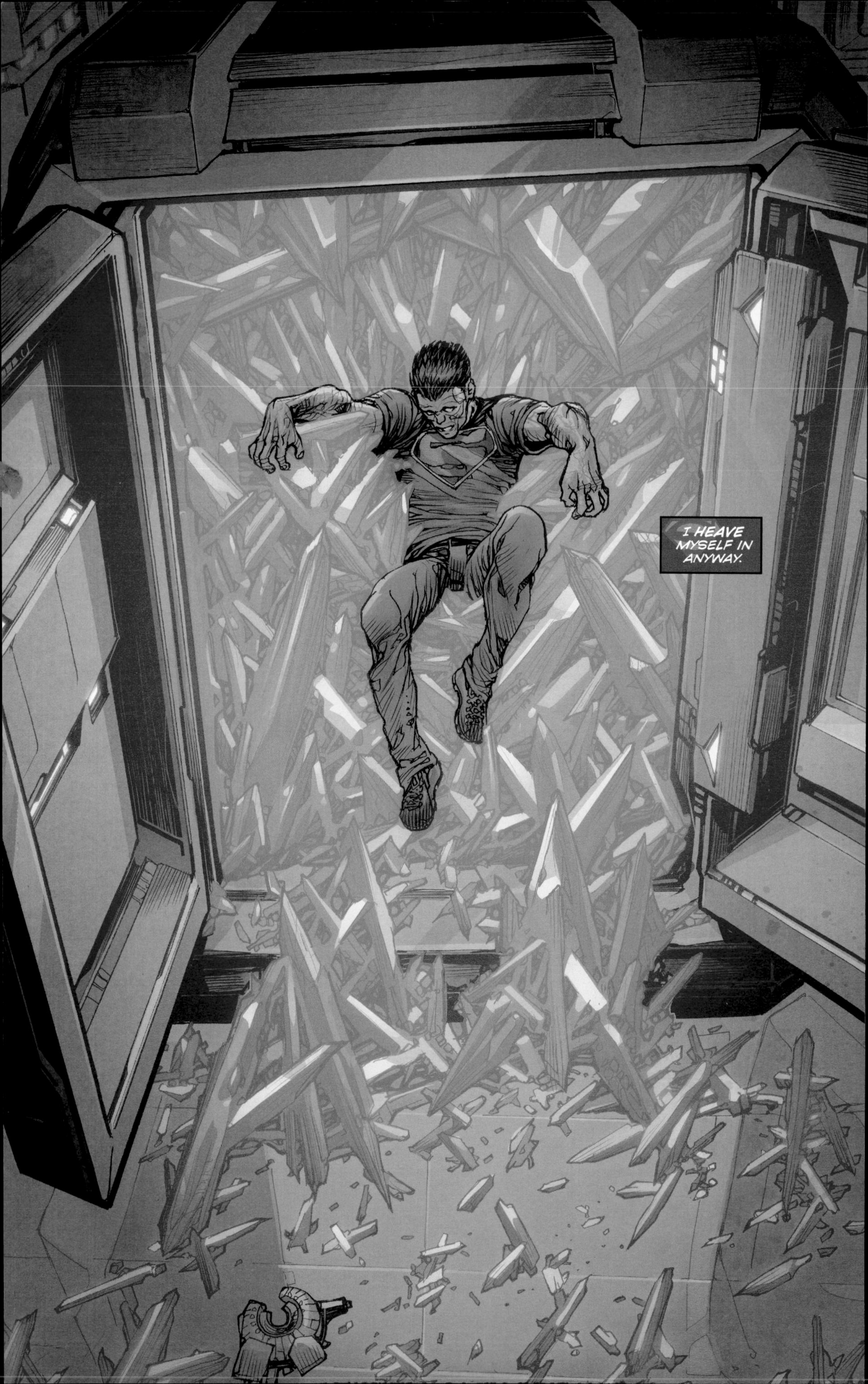
I HEAVE MYSELF IN ANYWAY.

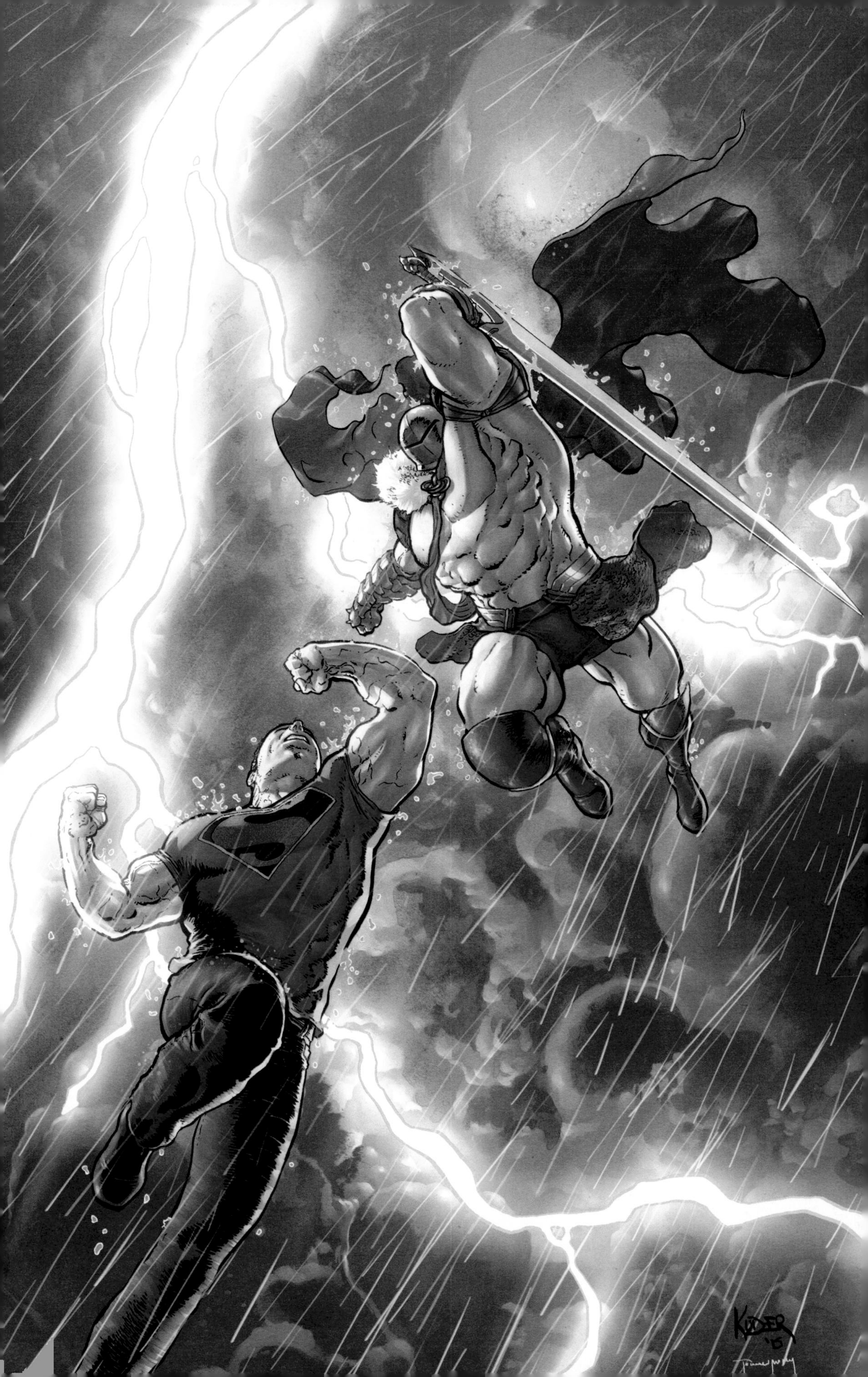

SAVAGE DAWN: IMMORTAL COMBAT

GREK PAK AARON KUDER writers **AARON KUDER** layouts **ARDIAN SYAF** penciller **JONATHAN GLAPION SCOTT HANNA SANDRA HOPE** inkers
TOMEU MOREY WIL QUINTANA colorists **STEVE WANDS** letterer **AARON KUDER TOMEU MOREY** cover

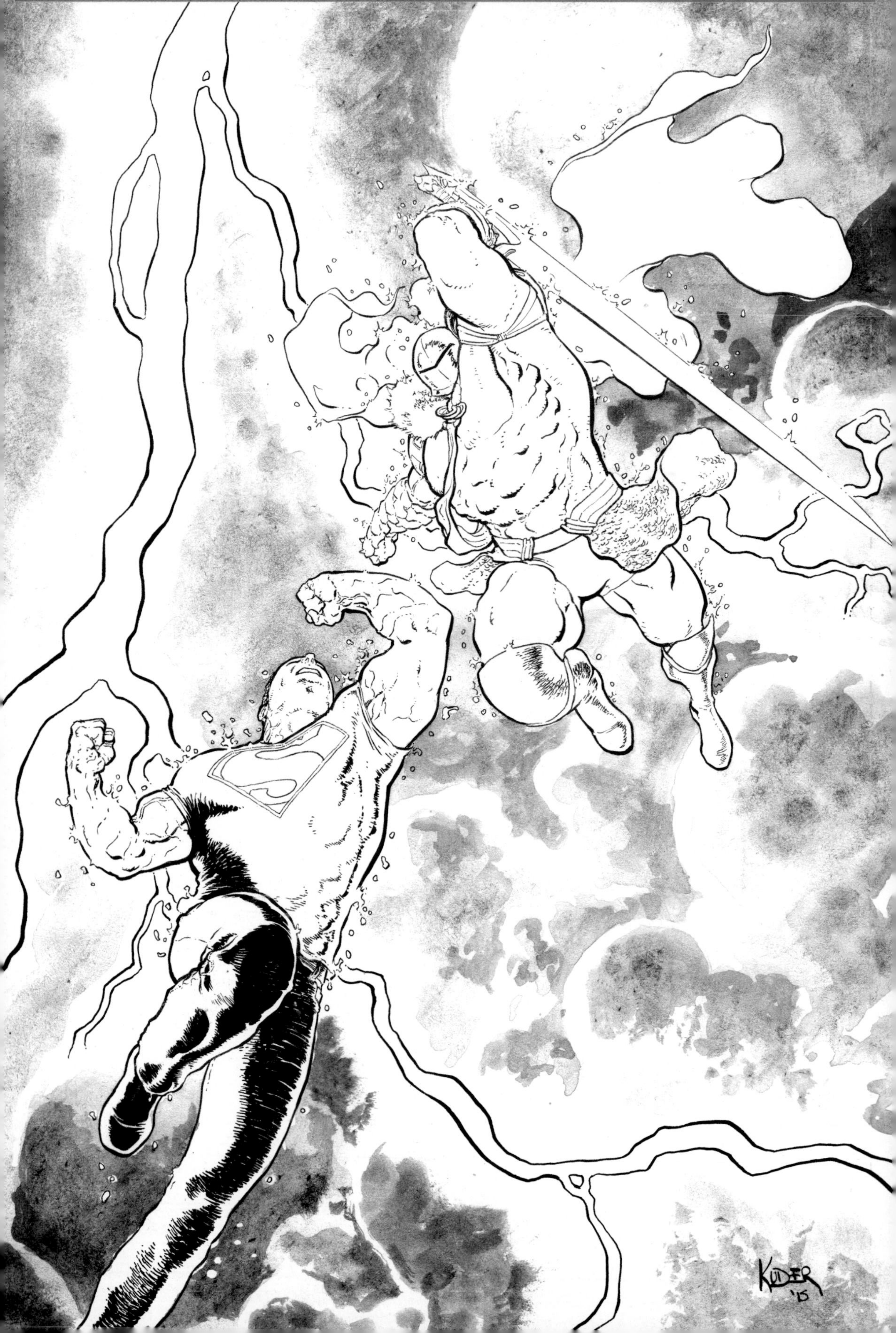
KUDER '15

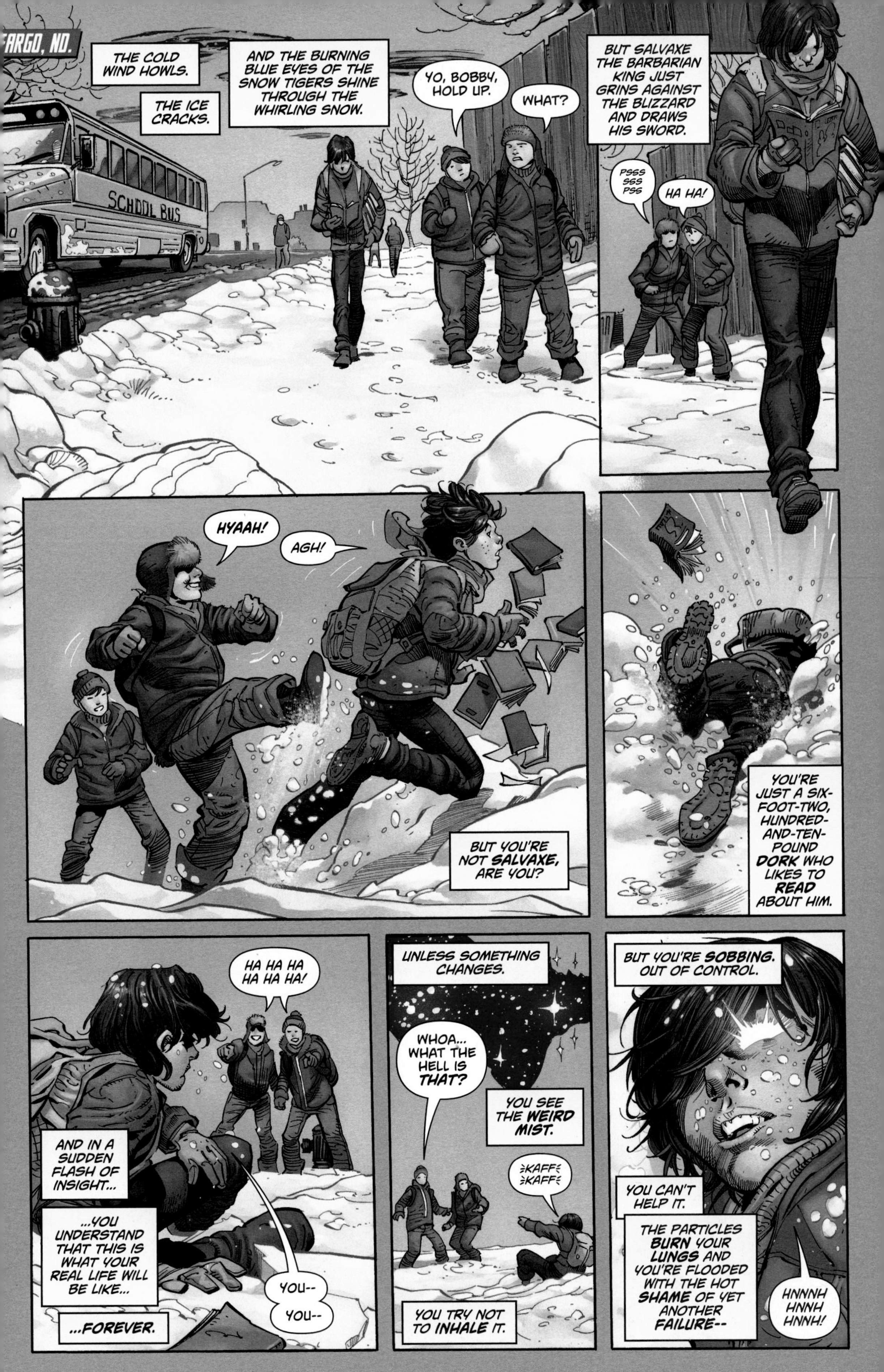
FARGO, ND.
THE COLD WIND HOWLS.
THE ICE CRACKS.
AND THE BURNING BLUE EYES OF THE SNOW TIGERS SHINE THROUGH THE WHIRLING SNOW.
SCHOOL BUS
YO, BOBBY, HOLD UP.
WHAT?
BUT SALVAXE THE BARBARIAN KING JUST GRINS AGAINST THE BLIZZARD AND DRAWS HIS SWORD.
PSSS SSS PSS
HA HA!
HYAAH!
AGH!
BUT YOU'RE NOT SALVAXE, ARE YOU?
YOU'RE JUST A SIX-FOOT-TWO, HUNDRED-AND-TEN-POUND DORK WHO LIKES TO READ ABOUT HIM.
HA HA HA HA HA HA!
AND IN A SUDDEN FLASH OF INSIGHT...
...YOU UNDERSTAND THAT THIS IS WHAT YOUR REAL LIFE WILL BE LIKE...
...FOREVER.
YOU--
YOU--
UNLESS SOMETHING CHANGES.
WHOA... WHAT THE HELL IS THAT?
YOU SEE THE WEIRD MIST.
KAFF KAFF
YOU TRY NOT TO INHALE IT.
BUT YOU'RE SOBBING. OUT OF CONTROL.
YOU CAN'T HELP IT.
THE PARTICLES BURN YOUR LUNGS AND YOU'RE FLOODED WITH THE HOT SHAME OF YET ANOTHER FAILURE--
HNNNH HNNH HNNH!

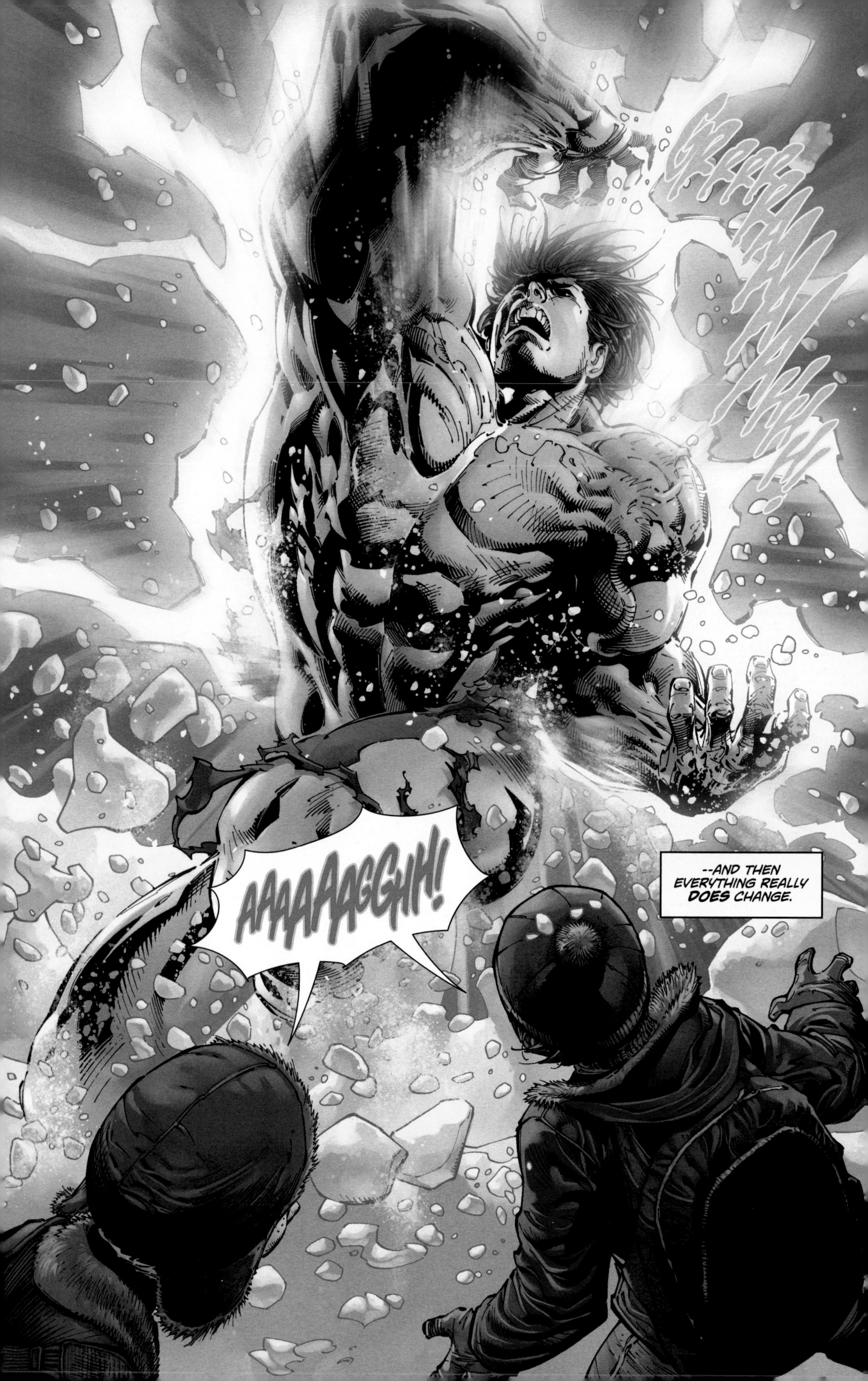
GRRRRAAAAHH!!
AAAAAAGGHH!
--AND THEN EVERYTHING REALLY DOES CHANGE.

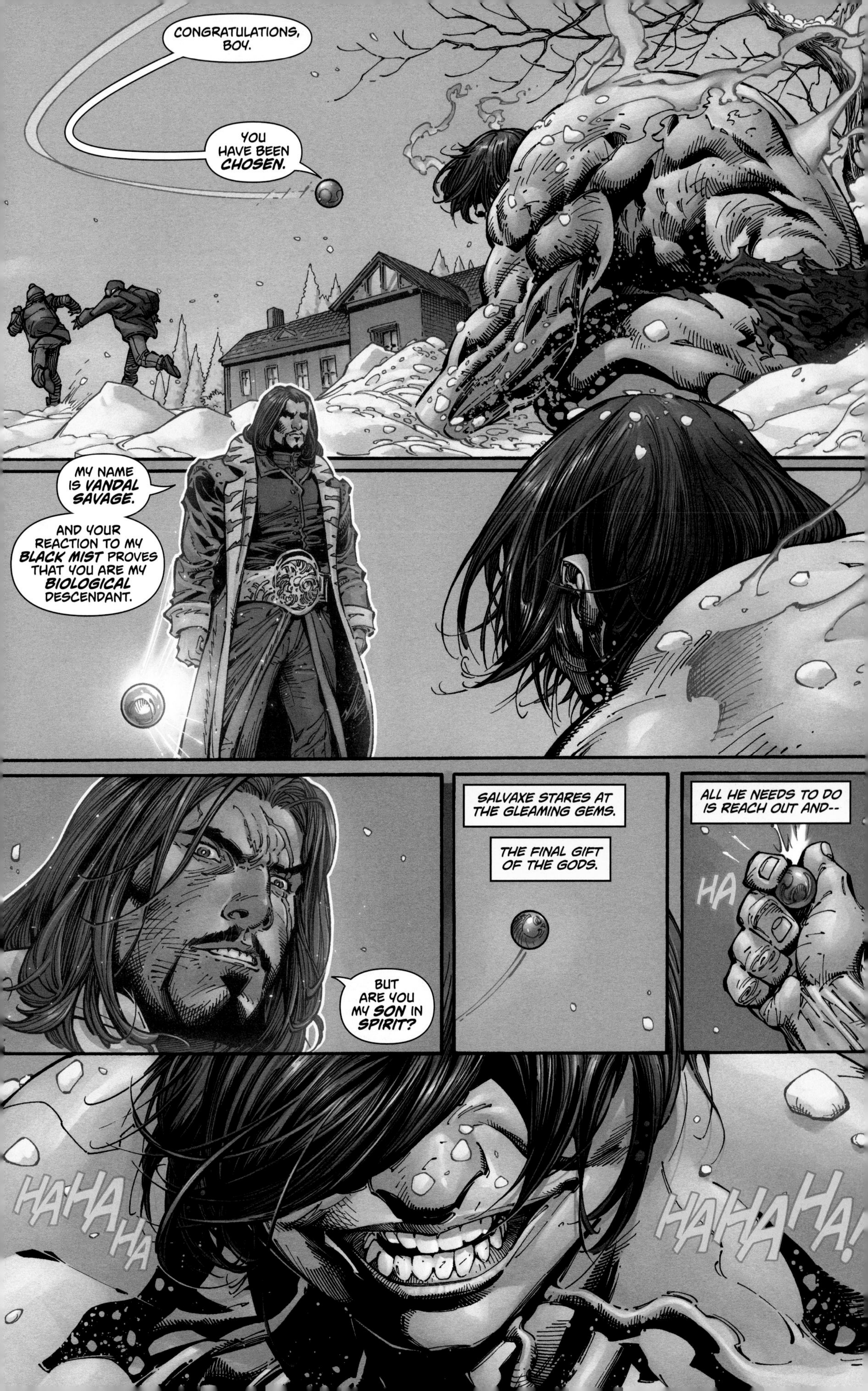
CONGRATULATIONS, BOY.
YOU HAVE BEEN CHOSEN.
MY NAME IS VANDAL SAVAGE.
AND YOUR REACTION TO MY BLACK MIST PROVES THAT YOU ARE MY BIOLOGICAL DESCENDANT.
BUT ARE YOU MY SON IN SPIRIT?
SALVAXE STARES AT THE GLEAMING GEMS.
THE FINAL GIFT OF THE GODS.
ALL HE NEEDS TO DO IS REACH OUT AND--
HA
HAHAHAHA
HAHAHAHA!

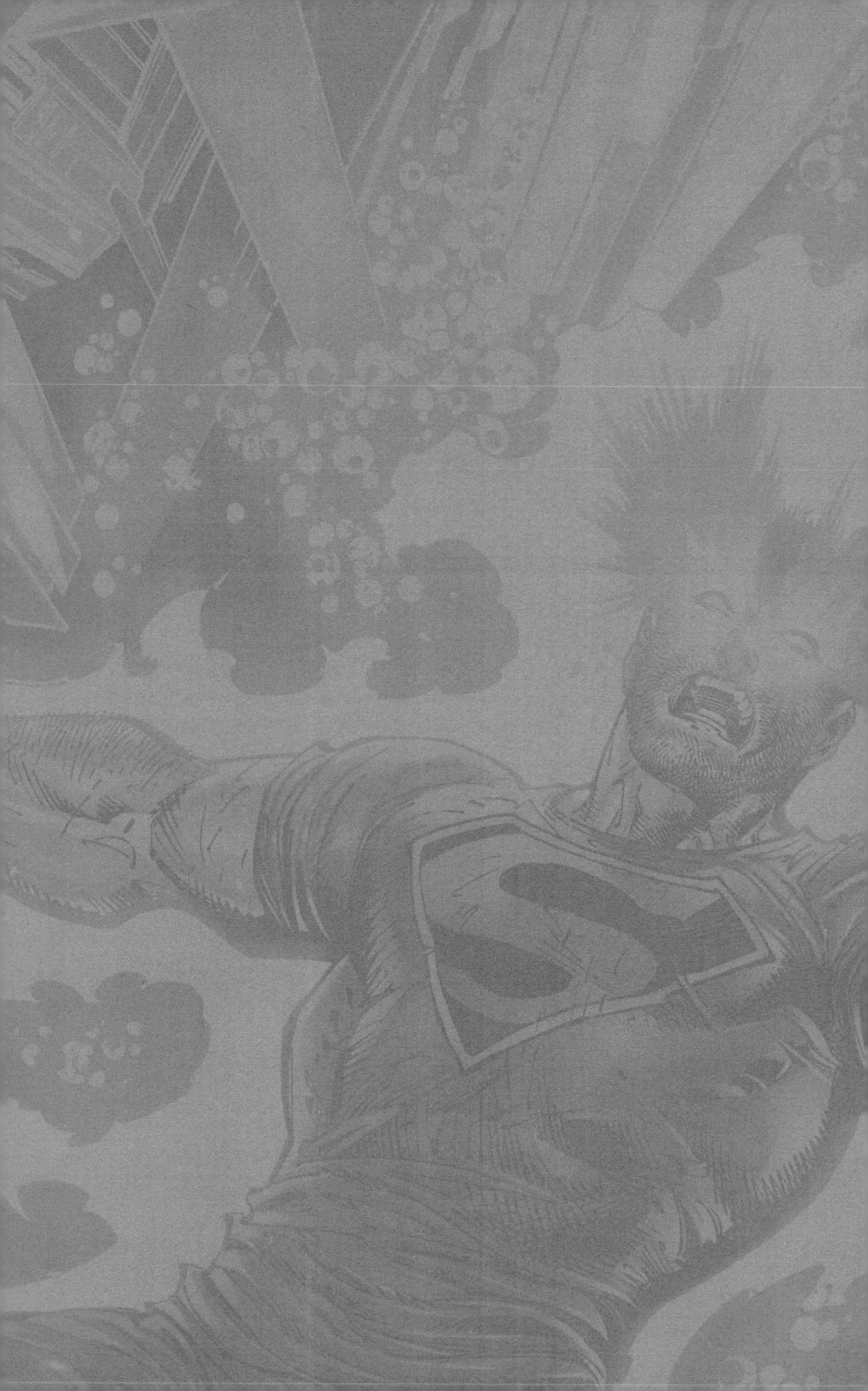

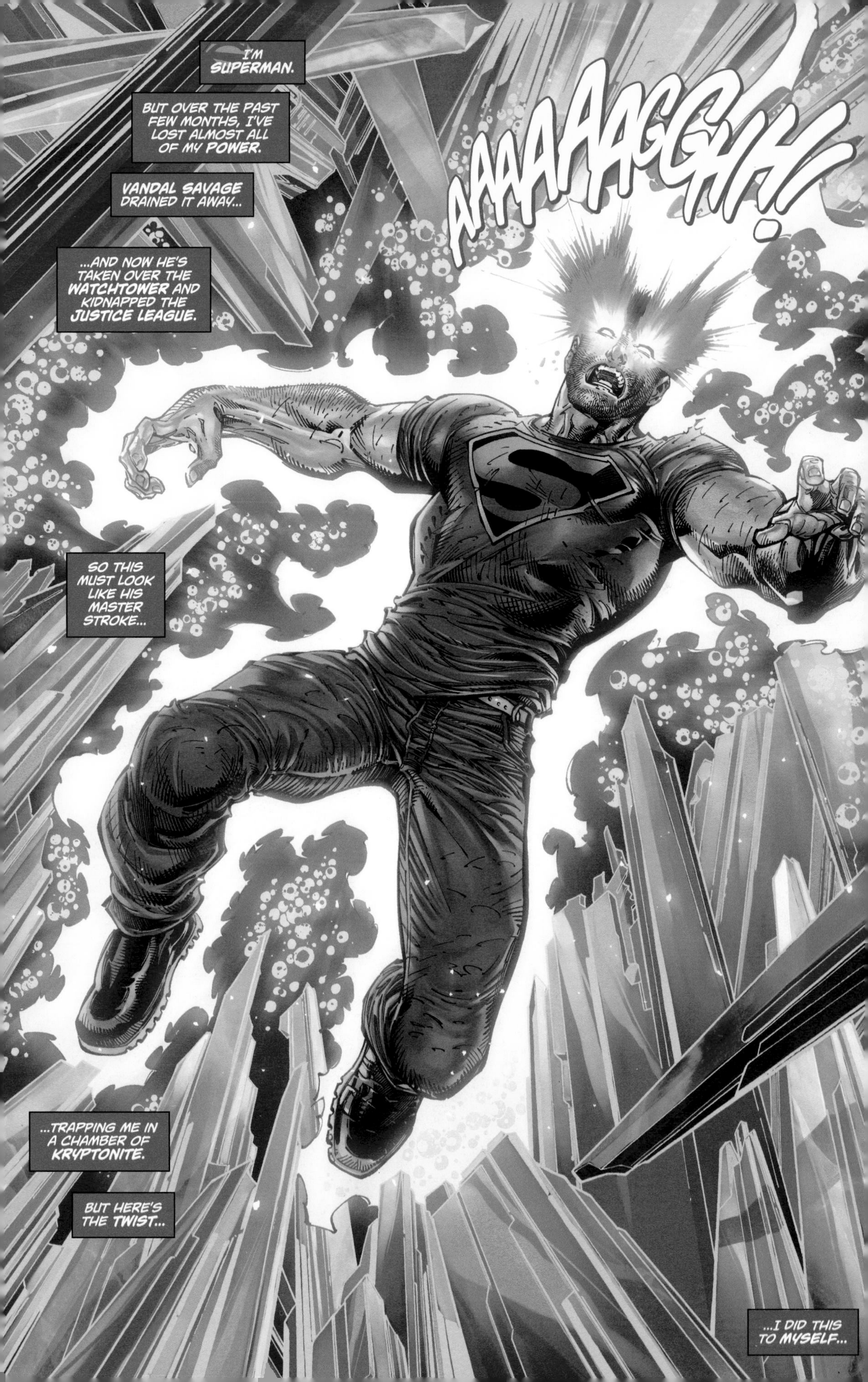
I'M SUPERMAN.
BUT OVER THE PAST FEW MONTHS, I'VE LOST ALMOST ALL OF MY POWER.
VANDAL SAVAGE DRAINED IT AWAY...
...AND NOW HE'S TAKEN OVER THE WATCHTOWER AND KIDNAPPED THE JUSTICE LEAGUE.
AAAAAAGGHH!
SO THIS MUST LOOK LIKE HIS MASTER STROKE...
...TRAPPING ME IN A CHAMBER OF KRYPTONITE.
BUT HERE'S THE TWIST...
...I DID THIS TO MYSELF...

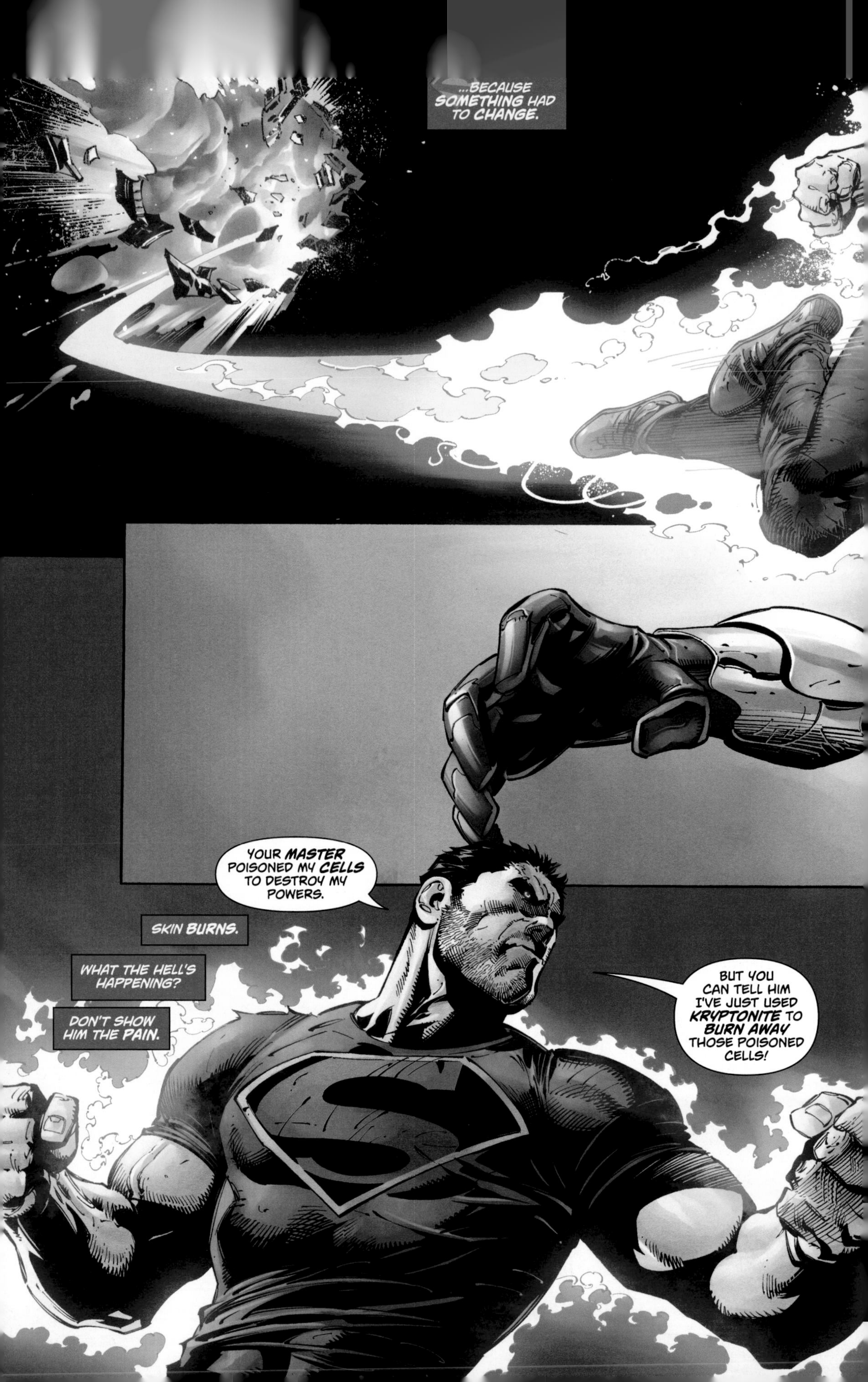
...BECAUSE SOMETHING HAD TO CHANGE.
YOUR MASTER POISONED MY CELLS TO DESTROY MY POWERS.
SKIN BURNS.
WHAT THE HELL'S HAPPENING?
DON'T SHOW HIM THE PAIN.
BUT YOU CAN TELL HIM I'VE JUST USED KRYPTONITE TO BURN AWAY THOSE POISONED CELLS!

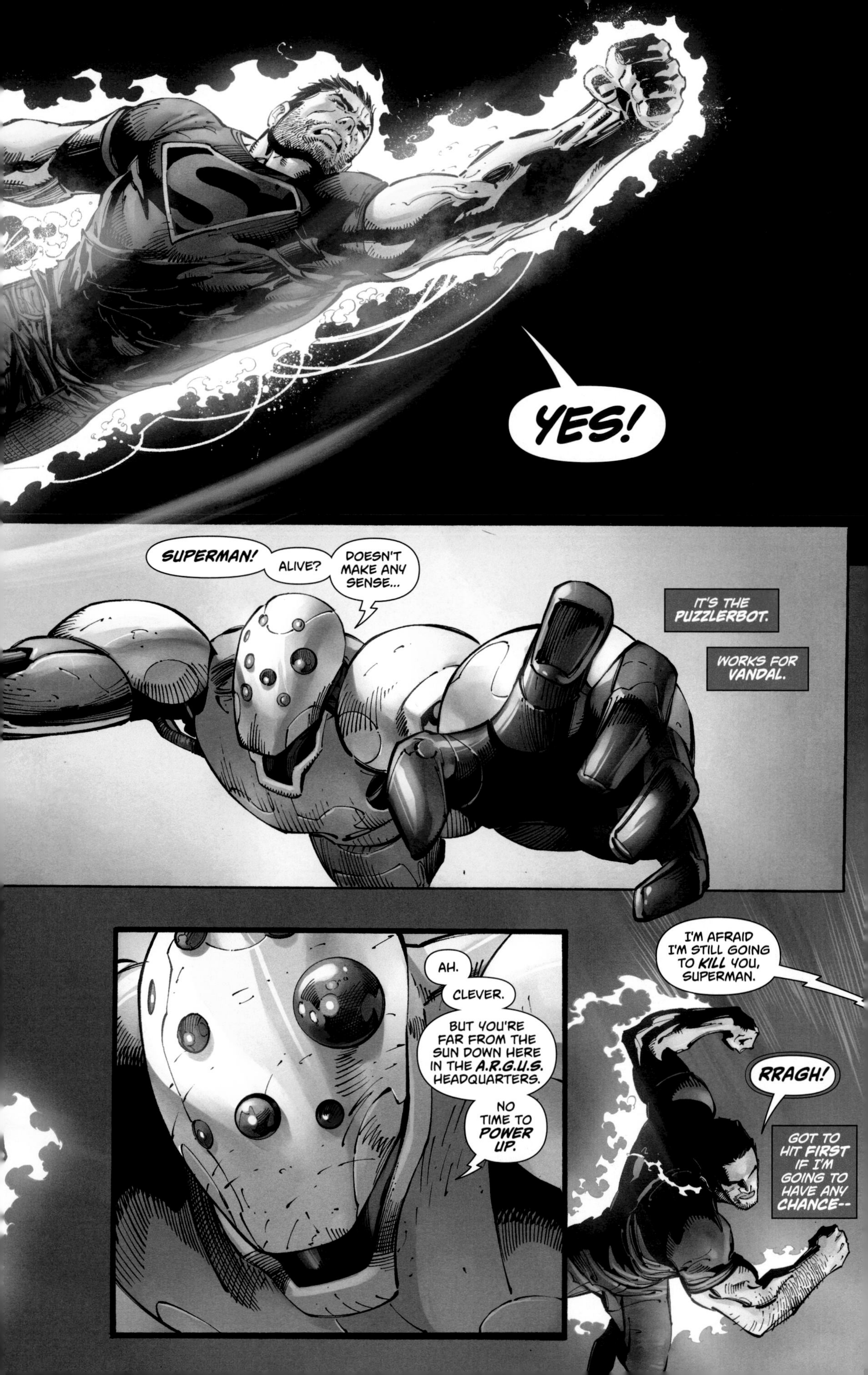
YES!
SUPERMAN!
ALIVE?
DOESN'T MAKE ANY SENSE...
IT'S THE PUZZLERBOT.
WORKS FOR VANDAL.
AH.
CLEVER.
BUT YOU'RE FAR FROM THE SUN DOWN HERE IN THE A.R.G.U.S. HEADQUARTERS.
NO TIME TO POWER UP.
I'M AFRAID I'M STILL GOING TO KILL YOU, SUPERMAN.
RRAGH!
GOT TO HIT FIRST IF I'M GOING TO HAVE ANY CHANCE--

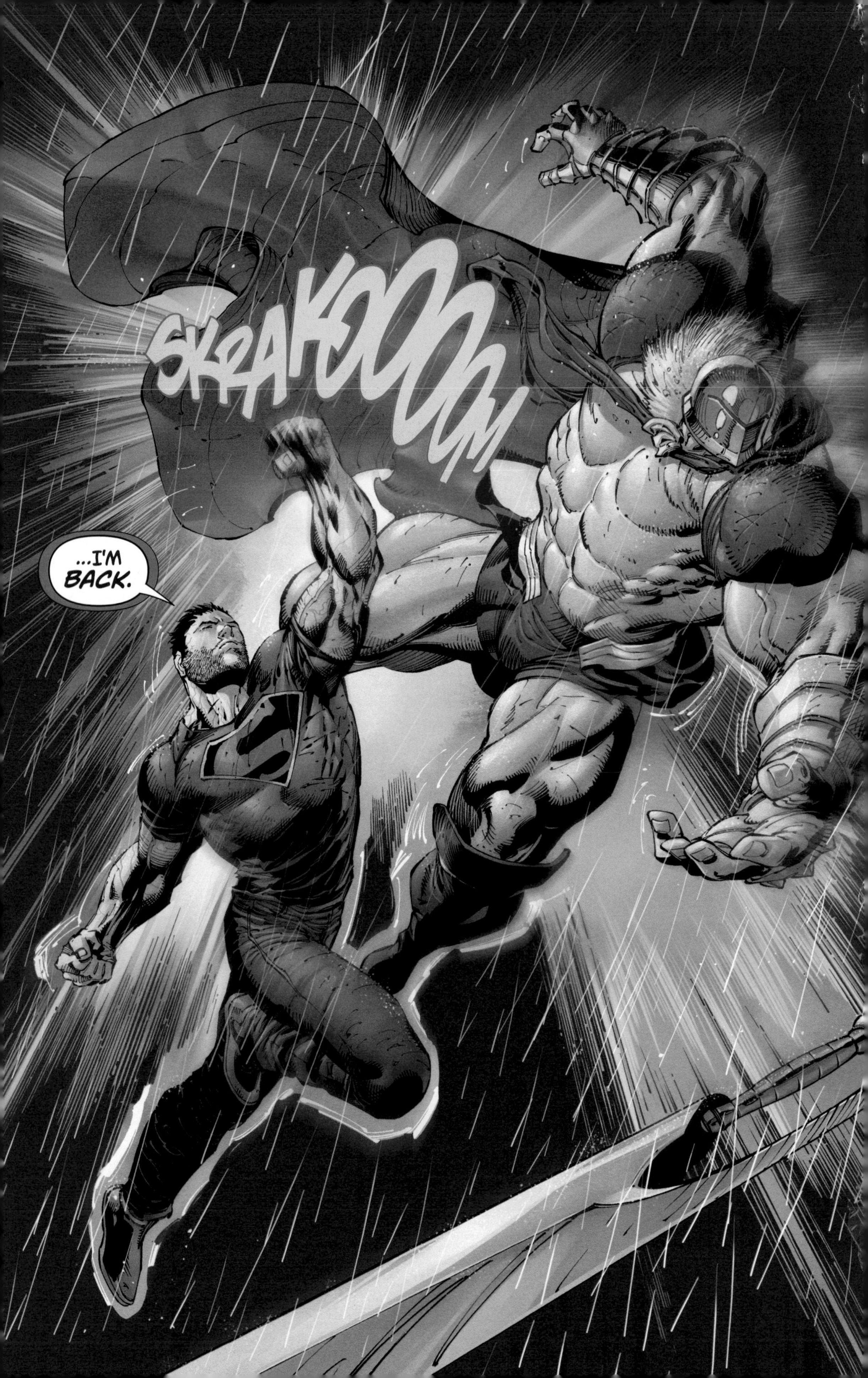
SKRAKOOOOM
...I'M BACK.

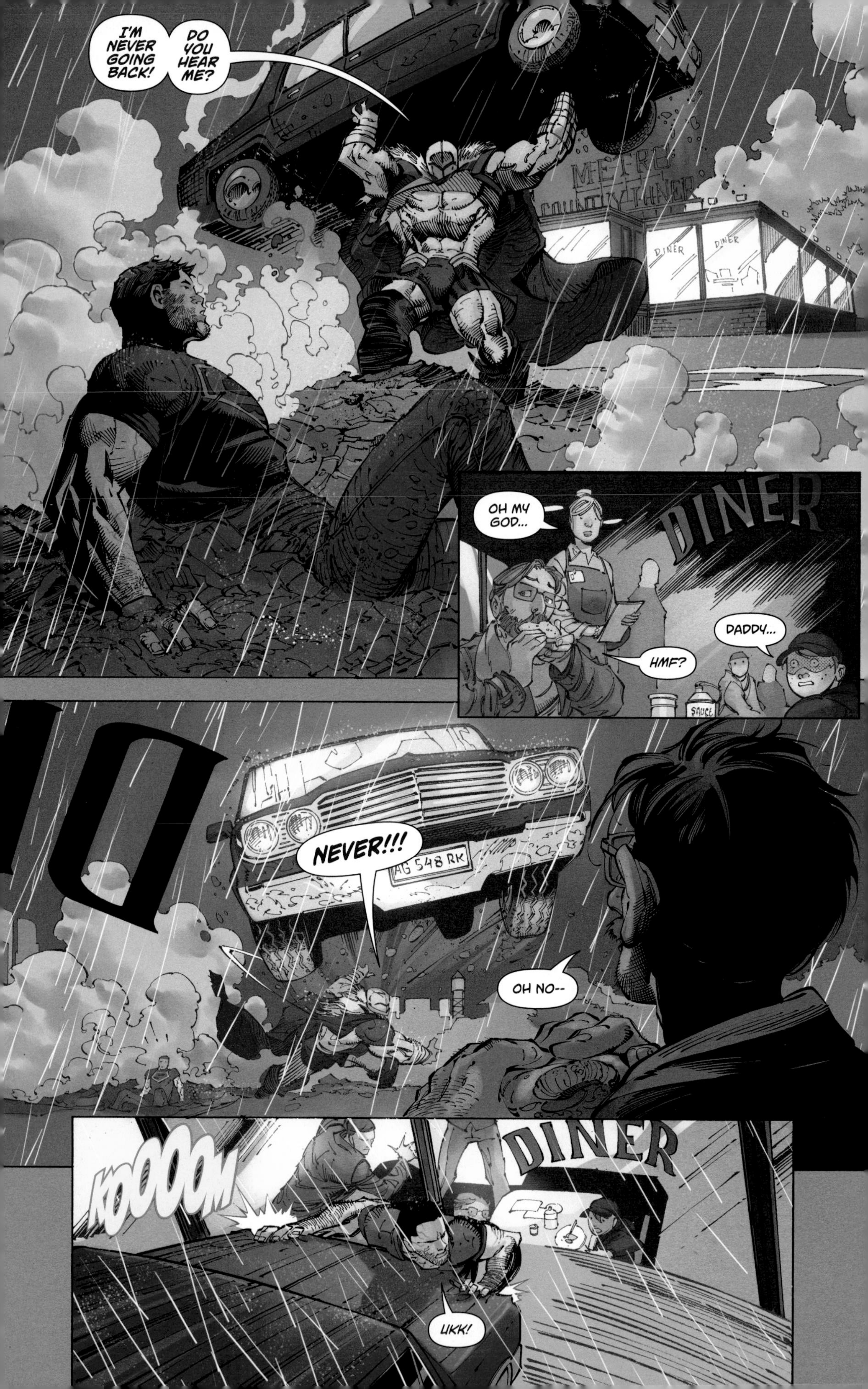
I'M NEVER GOING BACK!
DO YOU HEAR ME?
OH MY GOD...
DINER
DADDY...
HMF?
SAUCE
NEVER!!!
AG 548 RK
OH NO--
KOOOOM
DINER
UKK!

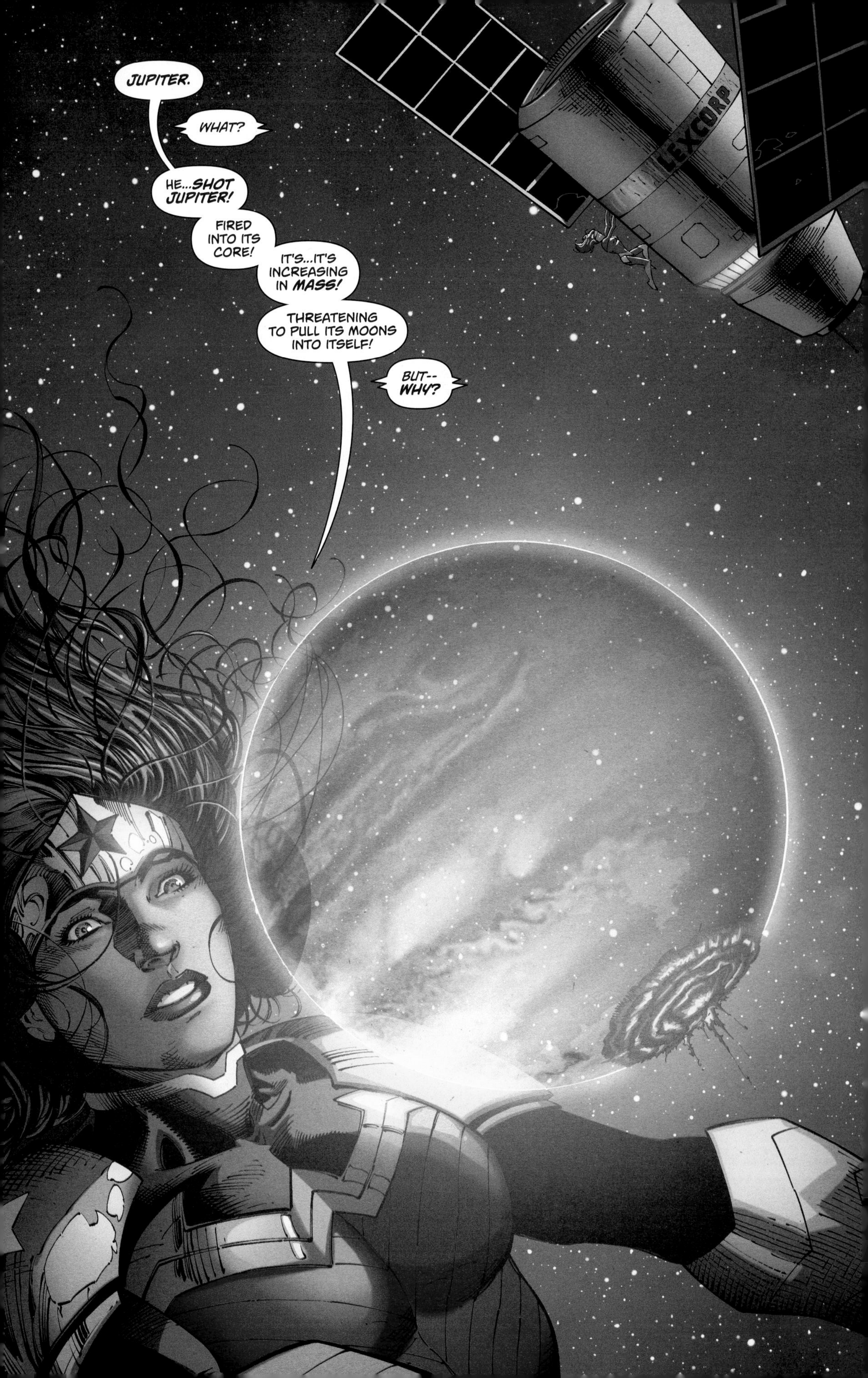
JUPITER.
WHAT?
HE...SHOT JUPITER!
FIRED INTO ITS CORE!
IT'S...IT'S INCREASING IN MASS!
THREATENING TO PULL ITS MOONS INTO ITSELF!
BUT-- WHY?
LEXCORP

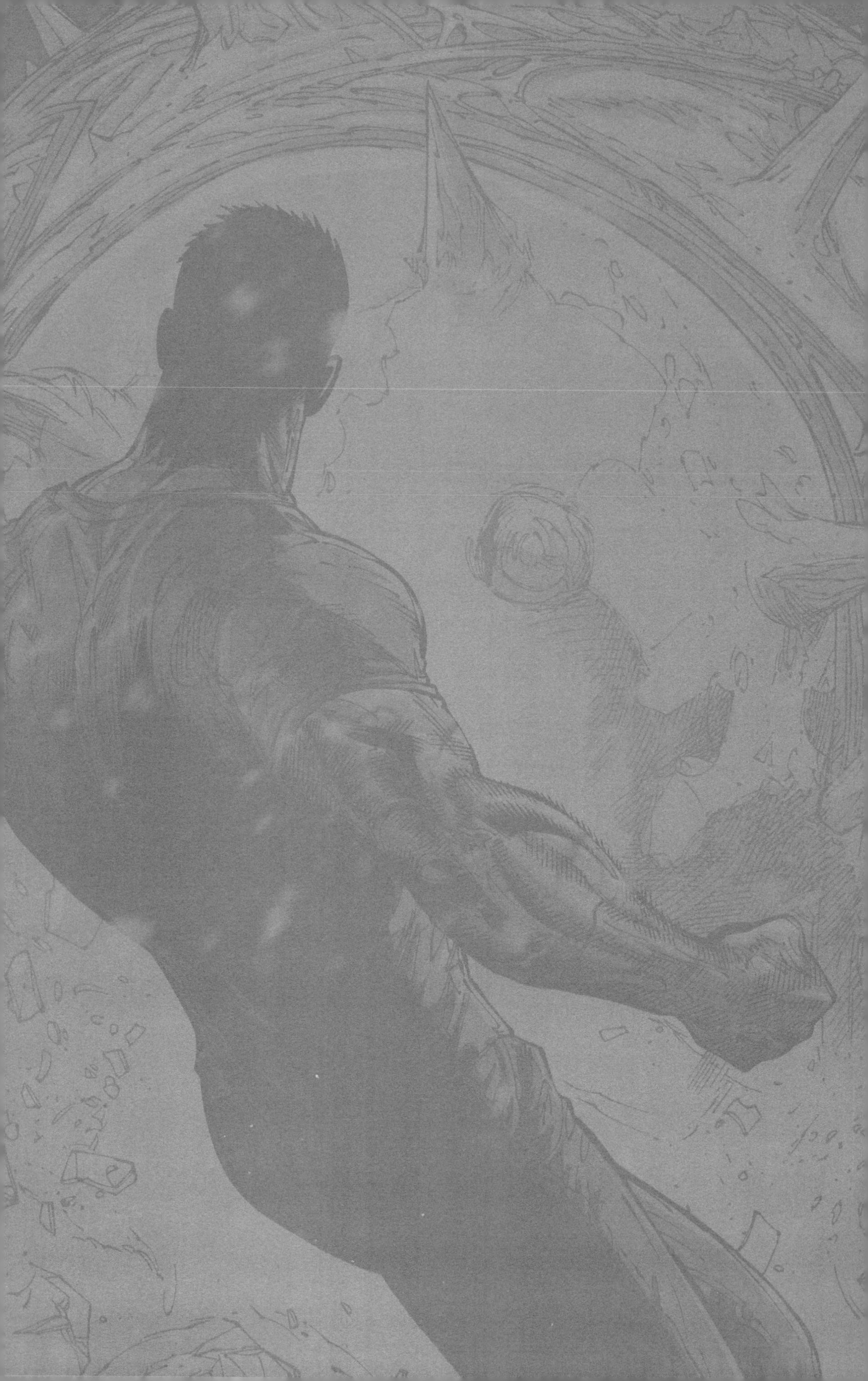

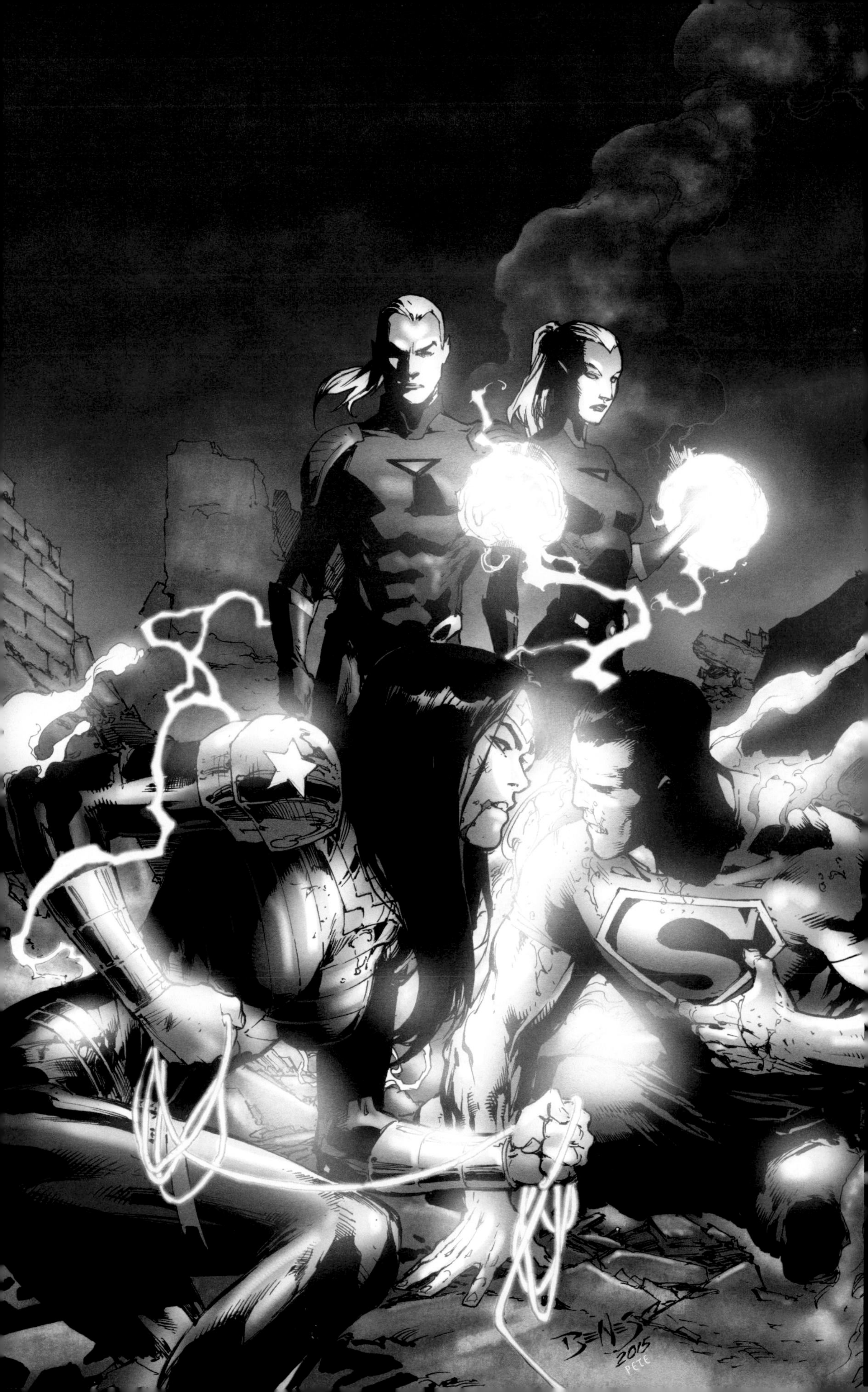
BENES
2015
PETE

SKYFALL

PETER J. TOMASI writer **DOUG MAHNKE** penciller **JAIME MENDOZA DOUG MAHNKE** inkers **WIL QUINTANA** colorist **ROB LEIGH** letterer **ED BENES PAT PANTAZIS** cover

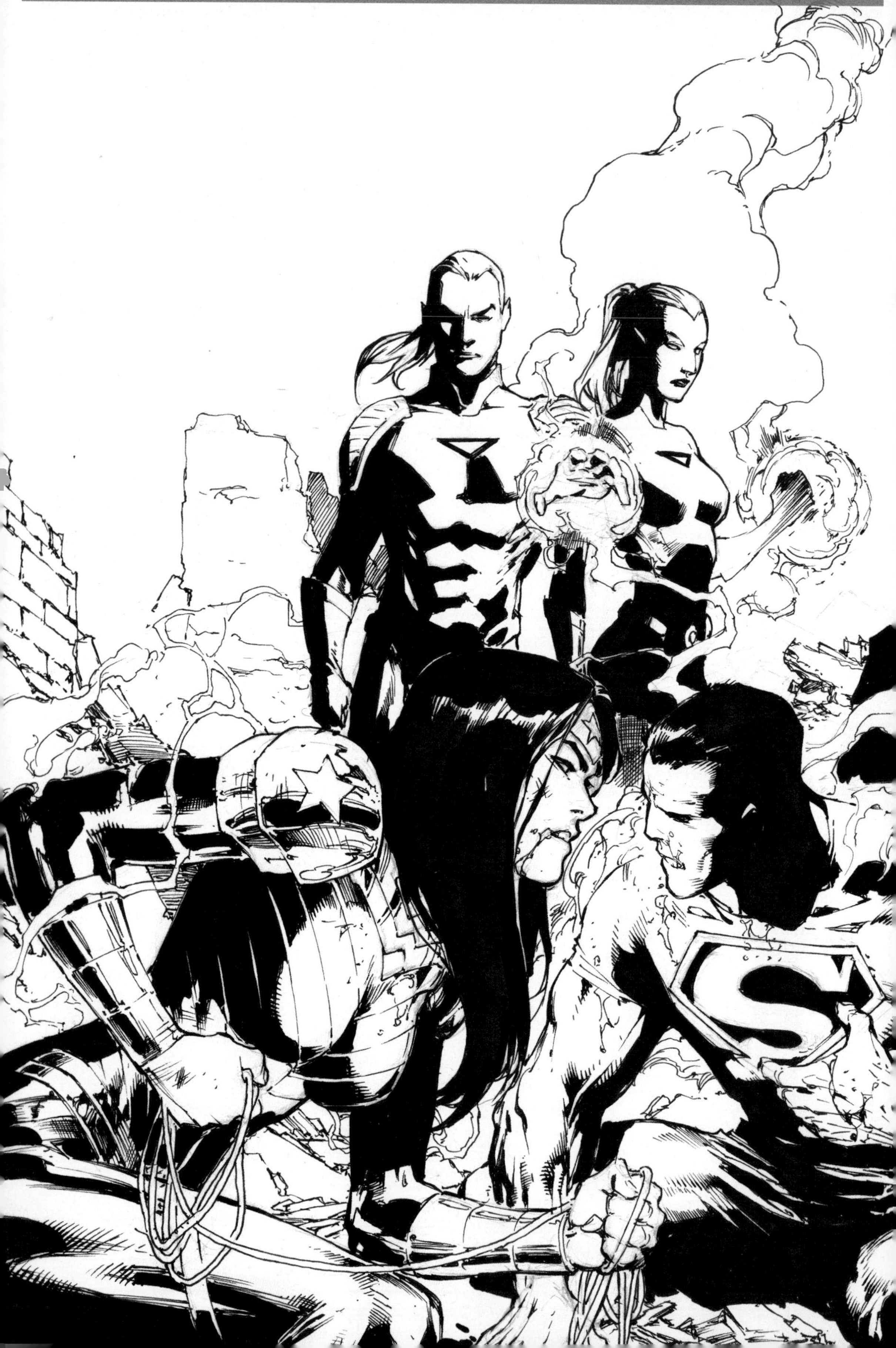

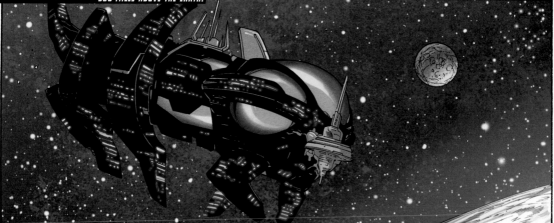

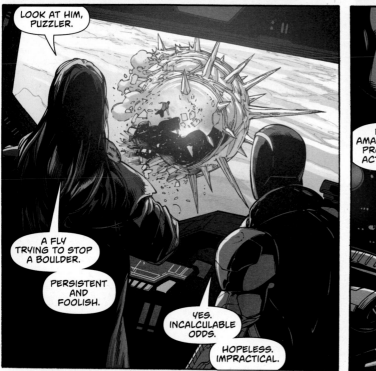

THE THERMOSPHERE.
500 MILES ABOVE THE EARTH.
LOOK AT HIM, PUZZLER.
A FLY TRYING TO STOP A BOULDER.
PERSISTENT AND FOOLISH.
YES. INCALCULABLE ODDS.
HOPELESS. IMPRACTICAL.
WITH THE JUPITER MOON REALIGNMENT AN UNQUALIFIED SUCCESS, IT'S TIME TO INITIATE THE FORTRESS MERGE ALONG WITH FUSING HIS DNA SIGNATURE TO THE ENERGY SHIELD.
FINAL AMALGAMATE PROTOCOL ACTIVATED.
TAKTAKTAKTAKTAK TAKTAK
COORDINATES ARE BEING COMPUTED, BUT I MUST INFORM YOU THAT ANOTHER MERGE IS RISKY.
I DON'T CARE.
HAVING FINALLY LOCATED THE FORTRESS, MERGING WITH IT IS THE ONLY WAY TO ENSURE THAT I CAN CAPTURE THE COMET.
LIFE IS RISK.

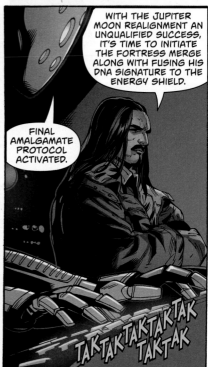

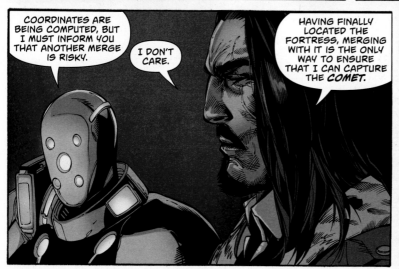

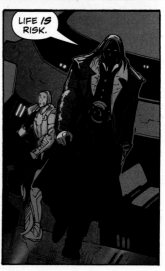

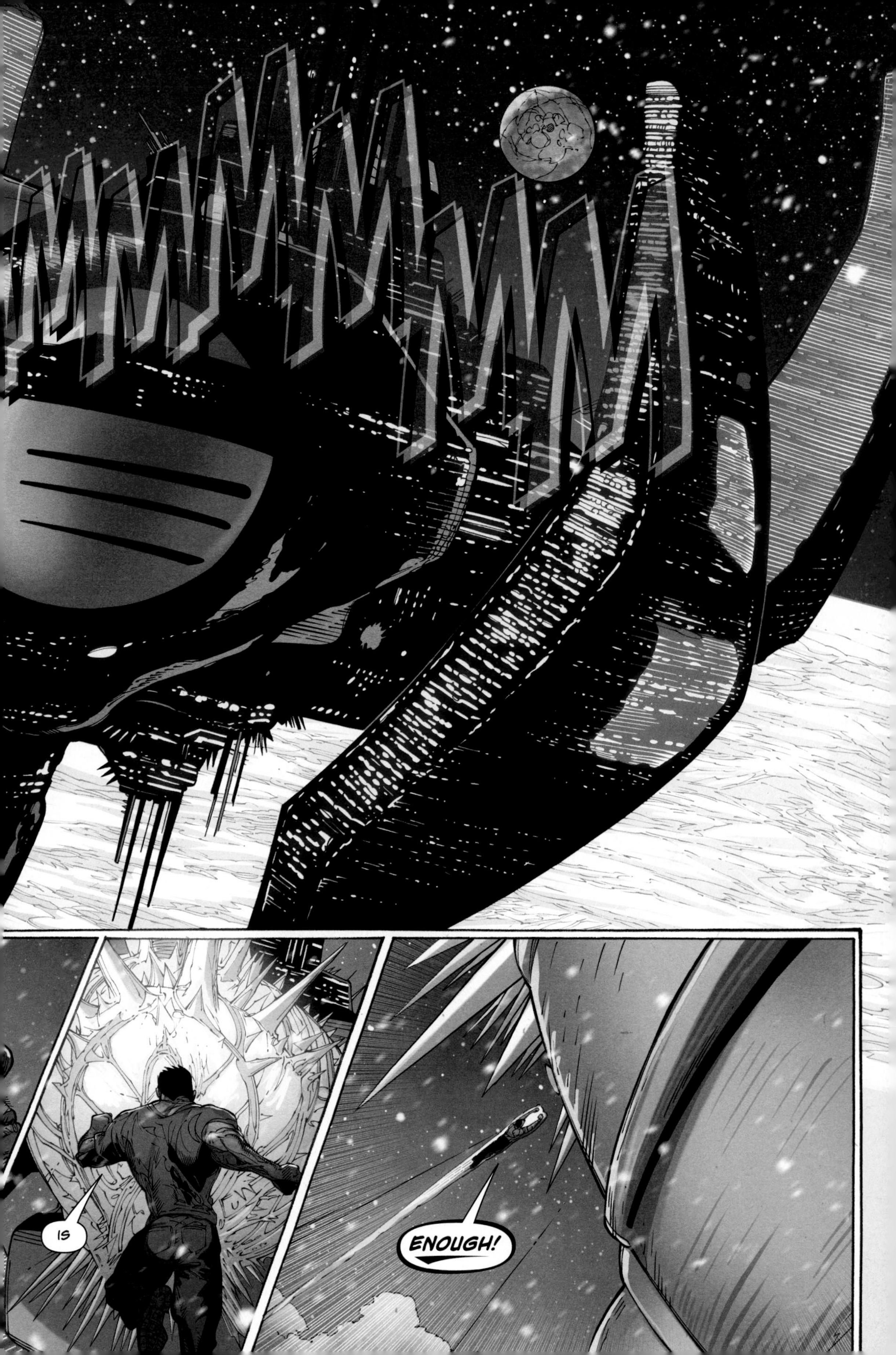
IS
ENOUGH!

THE MOONS OF JUPITER...

...SAVAGE HAS FINISHED MOVING THEM ALL...

WHERE THE HELL DID HIS BASE TELEPORT--

--TO?

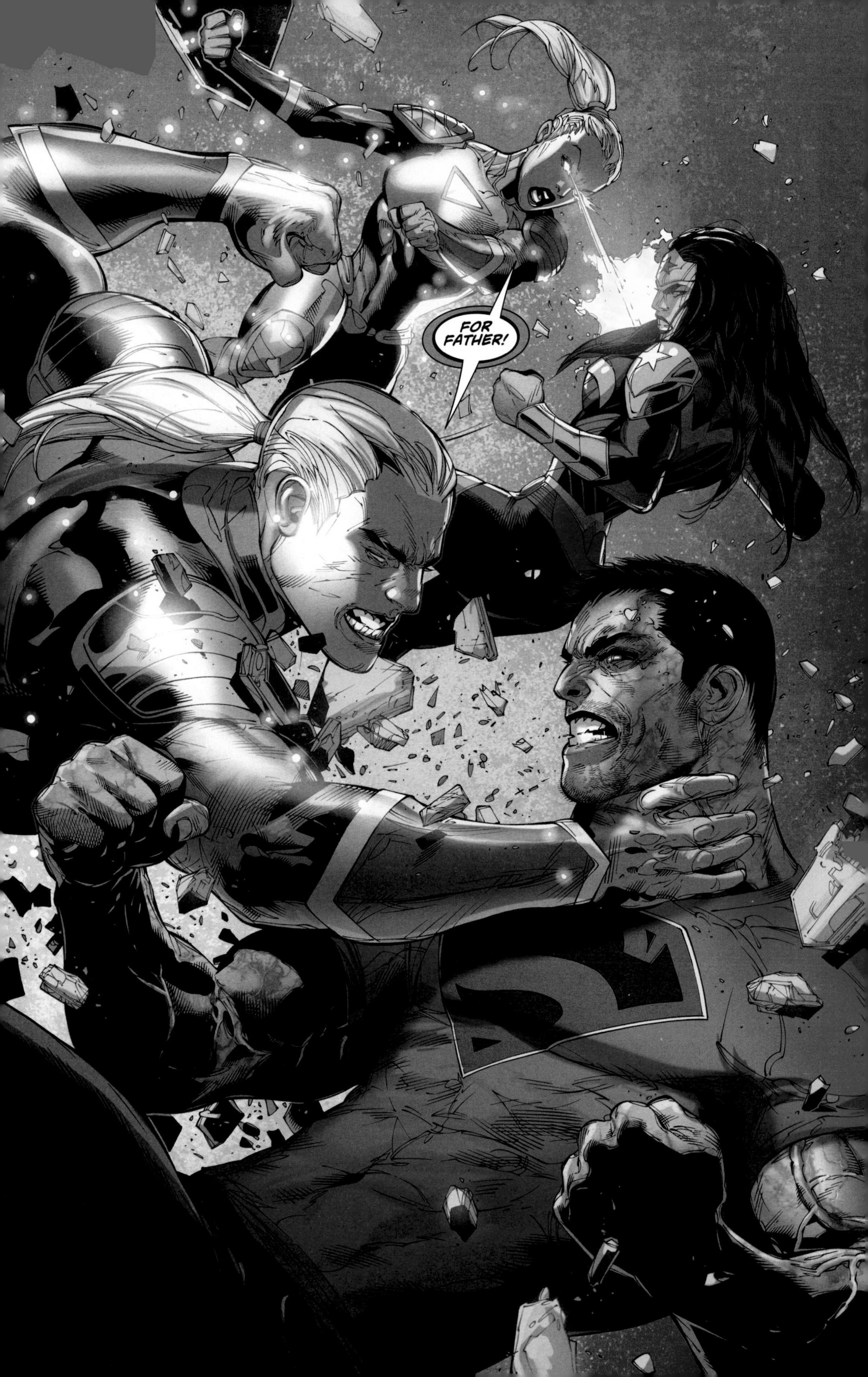
FOR FATHER!

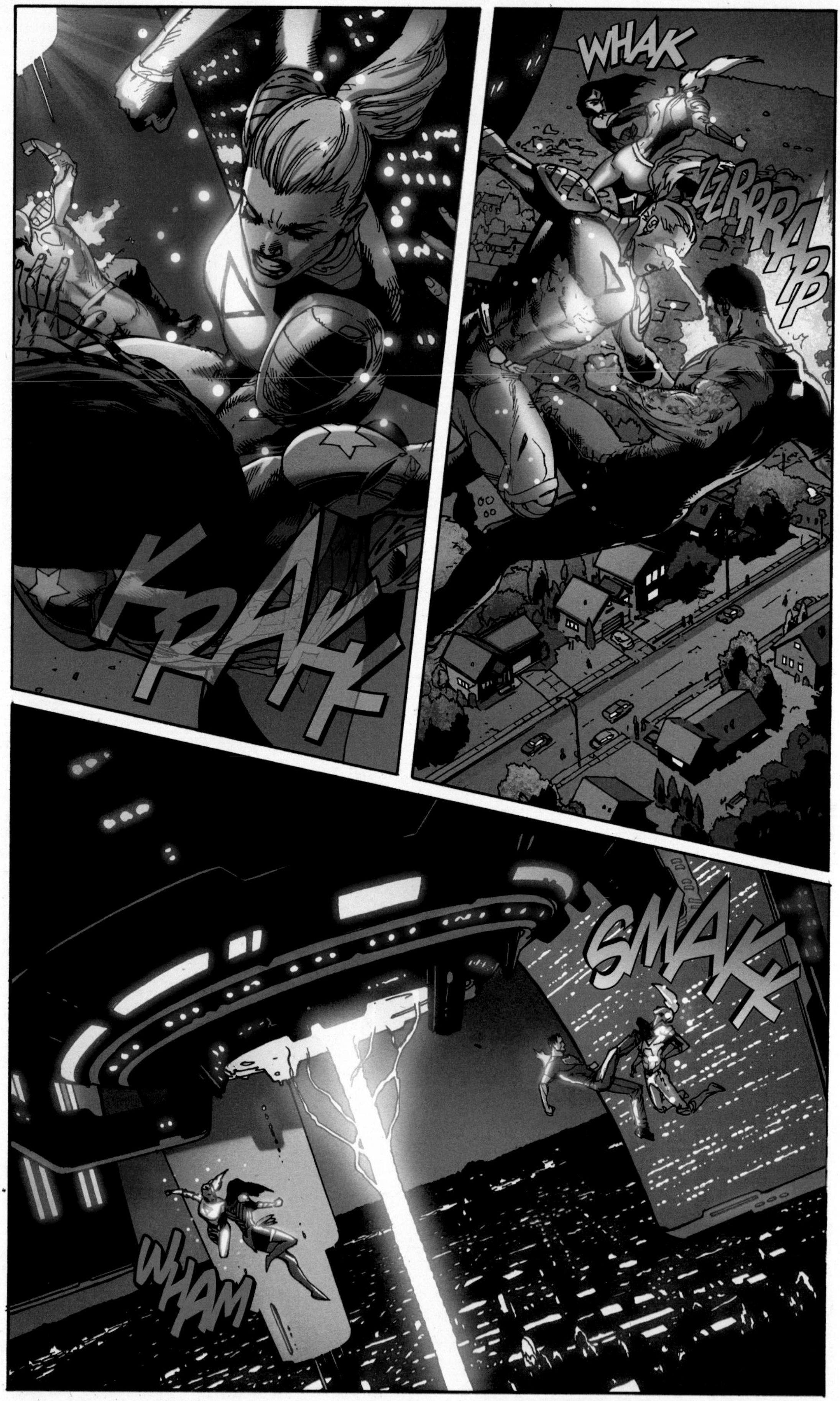
KRAKK
WHAK
ZZRRRAPP
SMAKK
WHAM

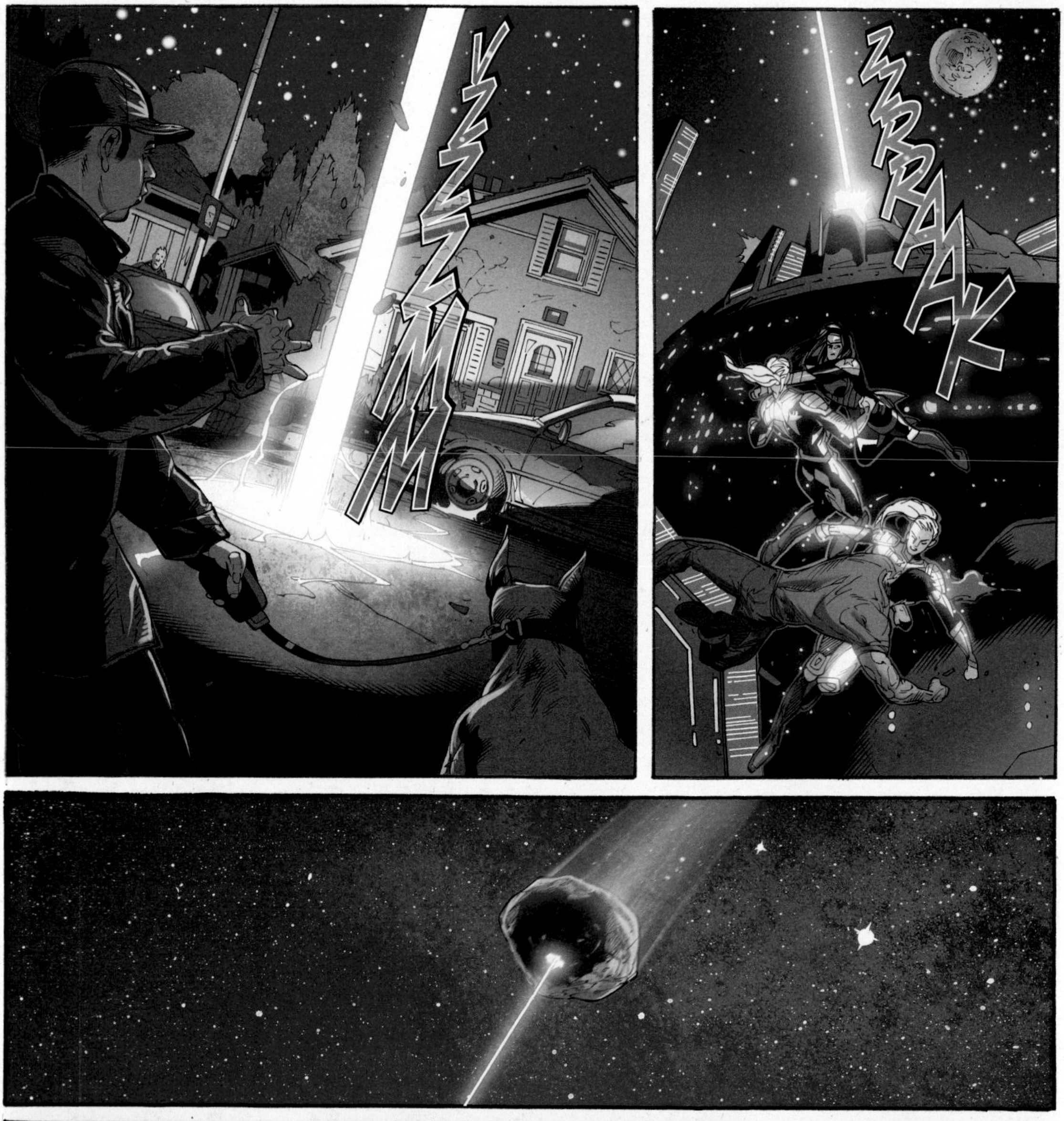
VZZZZMMM
ZZRRAAK

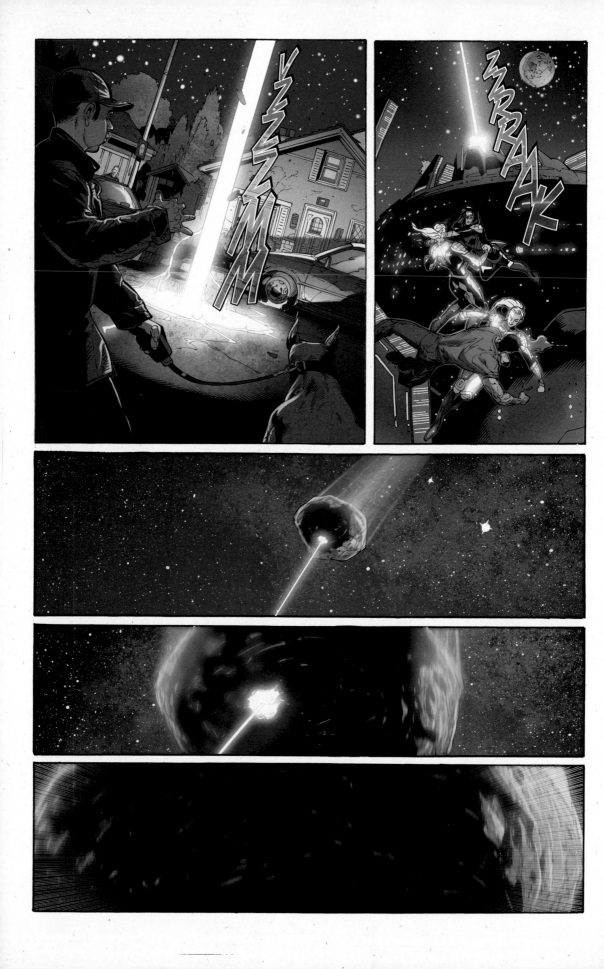

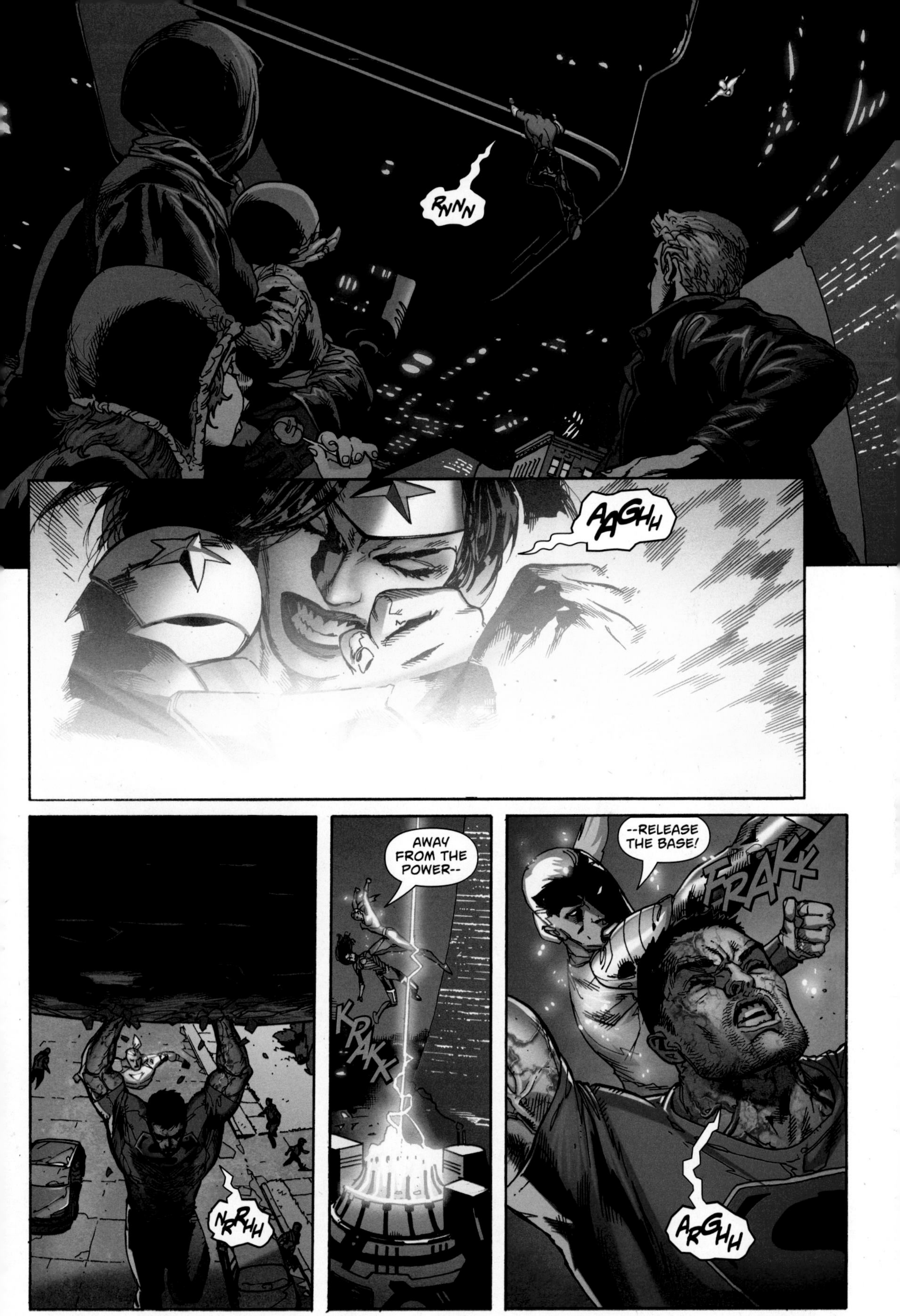
RNNN
AAGHH
NRRHH
AWAY FROM THE POWER--
KRAKK
--RELEASE THE BASE!
FRAKK
ARGHH

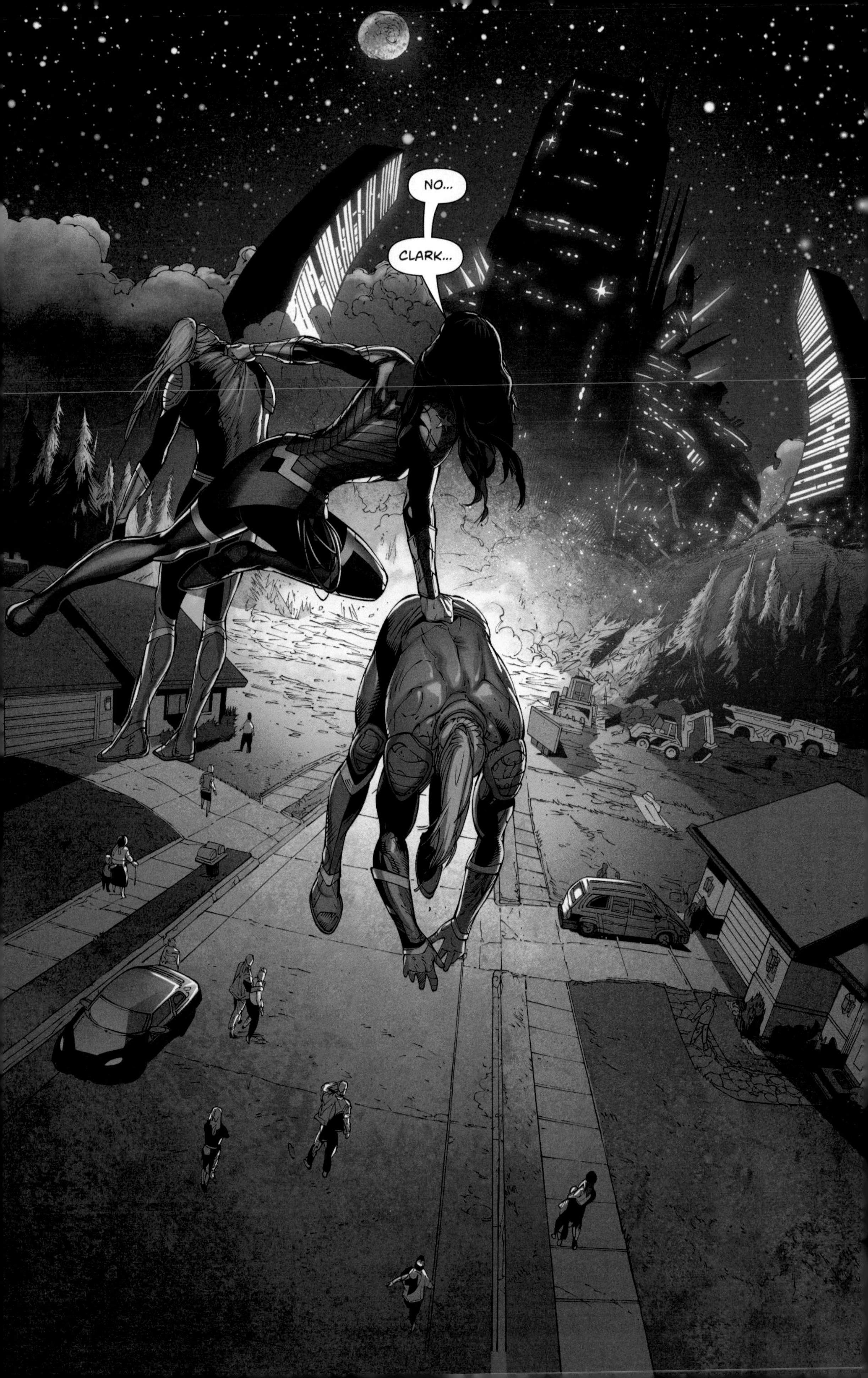
NO...
CLARK...

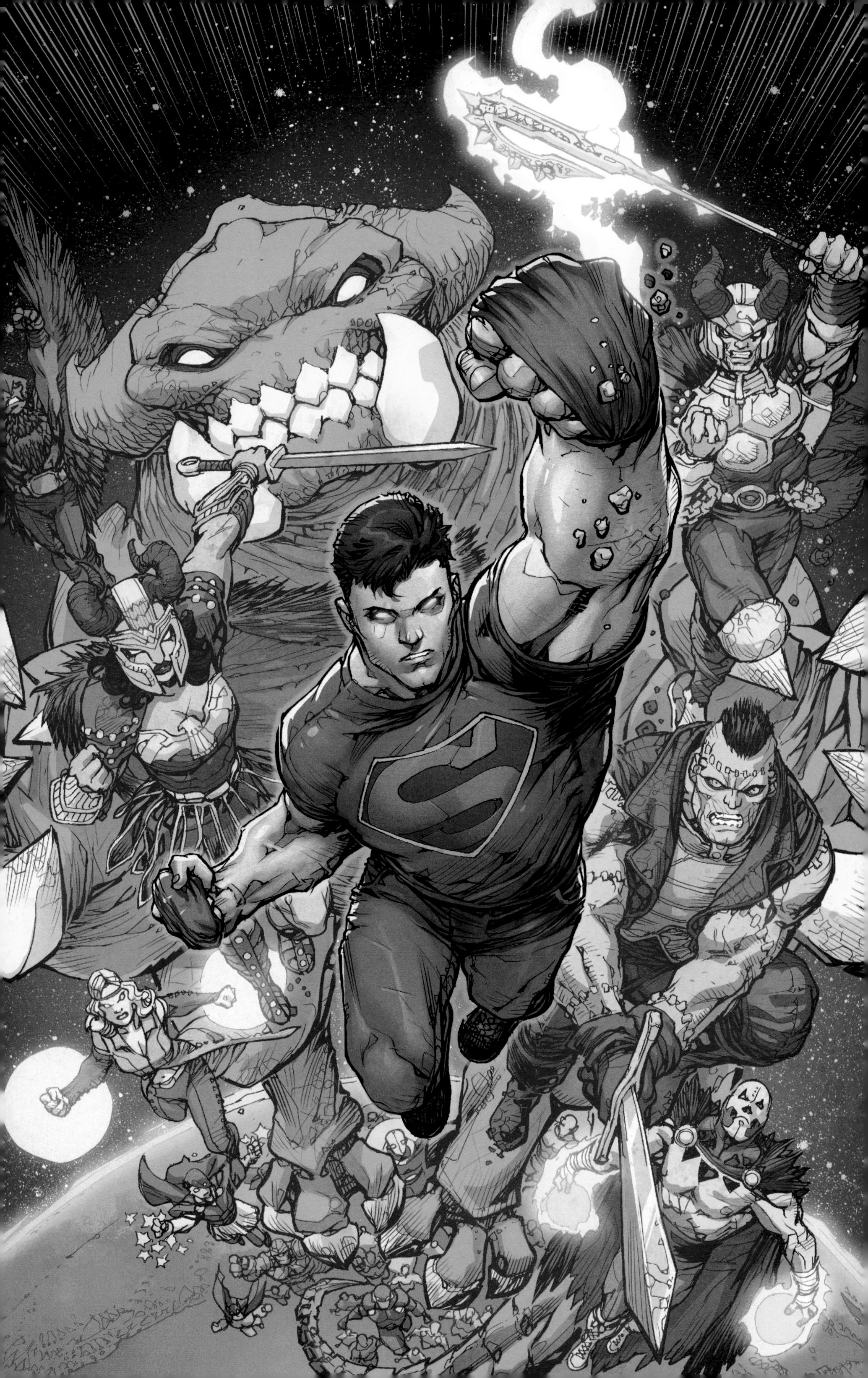

SACRIFICE

GENE LUEN YANG writer **JACK HERBERT** artist **HI-FI BLOND WIL QUINTANA** colorists **STEVE WANDS** letterer **HOWARD PORTER HI-FI** cover

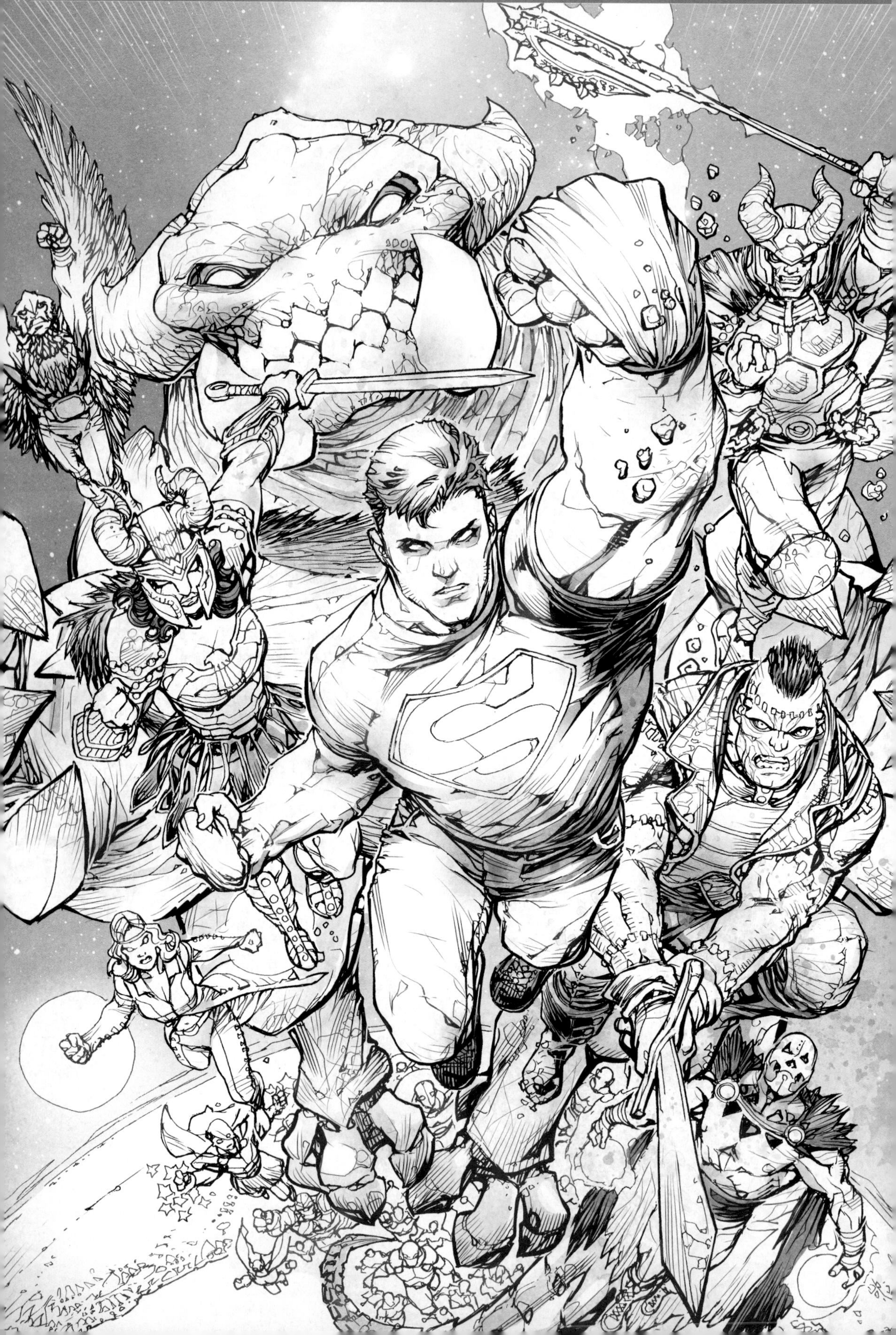

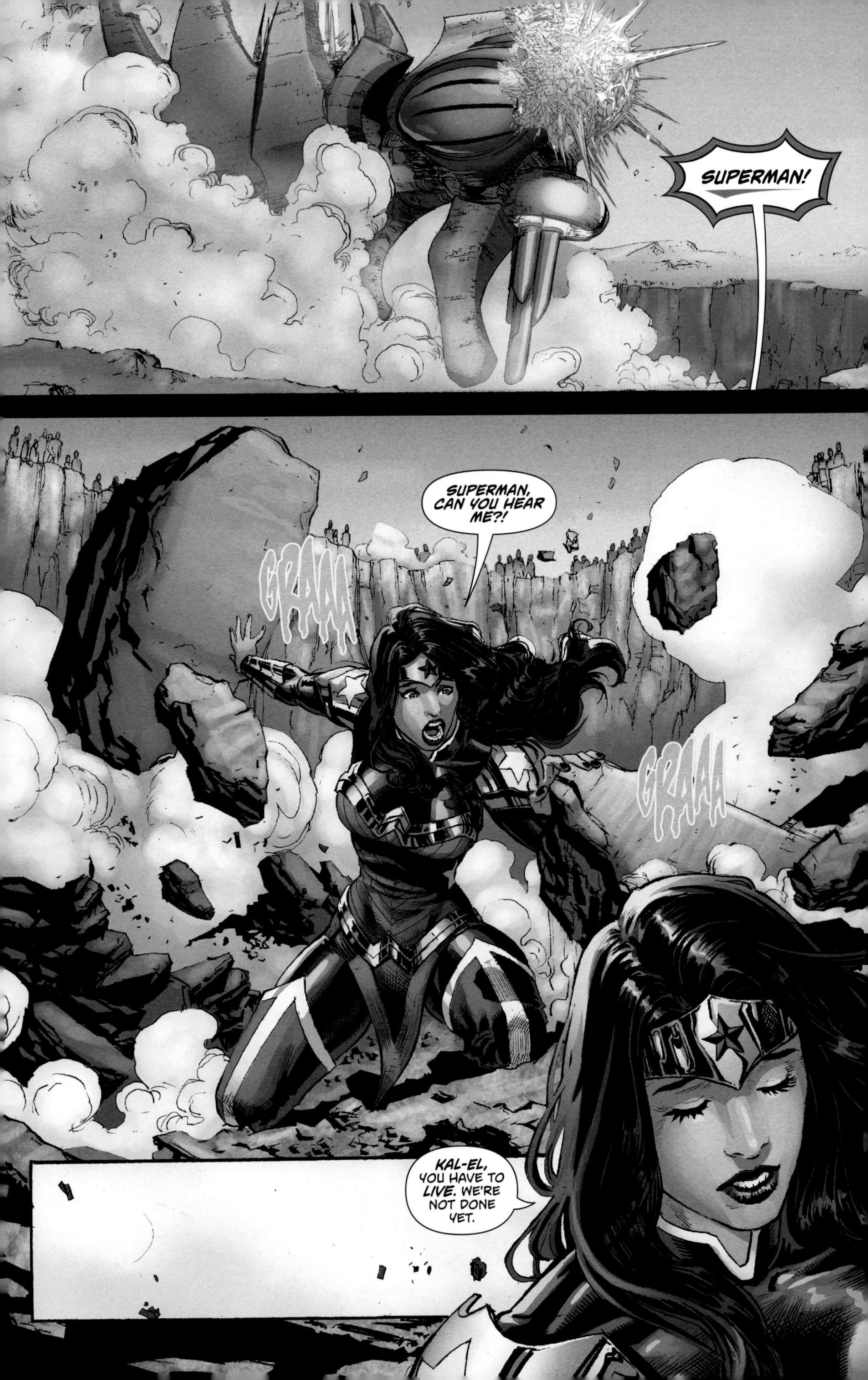
SUPERMAN!
SUPERMAN, CAN YOU HEAR ME?!
GRAAA
GRAAA
KAL-EL, YOU HAVE TO LIVE. WE'RE NOT DONE YET.

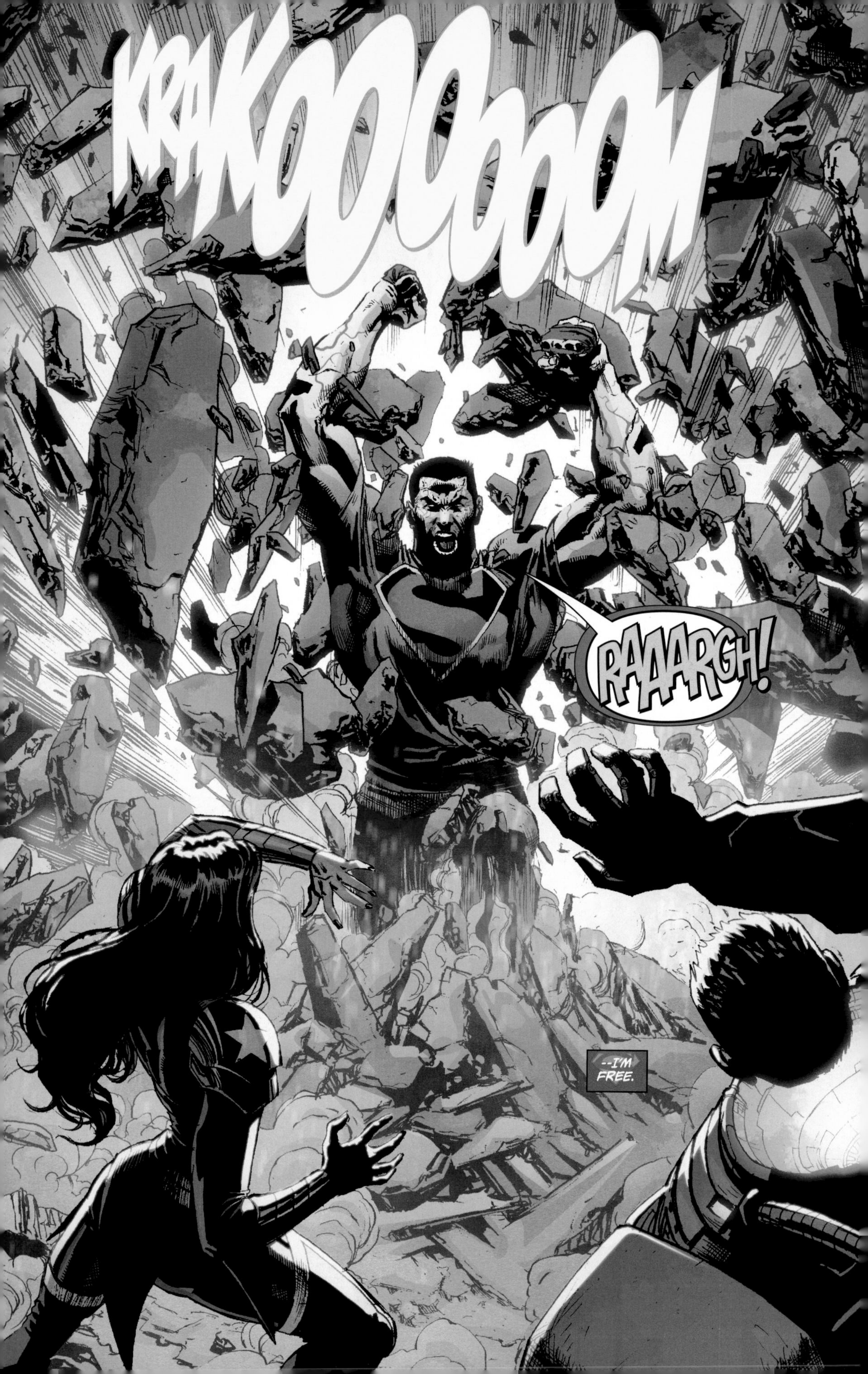
KRAKOOOOOOM
RAAARGH!
--I'M FREE.

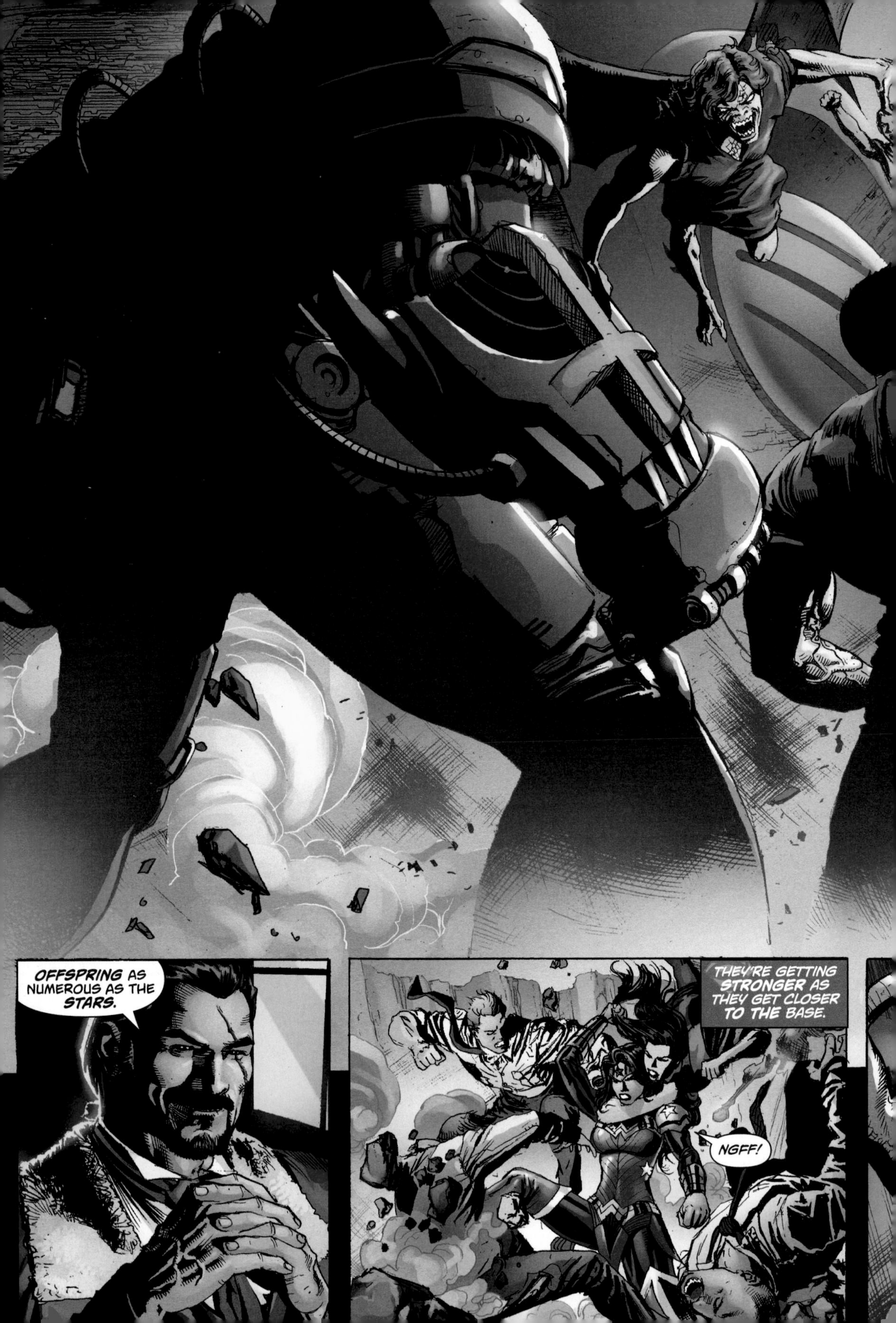
OFFSPRING AS NUMEROUS AS THE STARS.
THEY'RE GETTING STRONGER AS THEY GET CLOSER TO THE BASE.
NGFF!

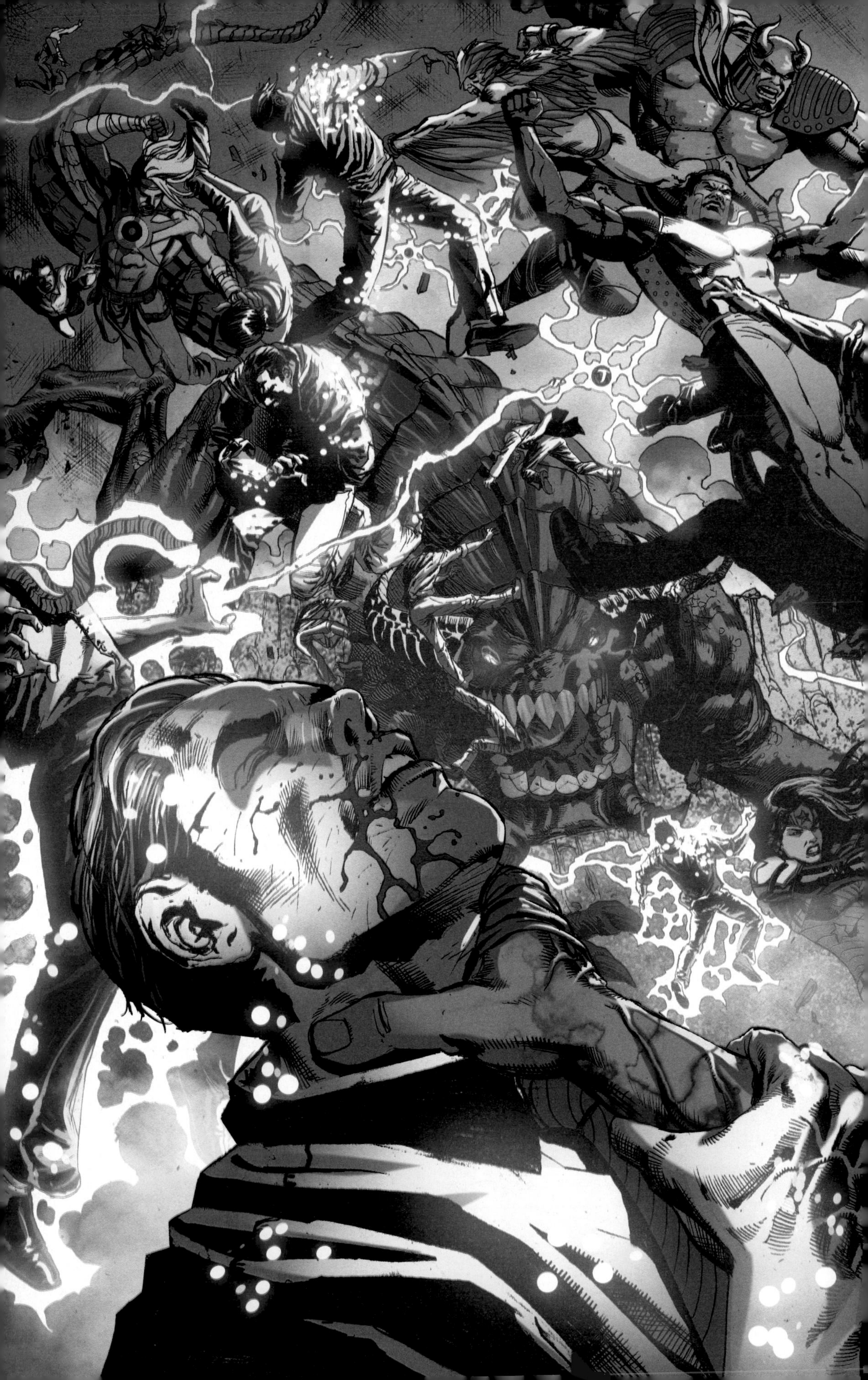

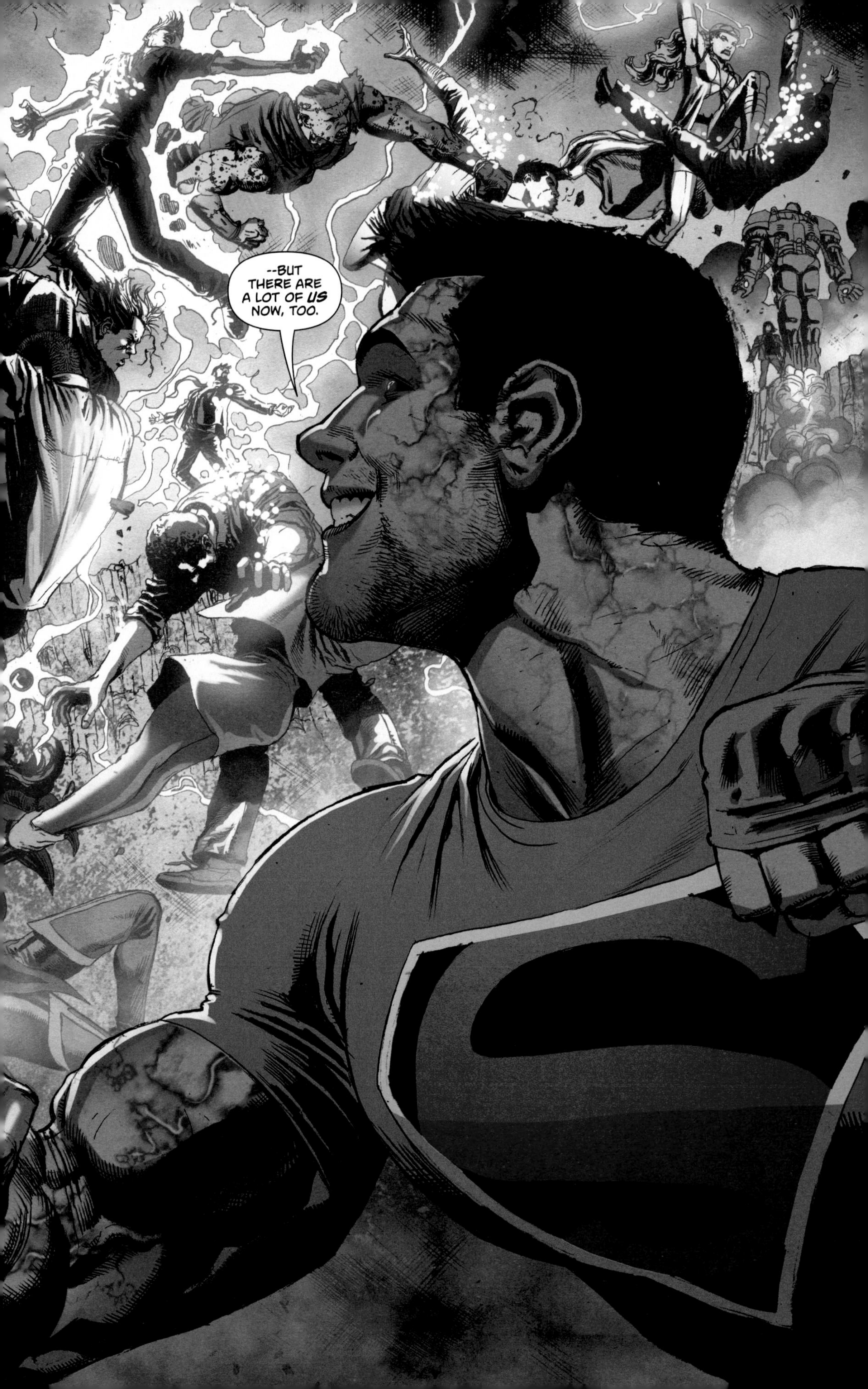
--BUT THERE ARE A LOT OF *US* NOW, TOO.

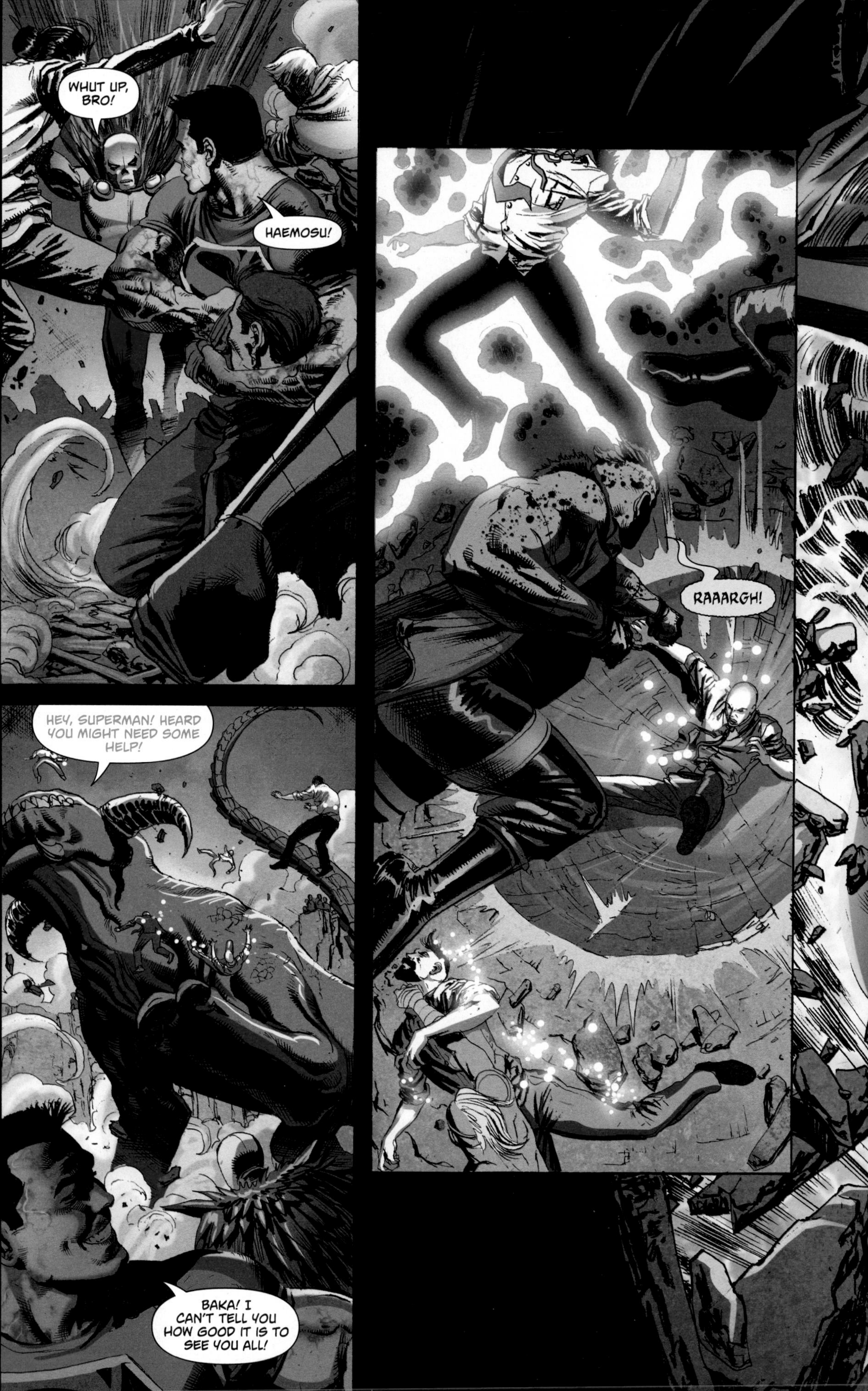
WHUT UP, BRO!
HAEMOSU!
RAAARGH!
HEY, SUPERMAN! HEARD YOU MIGHT NEED SOME HELP!
BAKA! I CAN'T TELL YOU HOW GOOD IT IS TO SEE YOU ALL!

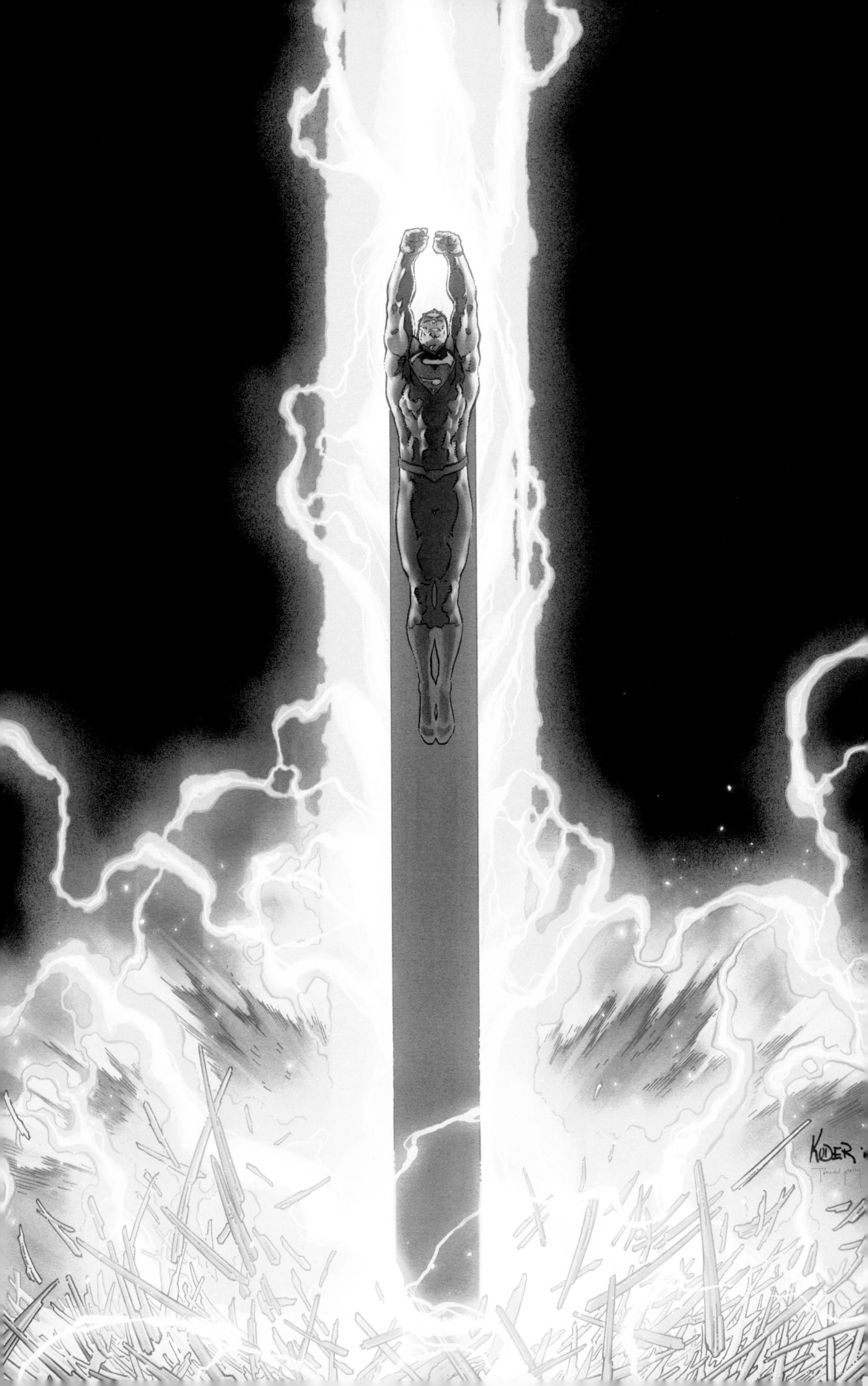

RESURRECTION

GREK PAK AARON KUDER writers AARON KUDER layouts AARON KUDER DAVID MESSINA JAVI FERNANDEZ BRUNO REDONDO VICENTE CIFUENTES pencillers
AARON KUDER GAETANO CARLUCCI JUAN ALBARRAN JAVI FERNANDEZ VICENTE CIFUENTES inkers TOMEU MOREY ARIF PRIANTO WIL QUINTANA colorists
STEVE WANDS letterer AARON KUDER TOMEU MOREY cover

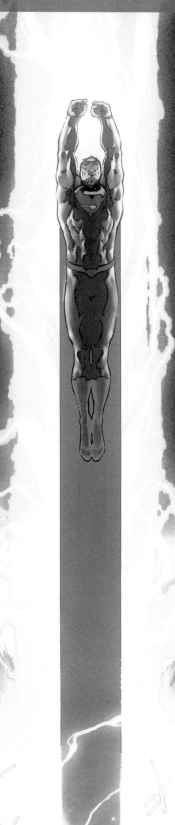

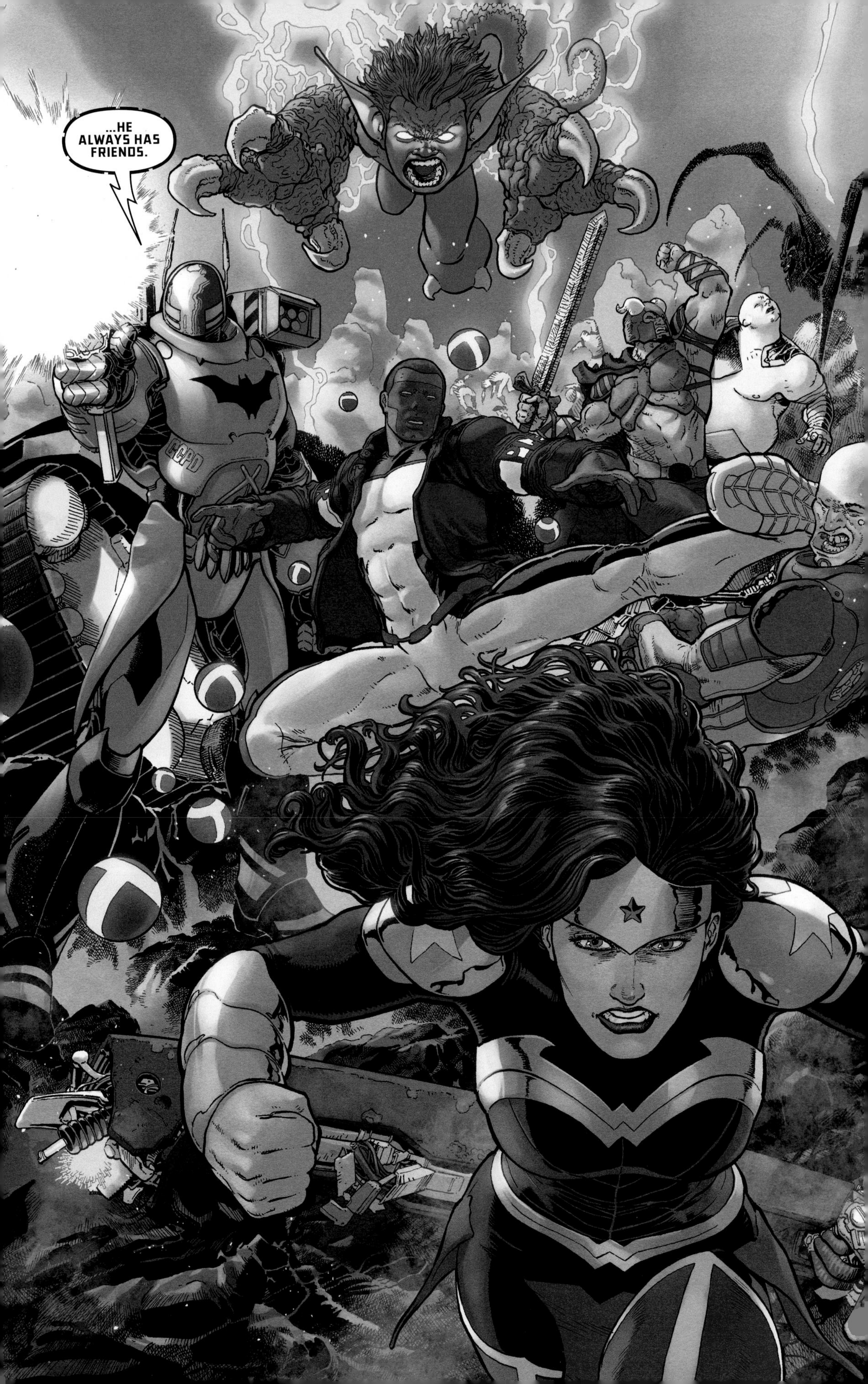
...HE ALWAYS HAS FRIENDS.

VANDAL DRAINED MY POWERS...

GRRRAAAA!

BRAAKOO MOOO

THERE'S NO WAY THESE LAST FEW HEROES SHOULD BE ABLE TO FIGHT HIM.

BOOOM

BOOOM

...TOOK OUT THE JUSTICE LEAGUE...

KTHOOOOM

...AND SHIFTED THE MOONS OF JUPITER WITH ONE BLAST FROM HIS MASSIVE WARSHIP.

BBOOOM

BUT NO ONE TOLD **THEM** THAT.

KKKRRAAAOOOOOM

HNH.

THEY CLEARED THE WAY...

HA.

BOOM!!

A CRACKLING BLITZ OF INFORMATION SURGES THROUGH MY BRAIN--

...BUT THEY'RE ALL ALIVE.

--VITAL INFORMATION FROM EACH OF THEIR CONTAINMENT UNITS--

--THEY'RE INJURED... WEAK... BARELY CONSCIOUS...

LANA!

AH, CLARK!

I KNEW YOU'D MAKE IT!

BUT... ...WHAT HAVE YOU DONE TO YOURSELF?

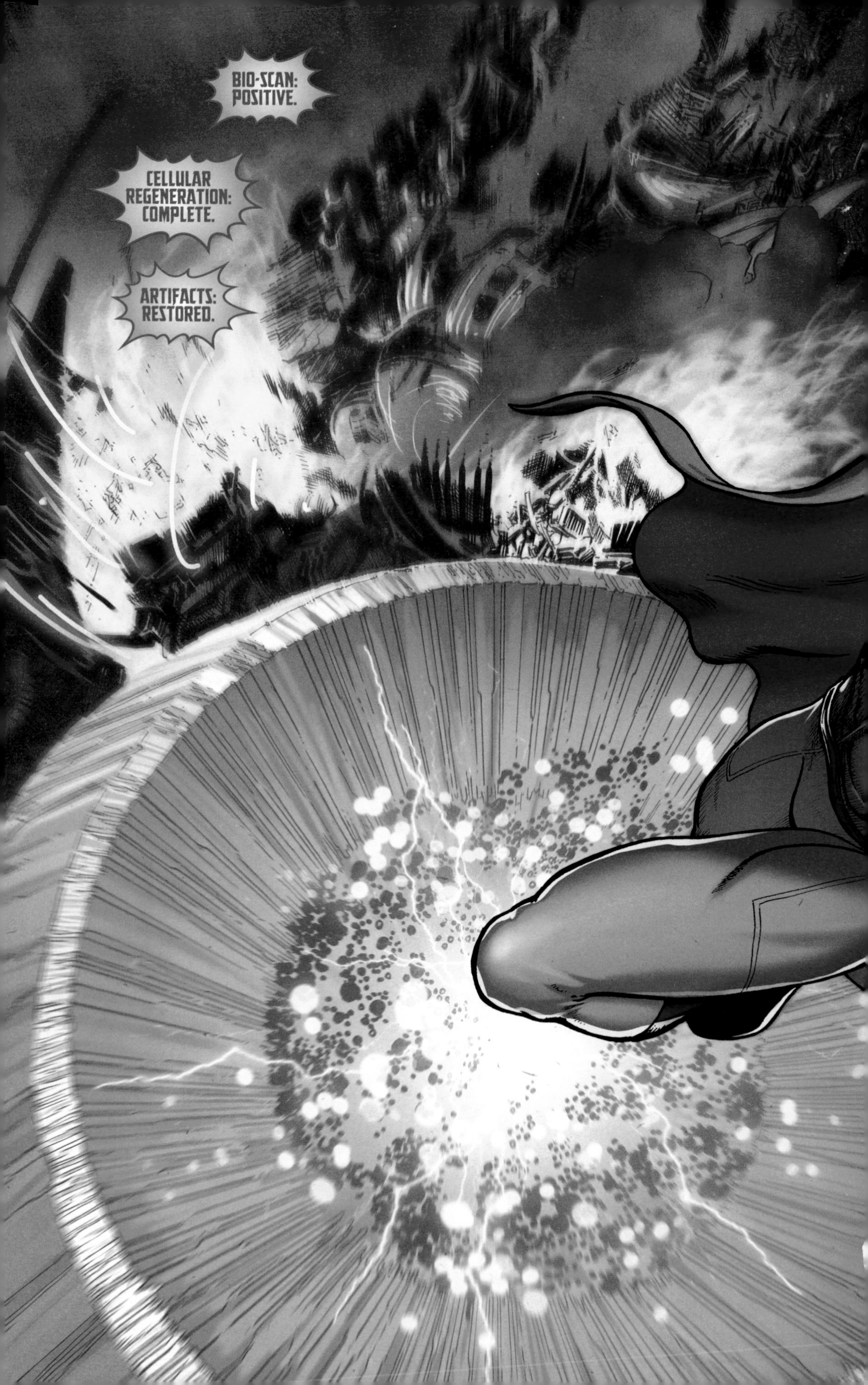
BIO-SCAN: POSITIVE.
CELLULAR REGENERATION: COMPLETE.
ARTIFACTS: RESTORED.

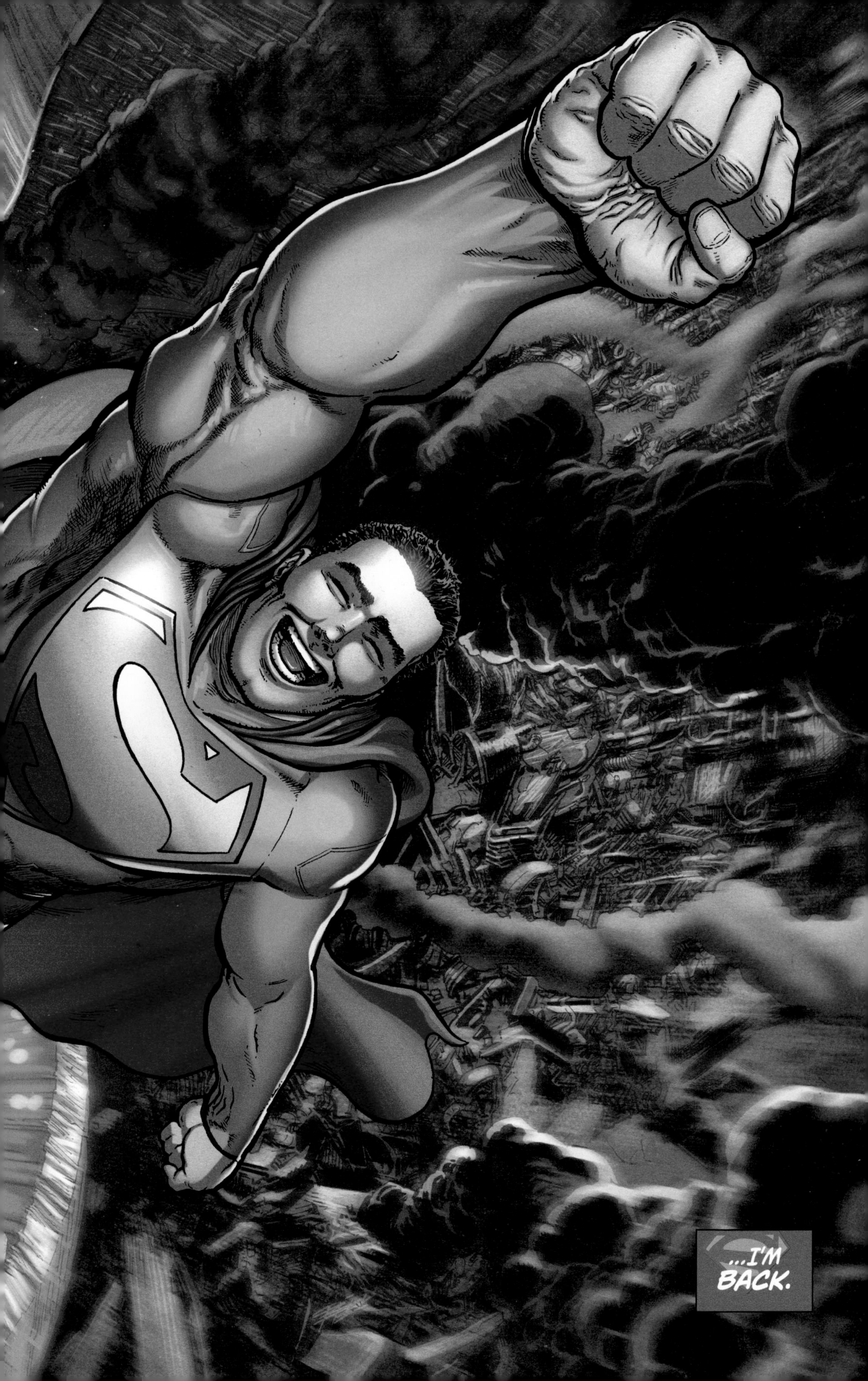
...I'M
BACK.

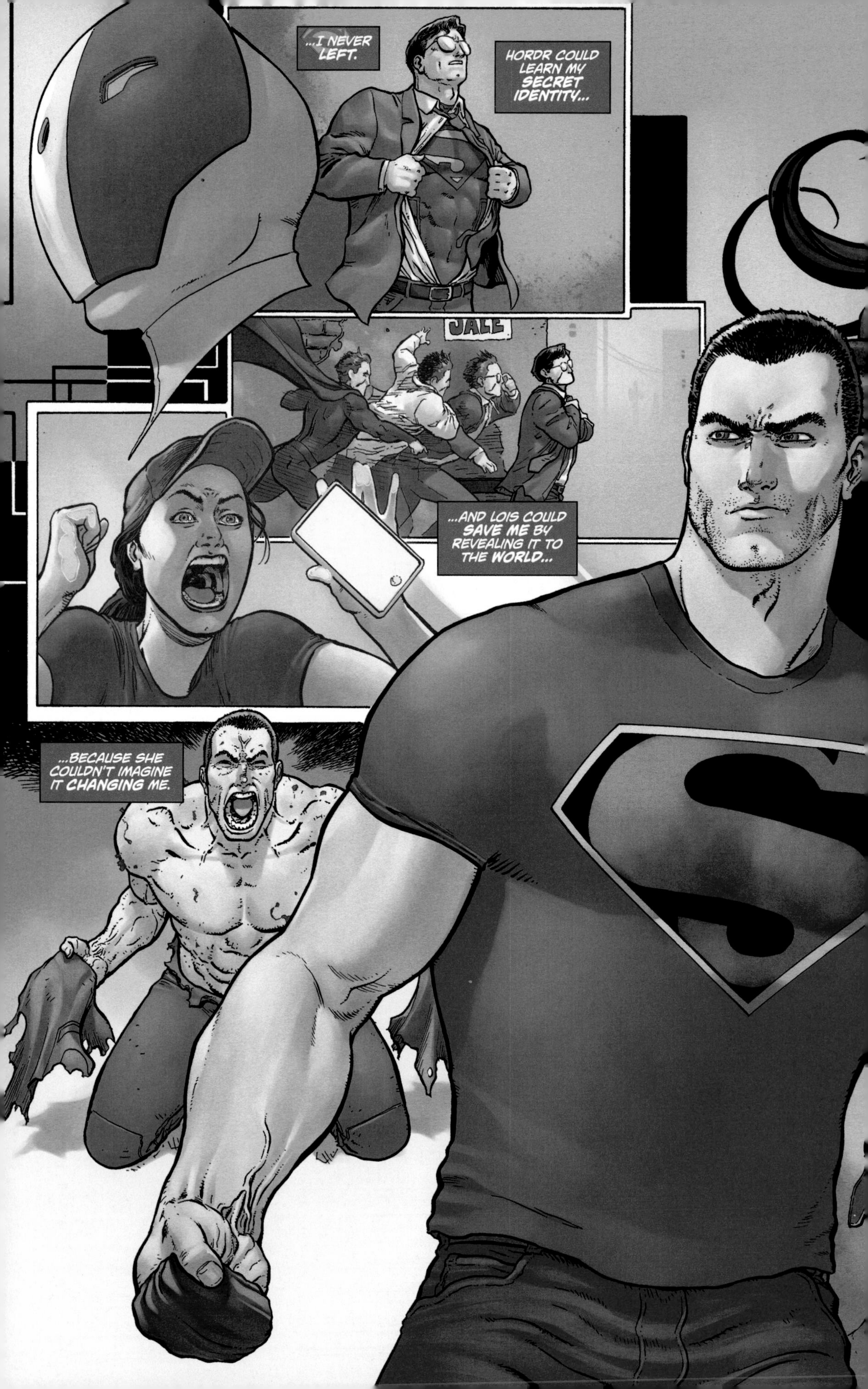
...I NEVER LEFT.
HORDR COULD LEARN MY SECRET IDENTITY...
SALE
...AND LOIS COULD SAVE ME BY REVEALING IT TO THE WORLD...
...BECAUSE SHE COULDN'T IMAGINE IT CHANGING ME.

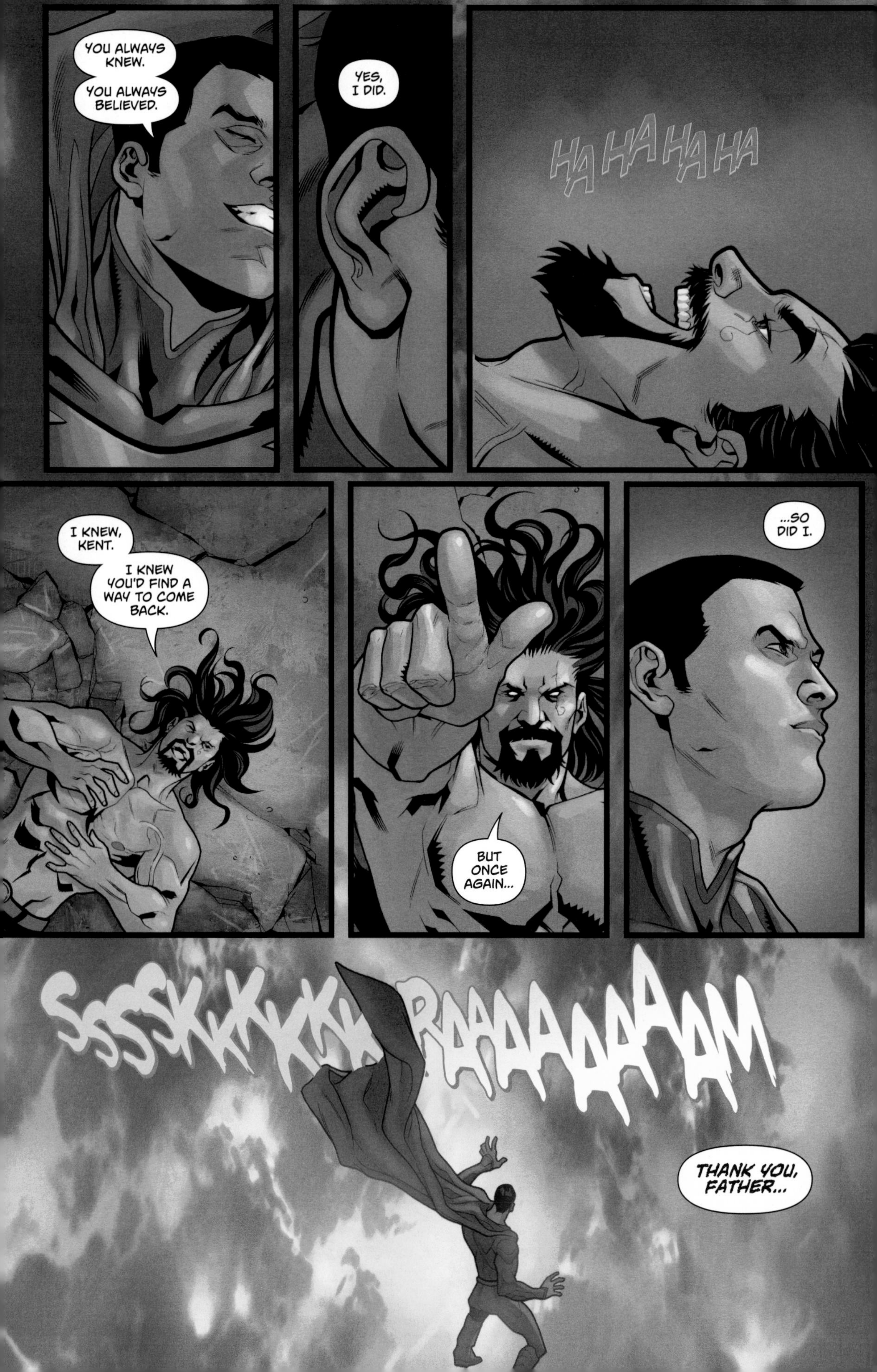
YOU ALWAYS KNEW.
YOU ALWAYS BELIEVED.
YES, I DID.
HA HA HA HA
I KNEW, KENT.
I KNEW YOU'D FIND A WAY TO COME BACK.
BUT ONCE AGAIN...
...SO DID I.
SSSSKKKKKRAAAAAAAAM
THANK YOU, FATHER...

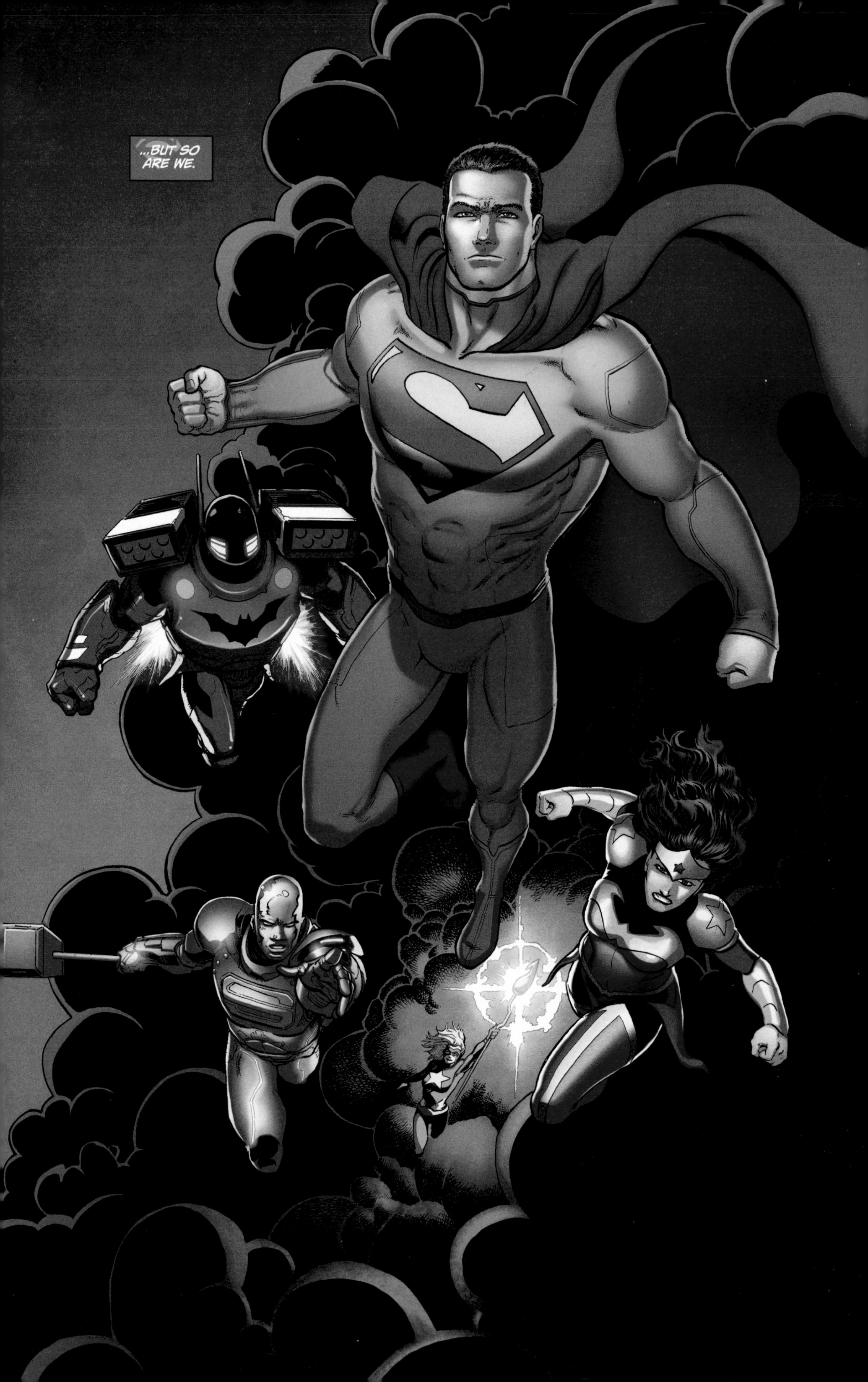
...BUT SO ARE WE.

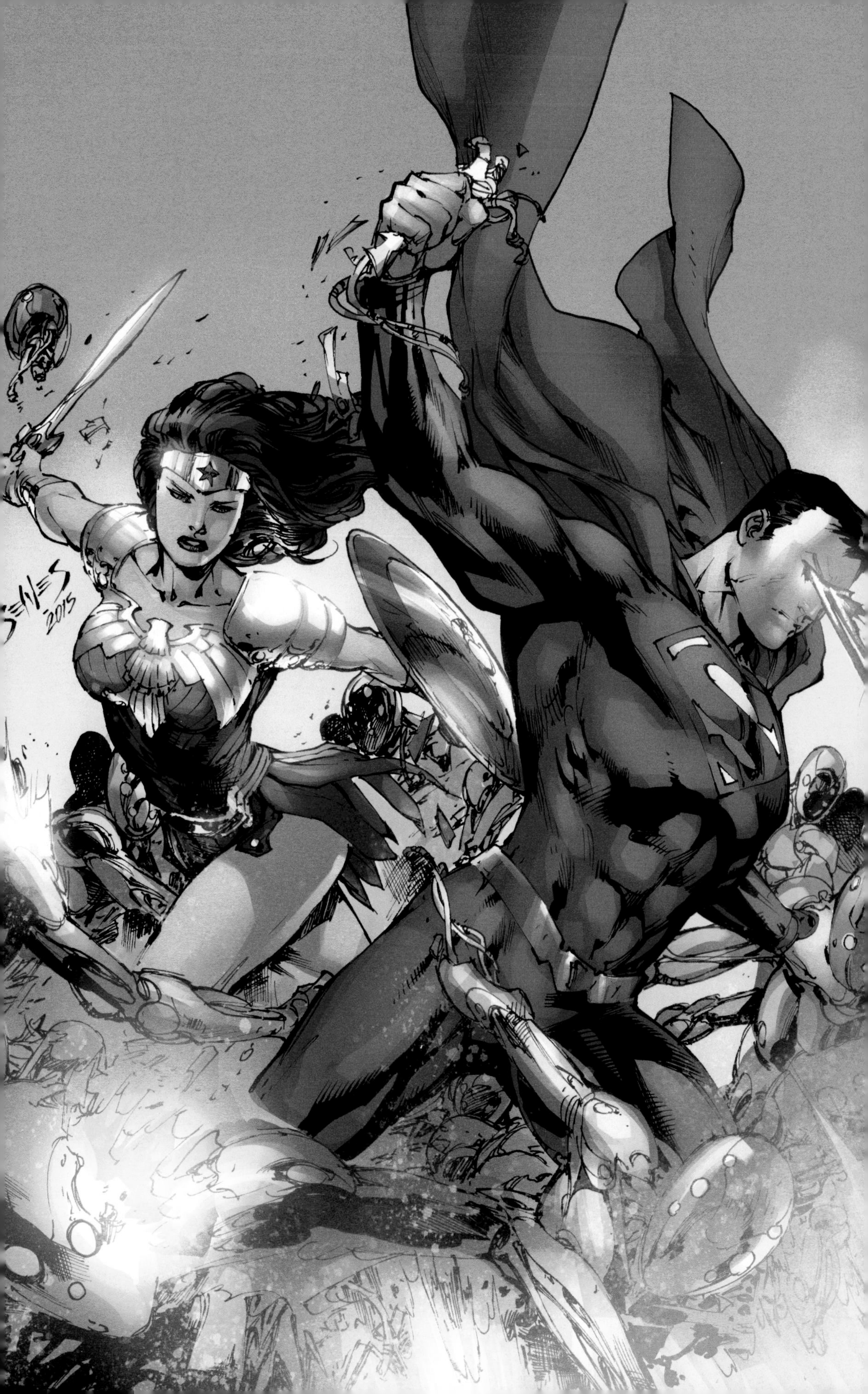

SLAM BANG

PETER J. TOMASI writer **CLIFF RICHARDS** artist **WIL QUINTANA** colorist **ROB LEIGH** letterer **ED BENES ALEX SINCLAIR** cover

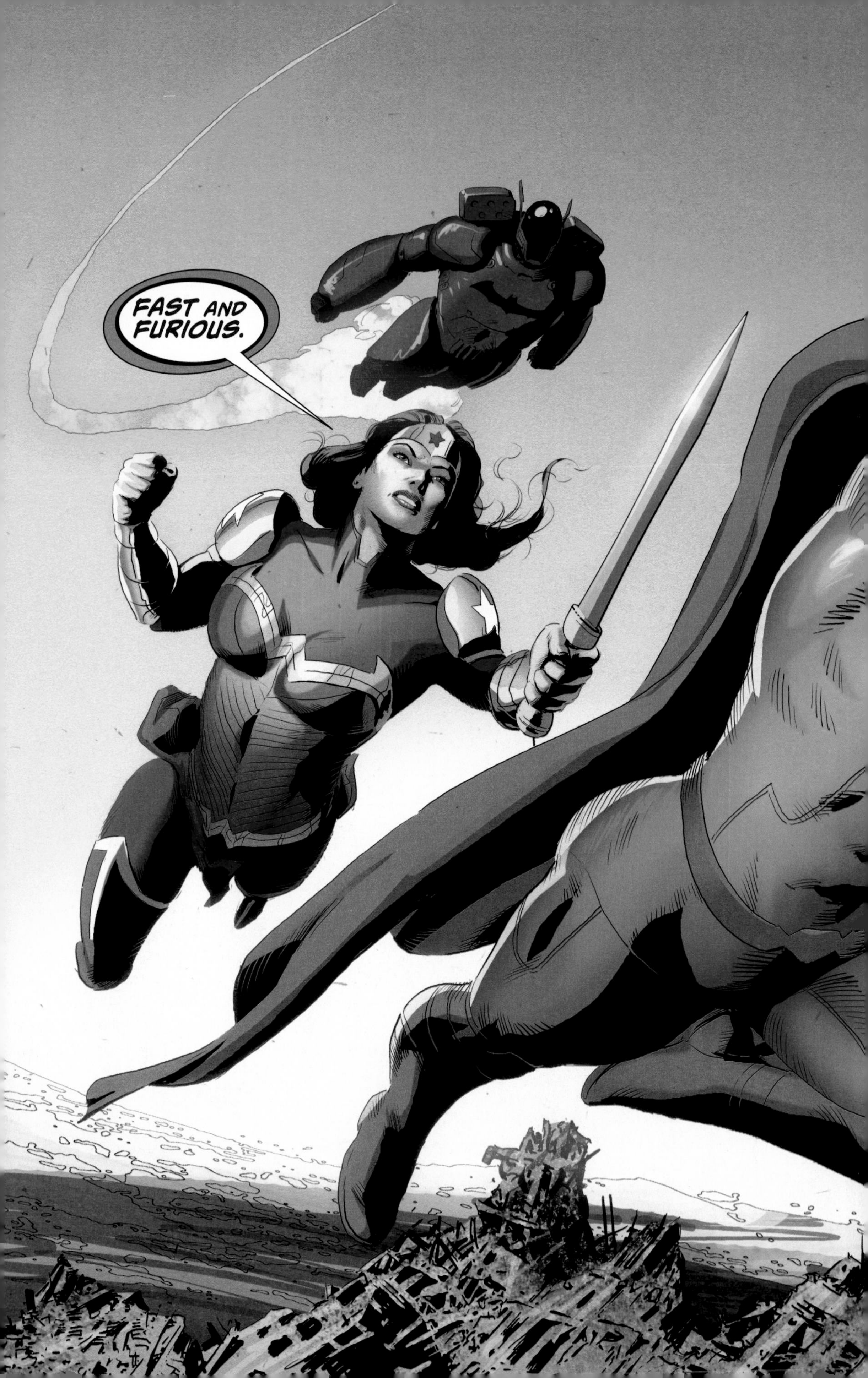
FAST AND FURIOUS.

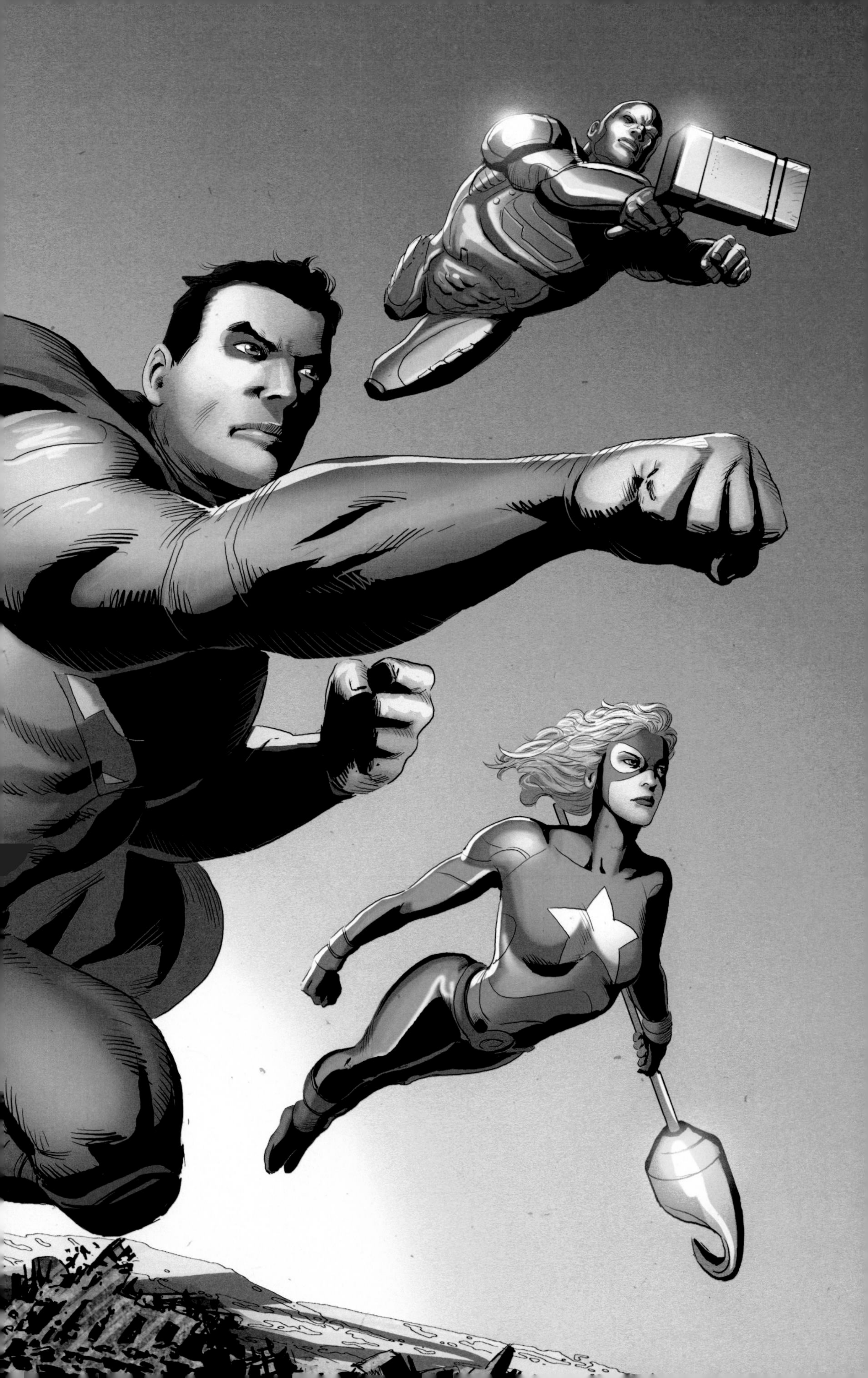

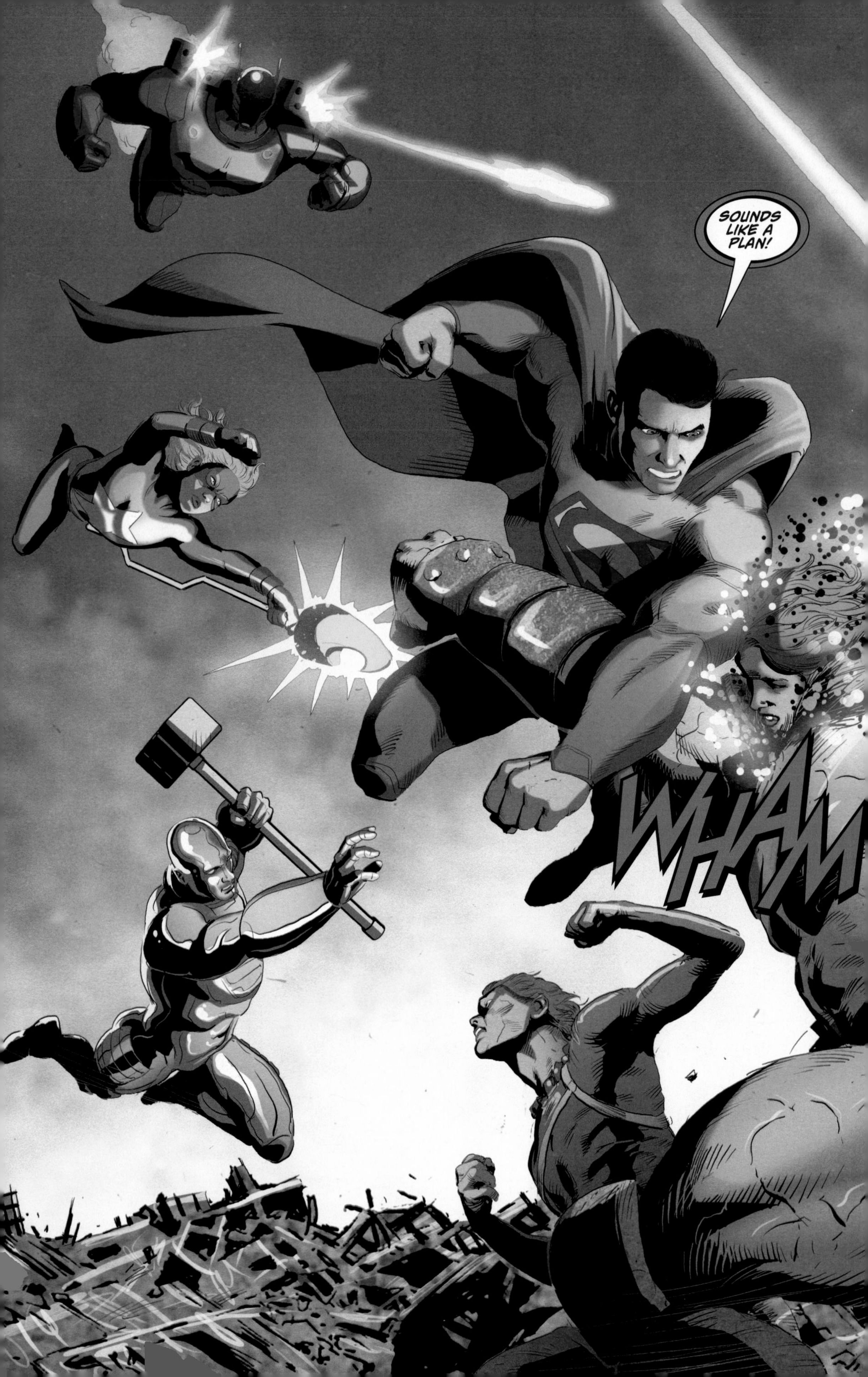
SOUNDS LIKE A PLAN!
WHAM

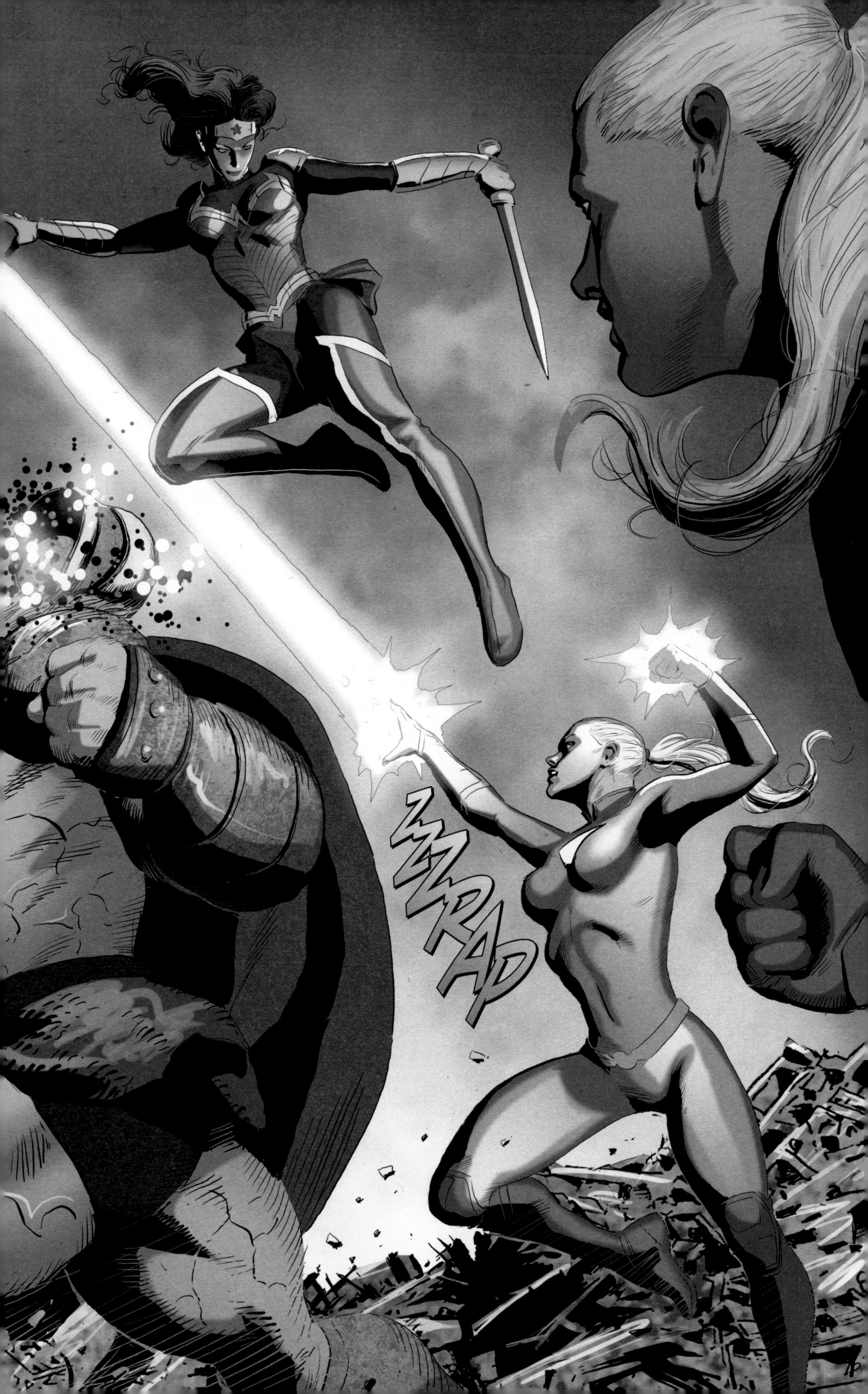
ZZZRAP

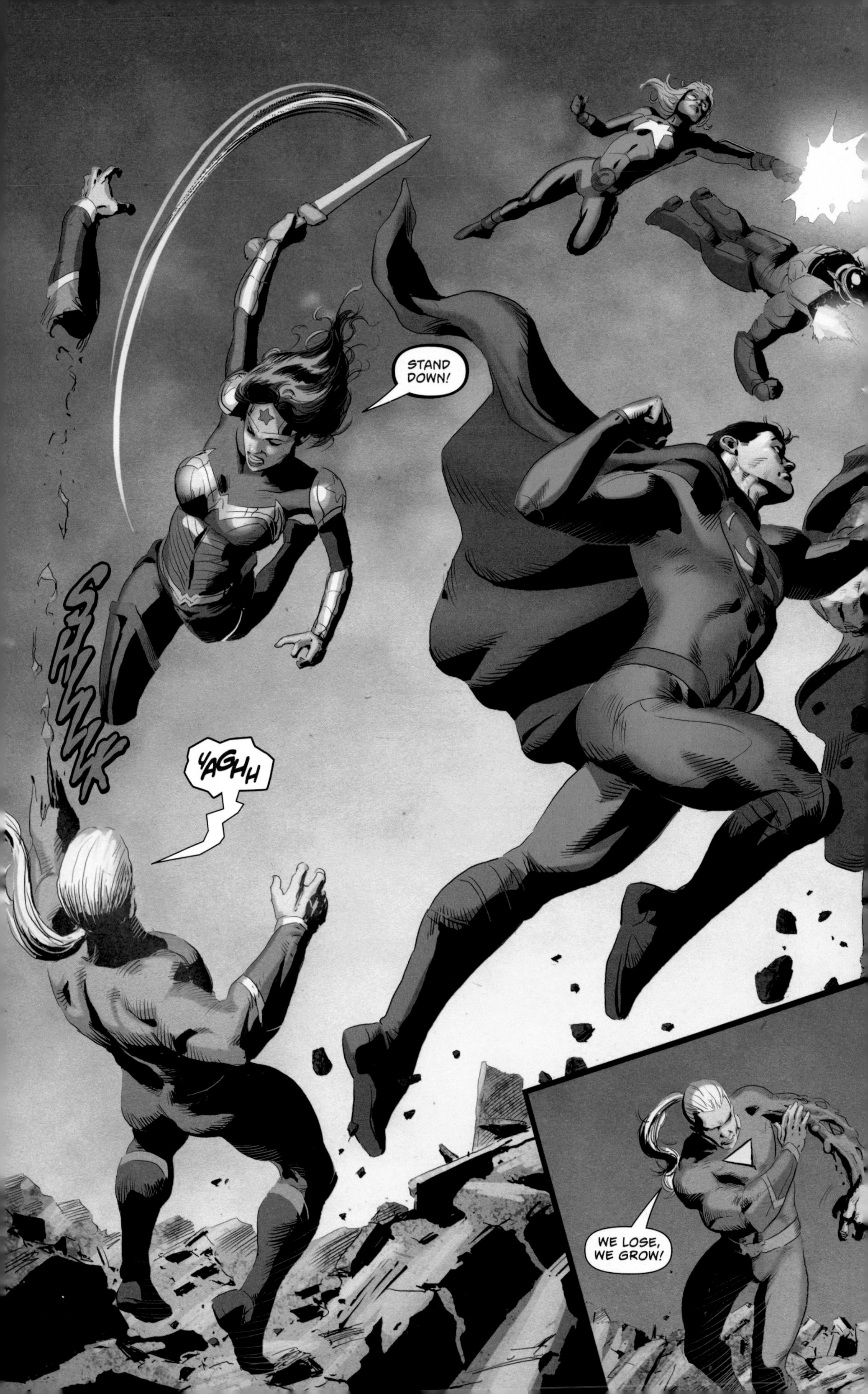
STAND DOWN!
SHHNNK
YAGHH
WE LOSE, WE GROW!

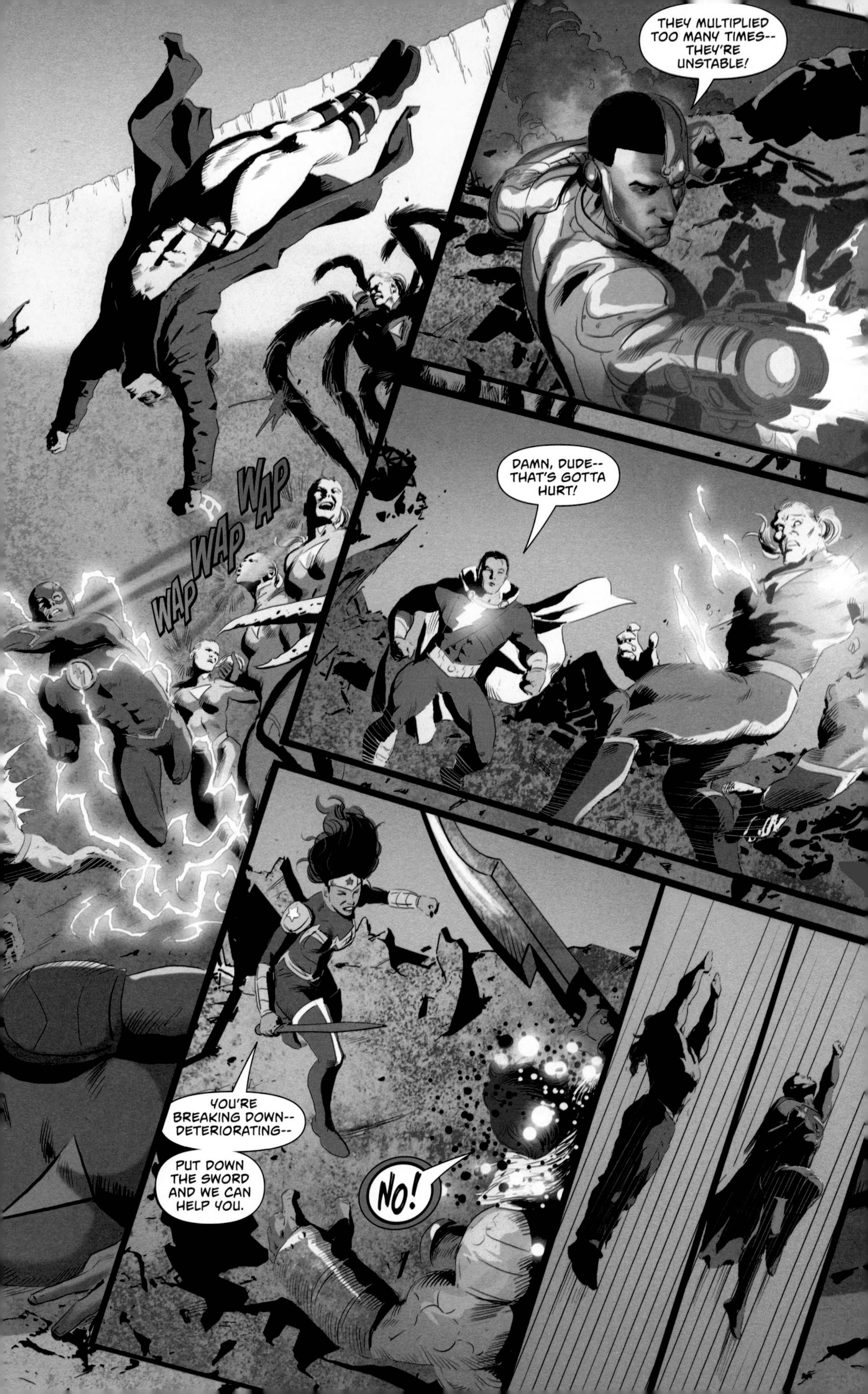
WAP
WAP
WAP
THEY MULTIPLIED TOO MANY TIMES-- THEY'RE UNSTABLE!
DAMN, DUDE-- THAT'S GOTTA HURT!
YOU'RE BREAKING DOWN-- DETERIORATING--
PUT DOWN THE SWORD AND WE CAN HELP YOU.
NO!

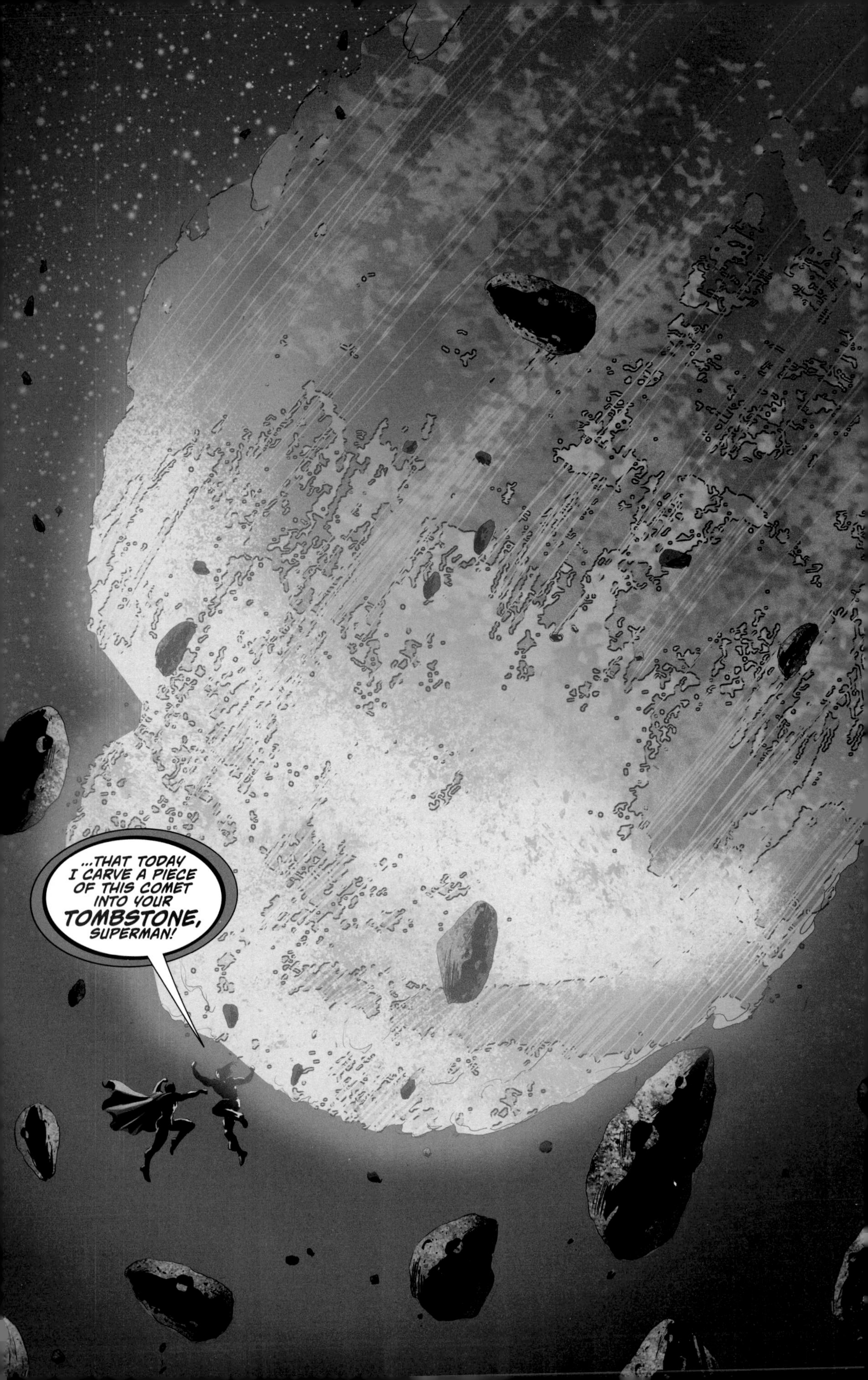
...THAT TODAY I CARVE A PIECE OF THIS COMET INTO YOUR TOMBSTONE, SUPERMAN!

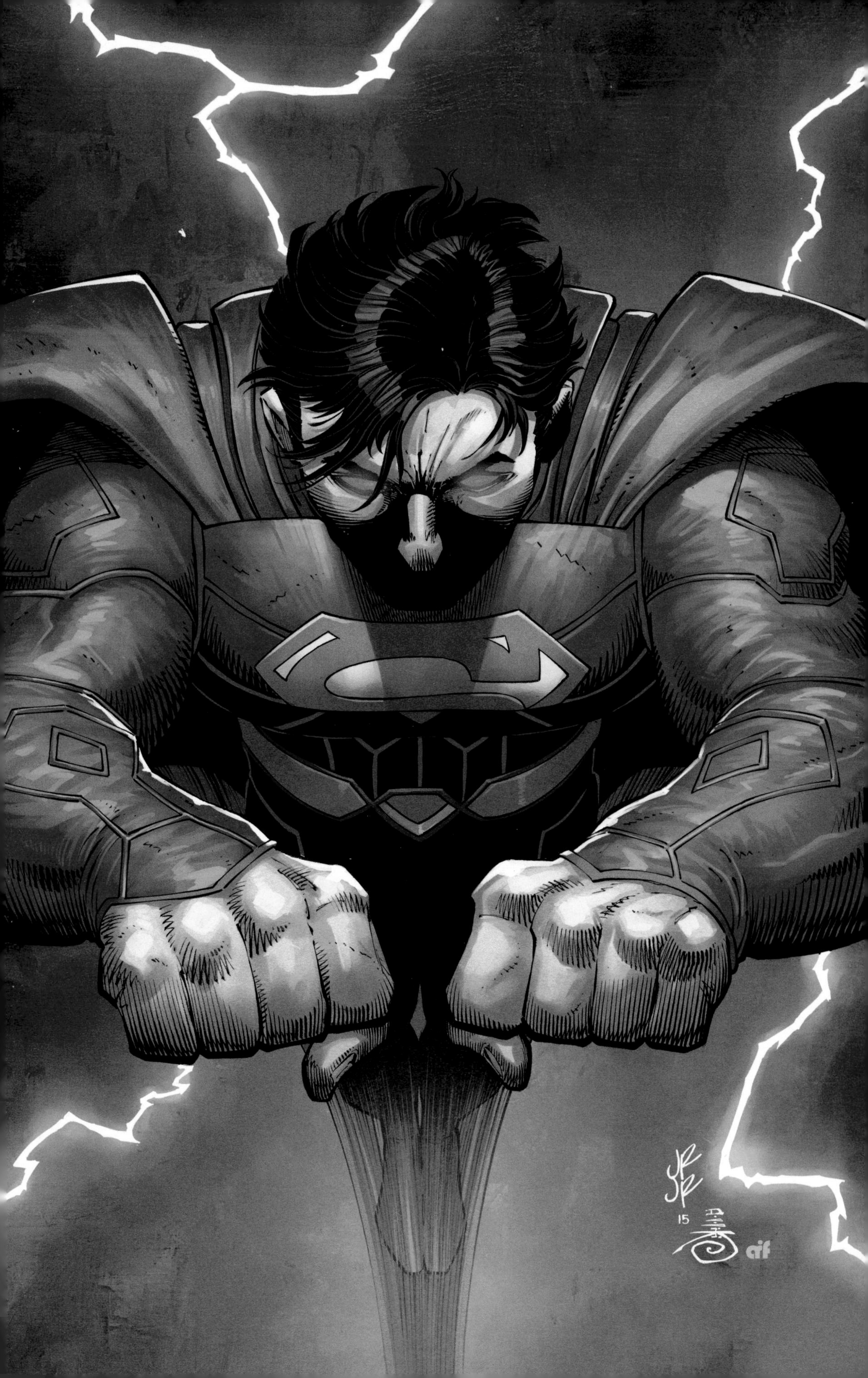

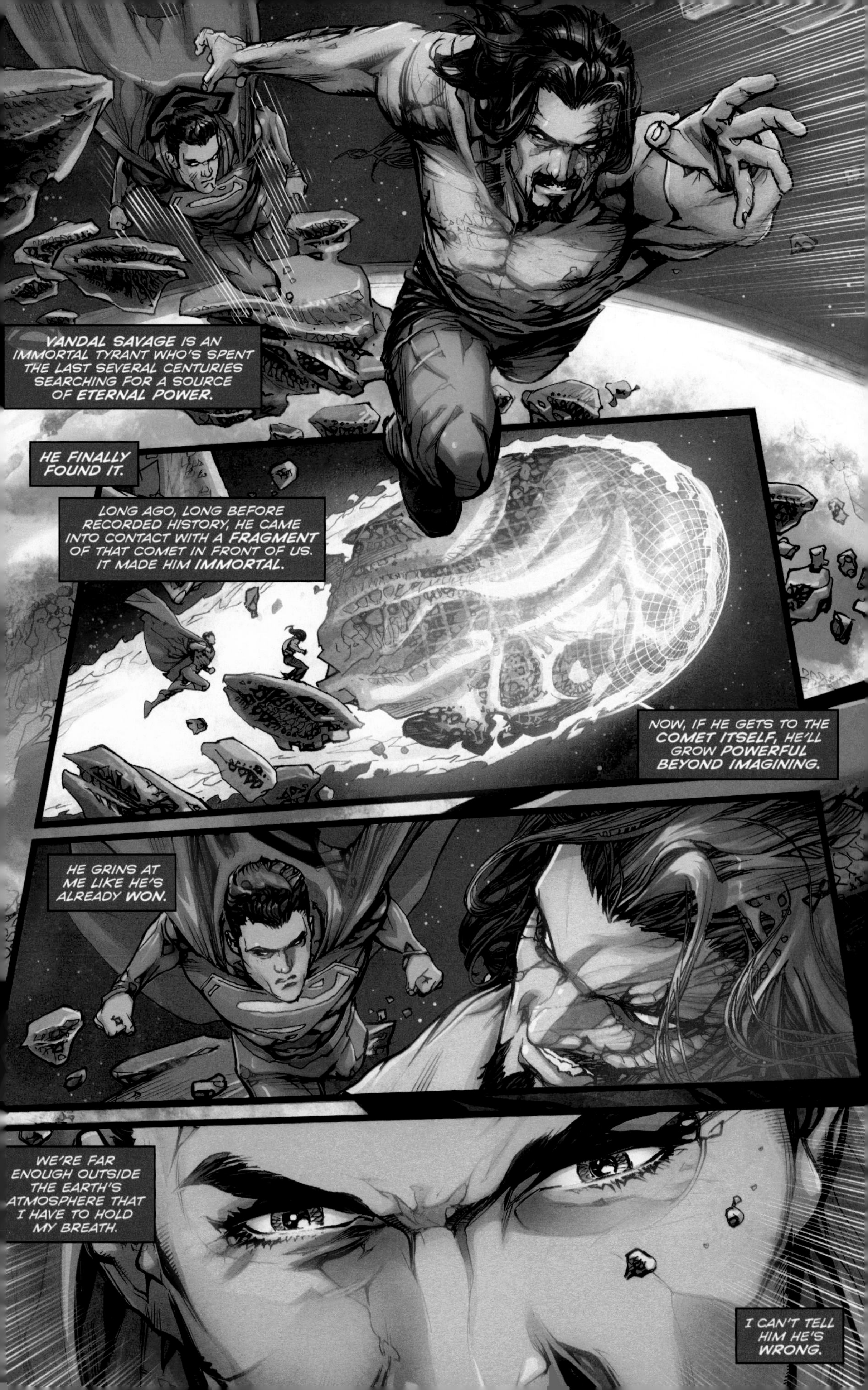
VANDAL SAVAGE IS AN IMMORTAL TYRANT WHO'S SPENT THE LAST SEVERAL CENTURIES SEARCHING FOR A SOURCE OF ETERNAL POWER.
HE FINALLY FOUND IT.
LONG AGO, LONG BEFORE RECORDED HISTORY, HE CAME INTO CONTACT WITH A FRAGMENT OF THAT COMET IN FRONT OF US. IT MADE HIM IMMORTAL.
NOW, IF HE GETS TO THE COMET ITSELF, HE'LL GROW POWERFUL BEYOND IMAGINING.
HE GRINS AT ME LIKE HE'S ALREADY WON.
WE'RE FAR ENOUGH OUTSIDE THE EARTH'S ATMOSPHERE THAT I HAVE TO HOLD MY BREATH.
I CAN'T TELL HIM HE'S WRONG.

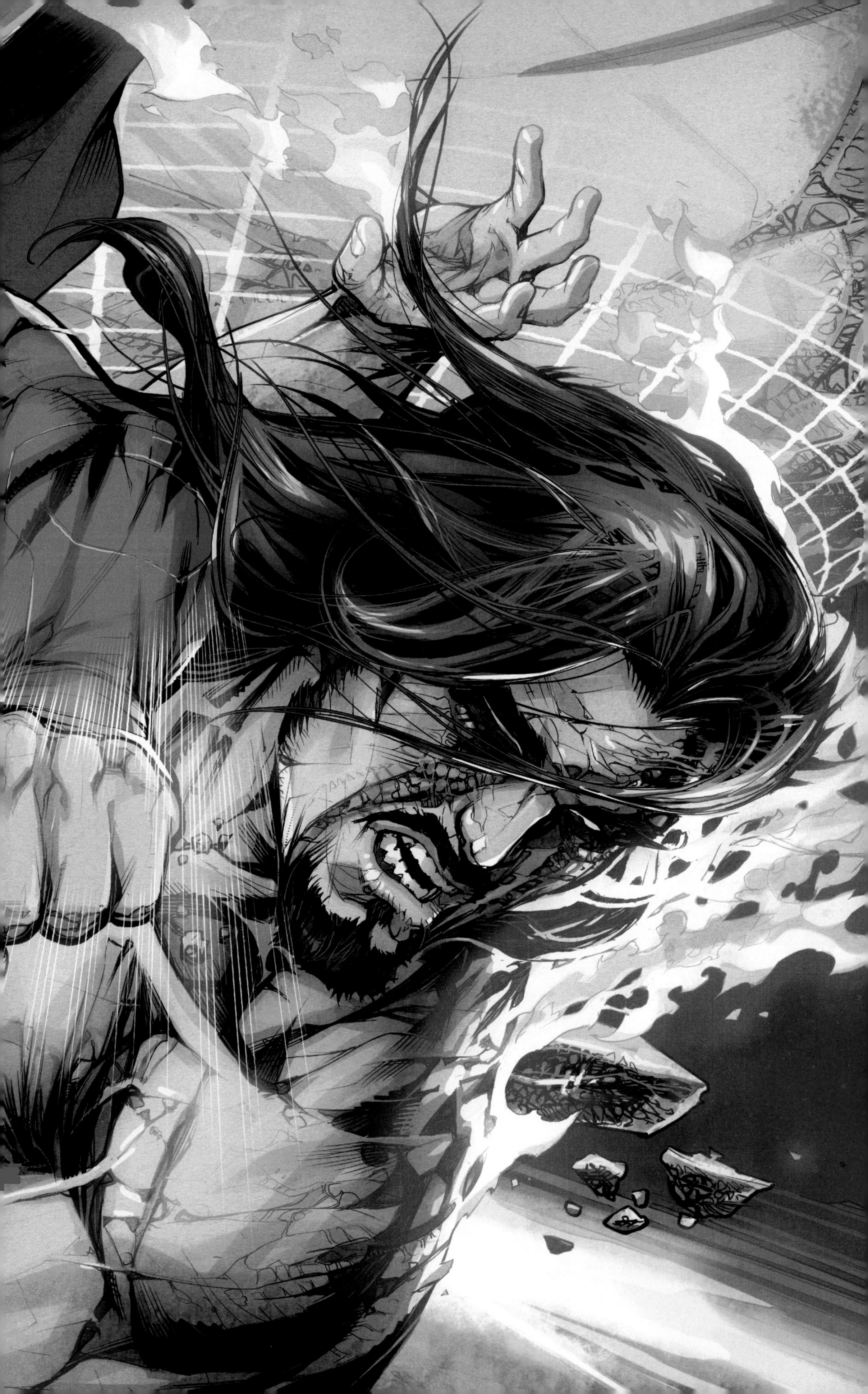

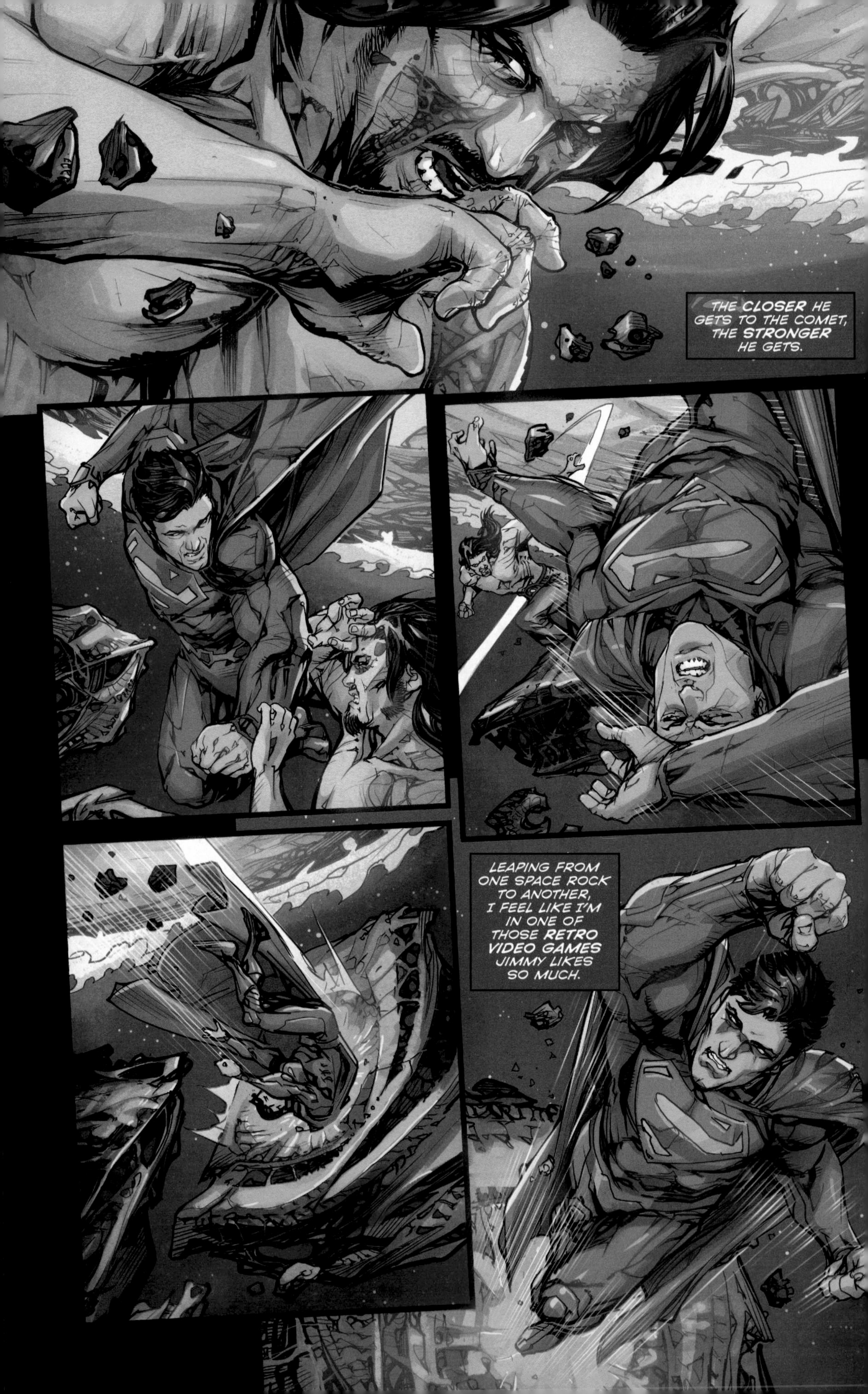
THE CLOSER HE GETS TO THE COMET, THE STRONGER HE GETS.
LEAPING FROM ONE SPACE ROCK TO ANOTHER, I FEEL LIKE I'M IN ONE OF THOSE RETRO VIDEO GAMES JIMMY LIKES SO MUCH.

KRoooSH

EVEN WITH MY POWERS BACK, THE IMPACT KNOCK'S THE WIND RIGHT OUT OF ME. I NEED A MOMENT TO CATCH MY BREATH.

Ngh

≈Huff huff huff≈

I CAN'T DECIDE WHICH IS GREATER: MY ADMIRATION FOR YOU--

KRUSH!

THAT LITTLE BOY...THAT'S ME.

Y-YOU SAVED OUR LIVES, STRANGER!

YOUR SON--!

YES, OUR LITTLE *KAL-EL.* BECAUSE OF YOU, HE'S *SAFE!*

THANK *RAO* YOU WERE HERE, MISTER!

"RAO"...?! KAL-EL, WHERE DID YOU LEARN THAT?! YOU KNOW THOSE ANCIENT SUPERSTITIONS ARE *FORBIDDEN!* THERE IS ONLY THE *HIGH CHIEF!*

I'M *SORRY,* MAMA. I M-MEANT THANK THE *HIGH CHIEF* HE WAS HERE.

THAT'S EXACTLY *RIGHT!* SURELY IT WAS *NO COINCIDENCE* THAT THIS MAN WAS IN OUR HOME AT THE *EXACT* RIGHT TIME!

THE HIGH CHIEF MUST HAVE KNOWN WE'D BE IN TROUBLE AND SENT HIM TO *SAVE US!*

ALL PRAISE TO THE HIGH CHIEF!

NO, NO ONE *SENT* ME. I'M NOT SURE HOW I GOT HERE. THIS WILL SEEM STRANGE TO YOU, BUT I CAME THROUGH THE *ROCKET SHIP* IN YOUR WORKSHOP.

THIS DOESN'T MAKE SENSE. BY THE TIME I WAS OLD ENOUGH TO TALK, I WASN'T ON *KRYPTON* ANYMORE. I WAS IN *KANSAS.* THIS *CAN'T* BE MY PAST.

THE ROCKET SHIP...?

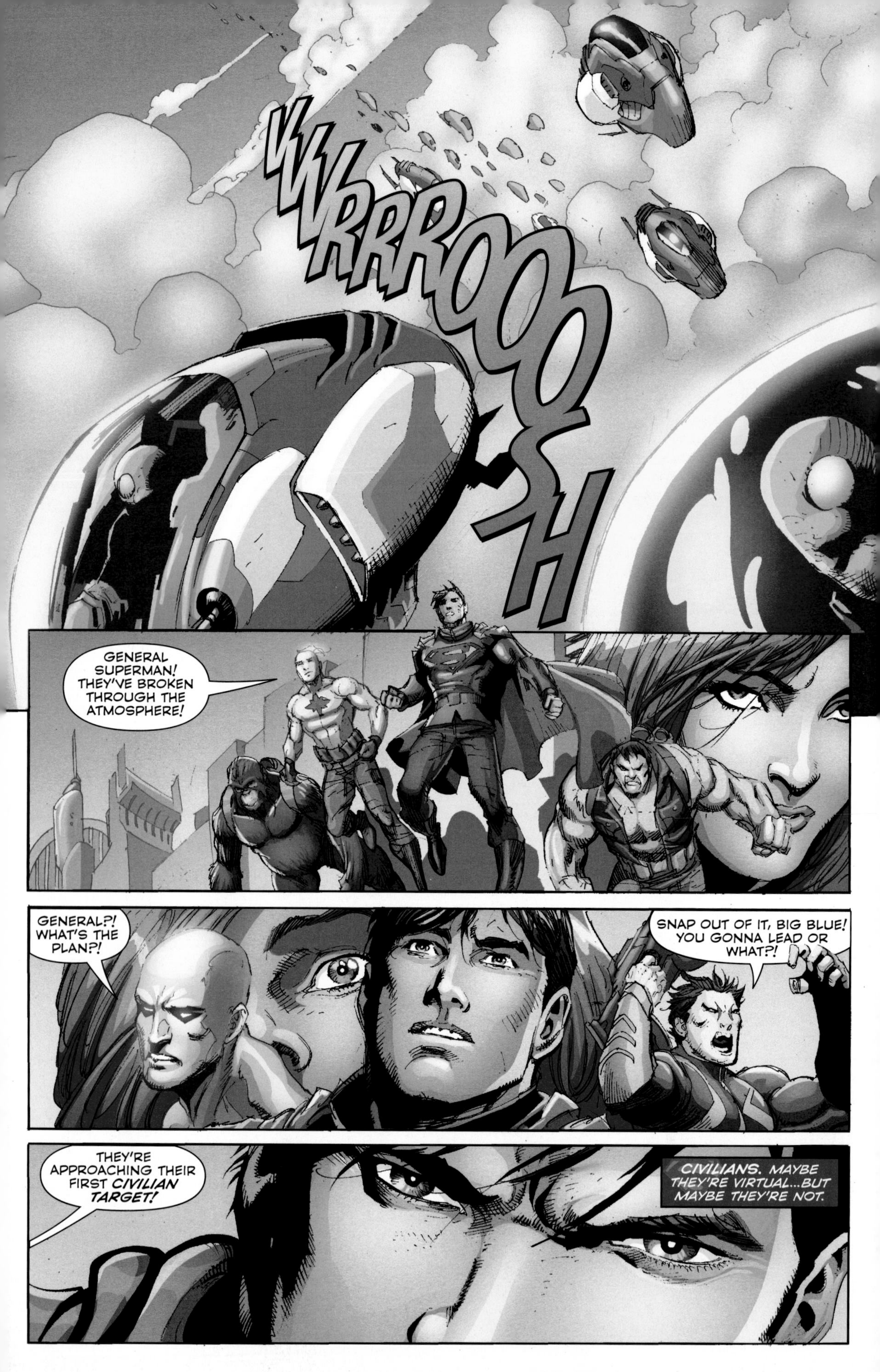
VVVRRROOOOOSHH
GENERAL SUPERMAN! THEY'VE BROKEN THROUGH THE ATMOSPHERE!
GENERAL?! WHAT'S THE PLAN?!
SNAP OUT OF IT, BIG BLUE! YOU GONNA LEAD OR WHAT?!
THEY'RE APPROACHING THEIR FIRST CIVILIAN TARGET!
CIVILIANS. MAYBE THEY'RE VIRTUAL...BUT MAYBE THEY'RE NOT.

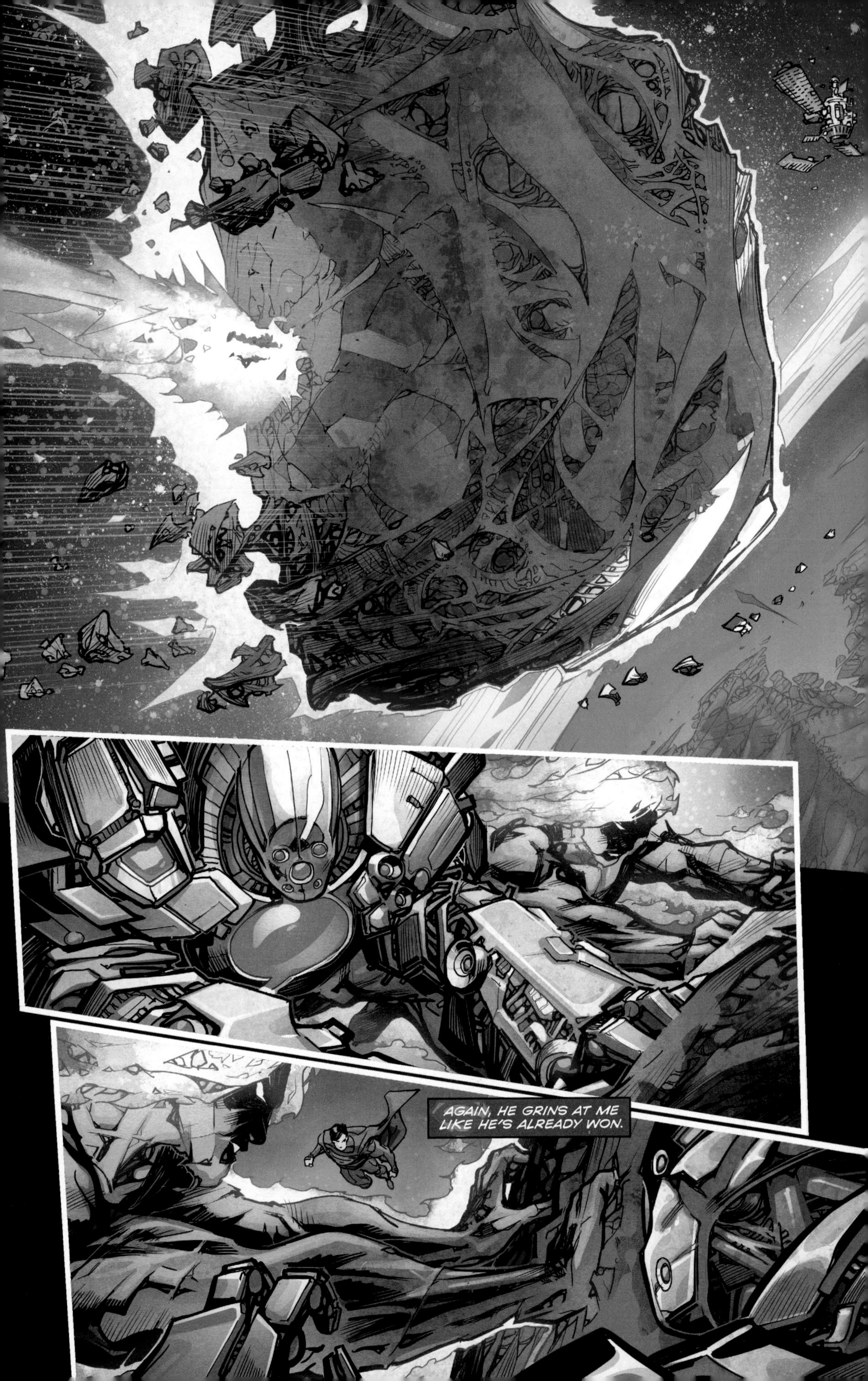
AGAIN, HE GRINS AT ME
LIKE HE'S ALREADY WON.

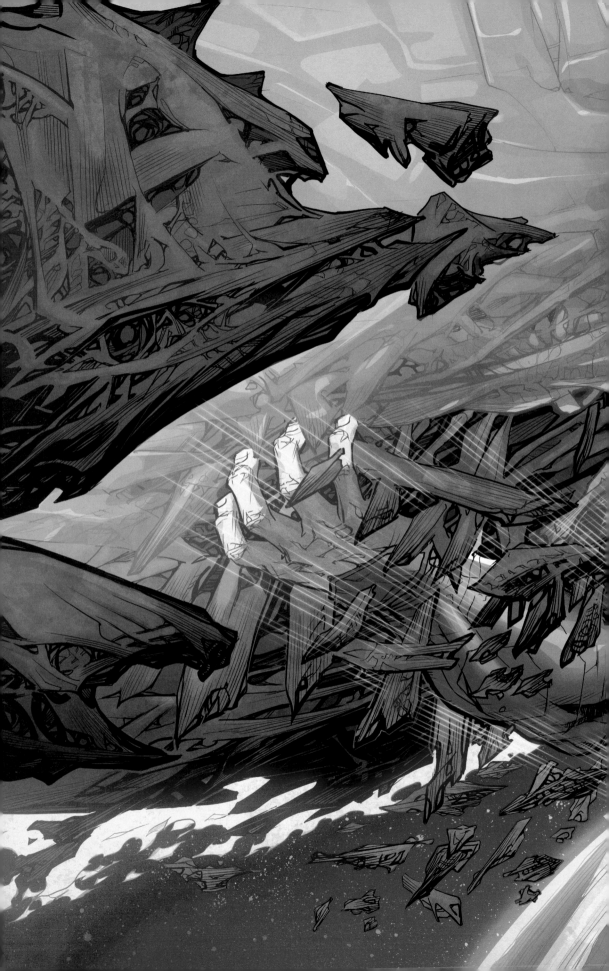

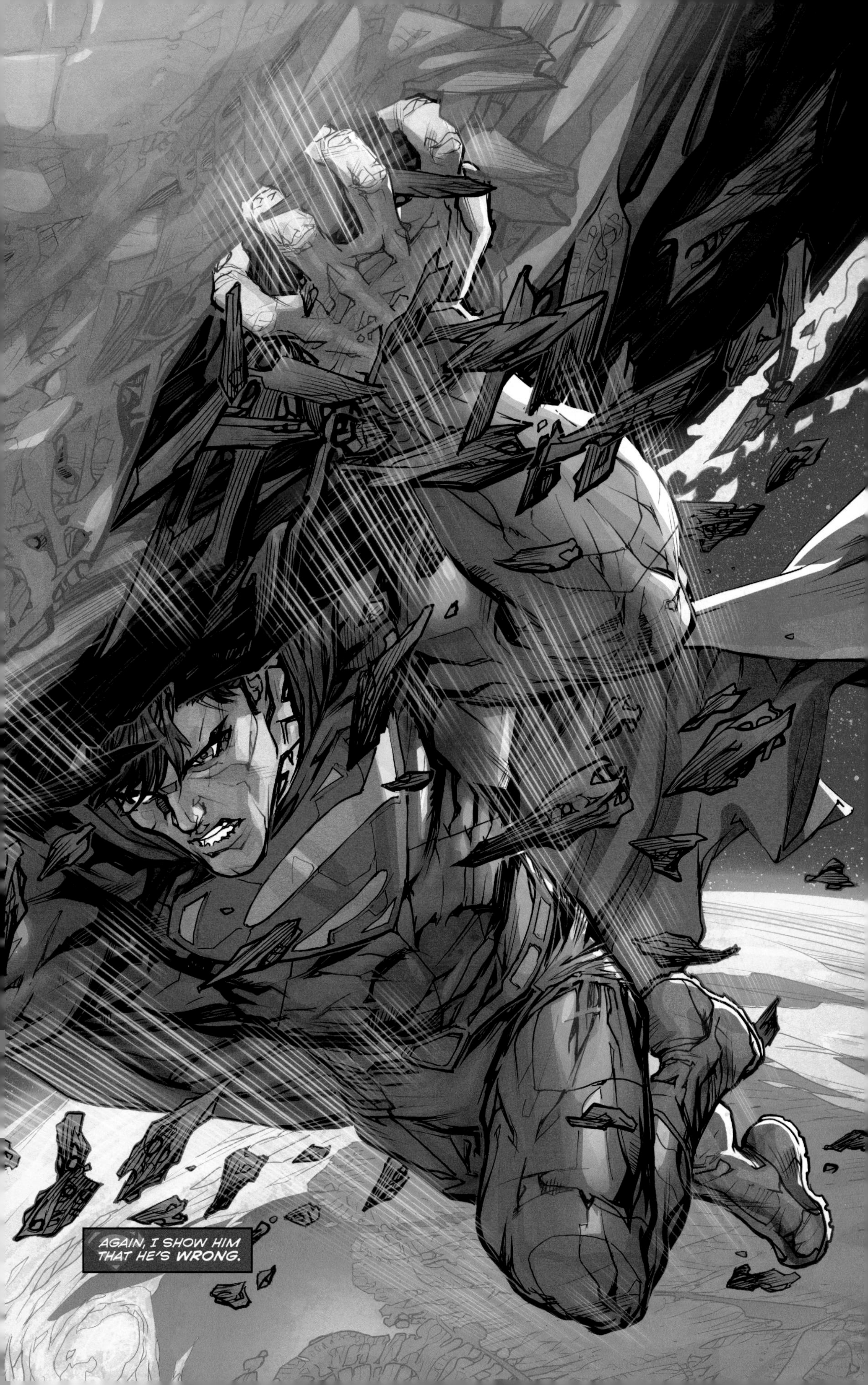
AGAIN, I SHOW HIM THAT HE'S WRONG.

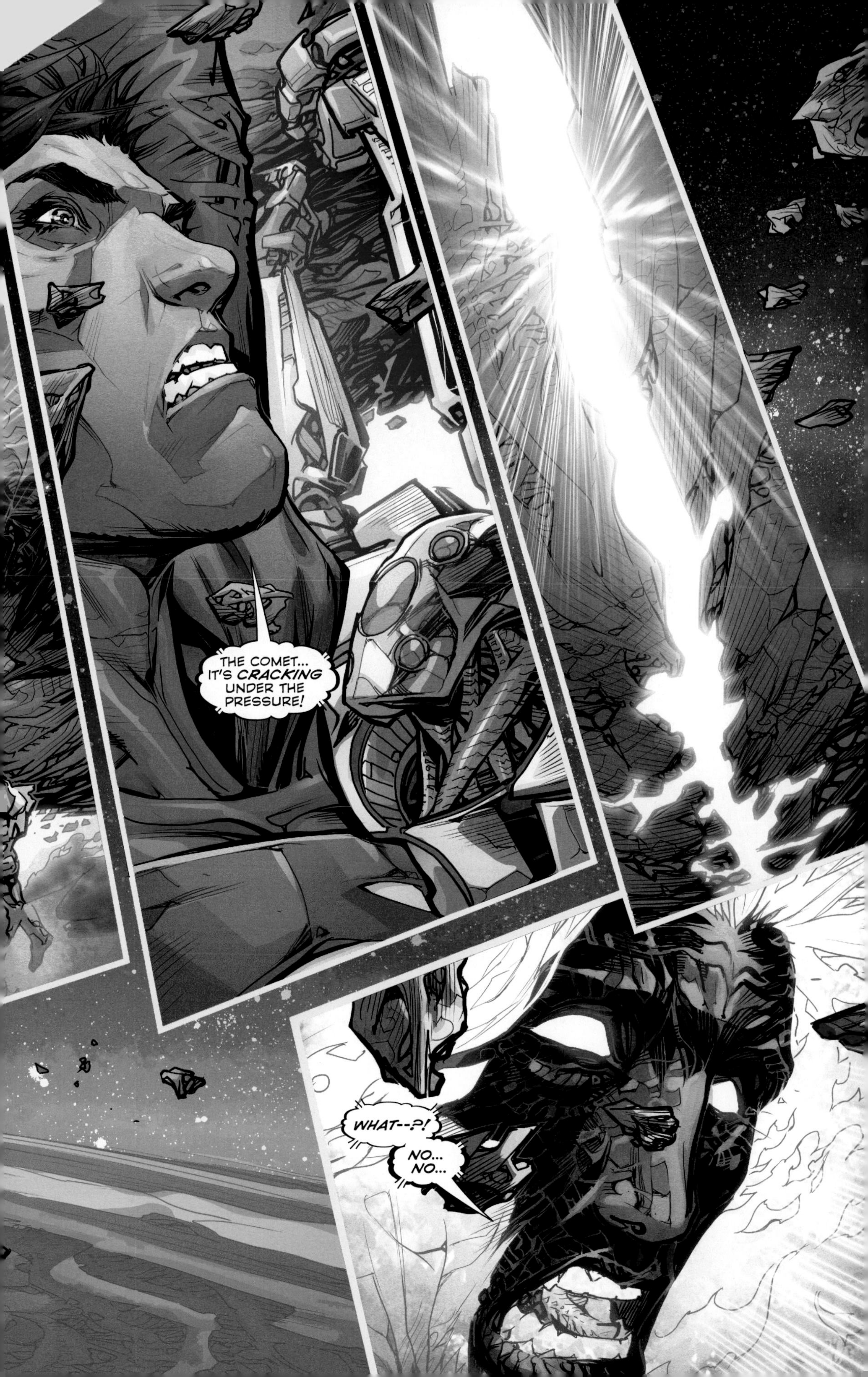
THE COMET... IT'S CRACKING UNDER THE PRESSURE!
WHAT--?!
NO... NO...

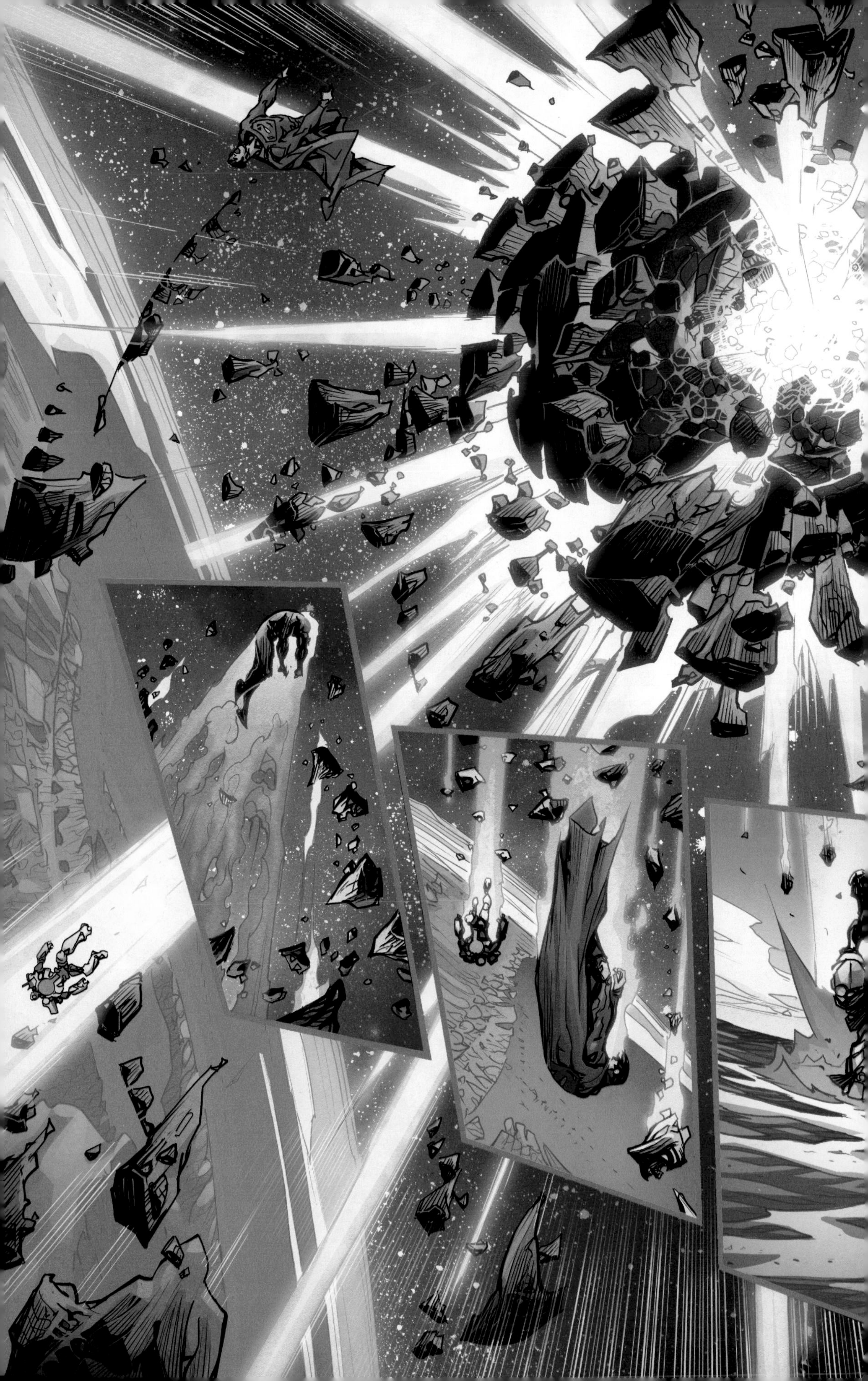

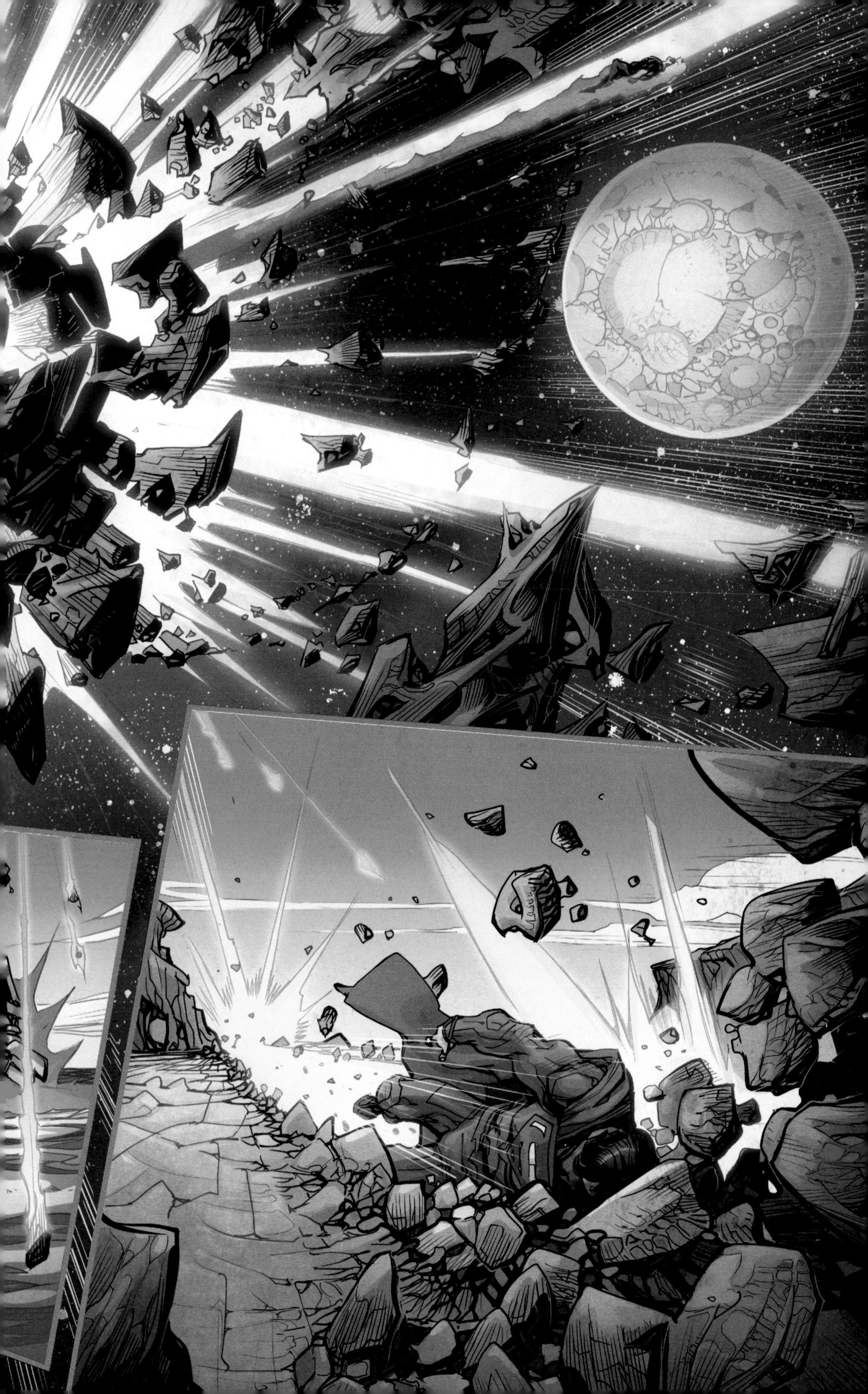

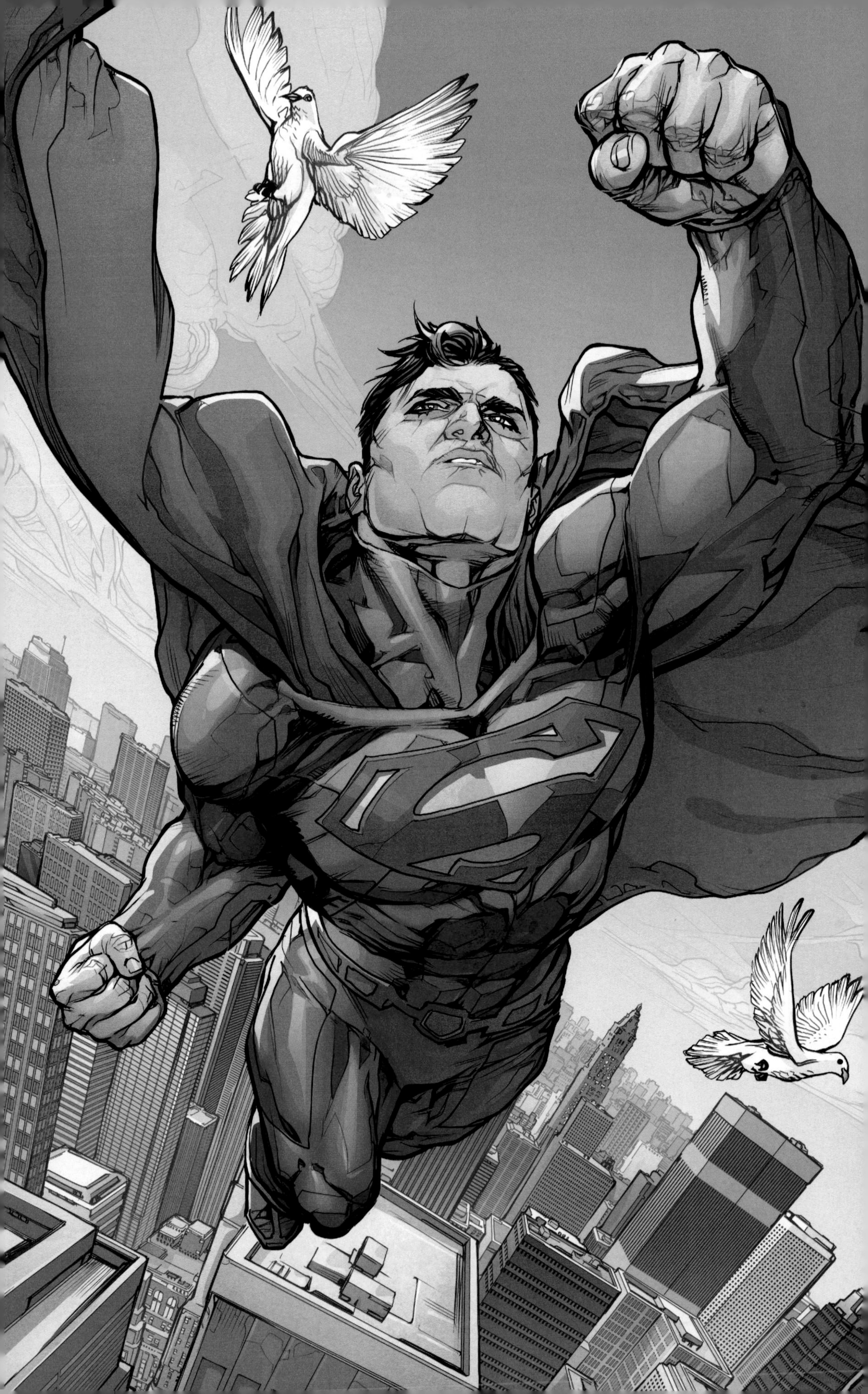

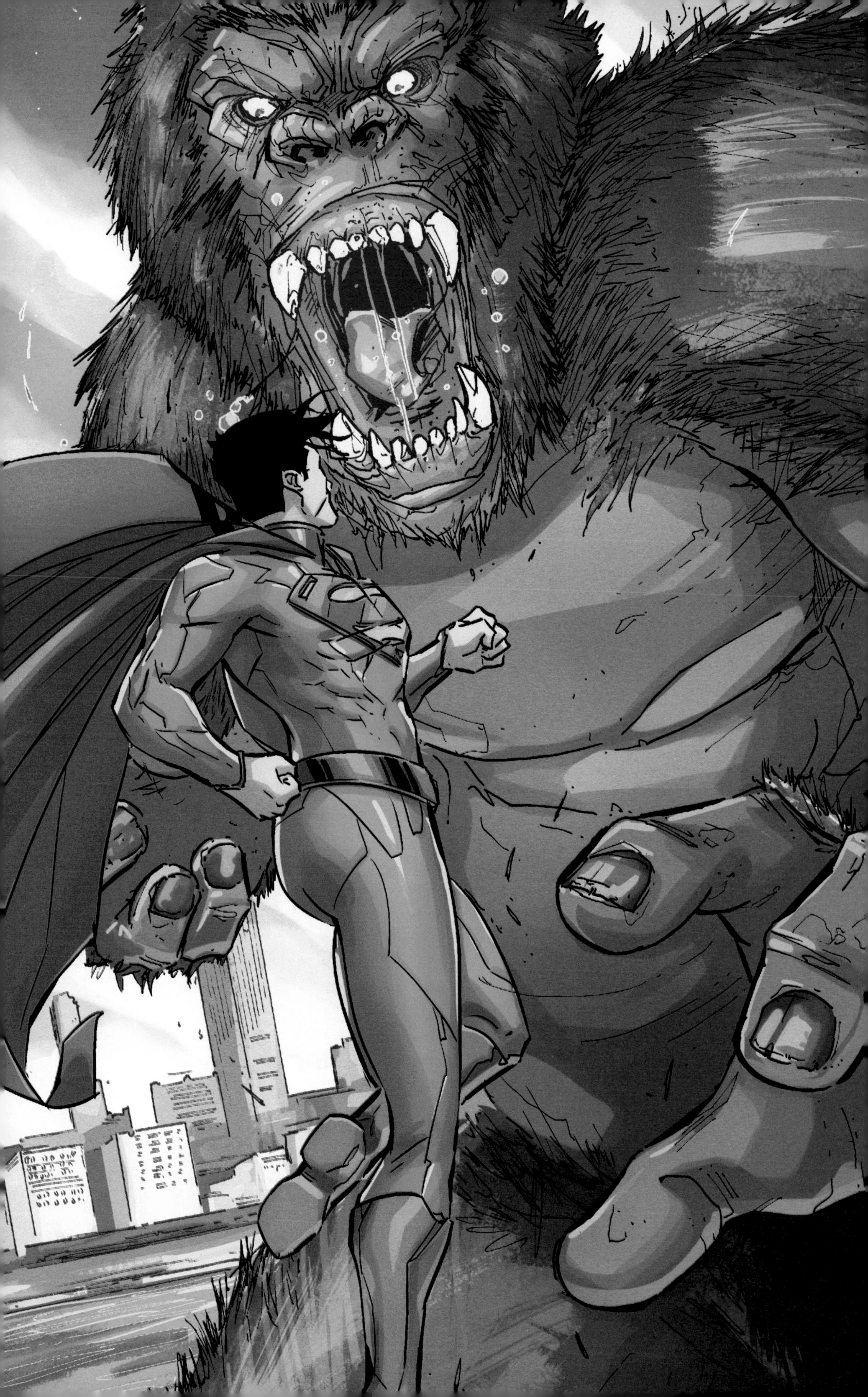

GRIEF

BRIAN BUCCELLATO writer GIUSEPPE CAFARO artist HI FI colorist TRAVIS LANHAM letterer

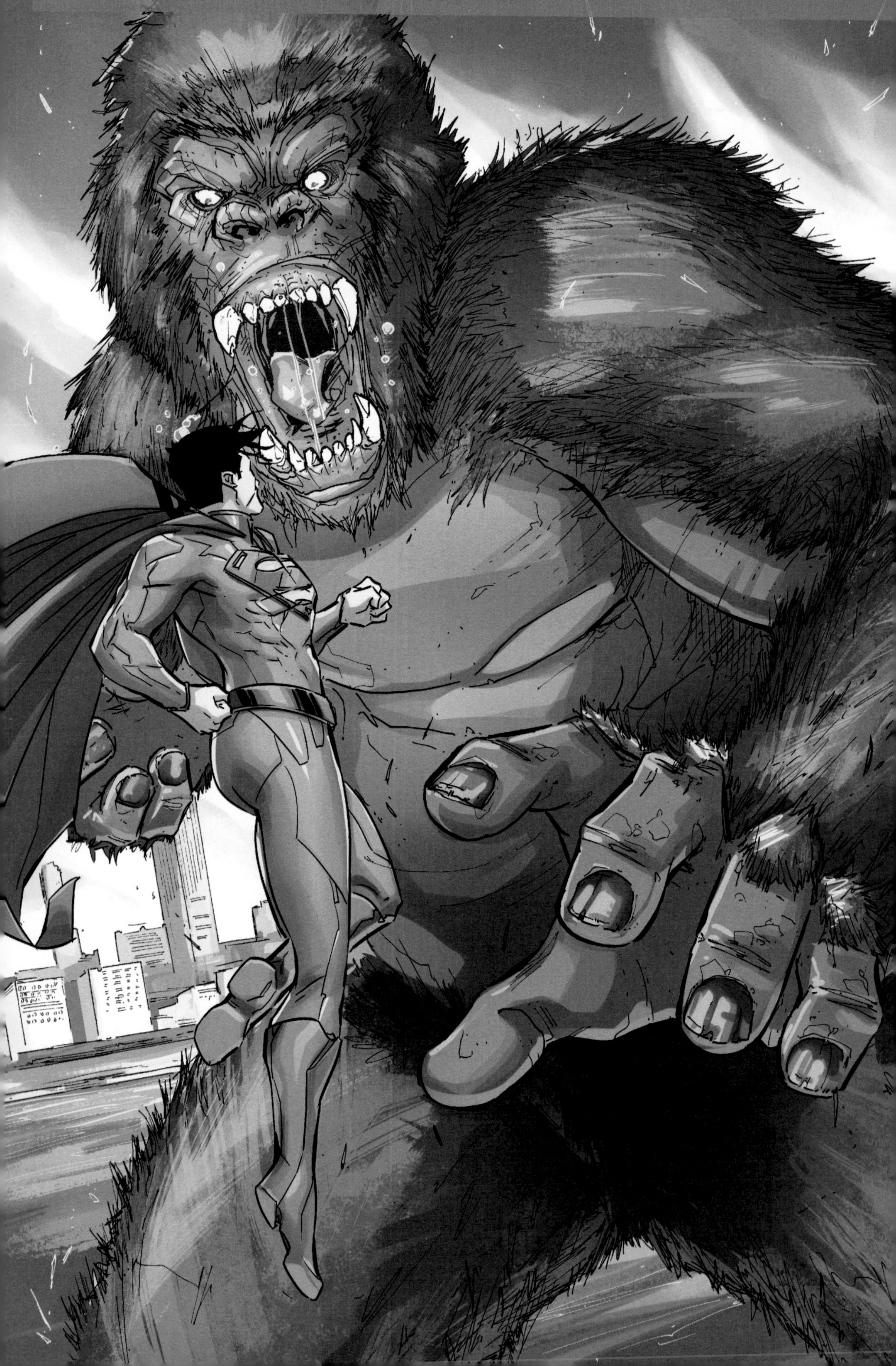

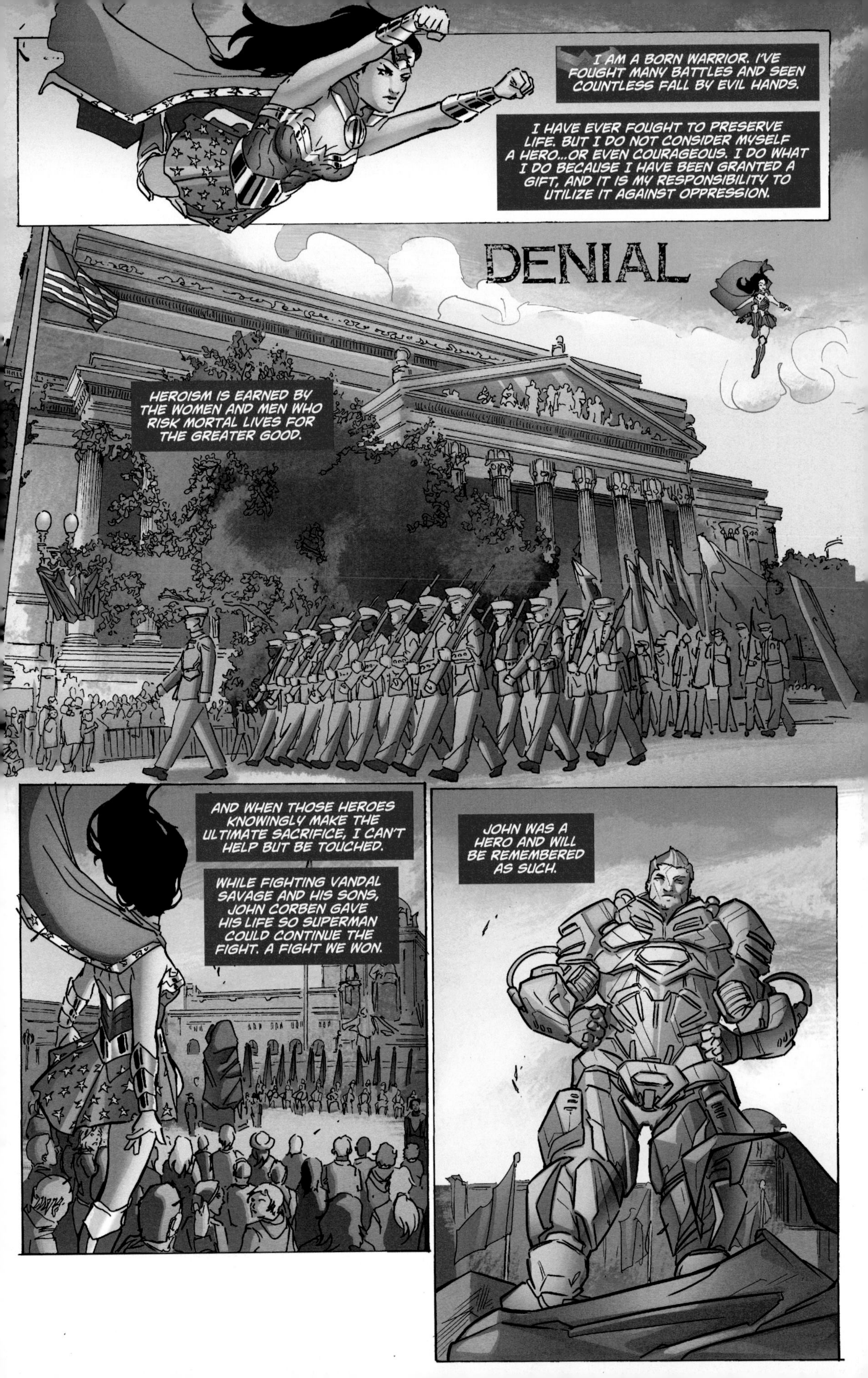
I AM A BORN WARRIOR. I'VE FOUGHT MANY BATTLES AND SEEN COUNTLESS FALL BY EVIL HANDS.
I HAVE EVER FOUGHT TO PRESERVE LIFE. BUT I DO NOT CONSIDER MYSELF A HERO...OR EVEN COURAGEOUS. I DO WHAT I DO BECAUSE I HAVE BEEN GRANTED A GIFT, AND IT IS MY RESPONSIBILITY TO UTILIZE IT AGAINST OPPRESSION.
DENIAL
HEROISM IS EARNED BY THE WOMEN AND MEN WHO RISK MORTAL LIVES FOR THE GREATER GOOD.
AND WHEN THOSE HEROES KNOWINGLY MAKE THE ULTIMATE SACRIFICE, I CAN'T HELP BUT BE TOUCHED.
WHILE FIGHTING VANDAL SAVAGE AND HIS SONS, JOHN CORBEN GAVE HIS LIFE SO SUPERMAN COULD CONTINUE THE FIGHT. A FIGHT WE WON.
JOHN WAS A HERO AND WILL BE REMEMBERED AS SUCH.

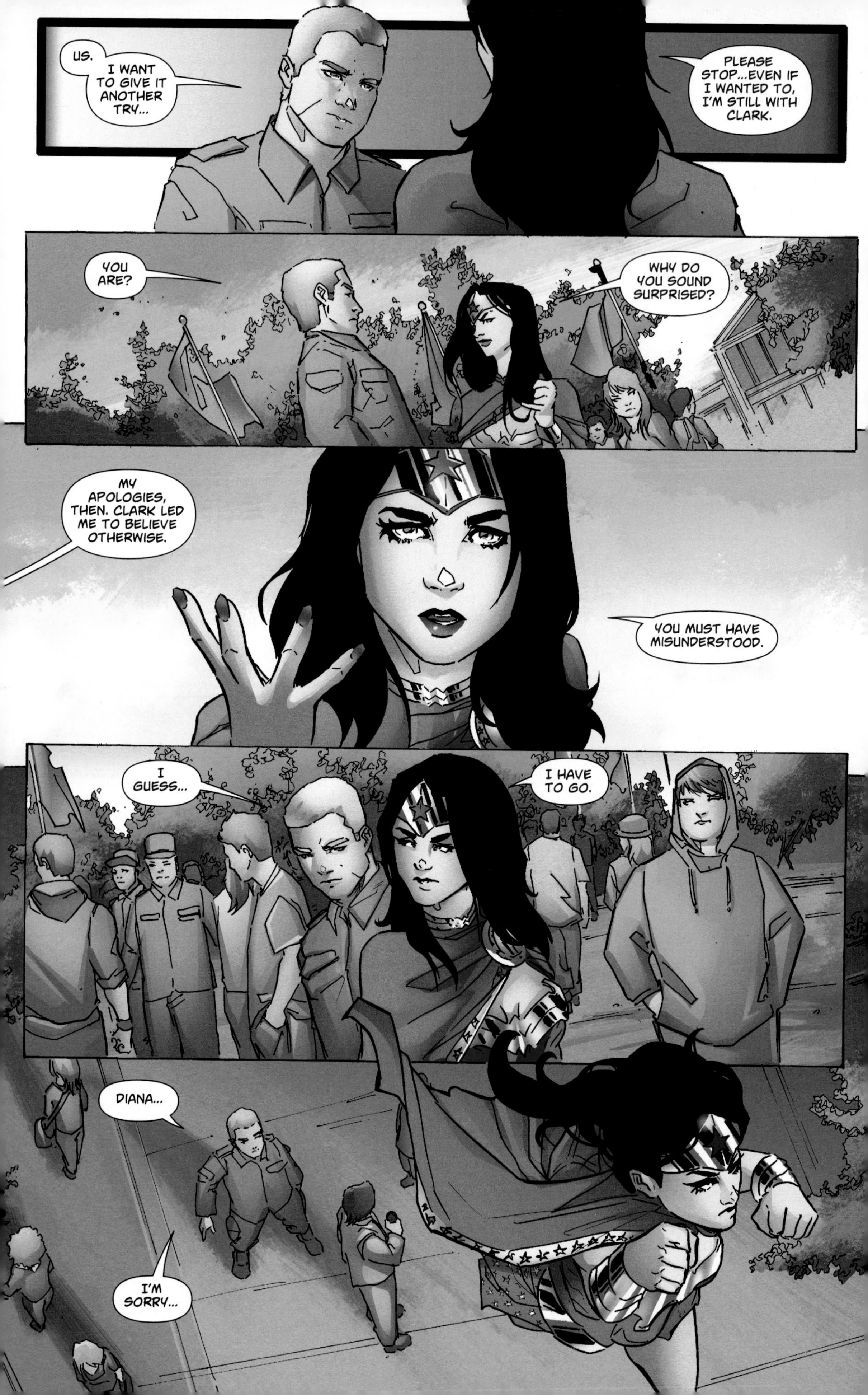
US.
I WANT TO GIVE IT ANOTHER TRY...
PLEASE STOP...EVEN IF I WANTED TO, I'M STILL WITH CLARK.
YOU ARE?
WHY DO YOU SOUND SURPRISED?
MY APOLOGIES, THEN. CLARK LED ME TO BELIEVE OTHERWISE.
YOU MUST HAVE MISUNDERSTOOD.
I GUESS...
I HAVE TO GO.
DIANA...
I'M SORRY...

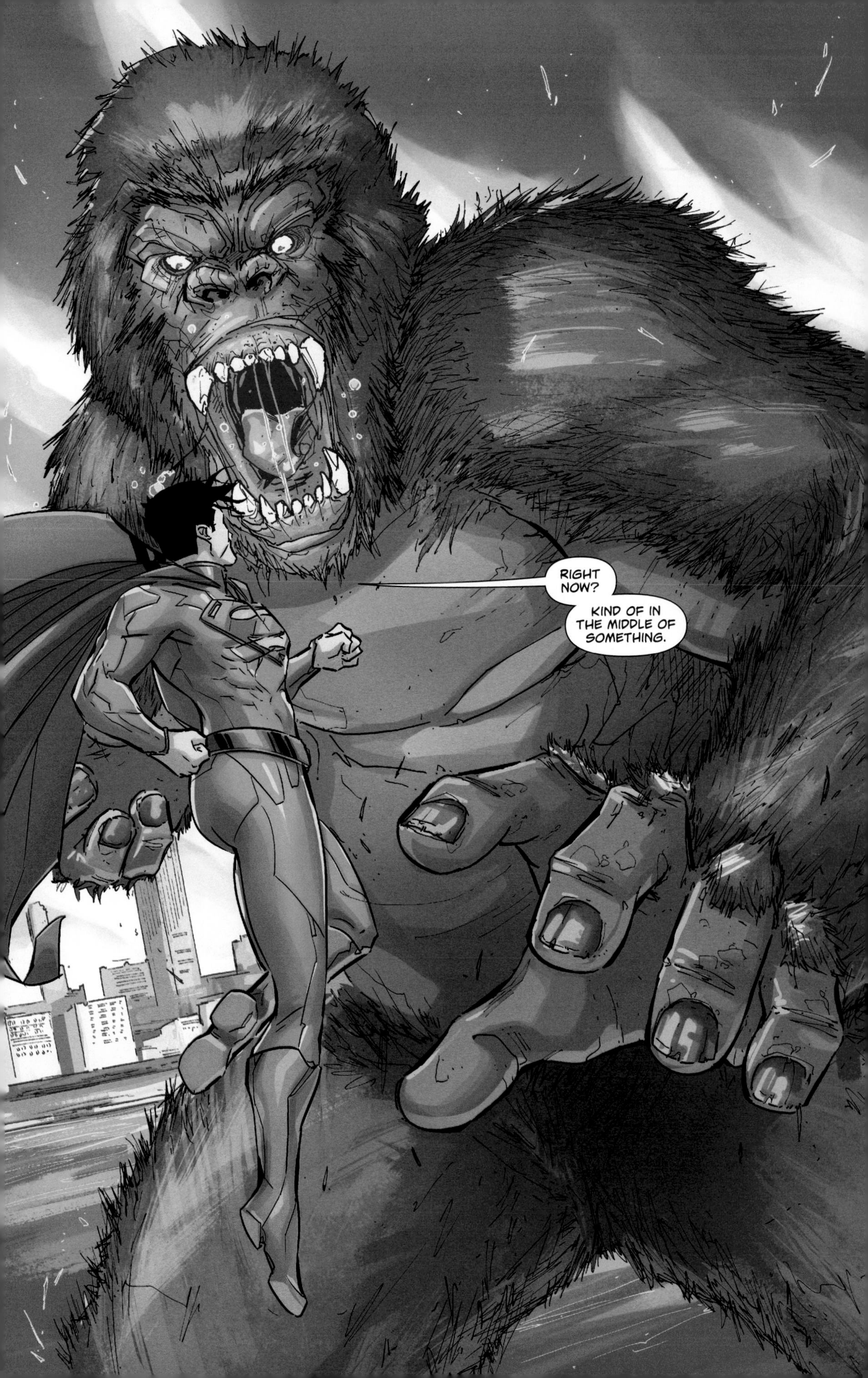
RIGHT NOW?
KIND OF IN THE MIDDLE OF SOMETHING.

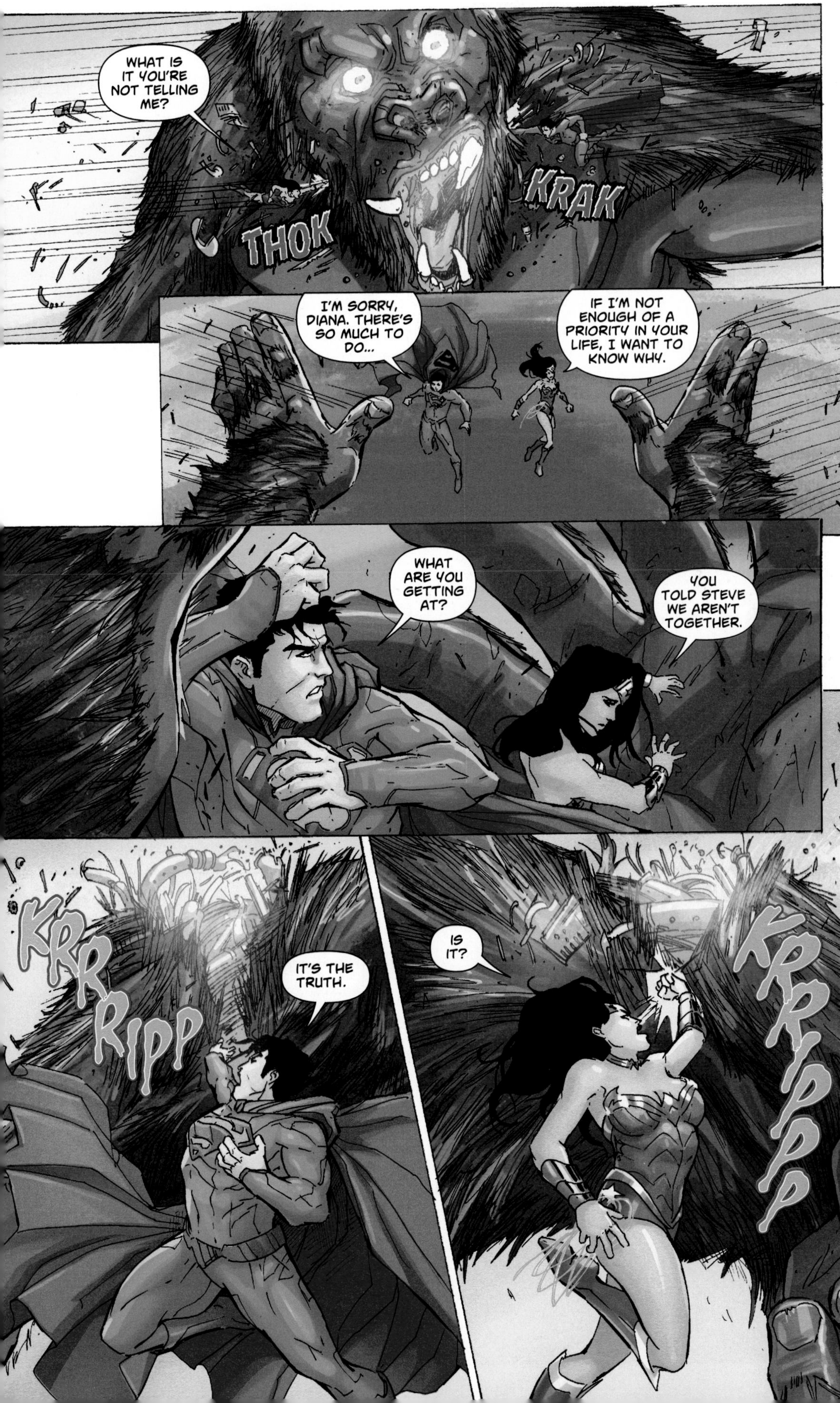
WHAT IS IT YOU'RE NOT TELLING ME?
KRAK
THOK
I'M SORRY, DIANA. THERE'S SO MUCH TO DO...
IF I'M NOT ENOUGH OF A PRIORITY IN YOUR LIFE, I WANT TO KNOW WHY.
WHAT ARE YOU GETTING AT?
YOU TOLD STEVE WE AREN'T TOGETHER.
KRRRIPP
IT'S THE TRUTH.
IS IT?
KRRIPPP

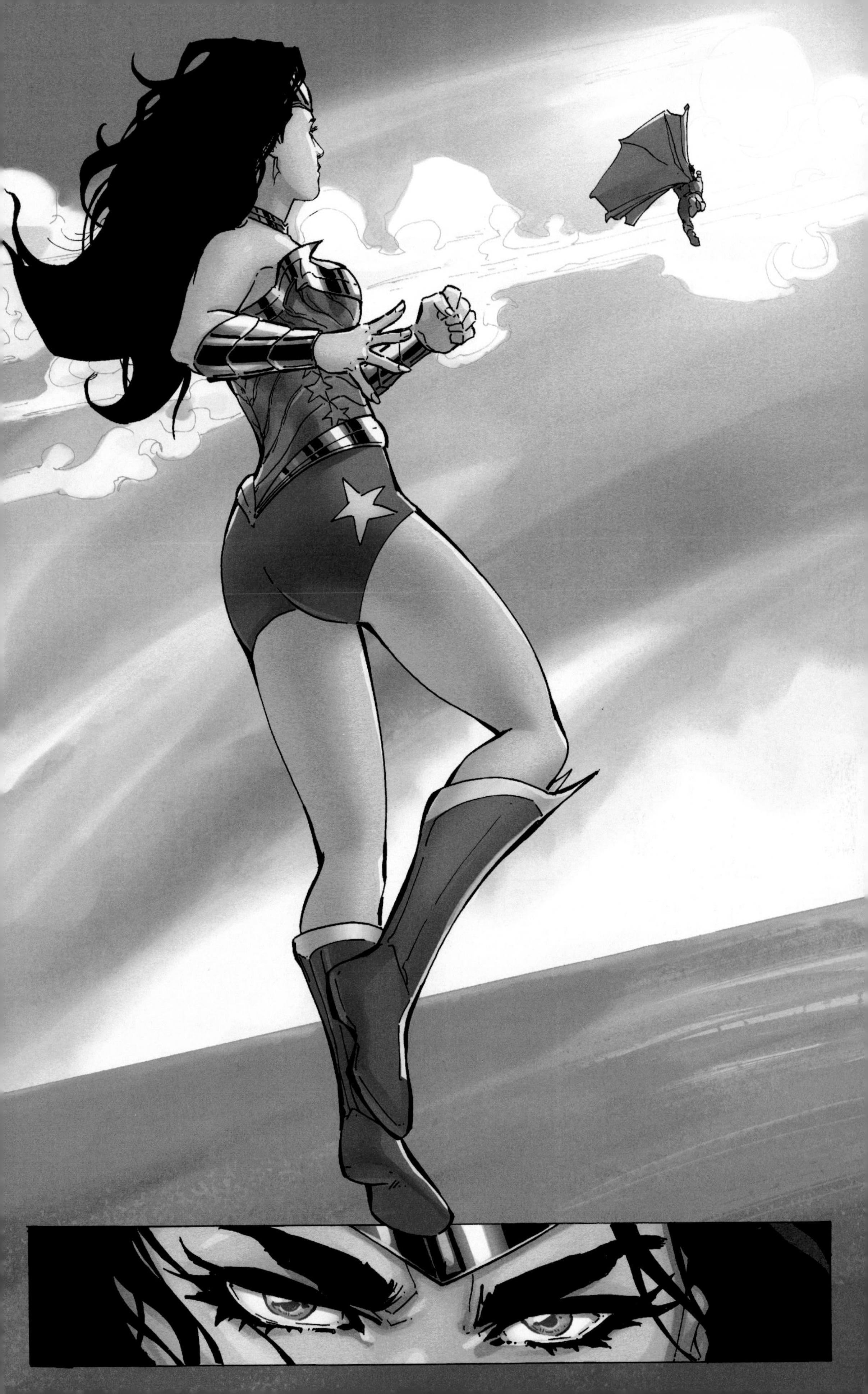

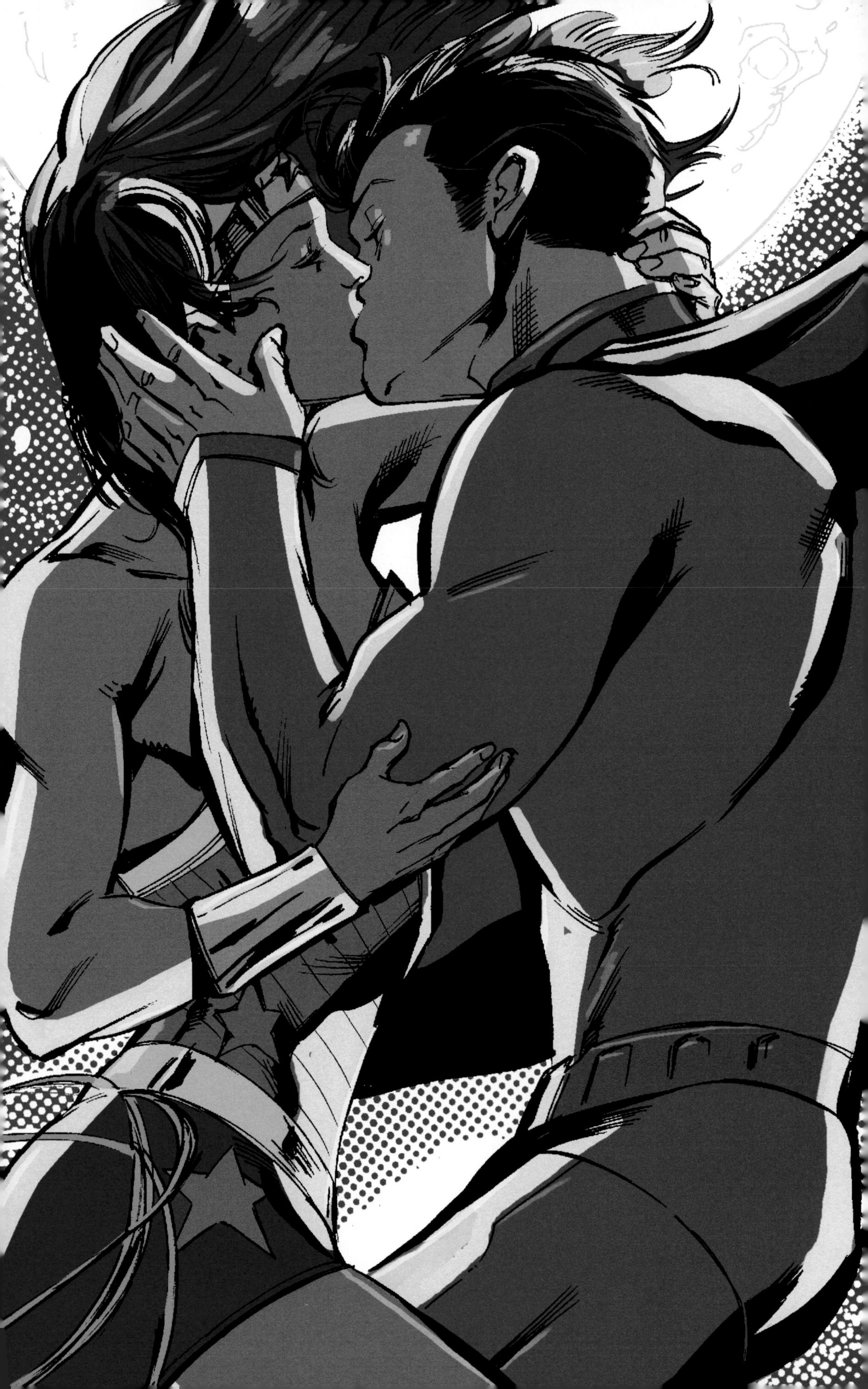

ACCEPTANCE

BRIAN BUCCELLATO writer GIUSEPPE CAFARO POP MHAN artists LEE LOUGHRIDGE colorist DAVID SHARPE letterer

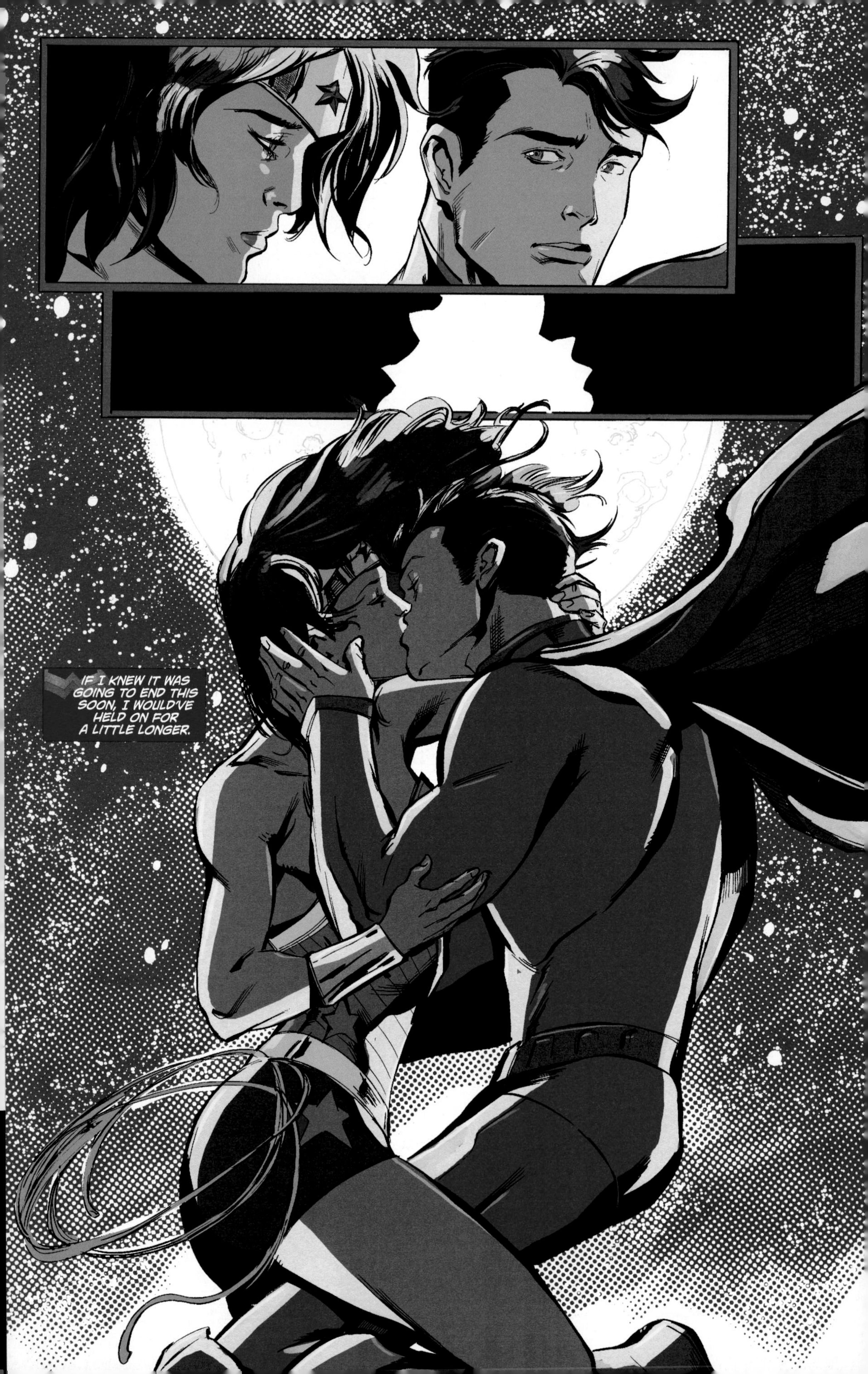
IF I KNEW IT WAS GOING TO END THIS SOON, I WOULD'VE HELD ON FOR A LITTLE LONGER.

WE HOPED TO KEEP IT A SECRET UNTIL WE WERE READY. BUT *CAT GRANT* BROKE THE STORY, IRONICALLY FOR CLARK'S BLOG.

WHAT DO YOU THINK ABOUT THE NEW POWER COUPLE?

SHE CAN DEFINITELY DO BETTER.

ONCE IT WENT PUBLIC, WE FACED TOO MUCH *SCRUTINY*...FROM OUTSIDE FORCES AND OUR FRIENDS.

OF COURSE, BATMAN WAS THE FIRST TO FIND OUT...AND THE FIRST TO LET US KNOW THAT HE KNEW.

YOU JUST NEED TO UNDERSTAND HOW THE REST OF THE WORLD--THE WORLD THAT DOESN'T KNOW YOU LIKE I DO--WILL *REACT.*

YOU'RE THE TWO MOST POWERFUL BEINGS ON EARTH. THEY'RE GOING TO BE GUNNING FOR YOU.

WE CONNECTED, BRUCE. IT JUST HAPPENED.

I'M HAPPY THAT YOU BOTH... FOUND SOMETHING TOGETHER.

WHO WILL?

WHOEVER IS AFRAID OF WHAT YOU TWO COULD DO.

SUPERMAN AND WONDER WOMAN A COUPLE!

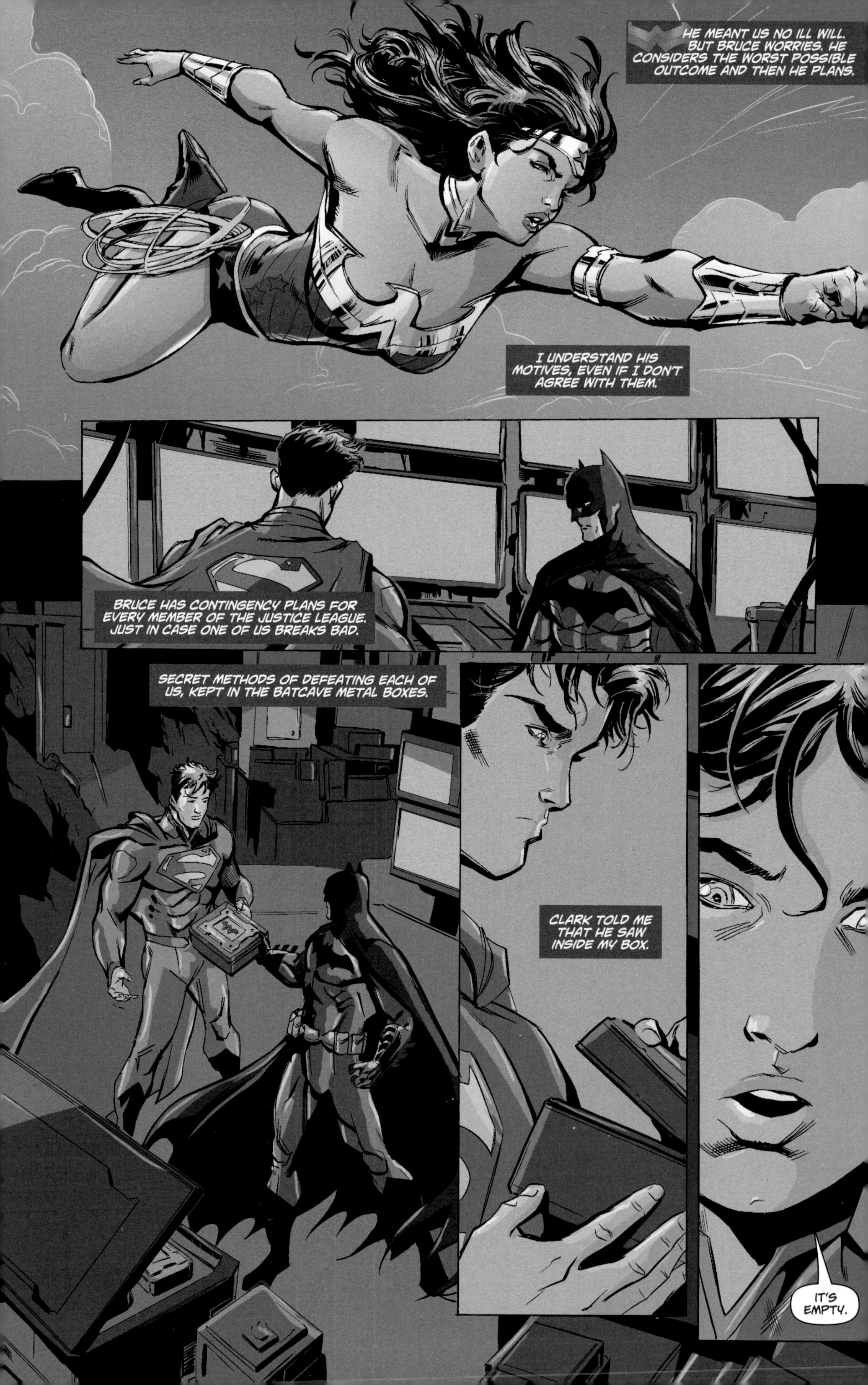
HE MEANT US NO ILL WILL. BUT BRUCE WORRIES. HE CONSIDERS THE WORST POSSIBLE OUTCOME AND THEN HE PLANS.
I UNDERSTAND HIS MOTIVES, EVEN IF I DON'T AGREE WITH THEM.
BRUCE HAS CONTINGENCY PLANS FOR EVERY MEMBER OF THE JUSTICE LEAGUE. JUST IN CASE ONE OF US BREAKS BAD.
SECRET METHODS OF DEFEATING EACH OF US, KEPT IN THE BATCAVE METAL BOXES.
CLARK TOLD ME THAT HE SAW INSIDE MY BOX.
IT'S EMPTY.

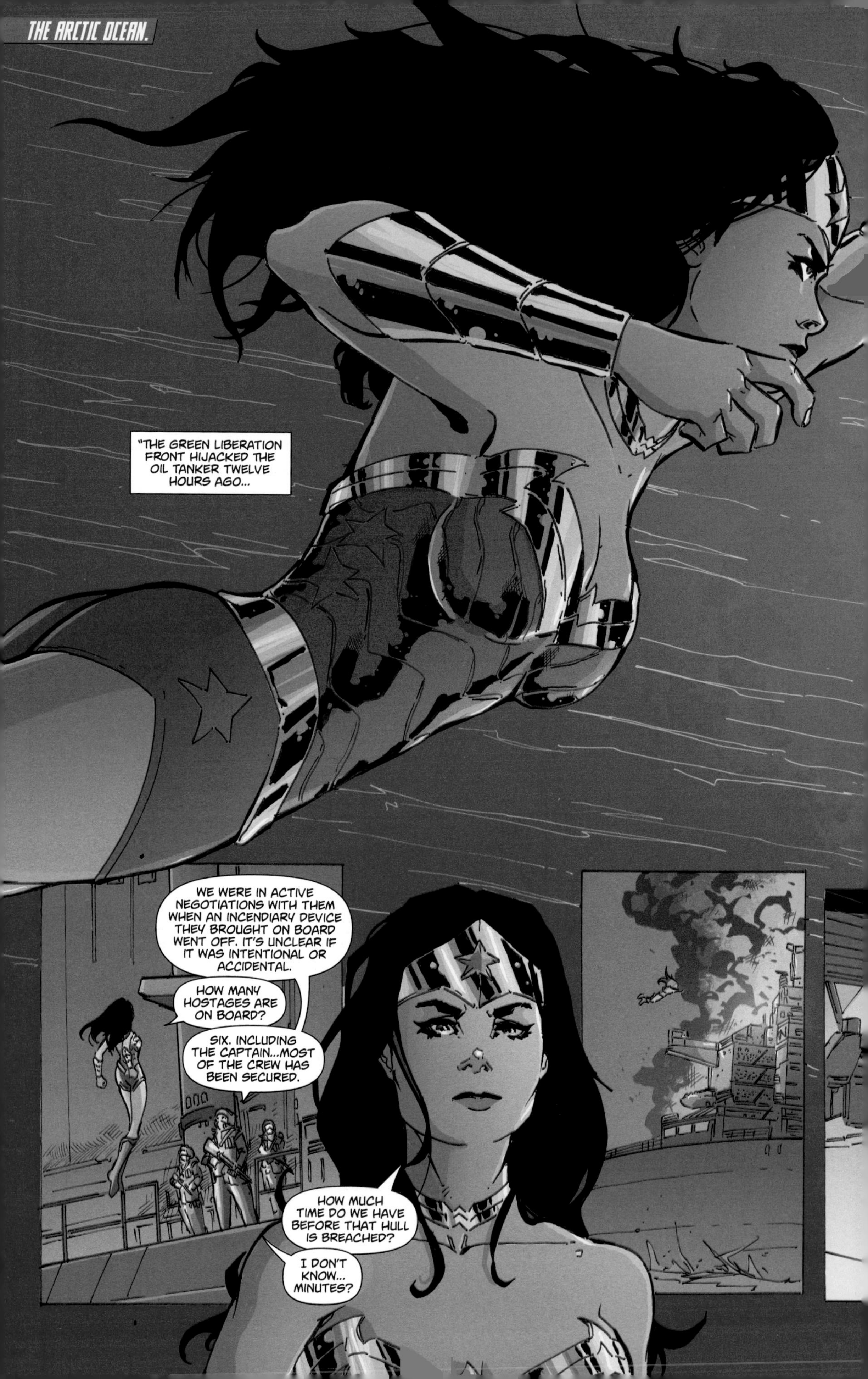
THE ARCTIC OCEAN.
"THE GREEN LIBERATION FRONT HIJACKED THE OIL TANKER TWELVE HOURS AGO...
WE WERE IN ACTIVE NEGOTIATIONS WITH THEM WHEN AN INCENDIARY DEVICE THEY BROUGHT ON BOARD WENT OFF. IT'S UNCLEAR IF IT WAS INTENTIONAL OR ACCIDENTAL.
HOW MANY HOSTAGES ARE ON BOARD?
SIX. INCLUDING THE CAPTAIN...MOST OF THE CREW HAS BEEN SECURED.
HOW MUCH TIME DO WE HAVE BEFORE THAT HULL IS BREACHED?
I DON'T KNOW... MINUTES?

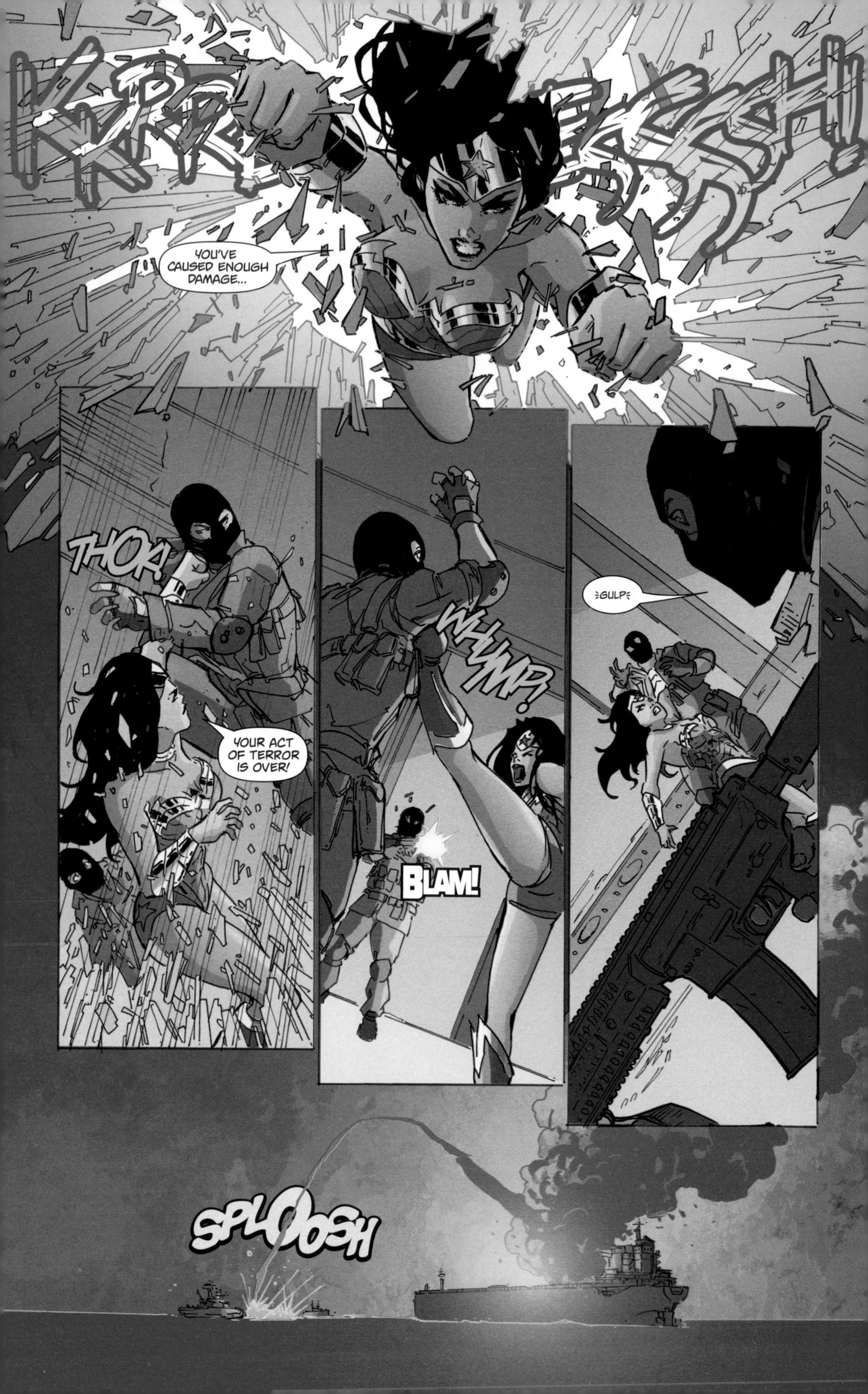
KRRRAAASH!
YOU'VE CAUSED ENOUGH DAMAGE...
THOK!
YOUR ACT OF TERROR IS OVER!
WHUMP!
BLAM!
GULP
SPLOOSH

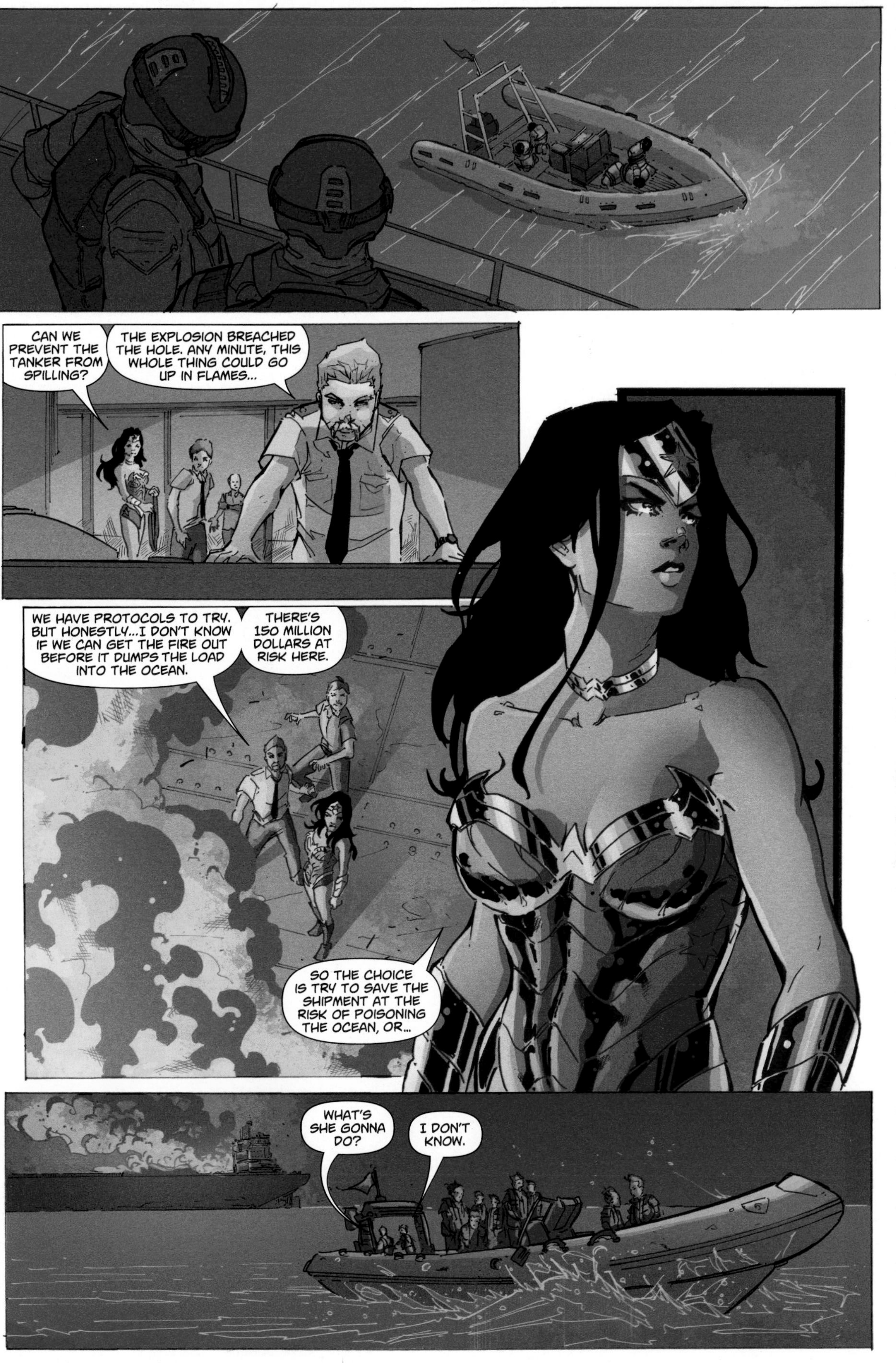
CAN WE PREVENT THE TANKER FROM SPILLING?
THE EXPLOSION BREACHED THE HOLE. ANY MINUTE, THIS WHOLE THING COULD GO UP IN FLAMES...
WE HAVE PROTOCOLS TO TRY. BUT HONESTLY...I DON'T KNOW IF WE CAN GET THE FIRE OUT BEFORE IT DUMPS THE LOAD INTO THE OCEAN.
THERE'S 150 MILLION DOLLARS AT RISK HERE.
SO THE CHOICE IS TRY TO SAVE THE SHIPMENT AT THE RISK OF POISONING THE OCEAN, OR...
WHAT'S SHE GONNA DO?
I DON'T KNOW.

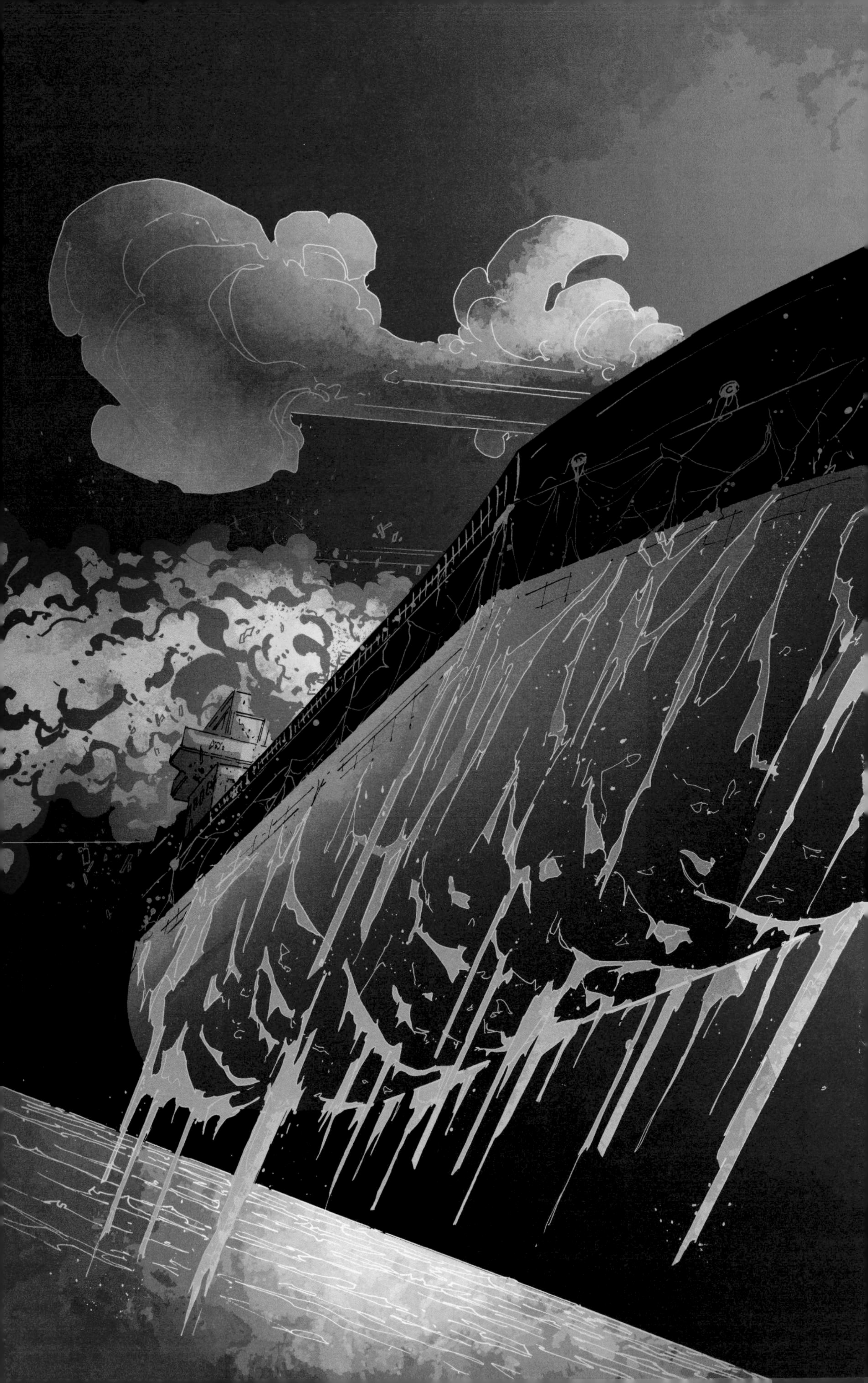

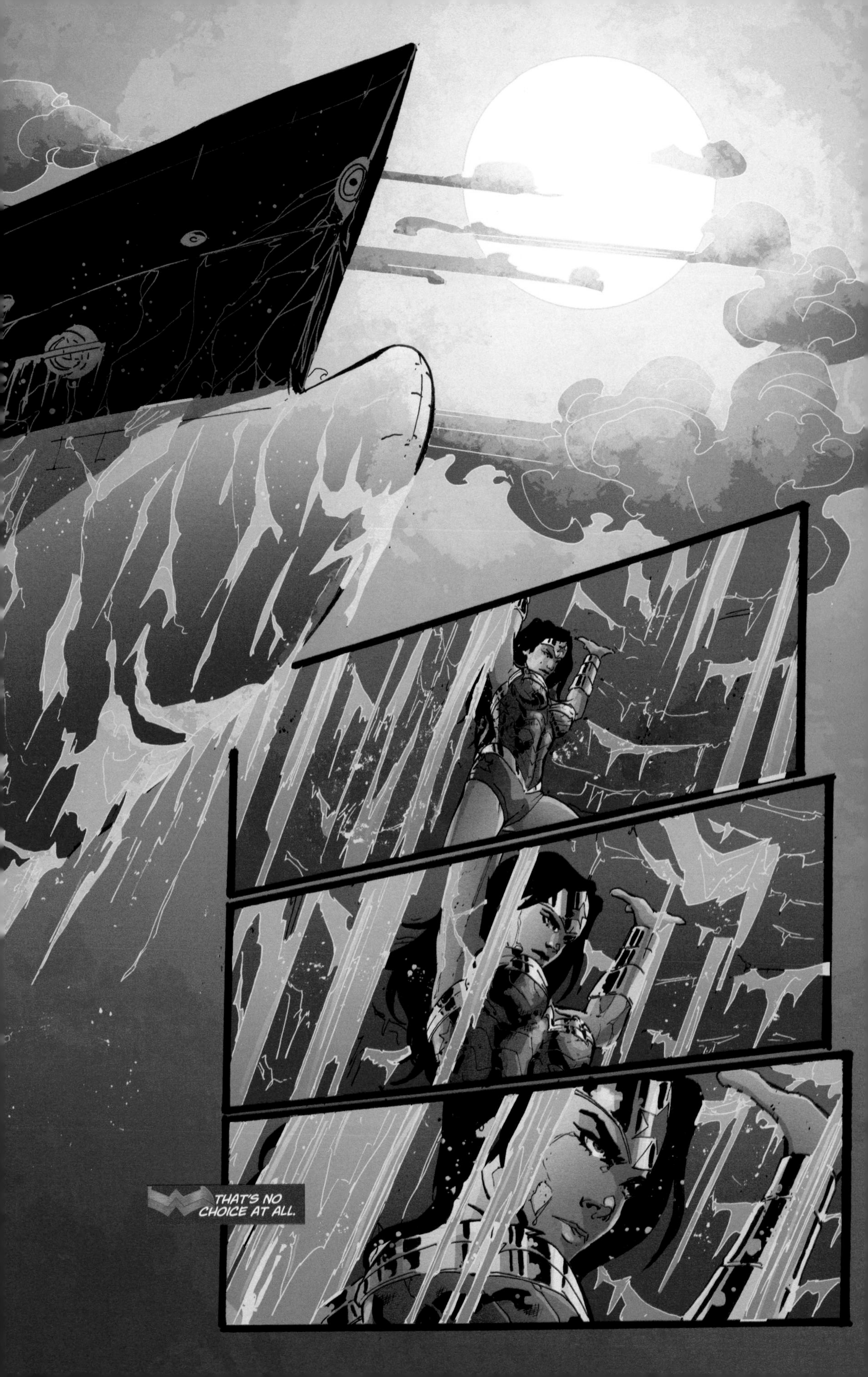

THAT'S NO CHOICE AT ALL.

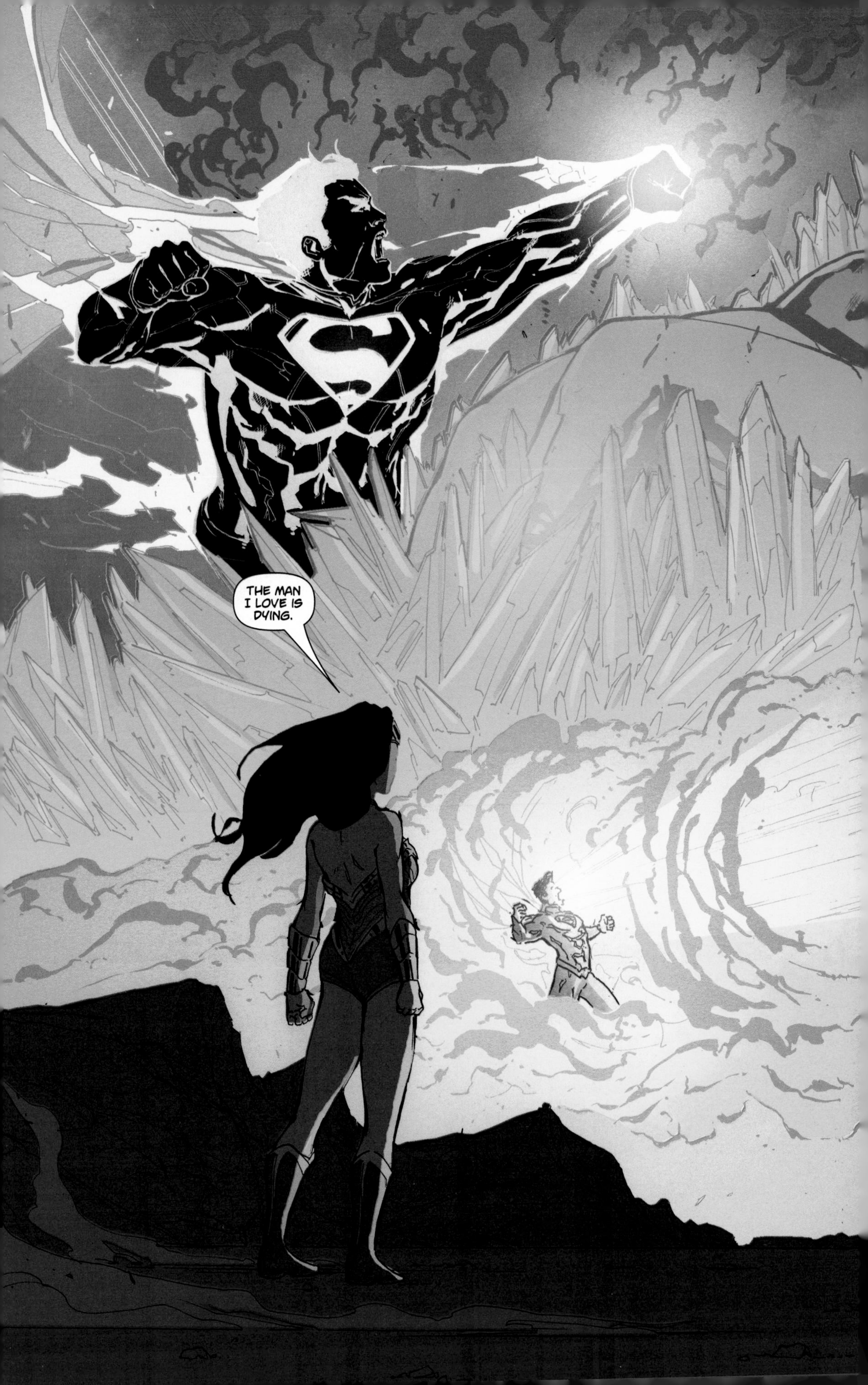
THE MAN I LOVE IS DYING.

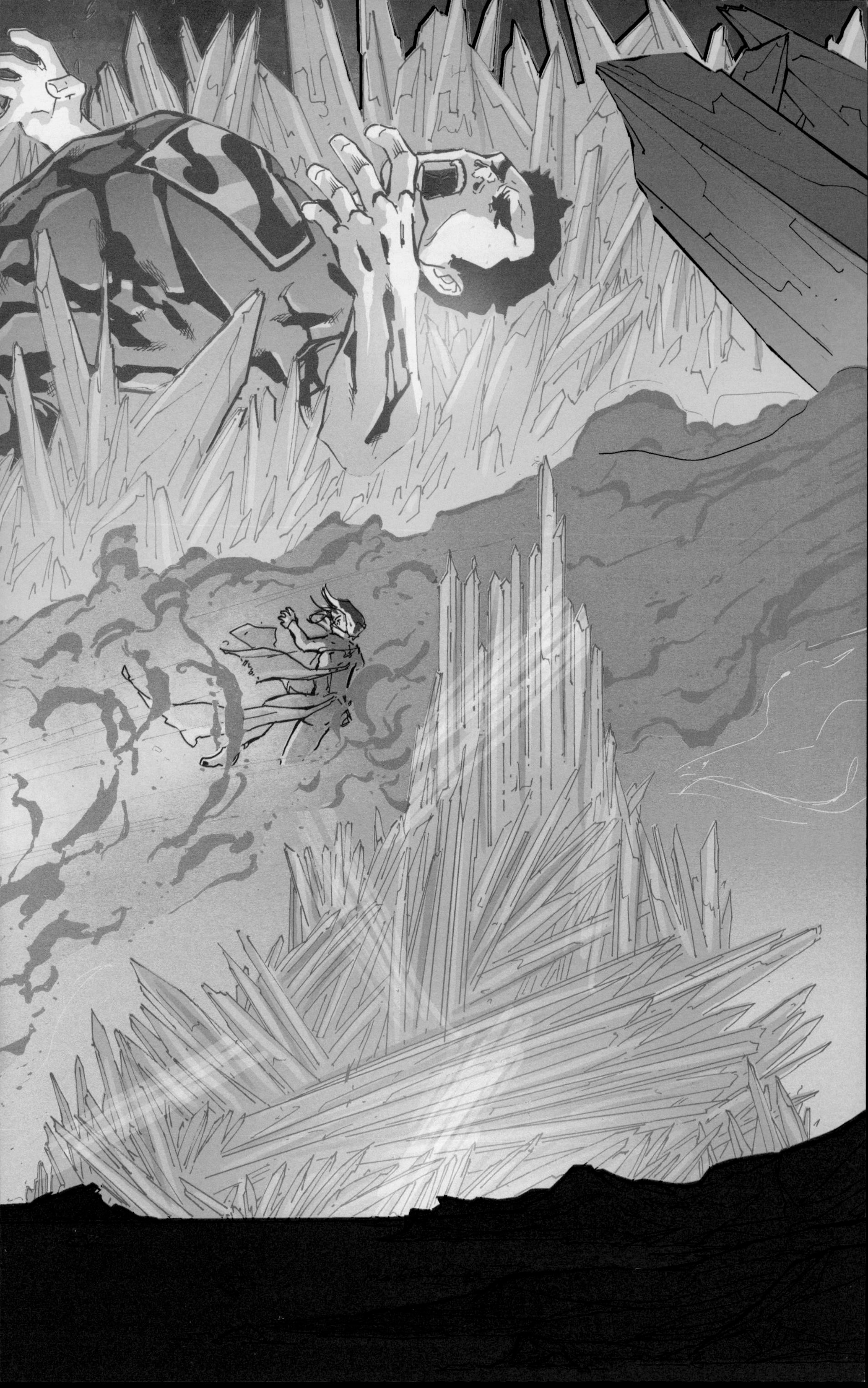

ART BY
DOUG MAHNKE
& JAIME MENDOZA

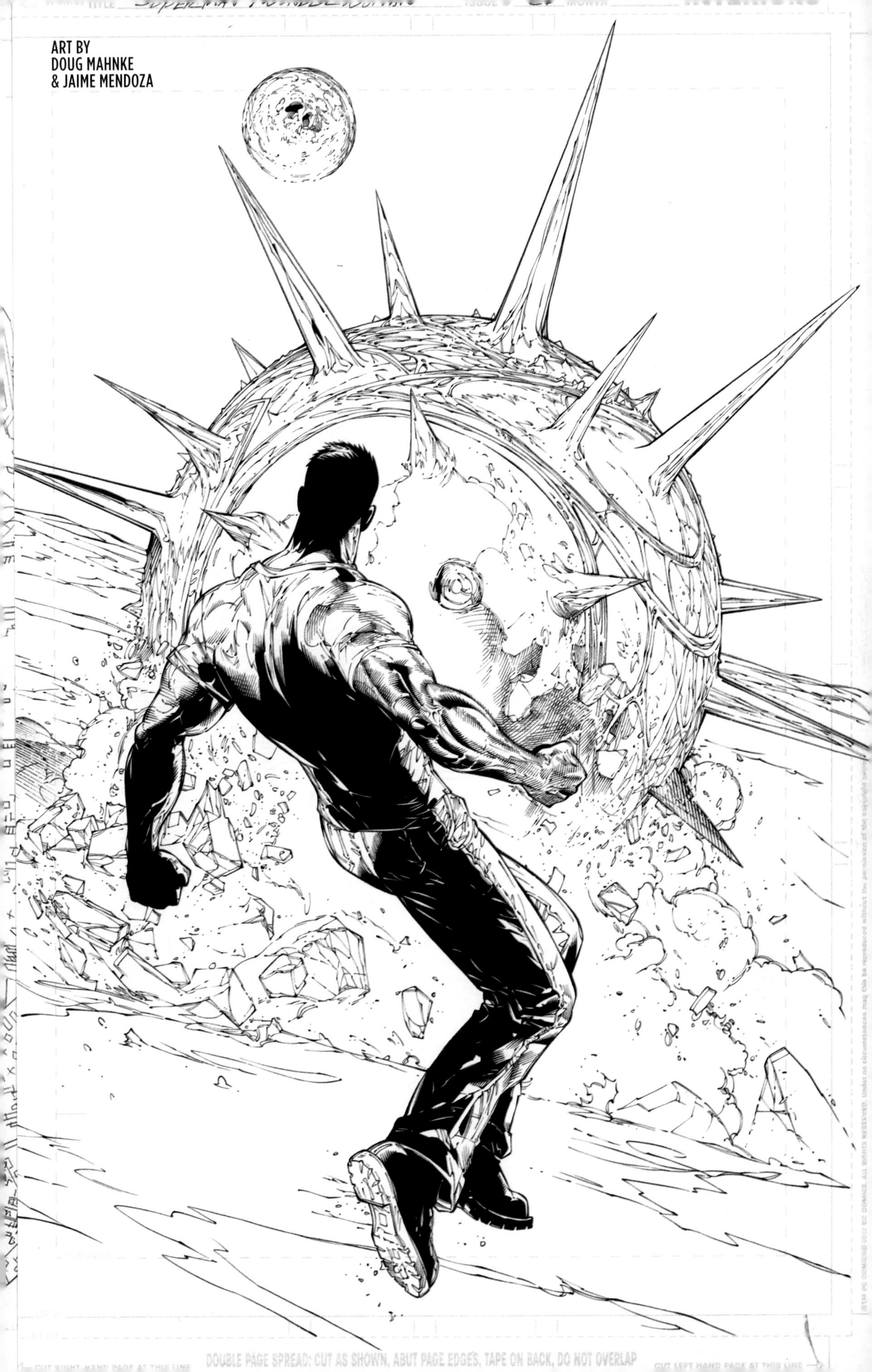
DOUBLE PAGE SPREAD: CUT AS SHOWN, ABUT PAGE EDGES, TAPE ON BACK, DO NOT OVERLAP

ART BY ARDIAN SYAF

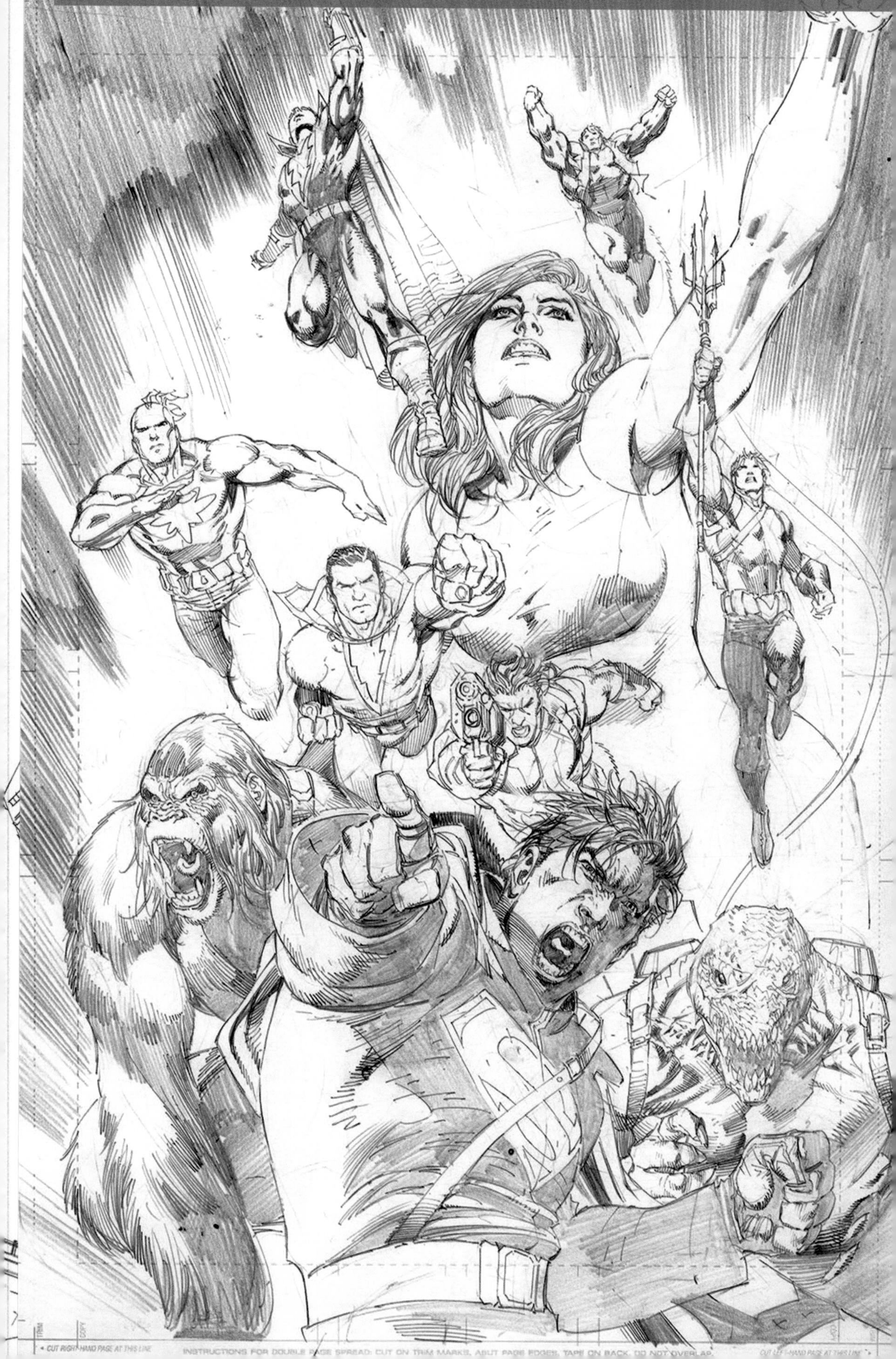

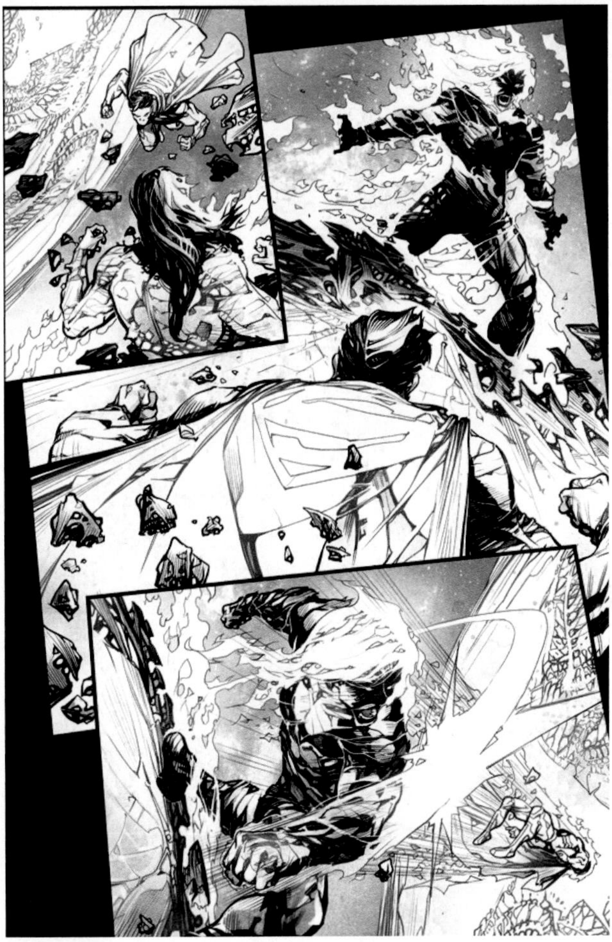

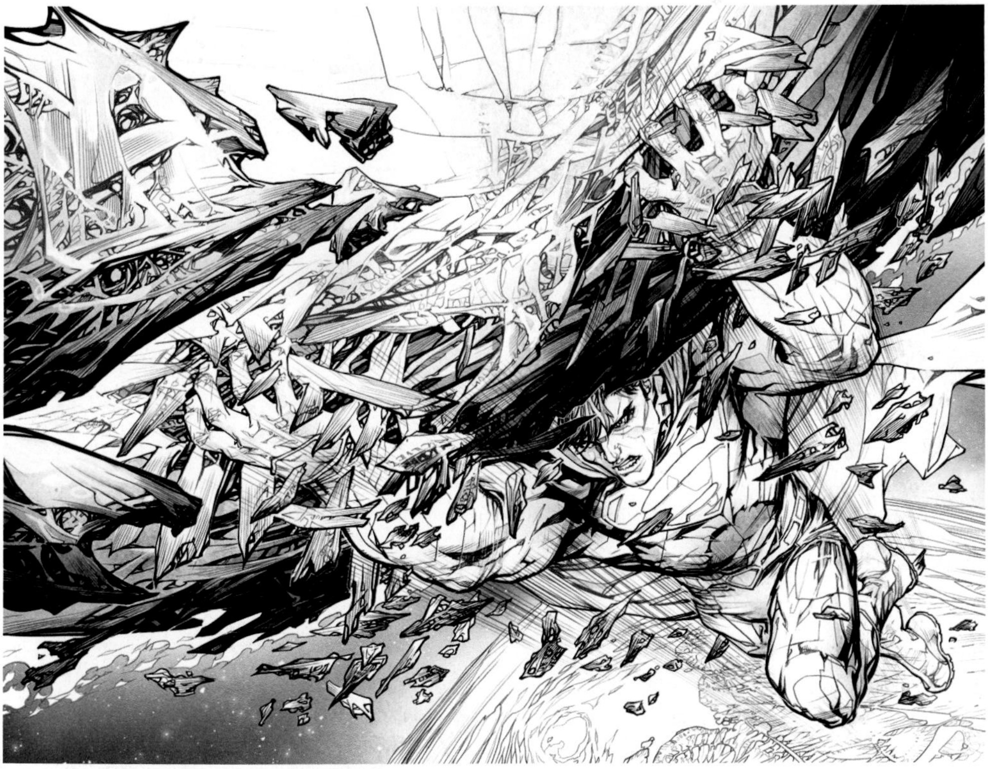

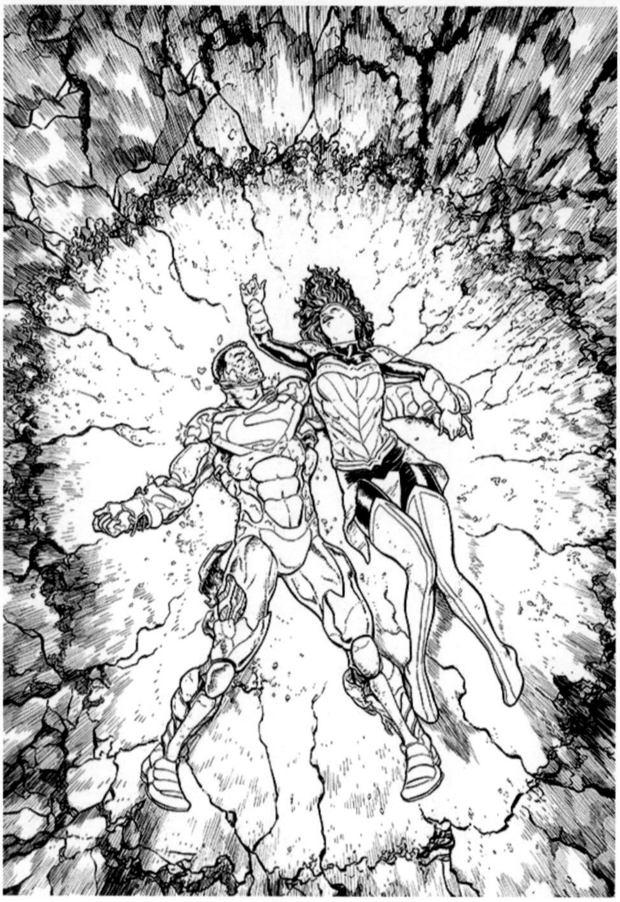

ART BY AARON KUDER

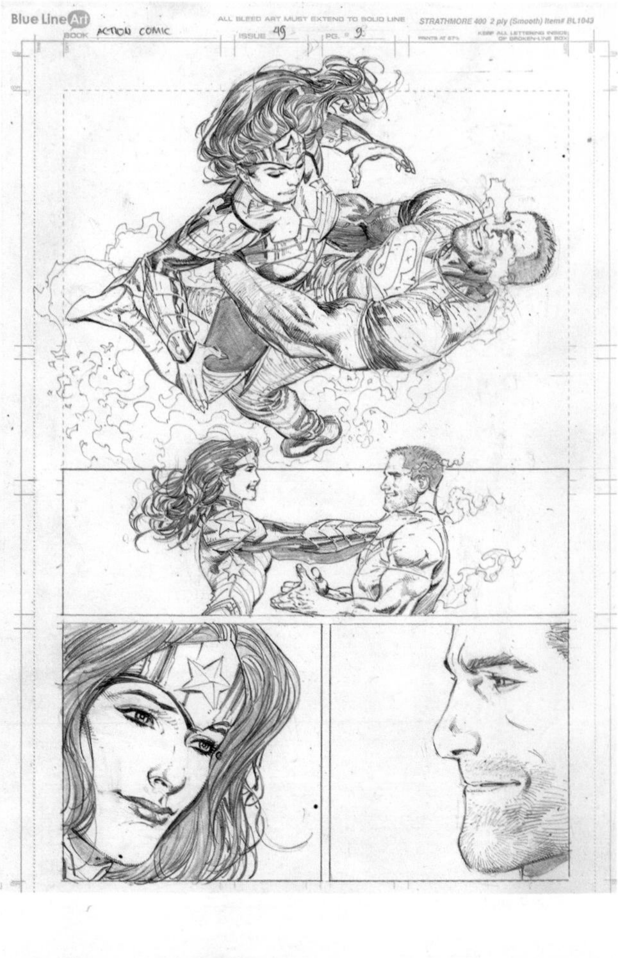
Blue Line Art
ALL BLEED ART MUST EXTEND TO SOLID LINE
STRATHMORE 400 2 ply (Smooth) Item# BL1043
BOOK ACTION COMIC
ISSUE 49
PG. 9

ART BY ARDIAN SYAF